A Christian Perspective
on Political Thought

A
Christian
Perspective
on
Political
Thought

Stephen Charles Mott

New York   Oxford
OXFORD UNIVERSITY PRESS
1993

Oxford University Press

Oxford New York Toronto
Delhi Bombay Calcutta Madras Karachi
Kuala Lumpur Singapore Hong Kong Tokyo
Nairobi Dar es Salaam Cape Town
Melbourne Auckland Madrid

and associated companies in
Berlin Ibadan

Published by Oxford University Press, Inc.
200 Madison Avenue, New York, New York 10016

Oxford is a registered trademark of Oxford University Press, Inc.

Library of Congress Cataloging-in-Publication Data
Mott, Stephen Charles.
A Christian perspective on political thought /
Stephen Charles Mott.
p. cm. Includes bibliographical references and index.
ISBN 0-19-507121-2. — ISBN 0-19-508138-2 (pbk.)
1. Christianity and politics. 2. Political science.
I. Title.
BR115.P7M58 1993 261.7—dc20 92-25045

2 4 6 8 9 7 6 5 3 1

Printed in the United States of America
on acid-free paper

To Sandy

Acknowledgments

I have drawn heavily upon the Christian realists, especially Reinhold Niebuhr, but also Paul Tillich and Eduard Heimann. The combination of their commitment to a transcending social justice and an emphasis upon the human being as both sinner and creation of God suits my approach well. Niebuhr had a formative influence upon my own development that has continued. His ability to examine critically all sides of an issue and his facility in supporting theological and biblical insights with current history and contemporary social theory continue to appeal. My approach also has emphases that differ. Some of these are due to other elements of my intellectual heritage, one of which is that of my doctoral professor in social ethics, James Luther Adams. His continual giving of himself to his students has meant learning as much from him since I formally studied under him as in that rich time a quarter of a century ago.

I want to thank Corinne Languedoc, then senior faculty secretary at Gordon-Conwell Theological Seminary, for once again contributing her skills to preparing final copy and for her collegiality during two decades of working together. John Hunt, my student assistant for three years, diligently carried out many research tasks for the book, and Nelson Copeland, student assistant in 1992–1993, prepared the author index. Many other students at Gordon-Conwell made their own contributions as we struggled together during the various stages of these materials. I want to thank the faculty, administration, and trustees of Gordon-Conwell Theological Seminary for the sabbatical year of 1990–1991 in which I wrote the book. I am grateful to the Lilly Foundation for the Faculty Development Grant that funded my research and travel costs during that year.

Professor Max Stackhouse and Professor Ron Stone helped set me in the right direction with careful comments upon early reading of the materials. Oxford University Press, with Cynthia A. Read as senior editor, Ellen B. Fuchs, managing editor, and Steve Bedney, copy editor, provided smooth and competent assistance. I have learned much about how to write from their careful editorial work.

Scriptural quotations from the New Revised Standard Version *(NRSV)*, copyright 1989, are used with the permission of the Division of Christian Education of the National Council of Churches of Christ in the U.S.A. Translations of biblical passages not otherwise identified are my own.

The book is dedicated to Sandra R. Mott, my wife and *copine*. She cares deeply, competently, and creatively for many people within a wide web of relationships to family, students, colleagues, church, and sick children and their own families. Knowing her gives me hope for my visions.

Beverly, Mass.   S.C.M.
August 1992

Contents

A Christian Perspective
on Political Thought

Introduction

The Importance of Political Ideas

Like air and water, politics is something in which everybody has a self-interest. Limits of supply also characterize its concerns; decisions must be made about them. Politics often even treats water and clean air. It deals with subjects in which the whole society has interest and which have consequences that affect the whole community or a substantial portion of it.[1]

Political action is influenced by ideals as well as by material desires and self-interests. People care about the nature of the society in which they live, not just about what it does for them as individuals. Widely shared values and collective purposes, even public moods, exert influence on political choices with a degree of independence from the actual needs of a citizen. For example, support for policies regarding health care or employment does not necessarily correlate with the degree of a family's needs in those matters.

People have a desire for public policy that is good by their standards. Public policies give expression to the public's general notion of the kind of society in which they want to live, what things are right and wrong, and what values the government should nurture and protect—whether these values are generosity, self-reliance, or courage. Racism and sexism in employment practices do not rise from market forces; rather, they reflect what the employer values, as well as what he or she wants to protect. Ideas of property influence how goods are distributed in the market. Conceptions about what is a fair wage and what rights exist for free education, free health care, or employment have a similar economic and political influence.[2] By their ideas about the way society should be, people have been deeply moved to hold on to their present arrangements or to struggle for change.

Ideologies provide a particularly powerful arrangement of ideas about society. *Ideology* is the picture of how society should be and how such a society is justified.[3] It is an interconnected set of ideas and beliefs that articulates how the basic values of a group of people apply to the distribution of power in society.[4] An ideology is the vision that gives a cohesive shape to social values and the dream of how the social order is to be organized by those values. Ideologies shape cultures in many ways that are not political, but law also gives expression to the society's social imagination and becomes an instrument of its realization.[5]

An ideology is possessed by a group, which uses it in relating to other groups and in dealing with conflicts within itself.[6] Values are both determinants of behavior as well as weapons used by contestants.[7] An ideology is not held with disinterestedness. It requires a commitment, even partisanship.[8]

The social import of social visions can be illustrated by an example that is

3

removed from our present vested interests. In June 1381 peasants incensed by the implementation of a poll tax marched on London with demands that included the abolition of serfdom. On one side was the massed rebellion of peasants with the potential of drawing discontended urban artisans to their cause; on the other side were the armed might and political expertise of the state and the aristocracy that formed it.

On each side the quest for or the use of power was motivated by a view of society and an ideal of how power should be distributed in a society. The lords had a corporal view of society. They drew upon the Apostle Paul's teaching about the church as a body. Society is a body. The head is the prince. The heart, eyes, tongue, stomach, and intestines are all the nobility and the officials. The feet are the peasants. In this body, of course, "the number of feet exceeds even the centipede." God was at the apex of the corporal hierarchy of society. From this viewpoint a difference in function meant a difference in privilege and power. Maintenance of this inequality was right and important. Society was a hierarchical reality independent of individuals, who had little import apart from their place within it.

The peasants had been stirred by the preaching of a priest, John Ball. He had used social images taken from biblical passages on the creation and the last days. Creation reflected the equality of all people in that they have a common Creator and are equal in the sight of this Creator. The proper application would be a classless society. The unequal distribution of property was contrary to the will of God; thus, the oppressed who overthrew concentrations of power were being obedient to the will of God. The time for judgment was here. John Ball had been preaching these themes for twenty years before the uprising.

In both the case of the lord and of the peasant the actions taken were governed by views that were felt to be grounded in Christianity, yet the differing social consequences drawn were momentous. This is often the case with ideologies. How is one to choose between them? In this book we will evaluate prevalent traditions of such views about life from the standpoint of Christian theology.

Part of the stagnation of the American governmental system at end of the twentieth century is the paling of ideology. People lack a compelling vision of what society should be and hopes of what it could be. Public visions are replaced by private visions of personal and family comfort. The future means little more than retirement. People do not possess a common dream that could motivate them to make personal sacrifices on behalf of the needy, schools, libraries, or parks, or even the infrastructure of their economy.

At the same time the collapse of the Marxist statist economies has opened up the questions of ideology. Is there clearly only one remaining vision, that of a mixed capitalism that has lost its barbs? Are there other visions that could better motivate action toward social goods neglected in triumphal capitalism? Is a fresh vision called for with new emphases and new approaches?

Politics Expresses Theology

This book makes two significant assertions about politics. The first is that politics is about theology. Politics summons and activates one's fundamental precepts about the nature of human relationships.[9] The French sociologist, Pierre Bourdieu, notes that in politics there is an oscillation between the general principles that one holds for the economic and social world and one's immediate experience of social life. Political choices more than any other "involve the more or less explicit and systematic representation an agent has of the social world, of his position within it and of the position he 'ought' to occupy."[10]

What constitutes good public policy in one's mind is influenced by upbringing, social class, and religious, ethnic, and regional identity.[11] The interplay between one's sense of social oughtness and one's own social position warns us that an argument for the importance of political ideas should not lead to slighting the influence of social relations. In asserting the importance of theology for politics, we do not ignore the Marxist awareness of how politics reflects the aggregate of production relations.[12] That the peasants and the lords in our example from the Peasants' Revolt held the views that they did and not vice versa is not surprising. There is a correspondence between one's visions and one's actions. The predominant cultural perspective of a society will be one that justifies its class structure.

People are influenced both by their social interests and by the cultural code in which they perceive and interpret them. Not all peasants or all lords would hold the views that surfaced in the Peasants' Revolt. In fact, most oppressed people acquiesce in a view of the world that justifies their predicament. The viewpoints of the major groups in our lives exert a great influence on our perspectives. While a group's outlooks are significantly swayed by the economic relationships of its members and other factors that are to its advantage or disadvantage, such forces are only part of the influence upon its values. In addition, individuals can separate themselves and transcend the prevailing views of their origins. Intellectuals from the bourgeoisie may struggle on the side of the proletariate.

When social ideal and self-interest are aligned, the impact upon motivation is powerful. Once a political ideal or a religious ideal is possessed by an individual or a group, it compels political action more strongly than do self-interest and deprivation alone.

Another way to express this tension is that society holds together by power as well as by its cultural values. For example, government is respected because it has power to enforce its laws and because respect for governmental authority is a value of the culture; this value has been given a universal basis.[13] In addition to various forms of power, political and social conduct is controlled by a common orientation to reality, nature, and human existence. As this orientation is grounded in religious belief, it expresses theology.

The science of politics from this perspective is not simply a study of order, authority, and efficiency. Since social ideals and moral values influence the public conduct of people, ethical categories are necessary for understanding political actors and government.

Government is not immoral. The conduct of monarchs, politicians, leaders of state, and citizens is not such that all behave on the level of the lowest possible moral denominator so that moral distinctions are meaningless.

Government is not amoral. To cite Thomas Aquinas' appropriation of classic political thought as an example, governmental action involves responsibility and a choice of means, and the means depends on ends that are moral.[14] The people engaged in poiltics are moral agents, attracted to both good and evil. They are confronted with challenges that go beyond the categories of technical efficiency. Because people are moral beings and need to integrate their world, they will defend their actions with reference to a broader and more abstract conception of reality and will be confronted with an image of what is right. Such an image is reflected politically as ideology. Since people will act morally or immorally as well as efficiently or inefficiently, a failure to deal with the basic ethical and theological questions of politics can lead to shoddy thinking or acting.

Charles McWhorter, an aide to Richard Nixon when he was vice president and later a loyal supporter, was interviewed during the Watergate crisis under Nixon's presidency. He was asked why there were so many charges of corruption flying about if, as McWhorter claimed, Nixon had been scrupulously honest when vice president. McWhorter responded, "There seemed to be an emphasis in the Administration on how to get results, and there were not enough people on the staff asking whether it's right or wrong."[15] In contrast, the classical view is that politics is the doctrine of the good and just life, a continuation of ethics.[16]

As Christians, we must be concerned about what is the proper expression of our faith. What elements of our theology do we summon for politics? What is the consistent expression of these elements? What do they say about the nature of the good life? What is justice?

The answers are not more relative than other forms of theology although they may be more subjective and more complex. God has an objective will for these matters too. There is truth to be secured in exegesis and theological thinking as they apply to political ethics. Christian theology must set forth a clear demonstration of the values and perspectives that Christianity offers for political decision making.

Politics means the selection of common goals and deciding upon the ways of moving toward them. It involves coordinating the activities of organized society on the basis of these common goals, not merely seeking effective responses to immediate circumstances. Simply "to follow the road" is not sufficient; to know where the road leads and to decide if that is the destination we choose is also necessary. Christian activism, therefore, must be preceded by theological reflection in order to provide what R. H. Tawney described as a "clear apprehension of the deficiency of what is and the character of what ought to be."[17]

This book pursues the theological and ethical tasks of discerning the structures of the common life and defining their direction. Paul Ramsey called such reflection and articulation the church's business in politics. Christian political thought clarifies the values of the common life and the range of legitimate alternatives in approaching them.[18] This study, therefore, is not a treatment of isolated political issues; rather, it is the development of fundamental elements of a social and political philosophy and a critical application of them to leading political standpoints.

Part I presents a Christian political theory. In it I set forth criteria that Christians should use to evaluate political theory. The criteria are the understanding of power, human nature, the nature of group life, justice and love, government, and time.

The emphasis in this approach is to develop Christian political theory by drawing substantially upon a theological and biblical perspective. In turn we attempt to broaden the perspectives of theological knowledge by relating it to the fields of political theory, public policy, and law. Other recent Christian writings on politics have a different strength in their helpful use of social scientific data to evaluate the effectiveness of political economic theories and of philosophical categories to clarify the arguments of their advocates.

One nevertheless cannot relate theological and biblical materials to political theory without fully engaging the social sciences, including history. A Christian interpretation of the fundamental elements of politics requires the religious sources of knowledge found in Scripture, theology, church history, and Christian experience. It also requires corroborating and expanding insights from political theory, sociology, anthropology, economics, psychology, and secular history.

Scripture provides essential conceptions for understanding the foundations and principles of politics. In using the Bible, however, one must be as much aware of where it does not apply as of where it does. I have described more fully elsewhere what might be called a dialogical approach to biblical hermeneutics.[19] Simply, the ultimate authority of Scripture as it has been heard and read in the Christian's basic experience of life creates certain unformed perspectives that affect how she or he perceives the social world. Such a perspective would include a sensitivity to the poor, for example. This leads to an awareness of the plight of the poor in one's own world. The Christian then reads Scripture more intentionally; because of this experience, relevant biblical materials that otherwise might be neglected receive attention. This new reading of Scripture guides further observations of current society. One returns again to Scripture with expanded questions and ideas. Careful exegesis reveals which of them are appropriate to the intentions of the authors of the Scriptural passages examined. The process of hearing, observing, and asking continues.

The interplay of hearing the Bible and experiencing society comprises only two elements of the dialogue. The careful use of reason, particularly as theology, guides the process. The thought and practice of Christians who went before in the history of the church, as well as that of fellow members of the present church, confirm one's interpretations. Observations of society include the tools of the social sciences. The guidance of the Holy Spirit must be prayerfully sought throughout the process of interpretation.

Part II of the book applies the critical framework to an evaluation of political ideologies. The ideologies treated are traditional conservatism, liberalism, democracy, laissez-faire conservatism, Marxist socialism, and socialism. In the epilogue we briefly use fascism as a case study to draw observations about the corruptibility of political ideologies and the readiness of the church to face such questions.

My approach is to deal with the ideologies in their fundamental, historic forms rather than in the mixed forms in which they are most present to us. I believe that this approach is helpful in disclosing the distinct ethical issues. A characteristic of this book is the theological and ethical evaluation of the ideologies in their basic forms. It also has a historical approach, concentrating on classical thinkers and ideas within each vision. In contrast, several recent Christian publications highlight thorough analysis of contemporary political and economic positions.

The stakes are high for achieving a valid application of Christian thought to politics. A wrongly conceived system of belief presents several perils for political thinking. One hazard is an incomplete or incorrect understanding of our theology. An example would be to consider justification before God by faith alone as granting release from responsibility for the world.

Another danger is to apply theological concepts that are not relevant to the political question at hand. The Calvinist doctrine that the number chosen by God for eternal salvation is limited does not settle the question of the inclusiveness of participation in political decision making, the issue of democracy.

A third peril is to ignore concepts that are relevant, such as the social justice of the Old Testament or the biblical concern for the physical body.

There also can be wrong applications of concepts that do have genuine significance for political thought. The concept of God's monarchy, which is a ground for criticism of human government, does not provide a model for authoritarian structures of human government. The commandment, "Thou shalt not steal," is not a refutation of socialism. Human dignity does not proscribe all forms of economic restraints by government.

The lack of thinking by Christians about the relationship of theology to politics produces naïve political thinking and wrongly directed political acts. The serious problem of the lack of Christian involvement in the struggle for social justice arises. Some Christians simply separate themselves from social questions. They find what Jacques Ellul describes as a cheap yet absurd feeling of relief from responsibility for anything public.[20] Other Christians have not withdrawn from political engagement yet have not examined what a Christian direction in politics might be.

Some Christians engage in politics very consciously as Christians yet their political positions do not appear to be in accord with a careful application of valid theological guidelines for Christian political thought. Christians can be very intentionally involved in politics as Christians without their politics being Christian. Differences will exist among the readers and the author in identifying to whom that description applies. Being genuinely grounded as a Christian means that this judgment must be made by a sincere examination of carefully established principles of Christian political thought, not by party or class loyalty or commitment to a particular issue or cause.

A disavowal of political ideology is a form of separation from politics. Idolatry and pretense to universality in any ideology must be challenged, but one must then not remove oneself from any association with current ideologies. Míguez Bonino correctly questions if it is possible "to claim a solidarity with the poor and to hover above right and left as if that choice did not have anything to do with the matter."[21] In a musical, Joseph says, "Any dream will do." He is mistaken, however, as he would be if he said all dreams are the same and equally illegitimate. "The content of the dream makes all the difference."[22] While rejecting any sacralization of ideology, we, again with Míguez, must recognize the place of "historical, analytical and ideological mediations" and "resolutely use the best *human* politics and economics at our disposal."[23]

Our purpose in analyzing different options in political world-views is not to identify bad ones to be discarded and good ones to be accepted. Rather, to deepen our understanding of social life and to become more effective political actors, we seek to evaluate critically all options, to learn from their strengths, to be warned by their weaknesses.

Such an eclecticism reflects a certain theology of culture. It assumes the unity of truth. All truth, although broken and scattered in our fallen world, is united in God and can be used by God's children. The human creators of political culture are made in the image of God. Although culture is fallen with the human race, there is a scattered perception of truth even apart from special revelation; however, it is imperfect for social life and insufficient for salvation.

Response to such evaluations may instead be commitment or recommitment to one of the political orientations or to reform it from within. It also may mean seeking new social emphases within a mixed system in which one lives. Emerson's observation of liberalism ("reform") and conservatism would be appropriate for this alternative. ". . . Each is a good half, but an impossible whole. Each exposes the weaknesses of the other, but in a true society, in a true [human being], both must combine."[24] From gazing at these visions, some might rather dream new dreams. They may search for a new form of society, drawing upon vital elements of past visions.[25]

Politics Is About Power

Politics also involves the collective effort to protect life from the threat that resides in the egoism of human groups. The common good cannot be guarded unless power is used against power. Accordingly, the second basic assertion that our treatise makes about politics is that politics is about power. Christian reflection must also expose the egoism in human group life and clarify the ground upon which government must rest.

By emphasizing the importance of politics in this study I am not returning to the old view of history that saw the elements of history as primarily the acts of individuals in and around political office. Politics is important because it is the expression of so much else, not because it is the single significant factor in history.

Theology gives direction to politics; the content of politics is power. The political process is the shaping, distribution, and exercise of power. Power is a handle that opens politics up to a broader perspective. It goes far beyond what we learned in high school civics about politics (knowing the names). Power is a concept that involves sociological analysis, economic analysis, and even theological analysis. Relationship to power is important in education, art, religion, and urban sociology.[26] Our concern is not a description of the political system—who are the members of the cabinet and who appoints whom—but an ethical comprehension of the sources of power, the distribution of power, and the validation of power.

Power is a critical component of both international and domestic political activity. The international dimensions of politics and political theory, however, are not treated adequately within this study. This is a limitation. The nature of politics and the role of political visions in these areas are not any less in need of such analysis.

We face a crisis of power. The first aspect of this crisis is the pride of power. In our lifetime we have repeatedly seen excessive power used for insignificant and questionable ends. As a consequence, there also is a crisis in the validation of power. Many feel the Christian position to be the rejection of power altogether. The mis-

uses of power lead to a moral repugnance about power and a retreat from power—
and in reality a retreat from politics. There never is a power vacuum, however. Simply to reject power allows the pride of power and the concentration of power to go
on unchecked. We need to understand power—its dangers, its checks, and its necessary and proper use. This understanding requires the perspective of Christian theology.

Value of Evaluating Political Theory

The study of political thought makes several contributions to effective leadership
in the church and in society. People are hurt by the way power is used. The exercise
of power, therefore, is a moral issue and thus a religious issue. The impetus of our
study is a moral and religious concern that life in society conform more closely to
goodness and justice.

Power is used according to different views of politics. Christianity is used to
uphold many of these views. People are hurt because of distorted views, supported
by bad theology. Christians are challenges to identify where they stand in the conflict of political ideologies. Accordingly, an alumna of my seminary, doing evangelism in Colombia, South America, wrote to me about the importance of this type
of study for students preparing for foreign missions.

To enact social justice is to shape the practice of power. Responsible exercise of
power for the sake of the Reign of Christ can be assisted by critical knowledge of
traditions of the employment of power. Christian citizens must know how to draw
upon their Christian resources in addressing political decisions. Members in the
church who are called to careers that involve influencing public policy require this
preparation in a special way. What is available often fails to be rooted deeply in
theology or Scripture. There is need within the church for substantial works that
address public values while drawing deeply upon biblical and theological resources
and the traditions of the church. Such a work would contribute both to theological
scholarship and to the understanding of faith and mission.

Finally, a mature understanding of political culture based upon Christian reflection will provide a more effective context for carrying out the dimensions of our
callings that are not political. We will more fully comprehend the needs of the people with whom we serve, teach, and disciple and the challenges of the society that
we share with them.

I

FOCUSING THEOLOGICALLY

1

The Goodness and Corruption of Power

Power in Society

> Many equate power with brute force. Today many Christians, misled by this identification, consider it unchristian to strive for the consolidation of power in organizations that aim at applying Christian principles to society. They believe that power may play no part among Christians. . . . A Christian may speak of love and justice with an unburdened conscience, but as soon as power comes into his purview he has probably lent an ear to the devil. (Herman Dooyeweerd[1])

Power is denounced frequently in religious circles. In the words of James Luther Adams, however, "Religion cannot be adequately described without employing the conception of power; likewise, power cannot be properly described without employing religious concepts. Power is the basic category of being and the basic category of social action."[2] Using power appropriately, therefore is both essential for political action and for the life in faith and society that precedes politics.

As social action, power emerges out of the many factors in life that can give one person an advantage over another. The most important factor in some societies is economic ownership, having more property than another or more significant kinds of property. Some people own factories; others own the shirt on their back. Another factor is knowledge. In a computer age, some have mastered the technology of information processing. A different type of knowledge is the ability to manipulate the processes of the community. Some people hold significant offices or know influential persons in the community. They know how to go about getting the good jobs for them or their friends and relatives. The ability to organize is a closely aligned factor. Economic power often rests as much in the ability to control the economic process as it does in economic ownership alone.[3] By knowledge and organization one can form ties with others that multiply the advantages that the person already has[4]; political power is one form of this ability.

Depending upon the type of culture in which one lives, other factors can furnish significant advantages. In some societies it is physical strength and military prowess. In others that role is provided by prestige derived from some particular cultural factor, such as respect for age, piety, or supposed descent from the gods, or, finally, having real or supposed access to supernatural forces. Time is an example of a resource that cannot directly control the behavior of others yet must be present for other resources to be of value.[5] People who work long hours at exhausting tasks have the disadvantage of not having the time (or energy) to use the resources that they already possess to affect the life of their society.

In a hypothetical society, in which these factors were held in equal balance, there would be no advantage and thus no power to harm.[6] In all real societies, however, the factors are distributed unequally among its members and groups. Power is produced by the structural process that distributes them unequally. This means that the advantages appear through the normal and customary ways in which the groups in the society interrelate and in which the basic tasks of the community are achieved. How much power a person has will be affected by his or her ownership or control of productive property ("means of production") or by having a job which is recognized as economically important for production in one's particular culture. One's power will be enhanced through membership in the governing elite or by having high status. The process by which society achieves order and organizes its life produces power.[7] In the relationships that have developed to carry out the tasks of society there is sufficient power to accomplish them, and those involved have different levels of control, access to resources, or remuneration; thus, Hawley can state that every social relationship is a power equation.[8] Knowledge, skill, competence, and ability are resources for power, but they are not necessarily power in themselves. One can have them without having power. They must be used by people in organized association with one another.[9]

Power accordingly is *relational.* It is a relationship between persons or groups in which one party is dependent to some degree upon another for an aspiration or goal.[10] Power is determined by where a person is in relation to other persons in society and by what one can do with respect to others. "If members of your community become poor in that their power[11] slips *with you,* you shall make them strong . . . that they may live *with you*" (Lev. 25:35–36; cf. p. 22). So the definition of power by Max Weber, one of the founders of modern sociology, is that *power is the chance to realize one's own will in a communal action even against the resistance of others.*[12] Bierstedt presents the same conception in other terms: Power, when manifested, reduces the options[13] for the recipient of power to do other than what the actor intends.[14] Power is the potentiality or capacity to have this effect even if it is not actually carried out. In *The Community Power Structure* Hunter gave examples of what power may do when it is carried out: removing an editor, determining who gets a job, influencing political decisions.[15]

Power is *structural;* it relates more to positions in the social and economic structure than to individual personalities. One possesses power primarily by the institutional position that one occupies in society—where one is socially, what notch one fills, not by who one is as an individual.[16] Jones can push Smith around not because she is Janet Jones, but because she holds the notch in society of being a banker and Smith holds the notch of being a semiskilled, low-wage worker. Smith may experience Jones' power in renting bank-owned housing that is inadequately maintained or in arrangements for paying off a loan. The prophetic critique included powerful *types* of people: large landholders, government officials, leading priests.

Whole groups of people share similar levels of power. That level of power may be called "a class." A group's level of power is determined by the total amount of economic and cultural assets it has and by how much of the total is made up of economic assets in contrast to cultural assets.[17] Cultural assets are formed in one's social origins in the family and in educational institutions. They include educational achievements, gender, ethnic origins, and mannerisms, interests, preferences, and ways of speaking and behaving that lead to being accepted and comfortable in a particular social situation. *Class* has traditionally been used more to describe the economic aspect of that level of power.[18] Those who belong to the same class have similar chances to advance economically; they have similar amounts and kinds of property and similar job opportunities. Their economic relationships are similar according to whether they are owners of productive property, have many or few employees, supervise others, or are wage earners.

The category of *status* describes the power classification of groups sociologically (i.e., in terms of social relationships). It treats the prestige and honor given to certain social roles by custom and law. Status is subjective in contrast to class. It has to do with people's opinions about others rather than with one's objective economic prospects. An example of status is prestige based on where one lives. Living on "the wrong side of the tracks" can be a source of negative status, a mark against you. Status can also be based on from whom one descended; the Daughters of the American Revolution have prestige in some circles. Status is associated with certain expectations about life-style.[19] More significant for our discussion of power, status can determine degrees of limitations on social intercourse, which we call *stratification*. Further, low or high status can be rewarded with different amounts of privileges, such as material goods or job opportunities. The clerical discount reflects the high status that the clergy have had as a profession in our society. Blacks lack power in American society because they have been doubly penalized in terms of both class and status. A high percentage of blacks belong to the lower income classes, and black skin is a negative ascription in much of the society.

The Three Powers

Defensive and Exploitive Power

Two prominent theological commentators on power, James Luther Adams and Paul Tillich, share a definition of power broader than that used by the sociologists whose conceptions we have been discussing.[20] Power is the ability of a particular existence to act in accordance with its being. It is the capacity to live out its life in accordance with its true nature. This capacity is possessed by virtue of the way it was created. Accordingly, power is a gift from God, the creator and sustainer. Human power exists as the way we make actual our possibilities of being. It is the way we respond effectively to these possibilities. This being is not abstract, but it is the being that God presents as a particular gift designed for each life.

An important contribution of this approach is that it establishes the goodness of power. Power is good, not basically tainted, because it is an expression of divine being. "Power belongs to God" (Ps. 62.11, *NRSV*).[21] Conceptions that start with power as a hindrance to a recipient's capacity to act have difficulty justifying power beyond the principle of the lesser evil.

This concept of power presented by Adams and Tillich initially may not appear to be stated sufficiently in social or relational terms. Similarly, biblical language of power does not necessarily relate immediately to the same process to which "power" refers in sociological discussion.[22] Many theological treatments of power describe it only as the ability to act (or "to move reality," "to make things happen," "to affect other people"). The idea of power as overcoming resistance, so prominent in the sociological tradition of Max Weber, which we have been following, is not inherent in these conceptions. Theological treatments built simply upon power defined as the capacity to act do not succeed in justifying power used in situations of conflict, such as political power. The basic definition does not bring the element of conflict to the surface. This issue is significant because how one defines power influences how one will deal with it.

Not all sociologists agree with the emphasis upon overcoming resistance in the definition of Weber, as stated earlier. There is a lack of agreement about power among sociologists. In fact, as we will see, a strength of an approach such as Adams and Tillich is that it provides a basis to describe the mutuality in power that some sociological critics see missing in the Weberian approach. Some also note the social justifications that disguise conflict from the dependent member. For example, in situations of manipulation, one might resist if the intent were not concealed.[23] Low income youths might not enlist for military service in such numbers if they saw that the career training advertised often does not become a reality. Even here, however, conflict is still present in the power relationship even though it is submerged. Further, power and social causation are not interchangeable although many theological treatments seem to assume that they are. Roderick Martin notes that warning someone to get out of the way of a car produces an effect, but it is not power over that person, such as occurred when someone was sent to patrol the Vietnamese jungle.[24] Highlighting the conflict within the power relationship is important for the Christian discussion of power because this approach exposes the controversial ethical questions of coercion, loss of freedom, and physical force. Showing how theological and biblical conceptions of power relate to the power described by sociologists is essential for Christian social ethics.

The ability to act in accordance with one's created being easily leads to the idea of others who would thwart the created intention. In the life of any individual or society, keeping its essential unity requires resisting tendencies that oppose it.[25] Tillich describes "the continuous struggle of power of being with power of being" that has various results ranging between the extremes of assimilating the other power and absorption by it.[26] In the actual human situation, sinful actions against others pervert the intention of the Creator. The gift of power is fallen with the race, and in all communities power is used overtly and covertly to the disadvantage of the weaker neighbor. With this perception, the definition of power as the potential to carry out one's will over the resistance of others applies to Adams' and Tillich's conception. The power of being is the potential to defend one's divinely created being from the contrary intentions of others. Our will is to maintain the integrity of our own being. Their will in this situation has the effect of thwarting it. The pressure of a gang upon a youth to join a form of street life is resisted by the youth's values, courage, and support within home and church. The power of being is a legitimate *defensive power* with the potential of carrying out one's will to be despite the resistance of others. Our personal resources and our ability to act in accordance with our beliefs are power as we reduce the interference of others with our course, which is to be the creature that we perceive God has created us to be.

Power in this way can prevent action, rather than produce action. Dennis Wrong, in describing power as producing the intended results on others, notes that inaction may be the effect of power. Issues are not raised in the community in anticipation of the reaction of powerful persons whose goals and interests would be affected by them.[27] State legislatures may turn down more progressive forms of taxation for fear that the wealthy and their businesses will leave the state. Although there is not much evidence that higher taxes actually do cause the wealthy to flee, "the threat has had more influence than the reality."[28] This dimension of power can be missed when one has only an operational view of power, treating it simply as behavior. Power then is understood primarily politically, as influencing decision making in a conscious attempt to manipulate. This approach inadequately observes the way in which power is frequently exercised "by inaction, by keeping issues from reaching the decision-making point, and by neutralizing potential conflicts."[29] This expression of power in producing inaction is an institutional way in which an elite is served while maintaining a low degree of visibility. The power of being, however, may also produce the inaction of exploitation of oneself or one's group that would otherwise occur.

A philosophical concept that goes back to Plato involves both active and passive powers.[30] They provide a mutuality of exercising influence and being influenced. This interchange is a form of social causation, but is not power. It lacks the involuntary character inherently present in power.[31] It is, however, an essential resource, framework, and goal of true power.

With passive "powers" one has the "power to hear." Part of one's power of being is the capacity to receive, be influenced by, and to participate in the creative powers of life. One needs a capacity to appreciate a great work of music or to be influenced by a great political leader. So Paul boasted of his weakness because through it he participated in the power of Christ (2 Cor. 12.9–10). By participating in the power received from the Creator and Redeemer, we are capable of not participating in a power that would abuse us.

Active and passive "powers" are also resources for mutuality in power, in which one participates with others in social life in order to achieve consensus and then to implement that consensus. Power indeed should be carried out in a framework that is lacking in "mere" unilateral actions that seek to dominate, control, and manipulate the recipients rather than to seek reconciliation in a higher form of community.[32] Intervening and defensive powers are incomplete and potentially exploitive if they fall short of bringing their recipients into effective participative power. The ultimate goal is "power with" instead of "power over." As creatures created to live in community, and who represent God with God's image, "to share power and to share in power is to be fully human."[33] Rollo May calls this form of power "integrative power." "My power *abets* my neighbor's power."[34]

An essential aspect of the defensive power of the weak is their ability to work together in resistance to exploitive power. Various weak individuals form a coalition to work as one for the social purpose, their need of which has placed them in dependency. They supplement their deficiency with numbers and organization in the vital resource that the more powerful party holds.[35] Historically, workers, too weak as individuals to negotiate effectively with powerful companies, have united to procure better wages or working conditions.

Since power is a relationship involving both active and passive elements, those who dominate need the consent of the dominated. The latter have the resource of withdrawing their consent.[36] The first step is rejection of the way the world is defined by the powerful. This disbelief and dissent requires a coherent creed that offers an image of the future that counters the reality of the present.[37] It is significant that American slave owners banned the reading of the Bible. As Frederick Douglass' master stated, "If he learns to read the Bible it will forever unfit him to be a slave."[38] The dissent is enforced by mutual support among the dispossessed. For women, "the first taste of liberation came with the discovery that other women felt as they did: it was liberation from the doubts about their own health and sanity." To prevent their slaves from being in touch with each other over time and over distance, the American slaveowners also enforced illiteracy.[39] The ability of the family of the slave and the ex-slave to maintain its remarkable cohesiveness despite slavery, violence, and dislocation was due to both the strength of marital values among the blacks and the supporting institutions of kinship networks and the black churches.[40]

Attributes that by themselves would appear to be but resources thus can be seen to be effective forms of power. Knowledge, competence, character, endurance, hope, faith, and friendships and social networks aid one in following one's personal purpose in life.[41] Much of the New Testament terminology of power has the character of this defensive power. "To them gave he power *(exousia)* to become children of God" (John 1.12) describes a resource that resists the sin, death, and demonic forces that would thwart the divine intent for those who receive Christ. "The gates of hell shall not have power [*katischuein*]" over Christ's followers (Matt. 16.18; cf. John 10.29; Col. 1.11, 13).

Defensive power is good since it relates to God's creational purposes. The absence of this power is evil because it gives space to actions that frustrate God's purposes. The elements of power, including our ability to know, to organize, and to work in cooperation with others, are good as gifts of God essential for human life in society.

Defensive power also includes material necessities, which also are given by God. Significant struggles of men and women in the Bible relate to economic survival. God gives power over [*šālaṭ* in the Hiphil conjugation] wealth and property for enjoyment (Eccles. 5.19). Conversely the situation arises where this defensive power [*šālaṭ* in the Hiphil again] is lacking and their wealth and property are in the power of a stranger (Eccles. 6.2; cf. Isa. 65.22; Ps. 128.2).

The special attention that Scripture gives to the plight of the widow, the orphan, the poor, and the resident alien reflects the awareness in Scripture of the potential for evil in powerlessness. God's vindication and compassion come when the people's "power has fled" (Deut. 32.36). In the center of Job's declaration of the injustices to these groups is the statement: "The powerful possess the land" (Job 22.8,

NRSV). Poverty is not merely a matter of material goods; it is also a matter of power and the lack thereof. (To be impoverished is to be "a-power-ished.")

> Again I saw all the oppressions that are practiced under the sun. And behold, the tears of the oppressed—with no one to comfort them! On the side of their oppressors there was power—with no one to comfort them. (Eccles. 4.1 *NRSV*; cf. Job 35.9)

So the poor person is defined[42] as one "whose power is insufficient" (literally, "his hand does not reach" [Lev. 14.21]). Oppression is to be "subdued under" someone else's "power" *(yād)* according to Psalm 106.42 (cf. Exod. 3.7-8 where slavery, a paradigm of oppression, is being in the power of another).

Along with the biblical attention to the power of being through creation is the profound awareness of exploitive power through the fall of the race. In evaluating power, we are forced to see it against the sinful world into which we are born in which the creation is marred and power is perverted. Our world is criss-crossed with the advantages with which one person exploits another. The conditions of destructive differentials in resources should never have existed but for sin, and power as a negative force never would have arisen. Sin, however, is a reality of our societies, and the power of being has been perverted into the power of exploitation, which then contests the power of being of others.

In operation power can be domination. It becomes the servant of our self-assertion versus the ability of others to assert themselves as God wants them to be. Tillich speaks of this aspect of power as preventing those who are dominated by it from acting spontaneously, so that they are treated as an object. Part of their personhood and ability to enter into community is lost.[43] Karl Rahner describes the chain reaction that is produced in another person's life by the interference of our act of power. Our action sets at work in the other's life a foreign law of action that somehow changes the whole sphere of that person's existence. The change is foreign to them because it is present by our will, not by the nature and being of that other person.[44]

Power increases sin, universally present in the human race, by allowing lust to work its will.[45]

> Alas for those who devise wickedness and evil deeds upon their beds! When the morning dawns, they perform it, because it is in their power. They covet. . . . They oppress . . . (Mic. 2.1–2, *NRSV*)

Thus the structure of unequal power leads to exploitation. A host of injustices exists (Ezek. 22.7, 9, 12) when the princes of Israel act "every one according to his power" (Ezek. 22.6 cf. Eccles. 5.8–9). In contrast is the future egalitarian age when power in the form of land is distributed to "every man according to his brother" (literal translation [i.e., "equally" *NRSV*], Ezek. 47.14; cf. 46.18).

The power of being, our defensive power, stands against such exploitive power. James Cone has stated, "The only limit to our oppression is our power against it."[46] As a fifteen-year-old black youth in Boston told Robert Coles, "They'll just keep on walking all over us. They always have. They still do. Why should they stop, unless we make them stop, *make them stop?*"[47] A black mother and maid found defensive power in her job and her attitude toward it,

> My daddy used to tell us: be a fighter, be like Joe Louis—hit back, hit back. Well, I've never hit anyone back in my whole life, but I can tell you, I try to hit back by getting up and down my work and not setting back and saying Oh, my gosh, and Oh, my gosh, until I'm just so low in my spirits that I'm no good to anyone and no good to myself either. . . . My husband is sick in the hospital with bad lung, tuberculosis. How could I live if I didn't work? How could my children eat? How could I pay the rent? How could I get us clothes?[48]

The absence of defensive power is a source of corruption. A twenty-year-old woman, a survivor of the 1982 Shatila Camp massacre in Lebanon, said, "Whoever they were, we know our revolution was the only security for us. When our fighters left our camp, anyone could kill us. And they succeeded."[49] Turning around the famous dictum of Lord Acton that "power tends to corrupt and absolute power corrupts absolutely," Adams states that powerlessness tends to corrupt.[50] The characteristics that the powerless often exhibit—apathy, proneness to seek immediate gratification, use of drugs, carrying out violence against themselves and their own group—cannot be explained only in terms of the inward conditions of sin. Reference must also be made to the external factors of power of which they and their communities are victims.[51]

Failure to perceive the pervasiveness of exploitive power as portrayed so forcefully in Scripture contributes to the advocacy of merely individualistic solutions or reliance upon natural harmonies. An important political implication of this chapter is that conflict and exploitation must be taken seriously in devising public policy. Trickle-down theories and supply-side economic approaches seek to help the poor by putting more material resources in the hands of wealthy investors, such as through changes in the distribution of taxes. The assumption is that the extra resources for the wealthy will be invested in industries that will provide more jobs for the poor. Wealth indeed is not a fixed quantity. The concern for the expansion of production is appropriate and usually should be a broadly supported public policy, but economic expansion does not necessarily mean an improvement in the situation of the poor. The weaker elements may even decline.[52] The expansion of wealth may not be significant enough to offset injustice in the conflict in society over its distribution, or its increase may even add to the injustice. The approach of relying on strengthening the economic hand of the wealthy to help the needy appears to be opposite to the biblical realism about power. It misses the genuine conflict between the powerful and the weak, and the destructive relationship of lust and power.

Power is needed as a barrier to sin. The defensive power of individuals and their communities is often insufficient against the magnitude of exploitive power. An intervening power is necessary to limit exploitive power. Rahner correctly sees this use of power as justified as the consequence of the sin to which it answers.[53] When power resources are broadly distributed, exploitive power is limited by the power of being. When they are grossly maldistributed, those who are weakest—whether peasant or refugee—are subject to injustice and violence. Where the inner resources of defensive power are distributed more evenly than the material resources, the psychological and spiritual intrusion might be thwarted, yet without a lessening of the physical assault.

Intervening Power

Life does not consist of a community simply divided among individuals, who are exploiters or victims. Within the biblical understanding, the individual is one who lives in community. True power of being includes a supportive network of relationships.[54] *Defensive power* includes a power of mutuality. We share power with others in establishing and maintaining a community that is just. Since it includes our social nature, defensive power overlaps with a third form of power, *intervening power.* Intervening power is an inherent part of social living, supplementing the inadequacies of an individual's or group's defensive power. It could be called "substitute defensive power"[55] with Christ on the cross as the great exemplar, as he defended helpless humanity from sin, death, and Satanic power. Intervening power stands in the gap between oppressor and oppressed.

In the Reign of God, which is present "in power" (1 Cor. 4.20), God is reasserting decisive sovereignty. In these "days of God's power," as Cyril Powell describes Mark's view of the ministry of Jesus, "there was power to deal with maladjustment and disease at all levels, physical, mental, and spiritual." "It was the power of a new life, enabling [human beings] to triumph over all manner of difficulties and disaster, and to face even death and what lies beyond it with a sense of victory." As the Letter to the Hebrews described it, they "tasted the powers of the age to come" (Heb. 6.5). In Jesus' acts of power (*dynameis,* especially in Luke, Acts), Jesus binds Satan, "the strong man," and plunders his goods. The power of Satan over human affairs and creation, which has brought misery, is challenged and broken (Matt. 12.22–30 par.; Luke 10.9, 17–18; 13.16).[56]

Intervening power is creative as it reestablishes power of being by thwarting exploitive power. *Defensive power* is the ability to retain one's created nature and purpose. The perversion of overcoming of defensive power is evil. *Exploitive power* that defeats defensive power is thus evil and an assault upon God's creation. *Intervening power* restores defensive power by defeating exploitive power.

Intervening power is creative in that its model and source is God. God in general and in special grace reestablishes power of being by overcoming the forces that pervert the creation. God's role as creator continues in the present and is not restricted to the beginnings. God did not grant powers of being and then abandon the creation. God is forming new life and re-creating destroyed life. God's role as creator continues in resisting the fallen forces that assail God's creation. God's redemptive acts are ultimately creative as they restore all things so that the glory of God will be known upon the earth.

The center of God's restoration is in the self-giving of God through Christ upon the cross; yet power is not excluded from the process. At the cross, Christ "disarmed the powers and principalities" of the rebellious cosmos that God is overcoming, and Christ reigns until they are destroyed (Col. 2.15; 1 Cor. 15.23–25).

God's creative love is expressed in acts of justice. God is working in history to overcome injustice and all other evil and unbelief in order to bring in God's final reign where love and justice dwell. Mention is made of God's care, which is present in the destruction of the power of the wicked, in the middle of a passage that celebrates God's creative power in the earth.

> Have you commanded the morning since your days began, and caused the dawn to know its place, so that it might take hold of the skirts of the earth, and the wicked be shaken out of it? It is changed like clay under the seal, and it is dyed like a garment. Light is withheld from the wicked, and their uplifted arm is broken. Have you entered into springs of the sea. . . ? (Job 38.12–16, *NRSV*).

God's power provides deliverance by shattering the destructive power of the enemy (Exod. 14.30–31; 15.6, 9). Yahweh exerts power as the defender of the poor. God does "justice for the orphan and the oppressed" (Ps. 10.18, *NRSV*) by "break[ing] the arm [i.e., power] of the wicked" (v. 15) "so that those from earth may strike terror no more" (v. 18). Intervening power provides justice by overcoming exploitive power. Yahweh empowers the needy to resist this power. Yahweh "stands at the right hand of the needy, to save them from those who would condemn them to death" (Ps. 109.31, *NRSV*).

God's normal way of exerting power is through human creatures, who are God's lieutenants on the earth. The created being of the man and the woman possessed the power to subdue (*kibšuhā*, v. 28) the earth, thus as God's vicegerent bearing God's image in their power (Gen. 1.26–30).[57] This mandate is clarified in the following chapter to be one of service *('ābad)* and care *(šāmar)* (Gen. 2.15).[58] Carrying out power faithfully is to share in one's human heritage and destiny received from God.[59] As Jesus taught in his sayings about the greatest being the servant of all, and as Jesus and Paul demonstrated in their lives, the purpose of power is to serve others.[60]

Power is thus a charge of God to use. The earth to subdue is now the world of the fall. It is when human justice fails and there is "no one to intervene" that God acts in more direct and extraordinary ways (Isa. 59.15–18). The proper situation is when the government and other human institutions are faithful channels of God's intervening power. The king receives God's justice to defend the poor by crushing the oppressor (Ps. 72.1–4; cf. Rom 13.1, 4, 6).

Power exists for the defense of our own being as well as for actions on behalf of the being of others. In Leviticus 25.35 a person who is poor is one whose "power slips" in relation to the rest of the community ("with you"). The divine mandate is to empower that person (literally, "cause him to be strong" [*ḥāzaq* in the Hiphil]). In the context the way of carrying out this responsibility is institutionalized as a proscription on exploitive power: "You must not charge [them] interest on a loan, either by deducting it in advance from the capital sum, or by adding it on repayment" (v. 36, *Revised English Bible*). The purpose is that the needy may regain their defensive power as mutually participating members of the community ("that your brother or sister may live with you") (v. 36). Sodom was condemned for not carrying out this empowerment of the poor, showing the universality of this mandate beyond the Mosaic covenantal community or theocracy. Sodom "did not make strong" (*ḥāzaq* in the Hiphil) the power *(yād)* of the poor and needy when it had the power to do it (Ezek. 16.49). As stated in the international wisdom of Proverbs, we are not to "hold back good from those who are entitled to it, when [we] possess the power to do it" (3.27).

The three dimensions of power are seen in Nehemiah 5, a chapter that provides a specific example of topics interrelated in Leviticus 25: loss of land, weakness, interest, slavery. The people, having lost control of their lands to creditors in their plight, were selling their children into slavery. "We are powerless [cf. Deut. 28.32], and our fields and vineyards now belong to others" (v. 5, *NRSV*). The diminution of their defensive power in the land had led to further exploitive power being exercised against them. As governor Nehemiah interfered on their behalf. He filed charges against those exacting interest, which had led to the loss of lands; and he restored the lands. The government as the intervening power acted against exploitive power to reestablish defensive power.

Paul, however, was jailed for agitating the city when he used his power of exorcism to free a woman who was being exploited by a demonic spirit and in turn by men. Paul's confinement by the city magistrates reminds us significantly that intervening power often becomes an exploitive power itself. Accordingly, intervening power must be limited and instrumental to creating a better distribution of defensive power. Defensive powers when present in excess also can be used to dominate others and become exploitive.[61]

Intervening power is guided and restrained by the principles of justice, to which the Scriptures frequently call the followers of God. Tillich states that justice is but the structure of power. Without justice, power becomes destructive.[62] Justice determines the proper limits and applications of power. It is these activities that give form to justice so that there is no justice without the exercise of power. "My power [*yād*] takes hold on justice [*mišpaṭ*]" (Deut. 32.41). "I put on justice. . . . championed the cause of the stranger. I broke the fangs of the unrighteous, and made them drop their prey from their teeth" (Job 29.14, 16–17).

Tillich also states that justice is power performing the work of love.[63] Love, as our desire to uphold the defensive being of others, conflicts with exploitive power; therefore, love requires resistance in the form of power. Biblical justice is not merely a mitigation of suffering, but a deliverance from the power that causes it. In the following text, "to exercise justice" could be better translated as "to deliver" (as does the *NRSV*).[64] "The Lord has given you justice *(šāpaṭ)* this day from the power of all who rose up against you" (2 Sam. 18.31; also 1 Sam. 24.15).

An exercise of power must be identified and evaluated by its purpose, as Adams argues. Such an end is to bring the marginal person into systems of power. As God brings people into relationship with God and with others in covenantal community, so, too, does intervening power give way to mutuality as it brings mutuality into being. The goal is to bring the powerless into roles of participation in the direction of their lives and community.[65]

Because of its view of human nature, Scripture sees peril in the lack of power (the lack of defensive power) and in the excess of power (the occasion of exploitive power). Reinhold Niebuhr rightly argued that since social injustice is supported by the self-interests of the powerful, it cannot be overcome by appeals of reason.[66] Power is never completely under the control of reason and conscience. Replacing regulation, inspection, and sanctions against industrial evils with self-regulation, dialogue, and negotiation is ineffective. Successful resistance includes power challenging power. Justice must be political as well as rational.

Power and Turning the Other Cheek

Power is often sharply criticized in Christian writings. Many of these writings are not in disagreement with the theology of power outlined here. By *power* these writers often mean exploitive power. They possess moral insight into the destructive possibilities of power, but are imprecise in articulating the dimensions of power. Other critics of power relate power to lethal force. They may also be in essential agreement with our treatise, however, once power is properly understood in broader terms. Many Christian pacifists advocate nonviolent forms of intervening power.[67]

Many traditions within the church, however, are accustomed to individualistic and personal responses that are confined to the inner resources of defensive power. A reasonable question arises about how the use of intervening power corresponds with Jesus' teaching in the Sermon on the Mount about turning the other cheek (Matt. 5.38–42 par.).

The understanding of oppression provided by Allan Boesak, a significant Christian leader in the struggle against apartheid in South Africa, is a helpful guide to the application of this passage. In *Farewell to Innocence* Boesak notes that the oppressed as well as the oppressor have a pseudoinnocence about the existence of oppression.

> The greatest ally of the oppressor is the mind of the oppressed. . . . [But] the affirmation of one's personhood is a powerful act that constitutes a farewell to innocence. . . . To ask blacks to love themselves is to ask them to hate oppression, dehumanization, and the cultivation of a slave mentality. It is to ask them to know that they are of infinite worth before God, that they have a precious human personality worthy of manifiestation. It is to ask them to withstand any effort to make them believe the opposite.[68]

Examined from this perspective, the passage in which Jesus taught about nonretaliation and Boesak's stance on hating oppression are found to be compatible. The Sermon on the Mount is not Stoic, such that these assaults on one's dignity and bodily life would not matter. In the same sermon in Matthew is the petition for daily bread, and Jesus' promise of God's provision of the material essentials of life, food, and clothing. Elsewhere, such as in the Nazareth sermon (Luke 4.18–19), we learn of Jesus' concern about oppression. In commenting on the long-suffering character of love in 1 Corinthians 13, Lewis Smedes states that these deprivations of basic needs are minideaths. We do not affirm them as good because death is the enemy (1 Cor. 15.26). We declare their evil while affirming life in the midst of evil.[69]

A slave mentality is also not present. We absorb the assault not because we are inferior to the oppressor. Again in the same sermon in the Matthean context our worth is emphasized. We are of much more value than the birds of the air and the lilies of the field, which also receive God's love and care. The oppression is instead resisted through the abundance of power of being that those who follow Jesus receive by grace. The resources of radical trust in God and the conviction of worth before God provide defensive power.

The response to the oppressor is that of those who live on the assumption that God is their Protector and Parent. We are not asked in this teaching to give up our created being. Rather, we are asked to give it up to God—a very different request. The "heavenly Father" in whom we are to trust radically for our basic needs is the same God who is revealed in Scripture as the defender of the poor, which is what one is in this distress. The Beatitudes of the Sermon, which in Luke immediately precedes the passage on turning the other cheek, once more assert this characteristic of God. The Reign of God is arriving with its final blessings as God intervenes on behalf of the poor (and in the Lucan form, with woes for their oppressors).

The mentality of those who receive these admonitions to nonresistance is one of deliverance and liberation. In love one does not assert certain prerogatives of defensive power. Instead, one trusts the intervening power of God, who will not rest with the exploitive power of humankind. As we have seen, however, God's ordinary way of carrying out intervening power is through the human agents and institutions of society that conform to God's will for justice. Waiting upon God, therefore, is also one of expectancy that God will work through others in the social community who will intervene to end the exploitation.

2

Doing Human Nature Justice

Reflecting upon politics as a Christian requires a theological and ethical understanding of the basic dynamics of life as they relate to politics. In the first chapter we encountered power, which involves fundamental aspects of society and the individual. Now we focus more broadly on the nature of human life. Human nature provides the roots of political thought. On one hand there is the objective reality of what human beings actually do have in common—biologically, psychologically, and socially. On the other hand, there are the various perceptions that people have of what that reality is, as well as the differing expectations for life that they relate to these ideas.

Political theory must be based on an understanding of human nature. Politics can be carried out only by human beings, and it involves the problem of how much power should be entrusted. A conception of human nature provides the political thinker with a means of evaluation. It is a standard of what is good for the community and for upholding the claims of the individual over against society.[1]

Not all who reflect upon politics are willing to claim knowledge of human nature because of doubts about the possibility of such knowledge. Normative political thought is hindered at the beginning by some current problems in political epistemology: Is there universal human nature? Can it be known? By presenting a Christian reflection on politics, we are intentionally starting from the standpoint of Christian faith. We are making the assumption that reliable truth is found in the Judaeo-Christian scriptures and in the natural world as created by God. We are building upon the Christian understanding of human nature without attempting the significant task of laying out the basis of its claims for knowledge. We are thus able to take a short cut into normative argument that those who do not make our assumptions would not take.

That Mysterious Mixture of Good and Evil

Human beings are neither simply inherently good nor inherently evil; rather, they are caught in a tension between two poles. The human race is fallen in sin, but it still reflects the nobility of its creation in the image of God. John Wesley described the mystery of these strange inconsistencies within us as "the wonderful mixture of good and evil, of greatness and littleness, of nobleness and barrenness."[2]

26

That it was in the image of God that the human being was created, a key element in the account of the creation in Genesis (1.26–27), identifies the human being as the representation of God on earth. To represent God requires a relationship with God; thus, in this passage humanity is addressed by God, hears God, and obeys God (Gen. 1.28–30).

To be made in the image of God also carries responsibility. God's address to those who bear the divine image assigns governing duties over the living things (1.26–30). The image of God itself implied rulership in two ways by its usage in the Ancient Near East: The king's statue proclaimed the king's domination, and it was the king who was the image of God.[3]

In turn the relationship and responsibility point to the spiritual, creative, and rational capacities needed for assisting in the continuation of God's creative work. To be created in the image of God is also to be communal: "In the image of God he created them; male and female he created them" (Gen. 1.27, *NRSV*).

Despite the fall of the human race in sin (Gen. 3), we retain the stature of those created in the image of God. In Genesis 9.6 capital punishment is decreed after the flood for those who kill a person: "for God made the human being in God's own image." James 3.9 appeals against wrong done to others on the grounds that they are "made 'according to the likeness' of God" (quoting from Gen. 1.26). The human being is still the capstone of creation. The image of God that it bears is now hampered and fallen, but it still displays God's image in consciousness, knowledge, feeling, and freedom.[4] Psalm 8.5 states that God has made human beings "little less than God (*'elōhim)* and crowned them with glory and honor." Yet because of sin the image needs to be renewed. According to Colossians 3.10 those who belong to Christ have "put on the new nature which is being renewed in knowledge after the image of its creator." The renewal presupposes the damage done to the old creation (vv. 5–8).

In Romans Paul has this same duplexity. In Romans 3.10–18 he quotes the sharp language of the Psalms to demonstrate that there are not different categories within humankind as far as sin is concerned: "All, both Jews and Greeks, are under sin's power, just as it is written . . ." (vv. 9–10). "No one is righteous." "No one understands." "No one seeks God." "No one exercises kindness." Paul's intent is to show the universality of the sin nature, not its totality in the sinner. His own wording in v. 23 is more measured: "All have sinned and are lacking the glory of God." Earlier in Chapter 2 Paul speaks more positively in describing the judgment according to each one's deeds (v. 6). Along with wrath and distress for everyone who does evil (vv. 8–9), "to those who by patience in well doing seek glory, honor, and immortality, he will give eternal life" (2.7). "There will be . . . glory and honor and peace for every one who does good" (v. 10). Paul speaks at least hypothetically of such goodness. In v. 15 he writes similarly: The Gentiles who knew not the Mosaic law but followed the unwritten law of their hearts, will be excused (or accused) by their conscience on the day of judgment.

The Biblical view of human nature after the fall is that it is in strange confusion. We have a capacity to do good, but we are unable to disconnect it from our capacity to do evil. Reinhold Niebuhr appropriately provides two criteria that should be used in assessing which political methods will provide the most good for society.[5]

The first criterion for a political strategy is: Does it do justice to the moral resources and possibilities in human nature and provide for the full usage of every latent human capability? The human being is not an animal; the fall is not complete. Politics should reflect this condition. Human beings are capable of making a certain rational evaluation of their own interests and even of those of others. A basic social disposition draws people together, and there is even a varying perception of justice.[6] Paul Tillich warns that every form of politics is necessarily destructive, which lacks the teaching that the human essence has not been completely lost, but rather continues as a norm and judgment even in the greatest aberrations of existence.[7]

With a lesser recognition, opportunities for persons to develop their potential will not be opened up. People will not be trusted to govern themselves; instead, there will be reliance upon dictatorial forms of government.[8] Cynicism also leads citizens to distrust each other, undercutting the essential practice for democracy of listening carefully to what people are saying.[9] Further, if our doctrine of human nature is so negative that further evidence of sin seems slight and negligible, then we will fail to feel proper compassion and anguish over current episodes of injustice.

The second criterion of Niebuhr for politics is: Does it take account of the limitations of human nature, particularly those that manifest themselves in our collective behavior? As Pascal said, "The human being is neither angel nor beast; and the misfortune is that whoever tries to play the part of the angel plays the part of the beast."[10] In his treatment of human nature, Niebuhr maintains this balance in exceptionally fine fashion in the tradition of Augustine, who spoke of the struggle within us between love and self-love.

The question may arise, "What about the Christian? Does our justification by faith warrant a different polity than what is necessary for the unbeliever?" The Christian life is not one of complete deliverance from sin. The New Testament usually refers to salvation as a process going on in the present or completed in the future. For example, Colossians 3.10, to which we have just referred, used the present (progressive) tense in the Greek to speak of our sanctification: "We are *being renewed* [*anakainoumenon*]" Paul, writing against opponents who claimed to be perfect, plainly stated that he had not obtained perfection. His hope instead was in the Second Coming when Christ would alter the weakness of his bodily existence (Phil. 3.12, 20–21). Not only are believers not perfect, but the New Testament is full of warnings regarding the carnal condition of many Christians and their capacity for enormous evil if they do not walk in the Spirit. Even the best efforts of the Christians suffer from the continuation of self-interest in our will and imperfection in our knowledge. The Puritan John Cotton saw that concern about the potentiality of evil applied equally to the church. "If a Church or head of a Church could have done worse, he would have done it [Jer. 3.5]. . . It is necessary . . . that all power that is on earth be limited, Church-power or other."[11] A Christian political philosophy has to be based on an understanding of human nature that includes the saint's capacity for evil.

Political theory must be *realistic,* which according to Niebuhr means that it should take into account "all factors in a social and political situation, which offers resistance to established norms, particularly the factors of self-interest and power."[12] Still with Niebuhr, it must be a *Christian* realism in the sense that it also has a vision of the present pertinence of social and ethical ideals and takes seriously all the factors in a situation that support them.[13]

The Lesson of Eden

The account in Genesis of the creation and fall of the human race presents graphically the dynamics of human sin. Eden shows that the source of evil lies in the very factors that makes us human/creatures, our freedom and our finiteness.[14] Tillich states that if one were to define humanness in a couple of words, it would be "finite freedom."[15]

In freedom we had the choice of eating or not eating from the tree of the knowledge of good and evil, and we failed. Tillich expresses well the correlation between freedom, sin, and the essence of being human. Dignity and risk are correlates. The person is truly human because he or she can be tempted. Freedom means having possibility, which is identical with temptation.[16]

Eden also shows the relationship between the source of evil and consciousness of our finiteness. In the garden we were tempted to overcome the confines assigned to us. Our limits were not to eat of the tree of the knowledge of good and evil. Our motivation was to become like God, as the serpent promised, "When you eat of the tree, you will become like God."[17] With our power of reasoning and self-consciousness comes the consciousness of our finiteness. By disobeying and eating of the tree we express our refusal to admit our creatureliness and to acknowledge our place as merely a member in the total unity of life.

The Edenic picture is not only important for political theory in its clarity about the nature of sin, it also shows that even when humanity was at its best, freed from a heritage of sin as a person and as a species, it still has the potential of evil. We have no way within history to move beyond the conditions in which sin arises. Rather, the capacity for sin is connected with our nobility. Sin arises in the very conditions of our being a creature, albeit a creature with the dignity of freedom and creativity. It is thus a capacity that remains no matter how good we are. Redemption does not come by extracting our true person from nonessential parts. The source of evil is not nature nor the human body, both of which people in the past have attempted to master in order to be rid of evil. The capacity for evil comes from the nature of our person as it was created by God, including our mind, body, will and emotions, all of which are positive in themselves. To seek salvation by freeing oneself from one's body or from nature or by humanizing the race thus tragically misses the mark as to the origin of evil. Sin appears in our very essence.[18]

Humankind does not have even the advantage of the neutrality of Eden. Because of the fall of the race, all people have the handicap called original sin, the negative influence of the fall on everyone. They all have a disposition toward sin. They develop in the womb of a sinful mother, they are nurtured by sinful parents, and they are socialized by sinful institutions. They are free in that they are still men and women, but that freedom is conditioned by the previous history of the human race. So all persons sin and receive the penalty placed on sin because of Adam. "Death passed to all persons because all persons sinned" (Rom. 5.12).

Because of our finiteness and freedom, we are insecure. We are insecure because of our finiteness lest we come to meaninglessness.[19] The reminders of our finiteness are intensified beyond the original situation of Adam and Eve in the trauma of birth and in the certainty of death because Adam and Eve were driven from the tree of life. We have wounds from personality development (e.g., a natural inferiority complex because of our constant early contrast as children with adults). John Wesley wrote to his brother Charles, "If I have any fear, it is not of falling into hell but of falling into nothing."[20] According to Tillich, we are "threatened by nonbeing," as is seen in our response to death, guilt, and error. This threat produces anxiety, which again to Tillich is a synonym for finitude—"finitude seen from within." Thus, anxiety is basic to our nature.[21] Our response to such insecurity is to seek to overcome our creatureliness.

We are also insecure because of our freedom. We are anxious lest we be not what we ought to be.[22] A human being has a fear of freedom, and seeks a false security by not exerting his or her created freedom. The servant who hid his talent in Jesus' parable found inaction superior to the risks of failure in responding to the opportunities presented by the in-breaking Reign of God (Matt. 25.26–30).

In face of such insecurity the human being has a choice. One can either trust God and find security in God's love, or one can continue in anxiety. Anxiety may lead a person to trust in God, and in that creative and redeeming relationship find the integrity of one's self. Then he or she no longer needs to dominate others, to be elevated above them, or to be dominated by them. The strengthened power of being does not draw its energy from false bases of security.

The recourse of trusting in God, however, may be rejected. It follows that unbelief, the rejection of God, not anxiety, is the root of sin. Unbelief thwarts our seeking refuge from our anxiety in the arms of the Almighty. Instead, we use our freedom in rebellion against the Creator, rejecting our position as creatures.[23] Evil arises in our will at the very center of our personality. Augustine stated, "By craving to be more, man became less; and by aspiring to be self-sufficing, he fell away from Him who truly suffices him."[24] When the spontaneous relationship with God is lost, spontaneous relationships with all others becomes difficult.[25] Other persons are no longer viewed as being intimately loved by God, and for the same reason the individual views his or her own being as an object to be manipulated or abused.

"You will not die," the serpent said, contradicting God. The serpent presented a distorted view of God as one whose commands are not fully on the side of human welfare. Sin involves assenting to a false view of God, or "rebellious unbelief," as Richard Mouw calls it. Sin lies deeper than ethical selfishness. It involves "love of the creaturely" rather than the Creator. Mouw states, "The kamikazi pilots' devotion to the Emperor seems to have been idolatry, but not selfish in nature." Because of pride, in our rebellion against the Creator, we are willing to trust in anything but God and will humiliate ourselves in bowing and scraping before brutal dictators and dumb idols. Sin involves misplacing the trust that rightfully resides in the love of God in some dimension of God's creation so that ultimate hope and allegiance is placed in, among other objects, economic systems and political ideologies.[26]

The insecurity involved in our rebellion against God also turns into aggression against threats of every kind. Our survival impulse has a spiritual dimension. We seek both to survive physically as an animal as well as to survive the threat of meaninglessness and nonbeing. We seek to overcome our limitations as human beings, or we assent to be less than fully human.

In the first form of false response to insecurity, we desire to possess power and glory. We have a will-to-power, to have power over others, and we seek prestige and social approval.[27] As a result self-esteem is bolstered as the basic drive in life. We become eager for all that will contribute to it. We are driven to build ourselves up at the expense of others.[28] We seek power to control others. We seek prestige in order to be considered better than others. A person compensates for his or her insignificance by pretensions of pride.

When we perceive other human beings having qualities or possessions that would make them seem better than us, we express our insecurity and inferiority in the rage of envy and resentment. Similarly, we begrudge with the same passion others who are gaining or surpassing what had been our superior position. The effort that envy precipitates is not to secure for ourselves the power or wealth of others, whether by an exertion of power or by a redress of injustices. We instead desire that they themselves be diminished by being stripped of assets, humiliated, or harmed.[29] The story of Eden continues in an account of sibling rivalry, the pyschological and social seedbed of envy. Cain was "very angry and his countenance fell" when "the Lord had regard for Abel and his offering." "And . . . Cain rose up against his brother Abel, and killed him" (Gen. 4.4–5, 8, *NRSV*).

The insecurity that remained unmitigated because of the rebellion against God perverted the spontaneity and mutuality in human relations:

"They knew that they were naked; and they sewed fig leaves together . . ."
"I will put enmity between you and the woman . . ." "Your desire shall be for your husband, and he shall rule over you" (Gen. 3.7, 15, 16, *NRSV*).

Their natural nakedness, of which they were previously unashamed (2.25), became the occasion of vulnerability so that the deepest human attraction became subject to manipulation to gain status or security, to flatter one's name, or to gain control over the behavior of others. As seen in simple form in marriage, the institutional life of human society became oppressive and manipulative. Accordingly, politics and technology became focused upon self-security, pushing back their intended objective of meeting the communal needs of humankind. The resulting conflicts between individuals and between groups were not just for physical survival; they were also competing expressions of power and pride. Power is pursued in order to feel secure by obtaining greater significance, fear, or respect. The very possession of power and prestige involved encroachment upon the prestige and power of others.[30]

Conflict thus became a stubborn factor of human life. People seek power over people because of their insecurity. The peril of a competing human will is overcome by subordinating that will to our ego and using the power of many subordinated wills to ward off the enmity which that subordination creates. A vicious circle is produced that intensifies the insecurity in face of aroused fears and enmities until the ego is finally fully involved in injustice.[31]

The fear of freedom leads to a course different from domination and elevation in seeking to escape insecurity. People instead secure new bondages and dependencies. Augustine speaks of the vanquished who readily succumb to their victors because they prefer "any sort of peace and safety to freedom itself."[32] Individuals flee from the isolation, powerlessness, insecurity, and lack of meaning and direction that are the "unbearable burden" of freedom. Writing during the Nazi era in which he saw millions of Germans "as eager to surrender their freedom as their fathers were to fight for it," Erich Fromm described the conditions in individual personality development and in the historical conditions of modern life that produce a longing for submission.[33] One recourse from this despair can be to plunge into a life that seeks security in legalistic conformity to moral and religious codes.[34]

A view of oneself as merely an object to be manipulated can also accompany a flight from freedom and be a form of rebellion. We assent to be less than the creature we were meant to be.[35] The escape from freedom appears as an inability to stand alone and to develop the potentiality that one has. Our whole life may instead center on a dependency upon another person, who is in turn manipulated by us in order to meet our needs and to be responsible for us.[36] For example, the woman who denies her created gifts in passive submissiveness to authoritarian patterns may be participating in the sin of failing to become a self, to take responsibility for herself, to make fully human choices. A person has freedom to actualize the possibility of nonbeing by choosing to lose oneself in the detailed processes, activities, and interests of existence. Such activity is sinful in the sense of orientation toward what is not God.[37] Similar to such "feminine despair" (although that phenomenon is by no means confined to one gender) is the mass person who loses oneself in secular matters so that he or she finds it easier to conform to others than to dare to be oneself.[38] John Raines observes that Marx correctly saw an element that was not sufficiently developed by Reinhold Niebuhr: Self-loss and passivity, not just self-love and pride, are sources of seduction.[39]

Our insecurity is heightened by the uncertainties of society and history that have play in our environment in the form of the lack economic stability, social recognition, or physical health. Our anxiety is increased by the power of human groups and the unpredictability of history. We are driven to control both history and our relationships in society as well as nature.[40] This intrusion of self-centered power into societal relationships explains our "cultural lag"—why we are unable to form a just or universal community. The lag is not merely a factor of culture; it has an ethical and spiritual dimension.[41] Humanity's insecurity will not be overcome by improvements in education, science, or technology. While presenting new possibilities for a just and secure community, advances in culture also introduce new threats of domination and submission. In part they reflect the power and interest of those who are in a position to influence the direction of research or to take advantage of its fruits. Our cultural dilemma has roots deeper than the education and science that grows with it.

Augustine is regarded by Niebuhr as the first great "realist" in Western history, who introduced a more Pauline note into the field of political ethics. Where Cicero had seen human government as a compact for justice made by rational men, Augustine saw it dominated by the love of self, formed by an uneasy armistice between contending forces.[42]

A Caution About Power

Where is the relevance for political theory in the presence of the will-to-power among the basic dynamics of sin? Politics does deal with how power is to be distributed. It includes putting power into the hands of certain people, those who participate in ruling.

We should note, however, that the power in the will-to-power is nevertheless usually *not* political power. It is much more comprehensive. In most people it is more subtle than political power. In a father it might be tied to sense of powerlessness in his economic roles so that he compensates in an authoritarian manner toward his children.[43] It might be reflected in insecurity regarding the outgroup, those who are independent of us, who are not in our sphere of power and who are a threat to our power—blacks, whites, liberals, Fundamentalists, communists, fascists, depending on where one is. It may come from resentment against pride or excellence in others or anything else that threatens our own will-to-power. The pertinence of understanding the will-to-power is a lesson that applies much more broadly than to politics.

We also are not saying that political ambition equals the will-to-power. Much of American culture does not need further reasons to be negative about those in government although we do need to understand better what is valid in our negativity. Political aspiration can be worthy. Kingship was a promise and blessing for Abraham (Gen. 17.6). We have noted already in Chapter 1 the positive aspects of power, which cannot be avoided without participating in another sin, that of social irresponsibility. There is (1) a legitimate defense of one's created being, (2) the limitation on rebellious freedom and the maintenance of mutuality and community, the healing powers of justice, and (3) the dispersing of power to the powerless, bringing them into the mutuality of power, that creates community.

Our intention is not to intensify suspicion of the bearers of political power, but rather to raise interest, concern, and caution for what is put into not only their hands. The same concerns apply to others to whom society grants exceptional powers, whether executives, corporate lawyers, establishment advisers, or other economic notables. It is not to be put there and forgotten by the child of conscience. For what is put into the hands of leaders is power and prestige, particular forms of that for which the ego craves in order to make itself secure in relation to other egos. It is "soul food"—ego food. Augustine wrote of the "appetite of the soul to hold other souls in its power [*sub se habere alias animas*]."[44] There is a mold in our sin nature—a desire for power—that power fits. Power is exactly what the worst part of us wants to use. Power is not sin in itself, but sin regularly expresses itself in the desire for power.

Ethical and rational approaches to controlling public behavior are insufficient. They do not deal with the substance of power. A warning that Christianity brings to politics is that political power, as well as economic power, is closely related to the most basic drives of the ego. Let us be sure that we understand the potentiality for evil that is presented. It is a possibility for any person, always latent within fallen humanity.

No Group Is Secure Enough

The lust for power is particularly obvious in those who are insecure, whether socially, economically, or psychologically. The danger of granting power to the insecure is evident. Should not power then be granted the secure? Power has been placed in the hands of those who would seem secure throughout most of human history—the wealthy, the mighty, the majority class or race. Should not the wealthy be trusted? After all they "already have the things for which wrongdoers commit wrong" (Aristotle[45]).

The Deception of Security

The person who is insecure seeks for mastery. The person who is secure assumes his or her self-mastery. The ego assumes itself to be the master of its own destiny and to be free from imperfection, but it is unaware of the self-centeredness of its own position. This position is unstable, however, because it is not observant of its own weakness and selfishness.

John Calvin was aware of the illusion that power creates. He viewed princes of small nations to be more humane than those of large states. Since those with more power reckon "their power to be unlimited, they set no bounds to their freedom of action and rush on, without restraint, wherever their passions drive them."[46]

Possession of power is an occasion for subtle but intense temptation. Power gives an exalted view of one's worth and accomplishments so that one can easily miss the sense of living under grace. Once power is established, "it justifies itself as necessary and earned."[47] In the disturbing and widespread Victorian racism, Anglo-Saxon imperial supremacy proved the innate superiority of the white to the satisfaction of many.[48]

The deception of wealth is a good example of this self-deluding voice of power. "Give me not . . . riches . . . or I shall be full and deny thee and say, 'Who is the Lord?' " (Prov. 30.8–9, *NRSV*).[49] In a powerful passage, Marx noted "the power to confuse and invert all human and natural qualities" that wealth has in an economy that responds to the ability to pay rather than to genuine need and real ability.

> Money is [considered] the highest good, and so its possessor is good. Besides, money saves me the trouble of being dishonest; therefore, I am presumed honest. . . I who can have, through the power of money, *everything* for which the human heart longs, do I not possess all human abilities? Does not my money, therefore, transform all my incapacities into their opposites? . . . It transforms real imperfections and fancies, faculties which are really impotent and which exist only in the individual's imagination, into real faculties and powers.[50]

Wealth does not provide a security that satisfies the desire for more. The president of Tanzania states,

> Man can only eat so much, and wear so many clothes, and live in one place at a time. That is why in rich societies an ever decreasing proportion of the national wealth is devoted to meeting these basic needs. But while human needs come to an end, the desire for power and prestige through the acquisition of material goods is insatiable.[51]

Plato sought to separate the combination of wealth and economic power by arrangements in which the rulers would have no material excess, or lack. They would not then become enemies and masters of their fellow citizens, fearing those inside the city state more than those outside.[52] The Quaker, John Woolman, said that the spirit that loves riches and gathers wealth defends its treasure with the power that the new advantage gives. "This is like a chain where the end of one link encloses the end of another." When even the smallest degree of this oppression "is cherished, it grows stronger and more extensive."[53] It is not surprising, therefore, that "one may look in vain for historic evidence that the rich have been more peaceful than the poor."[54]

The Insecurity of Having Power

Politically, socially, racially, economically, sexually, no one is strong enough not to be threatened and thus to be freed from seeking to selfishly dominate other wills. As we have seen, the lust for power, which often drives a person to positions of dominance, is rooted in weakness, not in strength.[55] The more we have, the more we have to lose, which results in the need for more power to retain it. Those who have obtained public acclaim are the ones who fear obscurity; poverty is a threat to the wealthy, not to the poor.[56] The need to defend power once it is obtained is politically and socially significant since its holders have the potential to carry out their will.

The more power that we have, the more conscious we are of it and threats against it. Joseph Conrad in *Nostromo* describes a South American strong man, Guzmán, who viewed the power of government as divine and "incarnated in himself; and his adversaries, the federalists, were the supreme sinners, objects of hate, abhorrence, and fear, as heretics would be to a convinced inquisitor."[57] The Watergate incidents that brought down President Richard Nixon are ironic in retrospect since such intrigues against political rivals were far from needed. The president's insecurity in his power was a far greater threat to his reelection than was the power of the opposing political party that he feared.

In the next section we will see that the factors that would seem to make types of people assured enough to handle power at the same time tend to blind them dangerously to dangers peculiar to the type of strength that they appear to have.

"Ideal Secure Persons"?

Out of fear of rulers who grasp for more power, some have suggested that the government should be taken out of the hands of the masses and placed in the safety of those who would seem to be the most genuinely secure—the wise, the virtuous, the religious.[58] Each of these groups could be considered as those who are most capable of being trusted with power. They would appear to be those best equipped to have power over others. We have seen that power gives a false sense of security and creates its own insecurities. What happens when power is given to these ideal groups? Are they immune?

The wise. Tolkien's story of the *Lord of the Rings* offers a profound critique of concentrated power. The ring, "the Ring of Power," must be destroyed before the evil Sauron can be defeated. It cannot, however, be used by the wise, powerful, and good—even if to destroy it. The powerful must not possess it because their power with the additional power of the ring would produce a new center of tyranny. This danger extends to the wise, even the heroic wizard Gandalf. As the elf-friend Elrond said, "If any of the wise should with the Ring overthrow the Lord of Mordor, using his own arts, he would then set himself on Sauron's throne, and yet another Dark Lord would appear." So those who are entrusted to carry the ring to its place of doom are the humble and unpretentious hobbits. Samwise, the hobbit, could withstand the temptation of the ring. "He knew in the core of his heart that he was not large enough to bear such a burden." All his need and due was the one small plot of a free gardener (not a garden swollen to the size of a realm), a garden toiled by his own hands (not the hands of others).[59] The wise and powerful would be deluded by their strength from maintaining this recognition.

The danger of false security for the wise is to lack awareness of the finiteness of their knowledge while pretending that it is final and ultimate. John Wesley argued, "Surely no fool is so incapable of amendment as one that imagines himself to be wise." He or she is like the self-righteous that Jesus addressed as not knowing their need of a physician. Their conceit is self-perpetuating because it prevents them from taking instruction from others.[60]

The possession of power makes an accurate perception of the limitations of one's knowledge even more difficult. "Irangate" involved secret shipments of arms to rebel forces in Nicaragua through the government of Iran. Reflecting on this incident of lying and lawbreaking within the executive branch of the U.S. government, the late William Shannon wrote,

> Reagan and the top insiders fell victim to a recurring illusion. They thought that because they had acquired exceptional power, they had also acquired exceptional insight. They confused secret information with secret wisdom. Because Reagan and his men believed they knew what needed to be done, they were prepared to violate the Constitution, the law, and the orderly procedures of government to make their will prevail. First came power and secrecy, next came pride and then came folly.[61]

Superior intelligence or knowledge does not eliminate the pervasiveness of sin, which affects all areas of the personality. Reason, too, is subverted.[62] Those who rely on their wisdom also become unaware that their knowledge centers around their ego and thus their social class. This is the social conditioning of knowledge. Niebuhr states that "reason is always, to some degree, the servant of interest in a social situation." Reason is defeated "on a lower level" in that prior to our cognizance it is

influenced by the perspective of the group to which we belong. The reason that sur-
veys the field of history is "an anxious reason, organically related to an anxious
ego."[63]

The university provides an example of the rule of the wise as it is expressed in an
actual institution. It is an institution that we can observe to determine how the wise
govern. The strife and criticism of the universities in the late 1960s disclosed the
degree to which the university was one with the forces of its culture, particularly the
powerful elements of that culture. Rather than being a socially neutral institution,
it engaged in housing practices that were detrimental to low-income neighbor-
hoods. It provided research and support for questionable practices of military intelligence and warfare abroad. In the years right after World War II, faculty members
who came under attack for leftist views or associations, even as mild as supporting
Henry Wallace's presidential campaign, were rarely supported by their administrators. Instead, out of concern for the public image and support of the institution and
for their own reputations, administrators were active in repudiating and dismissing
these faculty members. For this end, procedures designed to protect faculty members from administrative capriciousness were set aside. Executives of academic
institutions behaved no differently than did the executives of the movie industry.[64]

All this merely means recognizing the human nature of very cultivated men and
women. Academic or cultural refinement can include a reluctance to be open about
one's power. The business world can be more honest and more ethical than the
university. Langdon Gilkey observed that the more acute mind of the intelligent
person was able to rationalize its self-concerns with more plausible and elegant
beliefs than was the slower mind among the Westerners interned in the Shantung
Compound in China during World War II. He came to respect the open rascal: "He,
at least, was forthright in admitting his selfishness."[65]

A critical question about Plato's *Republic* is who will stand guard against the
guardians? Truth easily becomes the slave of power.

This possibility at least needs to be asked when research assumptions carried out
by members of a dominant group have results that negatively affect or ignore subor-
dinant groups. This was certainly a valid question when intelligence tests, already
under criticism as not being accurate across cultural and economic lines, were cited
still by some scholars in support of biological differences between races.[66] The desire
for a universal standard of measurement, as well as the desire for "scientific status,"
has led to continuing reliance upon test performance despite the criticisms of the
disadvantage to people of color and women. Yet the misuses are costly for those
negatively affected both in terms of lost positions for which the tests are used as
criteria of entrance and in terms of perception of oneself and by others.[67] Nevertheless, these examples are mild in comparison to the abuse of anthropology in the
late nineteenth century. "Almost all methods of classifying the human species . . .
whether by language, brain, physical features or colour resulted in the European
coming out on top."[68]

Our view of human nature warrants suspicion when members of a group that
possesses advantages present "scientific" arguments justifying their advantages—
particularly when the empirical base appears inadequate. An example occurred in
the early 1970s when some religious leaders opposed women's inclusion in lead-

ership positions by citing scholars, such as Steven Goldberg, who presented an endocrinoligical argument in favor of male leadership. They argued that male dominance was not due to cultural advantages, but rather to the acknowledgment by society of the biological reality that testosterone in men makes them more aggressive and thus stronger leaders. Yet data was available even then that testosterone makes males more aggressive only in the sense of acting to inflict physical harm upon others, which is not a leadership quality in human societies. Qualities that are related to leadership ability, such as competitiveness, dominance, timidity, or passivity, are not related to testosterone.[69] The fundamental problem is not a mental mistake in locating, understanding, and weighing evidence. Rather, truth has been subverted by the defense of white power and male power—probably without conscious dishonesty but at a lower, prereflective level.

Knowledge and academic experience do not make one especially safe to hold power. As T. S. Eliot wrote,

> Where is the Life
>   we have lost in living?
> Where is the wisdom
>   we have lost in knowledge?
> Where is the knowledge
>   we have lost in information?[70]

The virtuous

> One of the most sincere, dedicated and able men ever to occupy the White House. . . . He has set an example in self-discipline, family life, church attendance, et cetera, that is helping the country through a great spiritual crisis . . . and despite differences in certain political areas he deserves to be commended especially by Christians.

In these words Richard Nixon was supported before Watergate by an outstanding evangelist who had assumed that he knew the president well.[71] Some excellent Evangelical leaders felt burned when the Watergate revelations were made. They had thought that their close relationship to the White House under President Richard Nixon gave them a personal knowledge of the president so that they could give him political support by reason of his "personal ethics."

Virtue, in the private sphere and even more so in the public sphere, is a quality that is difficult to determine and to predict. How can it be forseen who has the virtue that can hold up in the midst of power?

> According to the proverb of Bias, "Power proves a man."[72] For many, while they remain of humble station, have all the appearance of virtue, yet fall away from virtue so soon as they arrive at the height of power. (Thomas Aquinas[73])

The political choice of a person who was genuinely wise, virtuous, or religious would have to be made on the basis of observation and reputation (and often institutional associations). Neither wisdom, virtue, nor piety is easily separated from its imitations—even less so in a body the size of a state.

The false security that tempts those known for virtue leads them to make their own tenets the standards for others. This is what happens when people begin to see themselves as good. Their standards become absolute standards of morality. Nonconformity becomes an evil rather than a disjunction and thus subject to the use of power. Efforts are made to form community by eliminating nonconformity in this realm. Some conservative Protestant schools have combined a commitment to the authority of Scripture in matters of faith and conduct with legalistic moral codes. In certain situations, students effectively challenged the biblical grounds for prohibitions such as the one against alcohol. The response to them by the administration was not on the grounds of biblical arguments but that these rules are necessary for forming the kind of community that they want. In effect, the transcending biblical grounds were abandoned in favor of the moral preferences of the administration and trustees. That these provide the best basis for community was regarded as beyond argumentation.

Plato stated that the worst crimes do not come from a weak nature. The possessors of the very qualities that constitute the philosophical nature do the greatest harm to communities and individuals, as well as the greatest good. The great virtues can corrupt their possessor when they are divorced from true wisdom. For example, once persons with qualities of outstanding potential for leadership become known for them, the resulting fawning upon them may corrupt them with pride and ambition.[74]

The religious. The false security of the religious person can be the extreme form of blindness. "The ultimate batte between human pride and God's grace takes place in religion."[75] When pride prevails, our partial achievements and standards become identified not only with the Good but with God. They receive not only ethical, but also divine sanction. When evil activity has transcendental endorsement, it can be pursued cheerfully and completely. Religious absolutes can veil particular interests.

What is most threatened can become most absolute. The unconditional character of some arguments about abortion is not despite, but indeed because of, the ambiguity of the biblical and medical evidence in establishing when human personhood, or soul, begins.[76] Similar observations could be made about some recent writings about the doctrine of Scripture. Uncertainty about one's own conformity to a given standard also may lead to abusing others for inadequately conforming to it.

The pride of religious dogmatism is contrary to genuine, living religious experience where the will-to-power is constantly being shattered by the love of God. God's mercy produces genuine power of being in self-acceptance and the ability to love.

Instead, the truth of God becomes our possession, not that which possesses us.[77] We become the possessors of the knowledge of the will of God. There is an abandonment of the human perspective. We fail to see the limitations of ourselves or of the forms in which religious absolutes are communicated to us. Here we get a glimpse of Eden—the desire to become like God. There is abandonment of forgiveness on one hand and of humility on the other. Donald Kaul in an editorial in the *Des Moines Registrar* wrote:

> When you are convinced you're doing God's work, it's only a short step to becoming convinced that everything that you do is justified. The Christian Voice people

are fond of quoting this line in the Bible: ". . . when the righteous rule, the people rejoice; when the unrighteous rule, the people mourn." To which I can only add, "When the self-righteous rule, watch out."[78]

This potential perversion of religion is sometimes actualized in cults. After the mass suicide in 1978 among the People's Temple members at Jonestown, Guyana, Stanley Cath, a psychiatric student of cults, stated that the process in which such violence can erupt begins with the conviction of many cult leaders and their followers about their special goodness. "Whenever people put hatred underground, deny they have it and project it onto other people, there eventually has to be some form in which it comes out." The corruptibility of the leader is denied. There is a vision of having sole control of truth, but it cannot be maintained. When a member has "a moment of lifting of the veil" and starts to doubt his or her continued participation, outbursts of violence often come as the members are knocked into line.[79]

The appearance of possessing genuine religious experience can delude the individual, let alone those who observe him or her. Only God knows God's elect. Great spirituality frequently has been a mask, and those who achieve this deception can be listed among the most dangerous of people. The peril lies in the powerful symbols they manipulate and the trust and loyalty engendered.

The lack of self-knowledge and genuine self-development in one wearing a religious mask is particularly hazardous. Because religious controls are not actually operating in the person, all the temptations of power continue without the equipment to confront them; the internal crisis is heightened by the self-deception. Jonathan Edwards noted that spiritual pride by its very nature makes dealing with it or any other area of sinfulness difficult. Since it is based in their own opinion of themselves, the possessors of this conceit have difficulty discerning it. Because it is pride about their religious state, it involves confidence in "their light and humility," which especially works against the discovery of pride. "The spiritually proud man is full of light already; he don't [sic] need instruction, and he is ready to despise the offer of it." The self-confidence drives away the necessary watchfulness to prevent succumbing to such temptation.[80]

In each of these cases—wisdom, virtue, and religion—security produces pride in security. The ego is identified with the base of security. Power is used to protect the base of security against any challengers.

True wisdom, virtue, and spirituality are difficult to locate politically and cannot be identified with particular human groupings. One cannot trust power centered in any of these groups. At the Massachusetts State House in Boston there is a statue of Mary Dwyer, a Quaker woman who was hanged in the Boston Common by the Puritans.

Lessons for Politics

We can learn two important lessons for politics from the human propensity for evil.

The Limitations of Politics

Self-love will not be destroyed until self-love is shaken to the roots, Niebuhr states. There is a permanent need for conversion. Seeing the depth of the human predicament forces us to remember our need of God. It was the rejection of God that led to the manipulative perversion of human relationships all along the way. Those relationships will not be reestablished until God's creatures accept God's merciful provision in Christ and are first restored to relationship with God. Accordingly, self-love (and self-fear) and their distorted products are a permanent factor in human history until, as Niebuhr states, the Lord of history finally and fully asserts sovereign majesty over the false majesty of the nations. We can receive a warning from Augustine: The whole human enterprise is more precarious than we realize.[81] Politics cannot remove the human propensity for evil.

The Permanent Need for Politics

If the will-to-power, and the will to be overpowered, are permanent, then power will permanently be in need of being controlled and redistributed. Otherwise, the weak will be consumed by the powerful.

The Christian view of universal depravity prevents reliance upon the benevolence of the economically powerful. As Victor Hugo stated, "There is always more misery among the lower classes than there is humanity in the higher."[82] This is why a Christian ethic becomes highly irrelevant if it lacks a dynamic political ethic that comes to terms with the evil misuse of power in human communities. It fails to come to grips with the source of suffering in the human quest for security as expressed in power. We need an ethic that comes to terms with the realities of power.

3

Groups in Society: Danger and Deliverance

Understanding human nature requires more than treating the individual. We must also understand the human groups in which individuals exist. The attention given to group life in biblical thought and the inseparability of group life from human existence stand in contrast to many Western political points of view, which treat individuals as by nature separate from groups; groups are formed secondarily and provisionally to meet individual needs and wants. A major weakness in the social thought of individualistically oriented forms of Christianity—whether liberal, existential, or Evangelical—is neglect of the importance of groups and their potential for both good and evil.

A social group is a structure of individual relationships that has the capacity of engaging in joint action or having common interests.[1] Thus, since it has its own structure and its own goals, a group differs from the mere sum of all its individual members. In addition, it has its own relations with other groups.[2]

The Biblical Importance of Groups

Groups are major players in the Bible. The "congregation of the children of Israel" acts and is a recipient of action alongside Moses, Aaron, or Eleazar. The Old Testament is a history of the conflict of nations, tribes, and families. Biblical ethics direct our attention to groups, such as the rich, the poor, the aliens, the royal court, the priests, the Pharisees. Bethsaida, Capernaum, Thyatira, Laodicea—cities as a whole and churches as one—are addressed.

To a large extent, God deals with people through groups. Most importantly, it is a group that is the channel of God's salvation. In the Old Testament this group is Israel. For example, in Isaiah 43 it is the group, Israel, that is chosen by God and is the object of God's love and redemption: "... Thus says the Lord ... who formed you, O Israel: Do not fear for I have redeemed you; I have called you by name, you are mine" (v. 1, *NRSV*). God promises it God's presence and protection (v. 2). The group receives a mission from God: God gives waters in the desert to "the people whom I formed for myself so that they might declare my praise" (v. 21).

In the New Testament the group that is the channel of God's salvation is the church. Baptism is a rite of initiation into a community. In 1 Corinthians 5 to

42

excommunicate someone from the Christian community is to deliver that person to Satan (vv. 1–5). It is the group—the church, those who are "in Christ"—that is the object of God's election. "Even as God chose us in Christ before the foundation of the world."[3] The New Testament uses many images to show our reception of God's blessings through this intermediate level. Individual Christians are parts of the body (of Christ), building blocks of a temple, branches of an olive tree, and sheep of a flock. Their identification and meaning come from a larger whole.

Paul, in much of his thinking, wrestled with the place of human groups in God's plan. For him the church is "not a sandheap of many grains, but . . . a great body with many members, all framed and knit together, growing up into unity and fullness of life . . ."[4] In Romans, he ponders the inclusion of the Gentiles into the church and the fate of national Israel. He also affirmed the priceless role that Israel had had as channel of truth, ritual, and access to God. To the Israelites "belong the adoption, the glory, the decrees, the worship, the giving of the law, and the promises. To them belong the patriarchs and from them, as far as human descent is concerned, came the Christ" (Rom. 9.4–5).

The group is an intermediate level through which God reaches the individual. God certainly does deal directly with the individual and sees individuals apart from the group. God, however, deals with the individual in terms of how God is dealing with a larger group of humankind.

Further examples of the biblical recognition of the reality of group life are seen in Deuteronomy 32.30 where one chases a thousand but two put ten thousand to flight. In Leviticus 4, to illustrate another aspect, the unintentional sin of the anointed priest brings guilt upon the whole people, whom he represents (v. 4). There also are unintentional sins by the whole congregation (v. 13). Rauschenbusch commented that there was something in the nature of the Jewish nation as a group that justified God treating it as a composite personality; God held it responsible for moral actions.[5] The potential of unified evil is seen in the story of the Tower of Babel. God confounds language and saves humanity from the self-destruction that would result if it united in proud sin. Yet in the Revelation of John, after Christ's redemption, the restraint is removed. The resulting "horrific global unity of deception and rebellion" is a precursor to the final judgment.[6] Collective life is a force to be dealt with. Where "two or three are gathered together" in Christ's name, Christ is present, authorizing judicial action (Matt. 18.19–20).

Individuals are evaluated in Scripture according to their membership in a group that is more permanent than they. Such a group is qualitatively different from a collection of individuals. Groups merit our attention in examining the bases of political thought. Theologically informed analysis should give attention to such aspects of human life beyond individual existence. Groups are essential to human life.

At the same time no earthly group is completely identical with the ideal that it is supposed to fulfill; this is why reformation is a permanent need. How the group is constituted and behaves is important. The group can be the means of departure from God, and the individuals in the group participate in the punishment of the group. "Prepare to meet your God, O Israel!" (Amos 4.12) is a word of judgment, not of invitation. We have a personal interest in the conduct of our groups.

The Social and Political Importance of Groups

The important place that groups have in the Bible is confirmed by social observation. We "work in groups, worship in groups, and in democratic society [we] must even seek to govern through groups."[7] Ethical perceptions, customs, and the sense of what is important are carried by groups and transmitted to the individual. Human beings cannot rely on instincts. Thomas Aquinas stated that no individual by one's own reasoning could attain all the necessary knowledge of what particularly concerns his or her own well-being.[8] "Nobody is strong, free, and creative enough to build [one's] whole life, every gesture and every word, in terms of strict personal self-expression."[9] Instead we live in the institutions of society, made manifest to us in groups.

Most of what we do, we do in proven and accepted ways without thought or choice. We can then concentrate our limited time and strength on what is personally important to us.[10] The tasks of social life are apportioned, resources made available, and wisdom shared. Our groups bring into the present other spirits and other ages. "Goodwill, self-mastery, self-renunciation, the Cross," as well arts and technical skills, are taught and learned "by one generation to another, by one generation from another."[11] The cultural values that are carried by the group provide the essential cohesion of society. In general people belong to several groups because no one group is sufficient to provide our varied needs for society.[12]

Groups reinforce the best of our human characteristics. For example, joy and exaltation in response to God is enhanced in group worship. Groups can support responsible ethical behavior that an individual may let slide. This contribution of group life was demonstrated in an experiment in Israel. In a caution against terrorists, the government had made many appeals that any suspicious objects be reported to the police. In the experiment, a box looking suspiciously like a bomb was planted, and the persons who did and who did not report it by telephone were followed and interviewed. Those passing through the area in groups reported the object significantly more than those who were alone. The other members in the group were providing moral influence not present to those who were alone.[13]

The early Calvinists recognized society to be characterized by associations, such as family, collegium (or corporation, such as fraternities and guilds), city, province, and state. The associations were ways of serving God faithfully by meeting fundamental human needs. The various aspects of human life were thus fulfilled. These associations were formed by covenants, which for the Calvinists were grounded in the fundamental purposes of life while making adjustments to the group's particular circumstances.[14] So Althusius, the culminating and most systematic of several Calvinists writers reflecting upon society and associations between 1556 and 1618, stated that "the simple and private association" is "initiated by a special covenant" according to "what is necessary and useful for organized private symbiotic life."[15]

Groups have a crucial place in the political structure. We live in what is called a *multiple group society.* Many different groups provide the arms of the total society. *Pluralism* is another term to describe such a society. In pluralism one group cannot be instituted to the exclusion of all others, and the individual is affiliated with many groups.[16] Power over the individual is limited when no association has hegemony over many aspects of its members' lives. The existence of the other groups makes pluralism possible. (It is important to emphasize that the reference for pluralism is groups rather than individuals.)

These groups are not aspects of the state. The state does not encompass the society, except in an extreme, totalitarian regime.[17] The word *totalitarian* indicates the extreme: the state "totals" the society. Independent groups between it and the individual have been removed.[18] Such a situation is an *overintegrated society*. It is significant that Hitler in gaining power quickly attempted to abolish all organizations that would not submit to him.[19] Likewise, one of the first acts of the military oligarchy in Chile after they gained power in 1973 was to abolish the labor unions. In an alternative form, in the former Soviet Union the party had manipulated the workers through its control of the unions.

In a healthy society the multiple groups are not only independent of the state; they are also controlled by their own members. The mediating structures even include regional and local tiers of government.[20] Medieval society was not totalitarian. The manor, borough, guild, university, or convent had a role in checking power external to them, such as the king. Medieval society was authoritarian, however, because the individual had little control over his or her corporate group.[21]

In the multiple group system the state is the product and servant of the community, one among many groups. According to Robert MacIver, the state is an association in society, not society itself.[22] In this usage *association* is distinguished from *community*. We create or are chosen into associations to pursue a particular interest on a cooperative basis. The association is voluntary, but we are born into the community, such as a village or nation. It is not a matter of choice. The family has characteristics of both association and community. The state (versus the nation) is an association, not a community.[23] The various associations of the multiple group society include the state, churches, economic enterprises (including both corporations and trade associations), labor unions, and political enterprises, such as parties and pressure groups. There are also associations for professions, education, sports, and entertainment.

The existence of groups provide a dispersion of power and increased centers of group creativity. James Madison, the early interpreter of the theory of the U. S. Constitution, confronted the potential for evil in human nature. He saw how it could rear up in the form of a majority holding a common interest that was threatening to the rights of other citizens or to the true interests of the community. In response he advocated the multiplicity of interests. "The society itself will be broken into so many parts, interests, and classes of citizens, that the rights of individuals, or of the minority, will be in little danger from interested combinations of the majority." The multiplicity of interests was part of the "auxiliary precautions" that supplement the control of the government by the people.[24]

The damage of the overintegrated society is not only political and economic, through the concentration of power. The destruction is also cultural in the withering of the creativity, enterprise, conviction, and devotion that cannot be created by external control. Rather, "every way of life and every way of thought is nourished from within."[25] As William Temple stated, the human being is more than social or political. A person "is also a seeker for knowledge, a creator and lover of beauty, a worshipper of God." Actions of the state to control these areas are destructive of values.[26]

The freedom from taxes that some groups, such as the churches, possess gives expression to the concept that the state is the creation of the community and that there are areas not in its right of control. There are familial, intellectual, friendship, and ecclesiastical bonds that have a special character distinct from the bonds of the state, and their separate character needs to be affirmed and preserved.

Christianity and Judaism have made important contributions to pluralism, particularly in the secularization of the state. In ancient Greek and Roman society there was little difference from the worship of the gods of the city states and the operations of government; the dividing line of the religious and the political was difficult to discern. The society was overintegrated. In this context the early church made a radical claim when it cited the words of Jesus that there are things that belong to God that do not belong to Caesar. A meaningful application occurred at the Nicene Council when it requested the emperor to leave the chancel. "You are not the mediator."

This limitation of the state's claim as an intermediary of truth was consistent with prophecy in ancient Israel. While not in reality a mediating structure in terms of a continuing organization, the Hebrew prophets did have an independent status in relation to the king (as well as to the people and cultus). They spoke solely in the name of God, often to their own political peril. Unlike the prophets in countries adjacent to Israel, who were attached to the courts, and to the false prophets in Israel, who simply served the king, the prophets provided an occasional bifurcation of power in times of crisis that opened in history a way of public criticism on behalf of religious reformation, ethical purity, and social justice.[27]

An *underintegrated society* is one where the freedom of groups is so extreme that it limits the state from acting for the general good; it is an anarchy of group formations. One group can then dominate the others, including the state. The business world posed such a threat in American society at the end of the nineteenth century in the United States.

The pluralism of groups requires that each group have independence from private groups as well as each from the state. A concern has been raised about the number of university scientists with commercial ties to industry, such as to the biotechnology industry. Universities and their faculties are a national resource, and their loss of independence decreases their sensitivity to the social impacts of science. This may have particular impact in decisions made by scientific advisory panels that affect public policy.[28] The point is not that industry is a source of corruption, but that autonomy of groups is needed in order that all legitimate interests be fully pursued and that each sector fully carry out its social purposes.

Voluntary associations can also provide freedom by standing between the individual and the family. The early church, composed of those who were willing, or forced, to leave parent and sibling for the gospel, broke the kinship pattern that dominates traditional society. The institutional incarnation of its kerygma was accordingly one of the great innovations in world history. It gave common people opportunity to learn the skills required for effective social organization. The capability of participating in social decisions in response to a transcendental purpose was dispersed to them. The individual, which the Reformation later freshly set forth as having direct access to God without mediations, was not to be wholly comprehended by community or state. This freedom, however, is articulated in the choices the individual makes in the context of association.[29] The Reformation, like the first Christian period, resulted in new or reformed churches, not in isolated individual experiences.

From the standpoint of the multiplicity of groups and the integrity of each type, the church is one among other groups in the society. From the standpoint of meaning and coherence, however, the church's role is unique. Because it is the channel of a faith that is comprehensive of all of life, the church clarifies the normative purpose of the other groups. It thus must resist identification with them or itself merely reflecting their understanding.[30]

Groups are channels for influencing society as well as for resisting domination. Groups, not isolated individuals, formulate public policy. The secondary groups or associations—lobbies, public interest groups, professional and trade associations— are where the matrix of public opinion and policy are formed. Through associations the individual can get a piece of the action by participating in the process of making social decisions.

Groups provide social space for freedom. Individual freedom of speech has a limited impact in thwarting tyranny unless it is combined with the freedom of association. Then when ideas are in conflict with the policies of the establishment, one has the freedom to organize a group to promote them.[31] Groups provide the institutional form of freedom that brings innovation or criticism to society.

The results of group influence on public policy can be positive or negative for a just and wholesome society. Our failure to pass effective gun control laws on both the national and state level is correctly attributed to the National Rifle Association, not to the "great numbers in our society who are hunters or marksmen." This situation may, or may not, contribute to democratic control. One association may predominate and infringe on the rights or interests of others to the point of doing them serious injury. The answer is not restriction of freedom of association or expression, rather, it is encouraging those affected to participate in politically effective groups.

In "mass society" where individuals do not have meaningful involvements in groups, social decisions are made by oligarchic groups while mass participation is chiefly in associations concerned with sociability, hobbies, prestige, or status. Democracy exists effectively or not according to whether the mass of society belongs to subgroups in the key organizations of the community. For example, Seymour Lipset's study of union democracy found that there is more participation and knowledge of the political issues facing a labor union when independent social and recreational clubs are formed in the union.[32]

By neglecting the associational involvement of their members, churches are often less effective in carrying out their professed mission of providing Christian influence on the institutions of their society. The churches tend to promote a merely

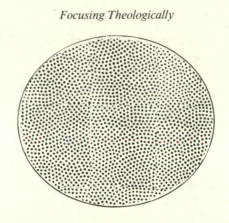

Figure 3.1.

personal ethic and to ignore nonecclesiastical associational responsibilities. When the members do participate, their associations are often not those that affect public policy; rather, they are those that are concerned with sociability.

The view reflected by this associational slumber of the churches is that society is a composite of individuals (see Figure 3.1). We have seen, however, that society would be more accurately viewed as a composite of groups in which the individuals are included (see Figure 3.2). James Luther Adams describes democratic society as "an association of associations."[33] The individual can be (and should be) in many of these groups and is influenced by all or most of them. Failure to work through groups in order to change society accompanies neglect of the importance of groups in the structure of the whole of society and of their consequential effect on the individual.

Adams has stated many times that history is not made by individuals loving each other, but by decisions requiring public policy; and public policy is made by groups, not individuals. There are certainly powerful and influential individuals in a society. Lane Kirkland of the AFL-CIO[34] has power, but his power lies in his institutional base. The power is in the seat, not in the person. Basic changes must deal

Figure 3.2.

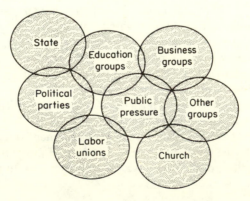

with the bases of power. One must deal with groups by working through groups. Edmund Burke wrote, "When bad men combine, the good must associate; else they will fall, one by one, an unpitied sacrifice in a contemptible struggle."[35]

Because of the role that groups have in determining the direction of society, we have to be concerned about groups, understand groups, and work through groups. We need to discern the ethical nature of groups just as we have to know the ethical nature of the individual.

Making Good Better and Bad Worse

The mysterious mixture of good and evil that characterizes individual human beings is true also of their groups. Such a consequence is not surprising, but there are aspects of group life that intensify the good and the evil so that just as groups are more than the sum of their individual members so too is their ethical nature.

The crucial contribution of groups to faithful human life should be clear from the first sections of this chapter. Groups provide the necessary context for moral living. Some groups are channels of God's blessing and power. God's choice and purpose for such groups means that their goodness is more than that brought to them by its individual members. In society groups are carriers of customs and values. In group life we have an emotional and supportive framework that encourages the expression of our best tendencies. The diversity of groups cultivates different dimensions of our personality. Groups provide contexts for creativity and enterprise. They furnish sanctions to help us to be what we want to be but for which we might not make the effort on our own.

Groups provide defensive power against the intrusion of other groups and exploitive individuals. Participation itself develops vital personal resources and self-esteem. There is a peril when masses in the society do not belong to significant groups. Kornhauser points out the lack of independent groups that is characteristic of mass society. Mass-oriented leaders do not have to compete with loyalties to independent organizations and can capture power by mobilizing large numbers of people. Mass society is highly vulnerable to totalitarian movements, in which conformity becomes obligatory. Identity with a dictator or with the total group provides the self-respect that normally should be found through participation in independent group life.[36]

Group life provides a means of involvement and mission. In groups we have the resources of mutuality to participate in the life of our society, and groups provide opportunities for intervening power in facing injustices in our communities.

Participation in groups can be an ethical action, an act of love. Group involvement can mean self-denial. The group has values that transcend its immediate interests. Participation in a group means joining a more inclusive community in which one must put the interests of others ahead of one's own. The group defines wider obligations that are more disinterested than the obligations discerned by the individual by oneself.

In the preceding sections discussing the social and political necessity of groups, the contribution of group life to sinfulness has been less apparent. Yet the nature of groups also intensifies the human orientation to evil. This characteristic of human groups is critical for politics. Reinhold Niebuhr, particularly in his classic, *Moral Man and Immoral Society,* shows groups to be a more pregnant source of injustice and conflict than purely individual pride.[37] The source of such immorality of groups is individual egoistic impulses.[38] In groups the cumulative effect of the uniting of individual vices is combined with certain dynamics of group life to produce evil. Participation in groups enhances individual sinfulness in several ways.

First, participation in groups can appear to decrease the contingency of one's own existence. Group life can be sought in the false attempts to overcome the confinements of finiteness, a phenomenon we have seen to be integral to human sinfulness (see pp. 29–30).[39] In the United States the security of the group is bolstered by the cultivated illusion of its not being dependent upon other nations. In this pheonomenon the ego becomes identified with a larger whole and finds security. Its successes becomes the individual's success. Its pain becomes the individual's pain. As a man from the hills of Kentucky unable to find work in Chicago stated, "But what the country takes is what I have to take: people say bad things to you, unfriendly things."[40] Seneca said, "No man loves his native land because it is great; he loves it because it is his own."[41] When the American hostages returned from Iran in 1981, Alan Richman insightfully compared the depth of our outrage over the treatment of this group with our responses to others who in during the same period suffered much greater injustices. He began his column with these words:

> There were fifty-two of them, a number easy to comprehend. It wasn't like 15,000 innocent people permanently disappearing in Argentina. They were Americans, mostly white males, and they looked just like us. The thousands in Chile's labor camps do not. They spoke our language. There were 3,000 people summarily shot in Guatemala last year who did not. They were us.[42]

Because the group's greatness mollifies the individual's insecurity, through their members or leaders groups make unconditional claims for conditional values for themselves. The group regards the values to which it is loyal as more absolute than they really are. National honor becomes the rationale for destruction, as in the Vietnam War. National security justifies violation of individual rights or of the constitutional processes of another society. Values associated with the United States, such as capitalism or democracy, are asserted as universal and timeless goods. (At this point I am not dealing with the validity of such claims nor am I suggesting that all who make them are subject to the motivation discussed in this paragraph.) "No nation today has a group consciousness that is merely mild patriotism, consonant with biblical principles, and free from racial pride and a sense of cultural superiority."[43]

Second, in a group there is less control of reason over impulse.[44] Studies have shown that decisions and goals set by groups tend to be more risky.[45] A group is often unified by momentary impulses and unreflective purpose. When a U.S. ship was reported to have been attacked by a North Vietnamese vessel, the U.S. Senate passed the Gulf of Tonkin resolution with almost no opposition, a decision that many senators came to regret. The emotional nature of the decision was highlighted by revelations of the Pentagon Papers, which indicated the extent to which the incident had been manipulated by the military.

Unlike the person, there is no national center of thought, deliberation, and decision; therefore, group-based thought is rasher. Tillich's reflections on this point would apply to other groups as well. He warns against personifying a group and notes the weakness of using a corporal image to interpret society. Such an image only partially represents social reality. The parts of the body do not retain their individual being and dignity as do the members of society. The government is not the soul or reason of a body. There is no such thing as a single will in a nation although much international theory assumes that national leaders do represent the will of their people.[46] The ruling group in society is not the center of the personality; rather, it is a part of society that is concerned that the whole society be responsible for that part's own existence.[47] Commenting on the tendency of power to increase power, Jacques Maritain states, it [power] would like to consider itself an end, not a means. "Those who specialize in the affairs of the whole have a propensity to take themselves for the whole; the general staffs take themselves for the whole army, the church authorities for the whole church; the State for the body politic."[48] The state thus tends to ascribe to itself a peculiar common good—its own self-preservation and growth.

Third, a group similarly has less capacity for self-transcendence, which is the ability to draw back from oneself in order to see oneself more objectively. Without self-transcendence, there is no self-criticism.[49] Without self-criticism, there is no ethical action since that requires reflecting upon one's own conduct in light of a standard.

In international group relations, a country that recognizes its own interests is more reliable to other countries in bargaining than one that operates in a moral idealism that shields its own interests even from itself. Garry Wills argues that the liberal doctrine of consent contributes to this hazard. The view that my country is right or ceases to be my country leads to seeking an integrity so high as to be irrelevant, or to assuming blindly that the country must be right, or to a hypocritical mixture of the previous two. "Once let a man identify his country with his fondest beliefs, with the very fate of freedom, with the hopes of mankind, and he is tempted to guard the moral claim at all costs, to rationalize failings, to invent lofty motives for the nation's policies. Puritan self-scrutiny turns, at that point, into puritan hypocrisy."[50]

A genuine sense of tragedy seems to be lacking in our government, and indeed throughout large segments of our society. In an editorial at the end of the Vietnam War, the *Boston Globe* asked, "Now, after Vietnam, can we accept the fact that deliberately and responsibly we did make decisions that were far more destructive of life and limb than we thought they would be, and that as a nation we are far more capable—in our own subconsciousness—than we had thought, of doing evil?"[51] The pardoning of President Richard M. Nixon made it convenient to avoid facing sin intimately connected to our national group. It reflected our inability to see one, with whom as leader of our nation we so closely identified ourselves, undergo public accusation of guilt, suffering for wrong done, or expiation. The timing of the pardon prevented legal charges from even being formally raised.

Fourth, a group has less ability to apprehend the needs of others. It is hindered by a lack of contact with others; this is particularly true of nations. The group lacks ethical perception.[52] The massacre by American soldiers of more than 400 inhabitants of the Vietnamese hamlet of My Lai in 1968 cannot be entirely separated from the policies under which they were operating. American leaders had approved of the general indiscriminate killing of Vietnamese civilians by air bombing, artillery, and small arms fire, especially in "free-fire zones." The distance from which these leaders made such decisions enhanced "their inability to *feel* what really goes on in a free-fire zone, what it is like to be a peasant in a premodern culture victimized by the incredible firepower released by advanced American technology of destruction, or, for that matter, how it feels to be a terrified, profoundly confused, and depersonalized GI doing the firing."[53]

Judgments when reached in groups often treat members of other groups in simplistic, stereotyped, or bipolar ways. While isolated racist individuals exist, racism is usually a group phenomenon. Nevitt Sanford and Craig Comstock relate a cabaret joke current in Germany in the early 1930s: "Show me one Nazi." "What do you mean? Here is a whole room full of Nazis." "Yes, but show me *one* Nazi."[54] The demeaning of another group is the basis of elevating one's own group, making oneself more secure. The negative stereotyping of women often is used to reinforce a positive evaluation of men.[55]

Belonging to a group thus can be the basis for receiving harm. Discriminating policies of Apartheid are not directed at individuals who happen also to be black, but precisely because they are black. Group-based harm does not come to individuals for reasons other than their being black or female, or whatever.[56]

Groups making serious organizational decisions at the top levels develop an atmosphere that discourages dissent. Policymaking groups, such as presidential advisers making some of the biggest decisions since World War II, have been victimized by this dynamic. These groups, perhaps to counter the stress of their roles, develop amiable relationships. The higher the degree of solidarity, the more powerful is the pressure on members to conform with the majority point of view. Disagreement or doubt is interpreted as lack of loyalty and a rupture of the cozy atmosphere. As a result critical decisions have been made with a false optimism and without thorough examination of alternatives and pitfalls. Yet we depend upon groups for decision making because groups, when functioning well, will make better decisions than would any individual working alone on the problem.[57] We would not prefer to have presidents abandoning counselors and making crucial decisions in their own dark solitude. Again, we have the dilemma of group life.

Fifth, a group is able to achieve effective self-consciousness in situations where the self-interests of the group are most threatened. Unity is found in conflict. Aristotle writes of how "common fear brings together even the greatest enemies" (*Pol.* 1304b23). Because the enemy or oppressor treats each one merely as a member of the group, rather than as a distinguishable individuality, the members come to care about how the other is treated. How the neighbor is treated is a strong indication of how they would be treated.[58] Thus solidarity is formed, as in the Golden Rule, by being able to put oneself in the place of the neighbor. This group solidarity, however, cannot extend beyond the group and the threat that it receives. Thus the group acts most cohesively when it is most selfish.[59] One can think of a white neighborhood that identifies itself and acts as a group because a black family moves in. A study was made of white parents of public school children in the three largest cities in Connecticut in 1966. Significantly, the study came before the time of the "white

flight" in 1967–1977, which was associated with increased desegration, racial violence, and black militancy. The researchers found that for 77 percent of the parents
(85 percent of the blue collar parents) the main reason at that time for being in favor
of a child going to a school in his or her neighborhood was a matter of practical
convenience, such as time and distance. The social bonding type of reasons, which
later prevailed, such as promoting neighborhood feeling, or children having friends
who are from the neighborhood or who are children of persons known to the parents, were not prominent. Yet after the increase in busing tensions, conservation of
the community had become the argument for the neighborhood school, which by
then was a nearly sacrosanct institution.[60]

Studies of racism disclose boundaries between groups to be strengthened when
members of one group compete with members of another group on a group level,
such as when white workers lost employment opportunities to black slaves. They
are lowered when members of different groups compete on an individual level, such
as blacks and whites in professional sports.[61]

Sixth, the larger a group is the more it seems to represent universal values,
broaching the problem of idolatry.[62] The group has so much more power, majesty,
and immortality than the individual; accordingly, it receives a reverence that is at
times religious in nature.[63]

The religious aspects of national loyalty come to a head in war. Max Weber
wrote, "War . . . makes for an unconditionally devoted and sacrificial community
among the combatants. . . . Moreover, war does something to the warrior which, in
its concrete meaning is unique: it makes him experience a consecrated meaning of
death which is characteristic only of death in war."[64] An example of the nearly religious address of the nation is seen in an advertisement in the Gastonia (NC) *Gazette*
during World War II (April 8, 1941), sponsored by twenty-two industrial firms:
"Believe only in Uncle Sam. Help him and rely upon him. That is the best of good
business. Whatever helps Uncle Sam, helps everything you hold dear. . . . Protect
him and you protect all." A prayer published later in the war called American pilots
"warriors of God," whose sacrifice resembled that of Jesus Christ.[65]

Group unity and power depend on maintaining this honor and respect. The reverence validates the group's sentiments, collective impulses, and claims to power.
Rituals, symbols, and ceremonies are consequently associated with the group to
stimulate and express the affection of the individual for the group. The bonds of
community are indeed strengthened. The flag and the Fourth of July serve this purpose. Mistreating such a symbol is a threat to the unit; it confirms the conviction
that the critic has separated oneself from the group; thus, the demand is heard,
"America—love it or leave it." Richard Neuhaus commented in an address in the
early 1970s on what was then the name of a significant Christian magazine of social
criticism, the *Post-American*.[66] He argued that we should not deprive people of
symbols of continuity and hope. More effective and still radical would be the
title, the *PRE-American,* beckoning a return and reappropriation of the nation's
symbols.

When the group is the nation, it seems to have a will independent of the individual's life. Its actions then often are not questioned even when they are counter to
moral conscience. In 1974 William Colby, director of the Central Intelligence

Agency, revealed to a congressional committee extensive activities by the agency in Chile to undermine the Allende government from 1964 to 1973, in violation of the principles of democracy and at least the spirit of international law. President Gerald Ford, while admitting the intervention, defended it in a news conference as "in the best interest of the people of Chile."[67]

On one hand the actions of the group may be equated with the well-being of the community or state. On the other hand its policemen, soldiers, or other officials may be seen, and see themselves, simply as representatives of the organization, rather than as separate, morally accountable individuals. It is "a condition of guilt-free massacre." To hold these representatives guilty for illegal acts is repulsive to those who share this outlook since that would reflect on the organization itself.[68]

The reverence for the group and the dichotomous nature of how group members often think of themselves in relationship to other groups encourage bipolar views in foreign policy and in conspiracy theories. Good and evil are cleanly divided between themselves and their enemies. As President Reagan stated, "The Soviet Union underlies all the unrest that is going on. If they weren't engaged in this game of dominoes there wouldn't be any hot spots in the world."[69]

Loyalty to the nation moves the individual to far-reaching sacrifices. The positive values of "uniting love which create and sustain the community" are the very ones that magnify the group and its leaders.[70] "Thus the unselfishness of individuals makes for the selfishness of nations. . . . Altruistic passion is sluiced into the reservoirs of nationalism with great ease . . ."[71] In turn, members are bonded even more strongly to the group for which they have made personal sacrifice.[72] Yet the individual's selfishness also lies buried under this sacrifice for the group and is not contested. One's own selfish concerns become absorbed in the ideology of the group. The person is not aware of contending for oneself. The engagement is only for the ideals of the group. A labor struggle is no longer on behalf of a higher salary for oneself; rather, the striker represents the whole working class and its glorious revolutionary goal.[73]

The family illustrates the combination of self-denial and self-aggrandisement that may be found in any social group, including the church. Commitment to the family may veil selfishness since the care appears to be for others rather than to oneself. The family, however, may be a means of advertising one's success and prosperity,[74] or perhaps one's intelligence, piety, or athletic prowess. This veiling may be particularly effective in an age in which there is legitimate concern about the neglect of the family. Many parents can identify with Michael Harrington's confession, "When I became a father, I discovered a willingness to be selfish."[75]

The family itself can be idolatrous in the sense of attracting to itself devotion that replaces other responsibilities to which God calls us. The form of this monopoly of commitment will vary by culture. Where material advancement hinges on the improvements in the status of the parent (or parents), involvement in group activity on behalf of the common good or other forms of mission may be eschewed if it interfers with the economic advance of the breadwinners.[76] The family thus can be the enemy of justice or evangelism in distracting from more public concerns and responsibilities. This is a subtle form of one group displacing others and undercutting the multiple group society. It is particularly dangerous in a harried and fragmented age when the family is sought as a refuge, and when there is a strong dichotomy between one's vocational and leisure time. If the family is not to be a springboard to dangerous social chaos, then loyalty to it needs to be tempered by effective wider loyalties.[77]

Whether it is the state, economic enterprise, or the family, the purpose for a group coming into being is a particular interest closely related to self-interest. A group cannot transcend it without threatening the purpose for its being.

Implications for Politics

Since social decisions are made by groups, and groups are selfish, social conflict is inevitable. The truce between contending forces that Augustine saw comprising society is a truce between self-loving groups as well as individuals. Niebuhr thus describes society as being "in a perpetual state of war."[78]

One implication of the propensity of groups for evil is a blow to optimism. Mere moral or rational persuasion is not sufficient to alter the behavior of persons in groups. Groups are governed by self-interest, not by reason or morality.[79]

Evangelism is also not sufficient, even though it is necessary to challenge effectively the self-orientation that feeds into group life. Individuals, not groups, are converted; we have seen that groups are more than the sum of their individual parts. Social conflict is between groups, not just between individuals; the depth of evil in groups goes beyond that of the individuals composing them. Change must *also* come in the structure of group life. "Group-based-harm," for example, will continue to threaten any member of the group with at least indirect or vicarious harm until the status of the group is changed. Ameliorating the situation of certain individuals does not suffice.[80]

In the midst of the oppression of groups, justice, therefore, requires the use of power and coercion. One of the most important political implications of this chapter is that ideologies that attempt to solve social problems by restraining the role of government and relying upon the interplay of the economy have failed to see the importance of groups in society and the social struggle which occurs between them. A statement of this insufficient analysis of group conflict and immorality is the following remarks by Ronald Reagan in his 1980 presidential campaign.

> My idea of an OSHA [Occupational Safety and Health Administration] would be if government set up an agency that would do research and study how things could be improved, and industry could go to it and say, "We have a problem here and we seem to lose more people by accident in this particular function. Would you come and look at our plan and then come back and give us a survey of what should be done.[81]

This position reveals a crucial theological weakness in understanding evil as it works on the group level.

The struggle with racism in the South provides an example of the need for strong government regulation. Civil rights advanced by coercion, the restraint of one community over another. In the years following World War II, including the first decade following the Civil Rights Act of 1964, voluntary compliance, conciliation, persuasion, and even law without an enforcement mechanism proved ineffective. "The problems of discrimination were clearly too complex and pervasive to be corrected without a dose of law carefully enforced." The only significant impact on employment discrimination came where the law required specificity of both wrong and remedy and used the enforcement mechanism of the courts.[82] The hierarchal denominations were more successful in integration than the more voluntary ones.

Yet the continual failures of coercion against racism indicate, on the other hand, the need for more than political solutions. They also show the strength of the immorality of groups versus the ideal of enforcement. Not until 1949 did a major Southern organization (the Southern Regional Council) oppose segregation.[83] The opposition to integration appears most strongly in groups, as in protests against busing; individual feelings are framed and heightened in the group action.

The other major political implication of this chapter, then, is the need to rely on more than the state. The state is, and must be, but one of the plentitude of groups of a mature society, each with its own significant contribution. A social philosophy and a social strategy must work through the matrix of group life. The state cannot be an effective agent for justice until its justice reflects the life of other groups of society. Such a group is the church, not only in terms of its own life, but also in terms of the meaning it is holding forth for the other groups of the community.

A way of summarizing would be to respond to an impulse that many feel after intellectual or experiential exposure to the evil in group life. The desire is to withdraw from groups; the larger and the more public the group, the stronger is the longing to separate. The distrust of institutions in our generation extends to the church and even to the call to ministry within the church.

I would offer the following arguments against attempts at withdrawal:

1. Withdrawal means neglecting responsibility for participation in community decisions.
2. Despite the egoistic tendencies inherent in group life, many groups have valid and necessary purposes that are achieved to some degree.
3. Groups are needed for self-realization. We are group beings.
4. Groups are needed for self-respect. The absence of group formations produces mass society, a society that is open to totalitarianism.
5. Withdrawal movements are often parasitical; they abandon the immoral social structure yet are dependent on it.
6. We are socialized by groups. We cannot simply separate ourselves from their influence through an exertion of will. Their imprint is already on our personality and attitudes. It is too late.
7. The necessary counterpart to the previous point is that individuals have the ability to transcend their group, a different matter from separation. The individual in the group can stand in judgment on group egoism, and one group on another group.
8. Belonging to many groups contributes to a balanced personality. The diversity of their influence and demands means that one is not dominated by any one of them. Since we cannot withdraw from the control of the state, other groups are needed to limit its effect.

9. The life of withdrawal presents its own dangers. It was in the desert that Christ was tempted.

10. Finally, but very important, we cannot escape the tragedy of human existence; our most noble efforts will still have wrong characteristics. The duty of tragic involvement is a biblical perspective as we go to Christ in the unclean place outside the camp and there offer the sacrifices of worship, sharing, and benevolence (Heb. 13.12–16).[84] The seriousness and the patience with which we approach social groups should be marked by corresponding hope and fear.

4

To Seek and to Distrust Government

Government often seems to be secondary to genuine human life. The state is not a part of most people's primary relationships. Its entry into our life often is experienced most obviously as an irritation at best, and at times as a severe oppression. Our resulting attitude can be to want as little government as possible, to disdain it, and not to seek it as a path of Christian vocation and mission.

Government, however, is an inherent aspect of human life. It is an aspect of community, and humanity always lives in community. Government is also God's intention for us. It is a necessary extension of our nature as beings with responsibility under God for creation and as beings who are sinners. Human society as a matrix of groups requires a group with an authoritative role. Government is an important expression of intervening power.

Yet as we began, government is also a significant source of exploitive power. It displays vividly the human social dilemma. We have a hard time doing with it, yet we cannot do without it.

The Universality of Community

In developing the theological framework of politics, we have been looking at progressively more expansive units after initially encountering the concept of power. We have examined the nature of individuals. We looked at the groups that are essential for their flourishing, but also in which they are buffeted. Now we briefly consider the human need to be bound together with others in patterns of behavior.

Aristotle wrote, "By nature a person is an animal who lives in a community."[1] John Calvin, like many other Christian thinkers, found this to be a fundamental truth about human nature: "A person is by nature a social animal."[2] Aristotle meant that we are brought together not only for the security of life itself, but even more for the common benefit of the good life.[3] Justice is a communal virtue. When people are sundered from law and justice, they are the worst of all animals. Yet our social nature shines forth in the fact that even when we seem to require no assistance from each other, we still desire to live together.[4] As William Temple stated, we need our neighbors' actual selves as the complement of our own.[5] Our social being is rooted in the family, based in part on the human being's long infancy and childhood.[6] Augustine wrote that God derived everyone from one individual so that they would have the similarity and ties of relationship, which would enable them to dwell together in peace and harmony.[7]

In the Bible there is a community as soon as there are two people. Eve joined Adam, and the two persons became one flesh. *Flesh* here represents human beings in relationship and solidarity with others.[8] Cain's punishment was to be a fugitive and a wanderer (Gen. 4.12). He eventually built a city (Gen. 4.17) in conjunction with God's promise of judicial protection (v. 15).[9] Cain as the founder of the city is thus an argument for the necessity of the city rather than for its condemnation.[10] The city synthesized several elements present before the fall including multiplication of people through procreation, cultivation of resources, and the authority structure of the family.[11] As assumed in Cain's punishment, the unnatural and undesired position is to be apart from community. Ecclesiastes put it this way: "Solitary individuals without sibling or child" spend their lives toiling for riches yet not understanding why they are not satisfied. They fail to ask, "For whom am I toiling?" (Eccles. 4.8; cf. v. 5). In contrast living in community with others provides essential power (cf. v. 1) and warmth:

> Two are better than one, because they have a good reward for their toil. For if they fall, one will lift up the other; but woe to one who is alone and falls and does not have another to help. Again, if two lie together, they keep warm; but how can one keep warm alone? And though one might prevail against another; two will withstand one. A threefold cord is not quickly broken. (Eccles. 4.9–12, *NRSV*)

"The community is as primordial as the individual."[12] There are no records of individuals living anywhere outside of a community structure. Malinowski, the noted anthropologist, stated, "The man of nature, the *Naturmensch,* does not exist."[13]

Community is universal because it is a human necessity. In the last chapter, in the context of understanding the contribution of social groups, we saw the essential contribution society makes to human life. We need not repeat those thoughts. We cannot live or live humanly without community. Even in a creative activity like art, the artist must avail oneself of the "tools and forms, of characteristic insights and styles" of her or his time and place.[14] The richness of that life that is human requires continuity from the past and a division of labor according to individuals' various gifts. So for Plato, the creation of the city lies in our needs (*Rep.* 369c). "We do not severally suffice for our own needs, but each of us lacks many things."[15] As Nigerians have vividly expressed the thought, "The hand of the child does not reach the top of the shelf above the kitchen stoves, while the hand of the older person cannot go into the bottle neck of the big calabash."[16]

Community is necessary for mental health. Alfred Adler taught that no one can separate oneself from one's social group and remain healthy. The structure of the personality is dependent on community. A lack of consciousness of fellowship with people produces high levels of anxiety. A person must be integrated with a community to realize his or her own unique personality.[17]

Academic disciplines have ignored humanity's irreplaceable dependence upon society at the risk of great distortion. In philosophy there is the "Cartesian Faux Pas"—Des Cartes' artificial abstraction of not only the mind from the body but also the mind from society so that, as Kolakowski put it, the thinker becomes nothing more than a "distilled intellectual substance."[18]

In psychology it was a half century before Alfred Adler, Harry Stack Sullivan, Karen Horney, and Erich Fromm expanded Freud's concept of the id to show social environmental factors. The individual is never apart from society. Even in the womb one lives symbiotically with one's mother. Developing as a human being involves socialization. One returns to the society from which one came and in the process discovers one's own identity, uniqueness, and moral responsibility. This individual as a creative and unique unit can then in turn affect society.

In political thought, as we will see shortly, artificial constructs have defined the individual as naturally isolated from community. Freedom is then defined as separation from community, and community becomes but an instrument secondary to the individual's self-fulfillment. As Juan Segundo states, however, "Society is not the end result of juxtaposing already constituted individuals. . . . From the very start it is a system of human reactions and interrelationships that constitute the individual and form part of [one's] total human condition."[19]

Christianity appears among us at times in the form of an individualism that relates with difficulty to community-wide and society-wide responsibilities. The individual is treated largely in terms of personal relationships with God and with other individuals and small groups. This piety fails to identify the influence of social groups upon the individual or the possibilities of impacting social institutions. It tends to be self-reinforcing since Scripture itself is read from that perspective and expectation. The biblical concern for the person in community and the creation-wide dimension of God's reconciling work is missed.

The Universal Need of Government

One prevalent theory of government, the social contract theory, can be understood as presenting government as a historical development, appearing as life became more complex. Espoused by thinkers like Hobbes, Locke, and Rousseau, it spoke of warring individuals putting aside their independent existence by contracting to have a society. With this society a government was formed, to which they transferred their individual rights.

The basic historical implication of social contract thought is not accurate—there never was such a solitary existence. William Ernest Hocking notes that it was used as a literary device to describe how the individual needs the state. The great exponents of the theory spoke hypothetically—"as if." The mythic form of history has an advantage over literally accurate history in that it can be told in terms of persons and their motives.[20] The form of the myth, however, still reflects an individualistic bias.[21] Individualism is primary (e.g., it is individuals, not groups, that form the covenant). Individuals, however, are neither historically nor logically antecedent to society. As social beings they are physically, emotionally, and rationally interdependent and have inherent duties of care and responsibility for one another.[22]

Instead, government is grounded in the need for some level of coercion or central authority in all forms of social cooperation beyond the most intimate. This coercion is present at least minimally wherever people cooperate in numbers.[23] Since community is universal and primordial, the basic roots of government appear in the foundations of human life.

In Genesis 4 the governmental function is already found in God's promise of judicial intervention to Cain (v. 15). Cain pleads that he will be denied God judicial oversight ("hidden from your face") and will be a prey to anarchic terrorism (v. 14). In response God vows that Cain will be protected by a judicial structure: "Whoever kills Cain will suffer a sevenfold vengeance." The form of these words is that of a Hebrew law. The account of the building of the city and the development of technology by the line of city dwellers then follows (17–22).[24]

Authority, corporate responsibility, and collective decision making are essential to every form of human life.[25] Hocking describes the permanent psychological needs that are served by human groups. The state represents an instinct to reflect upon instinct (power, authority, family ties) and to supersede it. It is an instinct, peculiar to human beings, that includes the impulse to become self-conscious in one's social purposes. Human beings have a drive to be the conscious arbiters of their own social destiny.[26] Law in this respect is largely a matter of making, keeping, and improving agreements.[27]

Government's Purpose Within the Matrix of Social Groups

The wholesome purposes of society are challenged by both individual selfishness and by its heightening in group life. Government responds to instinct at the group level, as well as the individual level.

Society holds together and resists the destructive effects of the immorality in competing groups, and coordinates their positive contributions, in several ways. Since our topic is the government, our attention easily turns first to the use of force and constraint. Governmental power, however, is only one form of social cohesion, and it is dependent upon the other forms.

The power of government is one of authority; it is power that has legitimacy. Authority means that power is voluntarily granted to an actor by the subjects for purposes supported by their values.[28] Even in discussing the power of the state, we have to include the values of the community and other forces. The state has power because of the legitimacy granted to it by the groups of the society that bear the most power. In addition to each group having a power of being, the government forms a center of action to give partial expression to the power of being of the whole community.[29] Power from the whole community is integrated to accomplish something together.[30]

Although the state's power requires the support of its subjects, it is still power. Civil authority is the centralized control in the community that has power to formulate and to enforce the basic formal rules of the society. Its power cannot be set aside by some other body in the society and still be the state. Those who disagree, agree to go along or are compelled to do so.[31]

The state is granted power to carry out essential purposes that cannot be carried out, or carried out as well, by other bodies without they themselves becoming government. There are some decisions that the central authority must make.[32] These include priorities of the community, such as empowerment of the weak. Much of the contemporary ideological differences are over what are the areas of appropriate state actions. One area of governmental initiative relates to "those acts which if left unrestricted would allow the few to control the many." An obvious example is the area of criminal law.[33] Augustine describes law (and education) as "tender mercies" of God in their restraint upon the cruel ills and ignorance which characterize human life, even though they themselves are carried out only through "labor and sorrow."[34]

The government not only restrains selfish, antisocial behavior. It also provides assurance for contributions that we feel a social impulse to make if we know that all others also contribute their share. National defense or traffic laws provide examples.[35] In this sense, the state gathers the community, rather than preserves it.

Social goals that cannot be reached unless there is collective action provide another area for the state's contribution to the cohesion of the community. Fire departments and protection of natural resources come to mind. Some matters are best done if there is only a single system, such water distribution lines, highways, foreign policy, or business cycles. There also are economic areas that go beyond the resources or interests of private enterprise. Space exploration, river improvements, and foreign aid programs may not bring negotiable economic returns to private investors. A further appropriate area of state contribution is where common action responds to major physical hazards that may strike any person through no fault of her or his own. Examples would include unemployment, death of a breadwinner, old age, sickness, crop failure, industrial accidents, and earthquakes or hurricanes.[36]

The other sources of social cohesion limit the power and importance of the state. There are many forms of regulation besides the state. Customs, traditions, and family training have a influential grasp on our behavior. In addition the various social organization and groups of the society have their own rules and forms of authority.[37] The state is but the central authority among other authorities throughout society.

Relatives, friends, and associates form common bonds that establish, continue, or terminate mutually recognized rights and obligations. These are *symmetrical* relationships. In them one is aware of how the actions of each affects the other, and the obligations are enforced by informal social and psychological sanctions. Gossip, ostracism, damage to reputation, and loss of the intimacy and trust of close associates have a powerful controlling impact. This network of reciprocal relations and sanctions is missing in contacts between strangers, or *asymmetrical* relationships. More control of the government is needed to protect the individuals in the relationships of strangers.[38] This need for more protection is reflected in the criminal justice system. To compensate for the fewer natural bonds, prosecutors, judges, and juries seek to punish killings between strangers more severely than those between friends and relatives, especially in the home. A study of 268 homicides in Houston in 1969, for example, showed that four times as many persons who killed a relative or a friend escaped punishment than those who killed a stranger.[39]

Society also holds together through its shared cultural values. Government, no matter how mighty, could not establish peace and order in society unless an element of order, community, and justice existed within the people.[40] A culture as a social system has a self-enforcing cohesive and integrating faith. Lord Devlin argued that without foundational agreement about good and evil a society will fall, and no society has discovered how to teach such common morality without religion.[41] The legitimacy of who carries out power and how it should be carried out is itself grounded in the people's common orientation to reality, nature, and human existence.

Finally, society holds together by a balance of power between the conflicting elements of society. The self-interest of the groups which can tear at the harmony of society cannot be ignored, yet it should not be simply suppressed. As we have seen, the groups are also the bearers of the values of the people. Instead the multiplicity of group life is encouraged so that the power of one nongovernmental group is able to counter the power of another group. In this way the selfishness of group life is harnessed, rechanneled, and directed apart from direct acts of governmental restraint.[42] The equilibrium in the tensions of society works for justice insofar as it prevents the domination of one group over another. The position of a group is maintained against the corrupting pressures of both excessive power and impotency. Groups also need defensive power.

There are two basic dangers in this jostling of groups, both of which result from the failure to reach a satisfactory equilibrium among them.[43] The first danger is anarchy. We have seen the powerful impulses toward immorality that become heightened on the group level. Inner checks are insufficient by themselves to control these drives but must be guided and supplemented by the government.[44] A situation becomes anarchic when tensions are unresolved and break out in overt conflict.[45] One part of society (the state) is not given sufficient authority over the other parts so that it can mold the balance of power by constraint.

The unprecedented number of financial failures of savings and loans institutions in 1990, which followed the extensive deregulation of the industry in the preceding dozen years, provides an example from one sphere of social life. When asked about the connection between the scandal and the deregulation, the coexecutives of a savings and loan corporation praised for its efficient management stated that the problem was not only greed. It also was hubris, they added, the conviction that the whole world is going one's own way, and that one can make no mistakes and do no wrong.[46] Irrationalities like greed and hubris break out of self-regulating strategies.

The attempt to replace certain aspects of governmental agency with voluntary programs also presents problems. James Luther Adams, the outstanding theologian, and advocate, of voluntary associations, wrote:

> The major crises of the past half-century, whether in international relations or in face of impending economic collapse, have demonstrated that voluntary associations are not omnicompetent alongside a "negative state." In face of serious economic maladjustment, or of major structural social needs, the appeal for voluntary associational solution of the problem is likely to be motivated by a class ideology. For example, Richard Nixon's theory of "the voluntary society" leaves it to people of tender conscience to cope with pervasive maladjustments by means of voluntary associations, thus relieving government, or the community as a whole, of responsibility. "Back to the grass roots" here in actuality means, back to the more intrac-

table power groups of the local or regional community. The first evil then, against which we need warning, is the evil of making too great claims for the competency of voluntary associations.[47]

The second danger is tyranny. Now the conflict between groups is reduced by the complete domination of one part (the state) over the rest. The society is maintained only by the authority element and not by a balancing of the tensions. Other centers of power are reduced.

One of the functions of the government is to preserve the equilibrium among the groups in society. A healthy society, as we have seen, is a matrix of a great variety of groups, contributing to different aspects of the individual and the community. The state presupposes this vitality of group life and serves as "the hinderer of hindrances." The business of politics then is to remove disharmonies that are thwarting the life of the groups and checking their vitality. The aim of the state's compulsion is "the setting free of the spontaneity which is inherent in the life of society."[48]

One way in which the government carries out its maintaining function is by arbitrating conflicts. An example would be the role the government has in business and labor disputes. This role requires the state to be more impartial than any other part. According to Maritain it is "a part which specializes in the interests of the whole."[49] The state also molds the process of mutual support among the groups.[50] For example, the government can encourage businesses to provide job training for low income people in exchange for tax breaks or adjustments in zoning laws. When such indirect approaches are not effective in restraining harmful group activity or in maintaining vital social functions, the state must act more directly in coercing submission to patterns of justice[51] or in directly carrying out vital services. The prospect of this compulsion supports the arbitrating and molding functions.

The objective of the state and of individuals seeking a peaceful society, however, is not merely to *maintain* an equilibrium of power in society. To maintain the balance between groups is to preserve the status quo, which may not be the best opportunity for justice. One cannot claim that any equilibrium is adequate as long as it maintains peace. The balance of power among groups is achieved in various ways with resulting degrees of justice. It may not be fair to all. The different groups may not receive the same benefits from the arrangement. One powerful group may be balanced against much smaller groups (see Figure 4.1).

There can be great disparity between the parts. In the equilibrium of the Middle Ages the peasants' position was maintained in part by the fact that if they starved, there would be danger to the economy and society. They did not get any worse or better. The powerful groups need the weaker groups the way they are.

The equilibrium of power is defensive power for its groups only to the degree that it maintains the life that God intends for each group and for the members of the community. The balance expresses exploitive power when it means that some are deprived of their basic needs on behalf of the superfluity of others.

"Any government that lives comfortably with the maladministration of the common good has lost the grounds of its own legitimacy." Where patterned, institutionalized maldistribution exists, the first duty of government is to correct it.[52] Advancing justice requires a change in the balance of power among the groups of

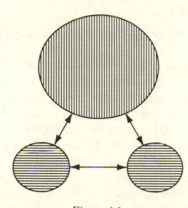

Figure 4.1.

the society. If the government seems inefficient or biased in favor of the more powerful elements in the current equilibrium, then it may not be a channel for just change. Class, property, and status are forms of power that contribute to maintaining the status quo, or the equilibrium.[53]

Shifting the balance of power upsets the uneasy social peace that rests upon it. One then may have to choose between social injustice with peace and the risk of violence.[54] The ethical dilemma is particularly difficult in a situation of just revolution in which arms are required to protect those using nonviolent means of change.[55] Change can at times come with minimal coercion by allowing units within the equilibrium to unite and act collectively. Labor unionization is an obvious example. It involves a change in the balance of power, and thus it usually is illegal at first: It is not allowed by the state, which seeks to preserve the current equilibrium.

The state functions to modify the society by reducing disproportions of power by conscious shifts in the balance of power. The taxing powers are used not merely for current revenue needs but also to decentralize the concentration of power through redistribution of income.[56] With criteria attuned to basic needs of the people, the state watches over the justice of the distributing operations of the economy.[57] The New Deal of Roosevelt following the Depression is an example. There was a significant shift of power in favor of the better organized elements of the working class. (Critics would argue that the basic motivation of the New Deal was really to *maintain* the broader structure of the capitalistic society in the face of threats of much greater shifts of power.)

Government can thus be seen as having two basic functions: nurturing the level of justice in the present balance of power and modifying it to achieve greater justice.[58] In these two functions the conflict between "law and order" and "justice" appears. Aristotle put it differently. The purpose of the state is not merely preventing mutual harm and providing the exchange of goods although these are necessary preconditions. The purpose is the good life, life that is full and sufficient (*Pol.* 1280b30–35; cf. 1252b30); it relates to proper needs, rather than to materialistic accumulation (1257b43).

Social Justice and the Purpose of the State

In the preceding sections several functions prescribed for the state presuppose a more basic conception of the state's responsibility for social justice. We spoke of the government's role in empowering the weak, correcting gross maladministrations in distribution, and modifying society to achieve greater justice. Many would not agree that such objectives are the proper business of the state. The idea of the social justice that impels the state must receive further grounding.

The state has a positive meaning of its own. Its purpose cannot be contained in a negative definition of restraining groups from moving out of their boundaries to prey upon other groups. This position would merely sanctify the present arrangements of groups or would provide no standard to identify unjust intrusions. The positive meaning of the state is justice. Its essence is to bear, posit, and enforce justice. The state, however, cannot be simply identified with justice nor with any other transcending value. In that it is secular. Yet it is not profane as if cut off from divine purpose and values.[59]

The positive purpose of government of advancing justice is seen in the biblical materials that present the ideal monarch. Behind these materials are principles for the proper conduct of government. Since they are presenting an ideal, these principles are normative for other forms of government to the degree that they are confronting perennial questions of civil rule. The ideal monarch is presented in two strands of material. The first is the ideal monarch in the royal psalms.

For example, Psalm 72, which Calvin liked to quote in expounding upon civil government, reflects the following purpose for the ruler: "May he defend the cause of the poor of the people, give deliverance to the needy, and crush the oppressor" (v. 4, *NRSV*). This task is identified as the work of justice (vv. 1–3, 7). Justice is understood as the use of power for deliverance of the needy and oppressed. To understand how this purpose of care and defense of the needy was carried out, we must understand the nature of the justice for which the monarch more than any other human office had responsibility (cf. Mic. 3.1). This conception of justice will be elaborated more fully in the next chapter.

In Psalm 72 there are oppressors of the poor separate from the state who need to be crushed. State power, despite its dangers, is necessary for society because of the evil of such exploiting groups ("on the side of the oppressors there was power" [Eccles. 4.1]). Without governmental power to counter such power there was "no one to comfort." Governmental power is to be used for the deliverance of the economically weak (cf. also Ps. 45.4–5; 101.8; Jer. 21.12; 22.15–16). The example of Nehemiah, cited earlier, is again helpful. The people in their economic weakness were losing their children into slavery. Nehemiah, representing the state, intervened and empowered them by restoring their lands (Neh. 5).

The purpose of government reflects the understanding of the nature of power, human beings, and society. An actively intervening state is a consequence of the perception of pervasive exploiting power in society motivated by the will-to-power. A theology of society that is more optimistic about the depth of power conflicts would substitute for the delivering model a more neutral referee model of the state.

The second strand presenting the ideal ruler is found in prophecies of the coming Messianic king. For example, Isaiah 11.4 (*NRSV*) states:

> But with righteousness he shall judge the poor, and decide with equity for the meek of the earth; he shall smite the earth with the rod of his mouth, and with the breath of his lips he shall kill the wicked.

Such an ideal ruler would take responsibility for the needs of the people as a shepherd: "He shall feed them and be their shepherd" (Ezek. 34.23). In Ezekiel 34 the failure of the shepherds (i.e., the rulers) of Israel to "feed" the people is described in v. 4. The same phrases are repeated to describe God's promise of justice.

> And I will make them lie down, says the Lord God. I will seek the lost, and I will bring back the strayed, and I will bind up the injured, and I will strengthen the weak, but the fat and the strong I will destroy. I will feed them in justice (vv. 15–16, *NRVS*).

This promise will be fulfilled by the Davidic prince (vv. 23–24). Similarly in Isaiah 32.1–8, the promised just and wise king is contrasted to the fool who leaves the hungry unsatisfied (v. 6).

The application of these materials beyond the limits of Israel in its unique role in salvation history is seen in that the monarch was a channel of God's justice (Ps. 72.1). God's justice extends beyond Israel (e.g., Ps. 9.7–9). All legitimate governments are theocratic in their proper functions of social justice. The cry, "Give the king thy justice, O God" (Ps. 72.1), is not only answered in the state provided for the people of God, but also in the fact that all rulers are instituted by God and are God's servants for human good. In justice they all are to be pipelines from God to their people. Romans 13 is structurally similar to Psalm 72.1 in viewing the ruler as a channel of God's authority, and the Old Testament material helps us to understand the nature of the good (*to agathon*, v. 4) that is the purpose of the state in Romans 13.

Daniel 4.27 is important for this question of the universal application of the ideal of the monarch as the protector of the weak. Nebuchadnezzar, the Babylonian king, is enjoined to carry out "justice and . . . mercy to the oppressed," the same kind of delivering justice as in Psalm 72.4. Similarly in Proverbs 31.9 King Lemuel, who is to "defend the rights of the poor and needy" (*NRSV*), is generally considered to be a northern Arabian monarch. "The general obligation of the Israelite king to see that persons otherwise not adequately protected or provided for should enjoy fair treatment in judicial proceedings and should receive the daily necessities of life is evidently understood as the duty of all kings."[60] The image of the ideal just monarch of Israel, whether in royal psalm or Messianic expectation cannot be restricted to a theocratic concern, which functions only to provide the promise of a Messianic reign that will be taken up at a future time. The demand for the same type of justice that delivers the needy from oppression was required at that time of a nontheocratic monarch. God's concern in the present and in the future, within Israel and outside of Israel, is that there be a community in which the weak are strengthened and protected from their foes.

Denial of the socioeconomic significance of the role of the ideal monarch is sim-

ilar structurally in thought to viewing Jesus' miracles only as proofs of divine mes-
siahship and not also as an expression of the care and deliverance of sick and
oppressed peoples, which is important to God in itself. In both cases external
assumptions, not exegesis, have provided the wrong kind of idealism in the sense
of the removal of the world of ideas from concrete human life. Miguez Bonino
rightly condemns this idealism as a distortion of Christianity because it removes
Christianity from its socioeconomic contact with concrete contemporary history.[61]

The literature of the nations of the Ancient Near East, as in Israel, presents the
hallmark of the ideal monarch to be this "special concern for the poor and helpless."[62] Psalm 45 provides an example that connects the justice of the ideal Hebrew
monarch with that of secular rulers. The monarch is praised as having "a scepter of
justice" and one who "loves justice and hates evil" (v. 6). This is the reason why he
is anointed (v. 7) Both of these ideas occur many times in Akkadian texts praising
the justice of the monarch. "The scepter of justice," used only here in the Hebrew
Bible, is used in Neo-Assyrian texts of a monarch whose pursuit of justice is
described in this way: "The king my lord has revived the one who was guilty (and)
condemned to death. The one who was imprisoned for many years is released.
Those who were sick for many days have got well, the hungry have been sated, the
parched have been anointed, the naked have been covered with clothes"[63] (cf. Ezek.
34.4; Ps. 146.7–9).

"To love justice—to hate evil" occurs several times in the inscriptions in connection with the promise of long and peaceful reign (cf. Ps. 45.10–15). The nature
of this justice is similar to role of the Hebrew monarch who delivers the poor. For
example, in one text that uses this phrase the monarch responded to a situation in
which "the strong used to plunder the weak, the rich used to take the property of
the poor. Regent and prince would not take the part of the cripple and widow before
the judge." Exorbitant rates of interest led to debt-servitude and the hopeless position of the poor. The monarch, however, was "not negligent in the matter of true
and righteous judgment." He drew up regulations and built anew the law court.[64]
Such a monarch was a legislator of just laws and the ultimate judge to whom
unjustly treated persons could appeal. In a similar vein it was customary for the Old
Babylonian monarch in his first full year to provide redress in a *mēšarum* ("justice,
just law") edict. This decree involved socioeconomic measures designed to alleviate
the destitute economic conditions of certain groups of the population in order to
prevent the collapse of the economy under too great a weight of private debts.[65]

This background to Psalm 45 is worth such detailed attention for two reasons. It
helps us to understand better the justice function of the ideal monarch in Israel. It
also shows that this ideal is not one restricted to theocratic contexts. The materials
are universal in that they already were in nonbiblical societies before they were
taken over with biblical revelation.

The strand of criticism of the monarchy in the Hebrew Bible is not directed at
the monarch as the deliverer of the poor. 1 Samuel 8.10–18 has been frequently
cited as an argument against a strong central government with its warning that a
monarch will be exploitive, taking the people's sons and daughters for his own military and domestic purposes, and securing substantial amounts of their property for
his private use (cf. Deut. 17.14–20).

The materials treating the establishment of the monarch in 1 Samuel are complex. 1 Samuel 11.12–15, for example, is quite positive toward the monarchy as there is great rejoicing in the renewal of the monarchic covenant. Many explain the conflict in terms of multiple sources. The antimonarchial passages (1 Sam. 8; 10.17–27; 12) themselves contain positive statements about the monarchy. Samuel is to listen to the people and provide a monarch (8.7, 22). It is Yahweh who has chosen the monarch (10.24; 12.1, 13).[66]

The two perspectives on a monarch for Israel are not based on the same conception of a monarch. The criticism in 1 Samuel 8 is not directed against the Davidic model of a monarch who is powerful in defense of the weak. The prophets take up the same criticism even while holding forth the promise of the future true son of David. The legitimacy of monarchy itself is not what is rejected. The reasons for requesting it and the type of monarchy that prevailed in that world are what Samuel condemns.

The monarchy that is criticized is the Canaanite model, where the monarch is the center of an aristocracy preying upon the people for its own consumption (cf. 1 Kgs. 21.7). Archaeological data from Alalakh and Ugarit reveal Samuel to be presenting an authentic description of the semifeudal Canaanite society as it existed prior to and during that time. This was a society with a warrier elite, monarchs active in loans and acquiring land through purchase and confiscation, tithe-taxes on products of the field and cattle in addition to customs and fines, and forced labor for roads, fortresses, palaces, and tilling crown lands. Samuel appeals to them not to impose upon themselves a Canaanite institution foreign to their way of life.[67]

The "manner of the king"[68] against which Samuel warns the people (1 Sam. 8.11–17) is countered by the "manner of the kingdom"[69] enjoined in the covenant with Saul; it is compatible with the continued sovereignty of Yahweh (10.25).[70] The delivering role of the monarch described in God's appointment in 1 Samuel 9.16 corresponds to the people's request in 8.20. Unlike the type of monarch criticized by Samuel, which centered on the use of office for personal aggrandizement, this view of the monarch expressed the need for government and deliverance. The people asked for "one to carry out justice *(špṭ)* for us" (v. 5). In the affirmative conception, the monarch continued the delivering function of the earlier judges, such as Deborah and Gideon. Like them, the true monarch delivers the oppressed. This monarch is a servant of the people (cf. 1 Kgs. 12.7).[71] Centralized governmental power is legitimate if the purpose of serving the weak is carried out.

John Calvin, more than most of the Christian theologians who preceded him, had such an activistic and functional view of the state. For him the state is a humanizing force. Because of sin it is a means of "a means of preservation, now indeed indispensable."[72] He cites the Old Testament passages regarding the rulers executing justice by delivering the poor and widow. The rulers were to "give aid and protection to the oppressed."[73] The purpose of government is the promotion of peace and well-being (*salus*[74]), as well as the glorification of God.

With the function of well-being Calvin thus goes well beyond the view that government primarily acts to keep order, to keep evil in check, or that it is an evil to be tolerated. When the purpose of government is seen as including happiness and a justice to be achieved, then government is presented as a modifier of society as well as a maintainer. Harro Höpfl demonstrates Calvin's position that if every Christian commonwealth were to do the duty of righteousness and piety, amelioration of the world would result. The church's duty was to urge magistrates to an ever closer conformity of human laws (positive law) with divine law. This would primarily be done through actual conformity to laws already in existence rather than by institutional changes or new laws. These laws included centuries-old concerns for the poor, just wages, schools, hospitals, and the critique of luxury.[75] Yet when necessity demands a change in the laws, God wants us to use the means that God has shown us and put into our hands.[76] Troeltsch rightly sees in these views an attitude rare and novel at that point in history "which desires to see society shaped and moulded for a definite purpose."[77] Society can be criticized in light of Scripture and reason.

This viewpoint can be the basis of a significant political activism when secular institutions are viewed more critically than they were by Calvin with his view that the normative institutional arrangements (e.g., war or private property) were divinely ordained in light of the necessities of the fall (technically a "relative natural law" theory). For the nineteenth-century Evangelical reformers, working in part in this tradition, promoting "public order and happiness through legislation was one of the indispensable means of doing good and saving souls." There are a multitude of wants and necessity that can be met only through the instrumentality of the government. Christians are bound to reform and uphold it.[78]

Divine Support of Government Authority

A government is capable of resorting to force to carry out its will; however, an expression of power in any society needs other grounds. We have seen that society holds together by its cultural values as well as by coercion. These values include those that support the arrangements of power in that society. Thus government needs prestige besides physical force.

Prestige derives from habits of loyalty and confidence. It is based in emotions, traditions, reason, and reverence. Reverence is a factor because the grounds of support for government are often metaphysical.[79] In preindustrial societies there often is little distinction between religion and government.

Romans 13 is a metaphysical support of government. It is not the form that equates the ruler with divinity; instead, it is one that shows the ruler to be ordained by God. It states that there is no authority except what is appointed by God (v. 1). The source of governmental authority is in God. God wills the principle of government. Abraham Kuyper argued that since all of us are equally human creatures, no one has a right to rule over another. Legitimate rule thus needs a source external to us: It originates in the authority of God (although God works through various human instruments of selecting rulers).[80]

The view of anarchists that the state is nothing but a set of relationships among individuals (engaged in actions tolerated for no other persons) is taken up by some laissez-faire advocates with the qualification that the state is necessary, but is to be endured like an appendectomy.[81] This perspective is incompatible with this passage. The state is a reality commissioned by God, an entity beyond the sum of the individuals carrying it out. Calvin thus refuted those who regarded magistrates "only as a kind of necessary evil" and called civil authority "the most honorable of all callings in the whole life" of mortal human beings; its function among human beings is "no less than that of bread, water, sun, and air."[82]

Further, what is basic to genuine governmental authority is justice, not force, which is only instrumental.[83] "The throne is established by justice" (Prov. 16.12). There is nothing essential to the state that prevents participation in it by those committed to justice. "When the just are in authority, the people rejoice" (Prov. 29.2). Beyond the state exists a transcending realm of truth, love, and holiness, which provide the meaning of community. This sphere is not the state, but it provides significance for the state that the state cannot produce or bear itself. Tillich perceived that this recognition lifts the state from being merely force and from arbitrary decision. The church is the community that discerns this sphere of values. The church groups must be free from the state so that they can carry out their function as the channel of meaning, but the state must recognize its need for this meaning which they bear.[84]

Does the grounding of governmental authority in God as in Romans 13 (and the similar passage in 1 Peter 2) exclude civil disobedience and revolution? Does the Christian have any choice but to give complete support to the actions of one's government? I have treated these questions in greater depth elsewhere[85], but some response to such practical implications of governmental legitimacy should be provided here.

First, modern questions of civil disobedience and revolution are foreign to the concerns of these texts. The concern behind Romans 13 is not to refute those whose struggles for justice come into conflict with unjust law. The problem that Paul encounters is antinomianism, the rejection of law on grounds that one possesses a spiritual status that rises above it. The principle of government itself is at stake. Paul must warn in this epistle against extreme interpretations of what it means not to be under the law but under grace. In Romans 6 he states that licentiousness means slavery to sin, not freedom. He now has to defend the civil law as well as the Mosaic law against this spiritual libertinism (cf. 1 Pet. 2.13–17, especially v. 16, "not using your freedom as a covering for vice"). The New Testament writers maintained against this extreme position that until society is completely regenerated (when, we should add, it nevertheless will be fully under the Reign of God [1 Cor. 15.24]), some sort of social, economic, and political control is needed to restrain and control evil persons.[86]

Second, Paul is presenting government in the ideal. It is the servant of God for good (v. 4). It honors the doer of good (v. 3). The passage (and what "good" means) needs to be understood in terms of Hellenistic Jewish conceptions of government. Philo of Alexandria, for example, is helpful. In this view of government the monarch is the shepherd and the father of the people (reflecting also the Old Testament view). He has the duty of caring for them. Government has many positive social functions, particularly in welfare. The ideal government distributes to "the necessary needs" of life so that there is no "excess for luxury" nor lack (Jos. 243 [cf. 2

Cor 8.13–15]). This is one side of the picture of government in Hellenistic Judaism. Here government is part of natural law and order. It is an expression of the Logos from God, a mediating force.

There is another aspect of the Hellenistic Jewish philosophy of government, however, that is not stated in the positive passages. From this vantage point government is the epitome of forces opposed to God. One sees a combination of obsequiousness and hatred to Rome in Philo.[87] The Revelation of John expresses the latter. Thus in other passages of Scripture we see the authority of government as often quite opposite to authority from God. What happens when the reality of government is seemingly for evil? What is one's responsibility when it does not meet the assumption of Romans 13 that government is a servant for good? The basis of civil disobedience is that the law under question is counter to the justice of God, and the basis of revolution is that the power refuted is not a legitimate government; it is not an authority.

Third, the concept of authority as appointed by God is two-edged. If God appoints, God is higher and separate.[88] At times, as in Acts 5, the people of God must cry out, "We must obey God rather than humankind!" Tannaitic Judaism (second century A.D.), therefore, while holding an attitude about government similar to that of Romans 13, taught that rulers are not to be obeyed if they command something that is forbidden by the Jewish faith.[89] As Abraham Kuyper proclaimed, seeing the source of true law in the eternal justice of God gives us courage to protest injustice in that name.

> And however powerfully the State may assert itself and oppress the free individual development, above that powerful State there is always glittering, before our soul's eye, as infinitely more powerful, the majesty of the King of kings, whose righteous bar ever maintains the right of appeal for all the oppressed, and unto Whom the prayer of the people ever ascends, to bless our nation and, in that nation, us and our house![90]

Martin Luther King stated that "noncooperation with evil is as much a moral obligation as is cooperation with good."[91]

We accordingly need to look at government in fact as well as in the ideal. The government can be the source of injustice. The groups that organize it have special power and stance in the community; it cannot be impartial although it is required that government be such. In Boston in 1988 there were 7.9 deaths per 1,000 live white births compared with 24.4 deaths per 1,000 black births. An inner-city physician commented that the legislators would not be able to understand the problem until the "issues of race and poverty are on the table." "If the babies of white suburban women were dying at these rates the problem would have been solved five years ago."[92] The groups that organize the government of the commonwealth of Massachusetts are not poor or black.

Government can also generate domineering impulses of its own. It magnifies the necessary prestige it receives, which is connected to the authority of the community and the majesty of true justice. Its order becomes order itself so that all rebels against its authority are rebels against authority.[93] A group that may have contributed to peace or justice when it first entered government becomes entrenched in power. It begins to receive more from society than its services require or, in struggling to stay in power, carries out measures that are harmful to the community.[94]

Power feeds on power, and exploitive power increasingly displaces intervening power. Acts on behalf of, or against, the political welfare of those holding power are identified with acts on behalf of, or against, the very safety of the society itself. In the Watergate crisis in the Nixon administration, the efforts of the opposition party to unseat the president were interpreted as threats to the security of the nation.

Government is created by a conflict of wills. The victorious will is partly fashioned and crystallized by the ruling groups. The danger of the self-interest of a monarch or oligarchy being associated with the good of the community is obvious, but a similar confusion can occur in a democracy. Niebuhr states that the general will of the people of which Rousseau wrote is but the myth of a final harmony of conflicting wills.[95] Marx argued that this concept reflected a cult of the people, a belief that the majority of the people of a nation had the same interests and the same understanding.[96] Unlike this imaginary people, the real people expressing themselves in elections are representatives of the different classes and groups in which the people are found. The victorious majority that organizes the government after the election will represent particular interests, and there may be inadequate checks to preserve interests of minorities that are in conflict with them.

Nevertheless, it was government in the first century, not a government before the fall of the race, that was declared appointed by God and a servant for good. James Madison wrote,

> What is government itself but the greatest of all reflections on human nature? If men were angels, no government would be necessary. If angels were to govern men, neither external nor internal controls on government would be necessary.
>
> In framing a government which is to be administered by men over men, the great difficulty lies in this: you must first enable the government to control the governed; and in the next place oblige it to control itself.[97]

To paraphrase Whitehead, government is a reality that we are "to seek and to distrust."

5

The Challenge of Biblical Justice

Justice more than any other concept provides the positive meaning of politics. It identifies what is most essential in life shared together in community and indicates the proper tasks of the government in supporting the common good.

Furthermore, justice is more than a principle of analysis. It is a rallying point. Justice is a powerful motivator. One should have a passion for justice. Justice points out the line where power becomes exploitive and indicates the objectives of intervening power. People accordingly devote their lives to justice, and Christians who are not pacificists state that it is only for justice that wars can be fought. Justice is also an attribute of God and a major mandate of Scripture.

Because justice defines the purpose of government, a person's understanding of justice will determine the direction of her or his political commitment. There are great disagreements, however, on what justice is.

What Is Justice?

People who discuss justice do agree that justice obliges us to do something that is good and that it is something which concerns other persons. Justice is a social norm, regulating the conduct of people in association with one another.[1] The disagreement among students of justice is over what good justice obliges us to do.

There are three basic approaches to justice reflecting broad differences in *Weltanschauung.*[2] The first approach is that of positive law. Justice is conformity to law. It equals legality. The second approach is social good. Justice is what is useful for the good of the particular society. Finally, there is the natural right approach to justice. Justice is what is due by a transcending principle of right.

Holders of the positive law position regard concepts of a justice over and above what is legal in the particular society as too vague and uncertain to be taken seriously as justice. This position is based on positivism, the viewpoint that moral or value judgments have no objectivity.

This approach is problematic for those who believe in special and general revelation and hold to the transcendence of truth and the knowability, at least in part, of this truth. From that perspective the positive law position has an unnecessary stringency in its requirements for truth that is not in accord with how most people think about justice.

More important politically, this theory of justice is uncritical socially. Because justice is contained in the legal definitions of the status quo, there are no grounds to challenge their adequacy. "Dread and fearsome are they; their justice and dignity proceed from themselves" (Hab. 1.7, *NRSV* [cf. 1.11]. Walter Kaufmann stated that Hitler's career did more than anything to promote skepticism about the moral authority of positive justice.[3]

In the social good theory the understanding of justice is dependent upon the traditions of the social group. It is found only in practices of society, including its social contracts.[4]

The definition of justice that results from this understanding often resembles that asserted in the natural right approach. This may suggest that the observer is really influenced by other evaluations of the individual than what he or she observes in social laws or receives in the social tradition. On the other hand one argument against natural law is that in reality it only expresses one's own social experience projected onto the cosmos. If, the concept of justice, however, comes from outside the society after all, or from a source more ultimate than the society, is it not really a natural law theory? If the concept of justice, is not over and above the society, what is the protection of the individual from the accepted standards of the society? If each social tradition defines its own justice, on what grounds could an international community criticize a society's treatment of its own members, as in the case of Hitler?[5]

In the natural right approach to justice the value of the individual is based on a rationally discerned definition of humanity that transcends legal codes or the understanding of the good of any particular community. These concepts can be understood by reason apart from special revelation, although special revelation may be seen as a crucial guide in identifying them.[6] Historically, this vision of humanity rested on religion and metaphysics, but in modern times efforts have been made to rest it solely upon rational grounds (e.g., John Rawls[7]). The end of justice is the good of the individual (under the glory of God). By stressing the individual, this position does not necessarily compromise our social nature. We are community beings while possessing unique value as individuals. Neither person nor community can be defined without the other.

Since we are concerned with a Christian political philosophy that includes belief in divine revelation, we have certain a priori moral judgments with which to work that are not necessarily available otherwise. Because we can operate with certain presuppositions about the nature of the person, as we have done earlier, we can use a natural law approach when others might not be able to accept its metaphysical assumptions. We see the person as a creature of God, in God's image, one for whom Christ died and thus of unique value and with corresponding rights required by God.

William Frankena provides an example of a modern natural rights position.[8] He argues in terms of the individual. He presents his argument in the form of an appeal to what is the most rational understanding of the notion of justice. He clarifies what we mean by justice when we think most clearly and consistently about it.[9] His elucidation is compatible with a biblical understanding of justice. I will summarize and to some extent restate his argument in the following paragraphs.

Many concepts that are offered as the meaning of justice lack sufficient content. They do not get to what is basic in the notion of justice. Such incomplete positions include the following statements: Justice is what is due; justice is what is due by law (the positive law position); justice is what is due by laws that conform to society's moral standards (the social good position); justice is rights and duties of the person (a simple natural law position). All of these, Frankena argues, are either too vague or fall back on something that could itself be unjust or nonjustice.

Justice involves distribution. What is distributed can be duties, opportunities, penalties, wealth, or liability to taxation. It deals with how power is distributed. The term *distributive justice* is usually reserved for the assignment of the advantages of living in society. It is positive in contrast to *retributive justice,* the assignment of penalties for violating the standards of the society. Retributive justice is also crucial for society, but our concentration in this chapter is on distributive justice, as we look at the positive meaning of politics.

Justice is also characterized by equality, at least in a formal way. Since its classic definition in Greek philosophy, justice has been understood as equality in the sense that similars are treated as similars and dissimilars are treated as dissimilars. Justice, however, is equality with a difference. Some dissimilarities do not hold in our modern conception of justice: obviously color of hair, but more importantly, gender or color of skin. To Plato and Aristotle justice did take into consideration degrees of personal ability or merit (e.g., amount of intellect).[10] This concept of justice supports aristocracy, which to them was understood in its etymological sense: "power to the best[11]." According to our modern concept, however, justice is not the equal treatment of equals but the equal treatment of all human beings as such. As Tillich put it, age, sex, race, intelligence, strength, and birth are accidental differences that should not prevail against essential equality.[12]

Moreover, justice is a hypersensitive form of equality. It takes into consideration certain handicaps that are hindrances to taking advantage of the opportunities of society. It looks for barriers that interfere with the chances to be equal in the good of society or to be participating members in the community. We would not consider a society to be just which did not distinguish sightless persons from other people. Because of their disadvantage, for them to be truly treated equally in life, they should be given more than others in some ways. Because of handicaps some people need to receive quantitatively more in order to be qualitatively equal. In terms of a whole lifetime they really are given no more than others. Some simply receive their gifts from life earlier.[13] The contribution of the community is proportional to the need.

The handicaps that justice considers go beyond individual physical disabilities and personal plights. Significant handicaps can be found in poverty or prejudice. As one judge said, "Loss of a leg is often less of a handicap than being born with a dark skin."[14] Justice takes into consideration differences in needs and capacities.[15] A full justice will be concerned to correct forces that create inequalities, rather than only to attempt to correct their damage.

We are working with a concept that goes beyond equality. It has more content than *procedural* justice, which is more equal in its thrust to open the processes of society to all its members. A just society has concern to consider and protect the good life of each person. It provides equal protection to all and removes any discrimination that prevents equality of opportunity. Considering and protecting the good life includes procedural justice but also gives special consideration to disadvantaged groups by providing essential social and economic assets when they cannot otherwise obtain. A just society also provides *substantive* justice.

The Character of Biblical Justice

Justice is a common biblical term even though English translations often veil the frequency and importance of justice in Scripture. As the accompanying chart shows, some words that have been frequently translated *righteousness* should often be rendered *justice*.[16] Other words are translated by *judgment* when *justice* would be closer to the meaning of the Hebrew or Greek term that is used (see Figure 5.1).

For example, the *King James Version* renders Jeremiah 22.3 as:

Execute ye judgment [*NRSV:* justice] and righteousness, and deliver the spoiled out of the hand of the oppressor: and do no wrong, do no violence to the stranger, the fatherless, nor the widow, neither shed innocent blood in this place.

In this context, which deals with proper relationships to oppressed groups in matters of access to social goods both the Hebrew words, *mišpāṭ* and *ṣedāqāh*, find their closest English equivalent in our word *justice*. A wooden, but yet conceptually faithful translation could read: "Execute justice and justice, and deliver the spoiled . . ."; but to take Olley's suggestion for *ṣedāqāh*, we would read, "Bring about justice and what is right and deliver the robbed . . ." The *King James Version* is more obvious, but the lack of clarity continues in recent translations. "Mighty acts of judgment" in Exodus 6.6, *NRSV,* should be rendered "mighty acts of justice."[17] While we know that the action did entail punishment on the Egyptian oppressors, the verse itself stresses freedom, deliverance, and redemption from burdens and slavery.

Hebrew	ṣedāqāh	mišpāṭ
	Translation in English Bibles: righteousness, justice	Translation in English Bibles: justice, judgment
Greek	dikaiosynē	krima
	Translation in English Bibles: justice, righteousness	Translation in English Bibles: judgment, justice
		krisis
		Translation in English Bibles: judgment, decision, justice

Figure 5.1. Biblical Words for Justice.

As Aristotle pointed out, the major Greek term for justice, *dikaiosynē*, also has a more general sense of the performance of all one's social duties.[18] Perhaps for most of our contemporaries *righteousness* has this sense of being socially upright rather than the other sense of being characterized by *right* or by just claims (i.e., *justice*). Some evangelical writers who reject a substantive social justice that includes benefit rights surprisingly do not treat the biblical materials on justice. One argument to defend this silence is a claim that the biblical uses of justice that speak of special care for the needy have the general sense of Aristotle's *dikaiosynē*.[19] Although the application of a distinction in a Greek term to Hebrew terms is improper, it certainly is true that the semantic field of *ṣᵉdāqāh* (and *mišpāṭ*) is broader than our term *justice*. *Ṣᵉdāqāh* does include the broader sense of one's total social obligation.

On the other hand, what is crucial is that very frequently *ṣᵉdāqāh* and *mišpāṭ* do overlap substantially with *justice*. A great number of their usages, as in Jeremiah 22.3, deal with justice proper in Aristotle's more narrow sense of recognizing conflicting claims in a situation of distribution of social benefits or penalties.[20] The following two passages are examples. "But it is God who executes justice *(šāpaṭ)*, putting down one and lifting up another" (Ps. 75.7). "They do not judge with justice the cause of the orphan, to make it prosper, and they do not defend *(šāpaṭ)* the rights [*mišpāṭ*] of the needy" (Jer. 5.28, *NRSV*). In this verse *mišpāṭ* [*NRSV* "rights"] does not describe the virtue of the needy but their valid social claims. We should note that Aristotle's particular justice itself was not merely retributive but also distributive in treating what was essential for the good life, which is related to "proper needs."[21]

The reader of the English Bible can use as a reliable rule of thumb that when *righteousness or judgment* is found in the context of social distribution or social conflict, *justice* would be a better translation. Ecclesiastes 5.8 furnishes an appropriate example: "If thou seest oppression of the poor, and violent perverting of judgment and justice in a province . . ." (*King James Version*) ("and the violent taking away of justice and righteousness" [*American Standard Version*]). Other indications that justice proper is specifically in mind include its relationship to state functions, to law, and to the use of power although justice is not restricted to a political context.

The nature of justice in the Bible will be presented in the following several categories that describe its crucial significance for our contemporary political understanding.

An Essential Characteristic of the Children of God

Justice is very important in the Biblical order of values.[22] It is a central duty of the child of God. This duty is so important that in several passages the people are admonished that their means of reconciliation and relationship to God will not be effective unless justice characterizes their actions.

Amos 5.21–24 may be the best known of these texts[23]:

> Even though you offer me your burnt offerings and grain offerings, I will not accept them . . . I will not listen to the melody of your harps. But let justice *(mišpāṭ)* roll down like waters and righteousness *(ṣedāqāh)* like an everflowing stream (NRSV).

Amos has already forcefully described the dire condition of the oppressed. The duty of justice to the afflicted is so central that if it is not fulfilled, God will not even accept the divinely ordained sacrifices and worship. When they fail to carry out justice, people do not have the true God as the object of their worship and devotion (Jer. 22.15–16).

Christ picked up this prophetic theme of justice and made its permanent imperative clear in Matthew 23.23:

> Woe to you, scribes and Pharisees, hypocrites, because you tithe mint and dill and cumin, and have neglected the weightier matters of the Law: justice (krisis) and mercy and loyalty (or faith [*pistis*]).

Christ's own understanding of the Old Testament is that justice is a central theme; he reiterated it in his preaching, thus applying it beyond the Old Testament theocracy.

Partiality to the Weak and Demand for Action

The most striking characteristic of biblical justice is its bias toward the weak.[24] "Bias" does not mean that God loves the poor more or that they should receive more than their just claims. It means that in the raging social struggles in which the poor are perennially victims of injustice, God and the followers of God take up the cause of the weak. In passage after passage the group to whom justice is to be applied is the oppressed—the widow, the orphan, the resident alien, and the poor. Throughout the Bible rulers and leaders are to exercise justice through concern for the weak and powerless.[25] Indeed, it is a standard of conduct for all of God's people.[26]

As it is frequently used in biblical texts justice is a call for action more than it is a principle of evaluation. Justice as an appeal for a response means *taking upon oneself the cause of those who are weak in their own defense.* Several phrases indicate the passionate and activistic character of this demand: "break every yoke" (Isa. 58.6); "I searched out the cause of him whom I did not know" (Job 29.16, *RSV*); "The Lord saw . . . that there was no justice and was appalled that there was no one to intervene" (Isa. 59.16, *NRSV*); "Execute justice in the morning and deliver from the hand of the oppressor" (Jer. 21.12, *NRSV*).

God's justice was the model. "All my bones shall say, 'O Lord, who is like you? You deliver the weak from those too strong for them, the weak and needy from those who despoil them'" (Ps. 35.10, *NRSV*). The Lord, the mighty creator is the one "who executes justice for the oppressed; who gives food to the hungry." This justice reaches out to the prisoners, the blind, those who are bowed down, the stranger, the orphan, and the widow (Ps. 146.9).

Continuity With God's Justice

The justice that characterizes God's defense of the poor is the justice that is demanded of humanity. In the Mosaic legislation the special care given to the socially and economically weak was based on God's being a God of justice. "The Lord . . . executes justice *(mišpāṭ)* for the orphan and the widow, and loves the strangers, providing them food and clothing. You shall also love the stranger . . . (Deut. 10.18–19, *NRSV*).

The prophets' protest against the economic oppression of the Israelite peasantry is couched in a warning about this active justice of God. God's justice is dynamic, demanding a similar response from the people of God.

> For the vineyard of the Lord of hosts is the house of Israel, and the people of Judah are his pleasant planting; and he expecteded justice *(mišpāṭ)*, but saw bloodshed; righteousness *(ṣedāqāh)*, but heard a cry! Ah, you who join house to house, who add field to field, until there is room for no one but you, and you are left to live alone in the midst of the land! The Lord of hosts has sworn in my hearing: "Surely many houses shall be desolate, large and beautiful houses, without inhabitant." (Isa. 5.7–9, *NRSV*)

There is a continuity between divine and human justice. Human beings receive justice from God for their decisions and responsibilities, and they learn justice from God.[27] It is methodologically necessary to look at the biblical materials describing God's social justice to develop the understanding of human responsibilities in justice.

Deliverance

Justice is rectifying the gross social inequities of the disadvantaged. It is not a mere *mitigation* of suffering in oppression. Justice is a *deliverance*. The terms for justice are frequently associated with *yᵉšûʿâ*, the most important Hebrew word for deliverance and salvation[28]: ". . . God arose to establish justice [*mišpāṭ*] to save [*hôšiaʿ*] all the oppressed of the earth" (Ps. 76.9; cf. Isa. 63.1).[29] "Give justice to the weak" and "maintain the right of the lowly" are parallel to "rescue the weak and the needy and snatch them out of the power of the wicked" (Ps. 82.3–4).[30]

Justice describes the deliverance of the people from political and economic oppressors (Judg. 5.11), from slavery (1 Sam. 12.7; Mic. 6.5), and from captivity (Isa. 41.1–11 [cf. v. 2 for *ṣedeq*]; Jer. 51.10). Providing for the needy means to set them back on their feet, give a home, lead to prosperity, restoration, end oppression (Ps. 68.5–10; 10.15–18).[31] Justice removes oppression; it does not merely help the victims of oppression to cope within it.

The same combination of justice and deliverance from the power of the oppressor is demanded of the ruler (Jer. 21.12; 22.2–3; Ps. 72.4).[32] Justice in the Bible is intervening power. God seeks for those who will "build up the wall and stand in the breach before" God in the land (Ezek. 22.30) over against the oppression of the poor and weak (v. 29; cf. Isa. 59.15–16).

Restoration to Community

We continually have before us justice as the correction of the situation in which the strong have exploitive power over the weak (pp. 18–24). In deliverance the people are returned to the situation of life in community which God intends for them. Justice is a restoration to community. As seen in the Jubilee and formulated in

Leviticus 25.35–36, the poor are described as being on the verge of falling out of the community because of their economic distress: "Their power is diminished *with you*."[33]

Elsewhere the poor are described as friendless and shunned (Prov. 14.20; 19.4, 7). Proverbs 5.9–14, describing the economic disaster that comes from a person's immoral conduct also highlights the communal nature of well-being: "I am at the point of utter ruin *in the public assembly*" (v. 14, *NRSV;* cf. Ps. 1.5).

The community's responsibility to its diminished members is "to make them strong" again, restoring them to participation in community (Lev. 25.35; cf. p. 22). The purpose of this empowerment is "that they may live *beside you* in the land." In Psalm 107.36 (*NRSV*) the hungry who receive God's steadfast love are able to "establish a town to live in." They can be active, participating members of a community once more. The concern is for the person in community and what it takes to maintain the individual in that relationship.

Recognizing community participation as the key criterion has important consequences for understanding justice. Participation in community has multiple dimensions. Its spheres include physical life itself, political protection and decision making, social interchange and standing, economic production, education, culture, and religion. Community membership means the ability to share fully within one's capacity and potential in each essential aspect of community.

Justice provides the conditions for participation in community. Individuals have responsibility according to their ability to transform those conditions into the reality of the good life. For example, justice provides the conditions of religion through freedom of religion, but it cannot produce faith itself. There is a huge gap beyond justice in this case.

The concern for each individual as a creature of moral and spiritual worth before God is that they be active agents of their own well-being.[34] Anything less diminishes community membership. Justice provides the conditions to sustain that agency. When justice produces dependency (as opposed to mutuality), it has not been successful in completing its task. Its deliverance is incomplete. Accordingly, the provision of land was crucial in Israel's social economy. Land was a condition of agency that distribution of food itself could not provide. Land furnished membership in the economic community, while food ensured access only to the physical aspect of community life (itself a task of justice, however, when lacking).[35]

From the perspective of God's universal justice, God as the common creator, and the death of Christ for all, the basic claims of justice for members of the Hebrew community are affirmed as valid claims for all people as members of the total human community.[36] The less universal communities that directly affect our everyday lives, however, remain crucial as the context for rights. Rights are the privileges of membership in the communities to which we belong.[37] Human rights, based in the universal community, are those that must always be respected by the concrete communities to which we belong.[22]

Basic Equality

Since membership in community involves a shared participation in all of its essential spheres, justice provides an equality in the fundamental elements of human life.

Biblical justice implies a relative equality. Because of a common creator, masters are to "grant justice and equality [*to dikaion kai tēn isotēta*]" to their slaves (Col. 4.1). Equality before God is reflected in the same social requirements placed on all of God's creatures, despite hierarchical differences among them (also Eph. 6.9); yet such categories of social status of their world were themselves challenged in light of God's singular majesty (Matt. 23.9) and the new creation brought into being by Christ (Gal. 3.28).[38]

Equality, however, is a shifty word in political science. Clarity is often better served by avoiding it, despite the noble traditions, struggles, and visions that it evokes. The term leads quickly to misunderstandings and stereotyped ideological assumptions. Niebuhr found that "equal justice" stated his thought better.[39] This term also needs qualification since, as we have seen, justice formally means treating equals equally so that "equal justice" does not specify the type of justice or equality one has in mind.

What we mean by equality as a special component of biblical justice is equality in basic needs. A basic equality does not mean a mathematical division of all property and power or a leveling of all social goods. Basic needs are limited and capable of being defined.[40] They are not infinite so that anything that is apt to be desired in society is subject to just distribution. The first priority of distributive justice is to meet the basic needs of every member of the community.

The principle of justice does not prevent unequal accumulations after the basic needs of all have been met. The biblical ethic of possession or consumption, on the other hand, was one of sufficiency.[41] Although this ethic was not presented in the language of justice claims, it would not differ from the implications of justice when part of the community was lacking in basic needs. The biblical understanding of human nature also raises alarm at the potential for evil in sharp differences in power among individuals and groups in the society. John Calvin described a "rough equality" in the Mosaic Law. Commenting upon the canceling of debts in the sabbatical year, he wrote,

> In as much as God had given them the use of the franchise, the best way to preserve their liberty was by maintaining a condition of rough equality [*mediocrem statum*], lest a few persons of immense wealth oppress the general body. Since, therefore, the rich if they had been permitted constantly to increase their wealth, would have tyrannized over the rest, God put a restraint on immoderate power by means of this law.[42]

In biblical justice special attention is given to the weak so that they can realize along with all other members the minimum requirements of participation in the community. The Bible treats this principle in several ways. The most interesting and significant is the distribution of the land.

The land, the common heritage from Yahweh upon which "all Israel" lived, from the greatest to the smallest,[43] was originally distributed proportionally among the tribes of the people according to the directions of God in the Book of Numbers. The principles of apportionment were first according to numbers (Num. 26.54) so that for each extended family a similar amount of land was available. The land was divided so that the more populous tribes got more and the less populous got less.[44]

Land, especially the diverse land of Palestine, however, varies in quality, and is difficult to distribute fairly. Breaking down the tribal land further and determining which land went to whom among the extended families and their protective associations was done by lot (Num. 26.55–56). Each unit had the same opportunity to receive the better parcels. Qualifications of family line or ability had no bearing.[45]

This distribution of land is the presupposition of the periodic return of the land in institution of the Jubilee. The Jubilee functioned to perpetuate the arrangement of assuring productive property for each of the most basic economic units (Lev. 25.28). Ezekiel prophesied a future restoration of this distribution of the land. The principle of that division was, "You shall divide it equally" (Ezek. 47.14, *NRSV*). Zechariah 3.10 and Micah 4.4 look to the time when once again all will sit under their own vine and fig tree, representing security and access to means of production.

Paul uses equality (*isotēs*) as the principle of material sharing between the different Christian communities (2 Cor. 8.14). Those who had excess contributed to those who were lacking.[46] Paul's model was the distribution of manna by God in the desert wanderings of Israel (v. 15). It was a model based according to need, not mathematical uniformity. No matter how excessive some were in the amount they gathered, each ended up with only "as much as each of them needed" (Exod. 16.18, *NRSV*). In presenting the ideal character of the early church in Acts Luke describes how the Christians had all things in common. The emphasis that "no one among them was needy," but what was shared "was distributed to each as any one had need" (Acts 4.34–35), may indicate that the thoroughgoing sharing was at the level of meeting the basic necessities for everyone.[47] Despite the Hellenistic format of the arrangements, the principle would then be similar to that of the Old Testament. They were carrying out the demand of basic sharing that John the Baptist had proclaimed as fruits of the repentance before the approach of the Reign of God. Those with excess in the basic needs of life should share with those who lacked (Lk. 3.11). Although the early Christian communities of the last days and the assembly living from the hand of God in the wilderness are special communities and their arrangements are not described with justice language, they still present an ideal of human relationships that should not be turned away from ongoing questions of proper human conduct.

Benefit Rights as Well as Freedom Rights

Access to all spheres that are essential to community as the meaning of justice requires a standard of justice for essential goods that are not in unlimited supply. The civil aspects of community, such as due process and forms of participation, can be distributed to all without taking from others. Economic matters usually do mean some form of redistribution to set things right. Substantive justice, which grants benefit rights, is accordingly controversial since it involves a partiality that many feel is contrary to the nature of justice.

The action of deliverance of the oppressed from the power of the strong in biblical justice, however, does mean action by the community that can be detrimental to the interest of the strong (e.g., Isa. 11.4). It may require adjustments in the community which, as in the Jubilee, takes back productive property that was legitimately acquired.

Achieving justice may also involve provision of material essentials of life, such as food and shelter: "The Lord . . . executes justice *(mišpāṭ)* for the orphan and the widow, and loves the strangers, providing them food and clothing (Deut. 10.18, *NRSV*). ". . . Who executes justice for the oppressed; who gives food to the hungry" (Ps. 146.7 *NRSV;* cf. 111.3–5; Job 8.6). "Food and clothing" is a Hebraism for what is indispensable.[48]

Job 24 describes the benefits that are taken away through injustice. Injustice starts with assault on the land, the basis of economic power (v. 2). It then moves to secondary means of production, the ass and the ox (v. 3). As a result the victims suffer powerlessness and indignity: "They thrust the poor off the road; the poor of the earth all hide themselves (v. 4, *NRSV*). The poor are separated from the bonds of community, wandering like wild asses in the desert (v. 5). They are denied basic needs of food (vv. 6, 10), drink (v. 11), clothing, and shelter (vv. 7, 10). These loss of benefits as injustice appear in other sections of Job as well.[49]

The connection of biblical justice to such material essentials of life in community stands in opposition to the concept of the purely negative state, which does not recognize benefit rights. In the latter interpretation justice only prevents the intrusions upon the rights of another. It prevents. It does not provide. The rights that are protected are those of property, person, and equal access to the procedures of the community.

These negative rights that are protected in this conception are indeed crucial to justice. A person who is denied these protections is cut off from the political and civil community and is not only open to abuse, but is diminished in his or her ability to affect the life of the community. Remedial or criminal justice is critical to protect the individual or group from intrusions upon their well-being. One example among many of retributive justice is the use of *mišpaṭ* for the judicial decision on one involved in involuntary taking of human life in Num. 35.12. The use of *mišpaṭ* in retributive justice is common. Procedural concerns are representanted in concerns about just *(ṣedeq)* weights and measures (Lev. 19.35–36), an emphasis in the prophetic and wisdom literature (e.g., Amos 8.5; Prov. 11.1). Due process is to be followed in judgment; there should be no bribes and neither the poor nor the rich are to be favored beyond their due claims (Deut. 16.19; Lev. 19.15).

The biblical conception of justice is foundational for such freedom rights, although our full understanding of them developed historically after the biblical period. They became more fully recognized as the experience of oppression was reflected upon in the light of biblical insights into human depravity and human worth.

Biblical justice, however, also includes positive rights, which are the responsibility of the community to ensure. Rather than the neutral and only punitive image of the ruler, the true ruler is one who strengthens the weak, heals the sick, binds up the crippled, brings back the stray, and seeks the lost (Ezek. 34.4, 16, 23).

Because of its economic and social focus biblical justice is continually associated with groups such as widows, orphans, resident aliens, wage earners, the poor, and slaves. Justice responds to economic need.

Violations of civil and property rights are also often involved. Economic deprivation often leads to vulnerability so that formal equality is perverted by substantive inequality. The situation, however, is not simply that the members of these groups have been denied equal civil process. If the concern were strictly a matter of violations of process and property, other groups would be also closely associated with justice. The most economically needy are not the only common victims of crime. Indeed, in such a situation of severe economic struggle the advantaged will be subject to crimes committed by the disadvantaged. "Give me [not] poverty . . . or I shall be poor, and steal (Prov. 30.9, *NRSV*). There is, however, no corresponding association of justice with wealthy groups, or other groups victimized only by crime (although biblical justice certainly does respond to these needs, too).

The widow, orphan, and stranger stand out in the depth of their basic needs. Justice is closely connected to them because its theme is to meet basic needs so that all can be included in community. The needs to which it responds are civil and political, but also social and economic.

The Law contained many benefit rights. Justice as an enforcement of the Law then would be a provision of benefit rights.[50] The law provided land to each extended family (Lev. 25).[51] Food was a subject of several of its stipulations. The poor received food in the sabbatical year (Exod. 23.10–11) and in what was passed over in the first harvest (Deut. 24.19–22; Lev. 19.9–10). The hungry were to be allowed immediate consumption of food in the grainfields (Deut. 23.24–25). By a transfer payment, every third year 10 percent of the harvest was put in storehouses in the towns for the poor (Deut. 14.28). Interest on consumptive loans was prohibited as a harmful economic activity which threatened a person's community status (Lev. 25.35–37). Similarly, holding as security a matter essential for life was proscribed as a matter of justice (*ṣᵉdāqāh*, Deut. 24.13).[52]

An Economic as Well as a Legal Focus

The goal in the restoration by justice is not recovering the integrity of the legal system as such. The community as a place where the basic needs of all are met is reestablished.

The wrong to which justice responds is not merely an illegitimate process (like stealing). An end result in which people are deprived of basic needs is also what is wrong. "You shall not oppress *('āšaq)* your neighbor *or* steal" (Lev. 19.13).[53] Certain forms of human relations are unjust in themselves even without consideration of the effects that they have on the lives of others. Stealing, cheating, and lying are immediately wrong and rightly restricted as much as possible by the law. Justice, however, also looks at situations in which people are deprived of what they need even if these intrinsically wrong actions are not present. Excessive power may take on the appearance of injustice only when it is perceived as having the effects of depriving others of their rights.

Justice concentrates upon fulfilling basic unmet needs. Justice as deliverance also resists human forces that cause that deprivation. It responds both to the oppressive use of excessive powers[54] as well as to perverting or violating the legal processes for similar ends. For the Bible injustice comes out of power combined with greed.[55]

The ability of the poor to hold their own can be destroyed without the law being broken. In some situations of oppression there are great inequities in power and resources, and the poor have little control over their lives. They have little choice but to enter into debts, which are foreclosed without mercy. Buyers controlled by their competitors refuse to purchase a person's crops. A small farmer is underpriced by the larger harvest offered to the buyer by his or her competitor. The owner of a small but profitable company is driven from business as his or her best workers leave for a larger company that offers them higher wages. That company may be less efficient but has broader resources to manipulate. Land reforms are thwarted by dividing the land among relatives and lackeys who are only nominal owners so that the landholding oligarchy is able to maintain its dominate position.

A striking example of this legal use of economic might occurred in the mountains of New Hampshire around 1900. The New Hampshire Land Company, possessing an increasing amount of timber land, refused to sell any of it to the native farmers, who earned income from logging. As they exhausted their limited tracts of land, they were unable to purchase any more. Their only recourse was to sell their farms to the land company for $1.00 or $2.00 an acre. Without legal violation the small loggers were destroyed, and the company sold the land to the big-scale lumber interests in lots not less than 10,000 acres.[56]

In Belize after slavery was abolished in 1838, private property remained highly concentrated. The Belize Estate and Produce Company owned about one half of all private land in the colony. Although it previously had been granted gratuitously, within a few months of emancipation the colonial office instructed that crown land was only to be sold; otherwise, the practice would "discourage labour for wages." The strategy successfully kept land out of the hands of slaves, who had only the theoretical freedom to choose not to work for their former masters in the mahogany forests.

The former slaves were hired with contracts for six and twelve months. The contracts were enforced by constables and the courts, which meted out three months of hard labor as punishment for absention from work without leave, "insolence and disobedience," and entering into a second contract before the expiration of the first. The laborers were given advances in pay at Christmas. These were quickly spent and the workers had recourse only to purchase supplies on credit at exorbitant prices at the employers' camps in the forest. To work off the debt the worker would have to sign another contract. Fifty years after abolition the colony's handbook stated, "Advantage has been taken . . . to keep them in debt by either supplying them with goods or drink for the purpose, and they thus have become virtually enslaved for life."

The contract system lasted for a century. In the 1930s the rations the workers received in the mahogany camps were said to be less that those given to slaves in the early nineteenth century. They lived in unsanitary conditions and suffered from medical problems associated with malnutrition, yet medical services were lacking. The laborers' legal status had been newly defined after 1838, but they "were not freed from the very real constraints of persistent power structures."[57] The oppression occurred, however, without violation of existing laws.

Eryl Davies argues that Isaiah does not condemn as illegal the acquisition of the land denounced in Isaiah 5.8–10. Through foreclosing of mortgages or through debt bondage, property could be taken within the law.[58] Isaiah nevertheless condemns the rulers for not defending the weak. He appeals to social justice above the law to which the law must respond.

The Bible gives attention to the content of justice or injustice—whether actions give life or destroy (seen vividly in Ps. 109.16)—rather than first of all the question of legality or illegality. The restoration is primarily to community, not to a legal position. Justice is not a measure of conformity to whatever the law may be. It is a standard of whether any social activity—legal, economic, social—brings people into supportive community or drives them out. Law is an effective and genuine social instrument as it gives expression to such justice.

Continuity With Love

One reason why some argue that there are no benefit rights in justice is that justice and benevolence (or love) are separate principles. Benefits belong to love not to justice. To claim benefits as rights is to confuse love and justice. Granting benefit rights additionally requires a partiality in justice. People have different need for matters like food or shelter assistance, and providing them necessitates taking from some in order to give to others. Such partiality, however, is contrary to the impartial character of true justice. It belongs rather to love, which is voluntary and which does not include the work of the state.[59]

Biblical justice, however, is frequently found in close association with love. As an example, love and justice in the following passage are interchangeable: " . . . [The Lord] who executes *justice (mišpāṭ)* for the orphan and the widow, and who *loves* the strangers, providing them food and clothing" (Deut. 10.18, *NRSV;* cf. Isa. 30.18).[60]

Not all benevolence is justice, but love that responds to unmet basic material needs legitimately calls forth justice. Such a loving, benevolent type of justice is not a confusion about biblical justice. It is the meaning of distributive justice in the Scriptures.

A Responsibility of Government

God's justice is to be that of the monarch and other rulers in particular. "The Lord has made you king to execute justice and righteousness" (1 Kgs. 10.9).[61] "Are you a king because you compete in cedar? Did not your father eat and drink and do justice and righteousness? Then it was well with him. He judged the cause of the poor and needy; then it was well" (Jer. 22.15–16).[62] We have already seen how social justice is required of monarchs both within and without Israel (cf. pp. 66–68).

The relationship of justice to the function of government is further indicated by the close tie of justice to law. "So the law becomes slack and justice never prevails" (Hab. 1.4, *NRSV*).[63] The relationship of power to justice reflects the connection to rule even further; we will return to that relationship in the following chapter (cf. also pp. 21–24).

Justice is almost universally accepted as the purpose of government although of course there is great disagreement on what the nature of justice is. As James Madison wrote, "Justice is the end of government. It is the end of civil society. It has ever been and ever will be pursued until it be obtained, or until liberty be lost in the pursuit."[64]

As Zeev Falk summarizes the biblical position, the chief function of the monarch was, as is well known, "the administration of justice and especially the assistance given to the weak against their oppressors."[65] This justice cannot be distinguished in its quality and direction from the justice required of others. The concerns of government and law include a substantive, material, and benefit-oriented justice.

Conclusion: Distribution According to Needs in Community

The description of biblical justice must take into account all of these factors: focus upon economic weakness, deliverance and restoration, the social priority of basic needs, participation in community, legal support of benefit rights as well as rights of protection and precedure, and continuity with the concept of love.

The traditional formulas of distributive justice prescribe the kind of merit that must be met to receive the minimal standard of that which is being distributed.[66] To work practically with a justice based on Scripture, one must decide which of these criteria best corresponds to the biblical data. By *worth* distribution is made according to differences of worth and status ascribed to different groups of the society, such as a nobility received by *birth*. By *social contribution* some groups deserve more of justice by the ascribed value of their contribution to society. A distribution according to *might* or *ability*[67] can be allowed to go on with considerable leeway in finding its own course. Distribution achieved by economic prowess, or by another form of ability, is understood to be just as long as certain procedural rules of the society are observed. By *contract* the focus is upon faithfulness to whatever agreements that have been made rather than to transcending standards for the contents of the agreement. It is thus procedural rather than substantive and will be a positive law or social good form of justice. Finally, there is distribution according to the *needs* of the recipients.

Among the traditional formulas of distributive justice the one most appropriate for biblical justice is distribution according to needs. These needs include both benefits and procedures and are oriented to life in community.

To state that biblical justice is distributed only according to needs would be to go too far. Some of the other criteria of distributive justice are at least assumed. For example, in every society achievement (or ability) has a role within the confines of the central concept of justice.[68] Once "just" distribution to the serf or lord is made, each achieves what one can within those confines.

When the biblical writers are being intentional about justice, however, and using justice terminology, it is distribution according to needs that prevails. This is the central direction for the conduct of the distributive systems. This intentionality about justice is not present in the narratives of great wealth for some individuals or in legal provisions that assume the existence of slavery. When justice is set forth, it is the basic needs for inclusion in community that are set forth; these concerns give direction to the economic, social, and legal ordering of the community.

6

Love Is Not All You Need

There is an actual phenomenon in life separate from justice that thinkers from a great variety of traditions identify as love.[1] Some Christian traditions regard it as providing a way of social conduct that is separate from justice and superior to justice (although this exclusion may be unwitting).

To understand the problem and the inadequacy of love without justice, we will describe how love appears as a distinct phenomenon. Genuine love gives expression to justice in order to complete love's social task. We will, however, momentarily consider love apart from its natural and proper continuity with justice. This is where a two-kingdom approach ends as it applies love to one sphere of life and justice to another. It is where a critic of that tradition like Reinhold Niebuhr begins. The dualism is not proper as either a starting or an ending point. Love, however, is not identical with justice. It is helpful to see the phenomenon of love as it appears without justice to understand the inadequacy of a strategy that depends upon such love for social responsibility.

The Distinctiveness of Love

Emotions are a constitutional part of what we would recognize as genuine love. Love includes feelings of identity with its object that cannot be reduced to an idea of the mind or an impulse of the will. We yearn for those whom we love. Augustine compared love to fire upon whose heat we float.[2]

Love is expressed in giving. According to Guy de Maupassant, "When two people love each other nothing is more imperative and delightful to them than giving: to give always and everything, one's thoughts, one's life, one's body, all that one has: and to feel the gift and to risk everything in order to be able to give more, still more."[3] Love is "an invariable thirst after [the loved one's] happiness in every kind."[4]

Love in some degree also means union with its object. The distinctions of mine and thine are dropped.[5] Fromm states that love is the only passion that satisfies the human need to unite oneself with the world while at the same time acquiring a sense of integrity and individuality. It is union with somebody outside of oneself, under the condition of retaining the separateness of one's self.[6]

These characteristics of love limit its application beyond the sphere of individuals

89

who are real and concrete to us. In Aristotle's ethics love is the extreme form of friendship. Since it seems impossible to be much of a friend to many people, loving many people would seem to be impossible.[7] Nicolas Berdyaev (probably under the influence of Dostoyevski) argued that love can only be directed to a person, a living thing, one's neighbor. "Humankind" never appears to anyone in daily experience. Only concrete men and women exist. Love cannot be given to abstract goods; thus one does not love humanity in general since that is an abstraction. Such abstract love, Berdyaev argues, has the danger of making people ready to sacrifice concrete, living beings for the abstract. This is the case of those Scribes and Pharisees who love the good rather than persons.[8] We could compare those who love America but hate Americans who disagree with them.

Sacrificial love is the purest love. Self-sacrifice as a description of love, however, presents significant difficulties. Gene Outka rejects it as the highest form of love.[9] It does not contain criteria to prevent sinful exploitation of oneself by others, and it does not help when the choice is between two neighbors rather between a neighbor and oneself. More satisfactory, he suggests, is love as equal regard. We are to love our neighbor *as* ourself. Self-sacrifice does need to be qualified.

Garth Hallet, however, shows that all of the different interpretations of Christian neighbor love entail extreme self-sacrifice, even the position that one should give more weight to one's own good than to the equal good of others. This position of self-preference would advise a crane operator to sacrifice his or her own life to prevent the crane from falling on a crowd of people.[10]

Self-sacrifice in genuine love is not oriented toward one's own needs for self-denial nor is it blind to anything about its object's situation. The self-sacrifice is instrumental. It is self-sacrifice for the good of the other.

Love draws upon the abundance of one's own defensive power. Sacrificial love does not come out of a vacuum of proper self-regard. It does not discount the created purposes that one possesses from God. As Jonathan Edwards held, it is a matter of the place of proper self-love, not its absence. Self-love is set to the side, but it is not eclipsed entirely by pure love devoid of egoism. Proper love for oneself occurs in the larger context of love for the excellency of God, which is the most basic foundation. We love others in hope that we will also receive the added good of reciprocated love, but we love even when the certainty of that return is lacking.[11] There is a depth to love, therefore, that goes beyond equal regard.

The golden rule simply provides a way of discerning what I consider to be good in contemplating my obligation to others; it does not comprehend the fullness of love.[12] Love is more than the equal regard that this principle implies. The difficulty that love has in distinguishing between the claims of neighbors is indeed real. Love has to engender principles of justice to guide such choices.

Hallet argues convincingly that self-subordination most adequately describes the relationship to others and to one's self in New Testament love.[13] Only on the condition that maximum benefit to others has been assured should one give independent consideration to one's own benefit. The texts that speak of Jesus and his followers as a servant and slave are particularly supportive. We are to be servants just as Jesus came "to serve and to give his life as a ransom for many" (Matt. 20.26–28 par).[14] We have previously examined love's ability to surrender defensive power for the sake of others in the Sermon on the Mount (Matt. 5.38–42).

Love, however, as a passionate yearning for union with its object that is ready to subordinate itself to the good of others presents political problems when it is cut off from justice. The attractiveness of equal regard is that it is closer in nature to justice, smoothing the transition from love to justice. Acknowledging the existence of the more distinctive aspects of love sharpens our realization that justice that rises out of love is socially necessary.

The Need for Justice

Justice is different. It does not give; rather, it fulfills claims and rights. This usually also means taking. One receives from justice that which is one's right as a human being under God. Love is a gift, reflecting a choice by the giver. William Temple referred to the "banner so familiar in unemployed or socialist processions—'Damn your charity; we want justice.' " He notes that in such a situation charity in place of justice would be virtuous only on the supposition that the present order is sacrosanct.[15] In such situations justice is a morally necessary altering of the structures while love is a voluntary giving within the structures. Love is "giving another person what belongs to you" while justice is "giving another person what belongs to him or her" by right.[16]

One encounters justice more commonly in one's relationships with those who are not one's neighbors. Justice is first of all abstract and objective. The context of justice is the selfish conflict of group versus group, individual versus individual, that comprises society. Justice is a guide for reaching a proper equilibrium in the midst of the conflicting claims upon our love.[17]

Because the egoistical passions are so strong, justice must use power to achieve a fairer balance of power.[18] It must throw up defenses against the inordinate expansion of defenses. Nature has built-in compensations to allow a species to "escape the death that lurks everywhere for the undefended."[19] Fish and insects survive by producing thousands of eggs. The human species protects itself with an ethical norm to shelter its weak from the strong.

The claims that justice adjudicates include those of oneself and one's group, or the group that one represents. Justice means not surrendering them but reaching the point where all receive their proper due.[20] Thus while "love achieves oneness, justice maintains distinction"[21] (which indeed is a component of love).

Again seemingly moving beyond the purity of love, justice includes punishment. As Míguez Bonino states, love operates by establishing justice, redressing the condition of the weak. "Judgment, therefore, is the unavoidable shadow of love as it meets human arrogance and inhumanity."[22] With such characteristics justice means getting knee-deep into the conflicts of the world. When viewed this way, justice seems far from the simple giving of love. It is not surprising that many Christians are warm on love and not too hot on justice.

Love, cutoff from its implications in justice, however, is not biblical love. H.

Richard Niebuhr corrects his brother, Reinhold Niebuhr, in the latter's acceptance of the liberal interpretation of Jesus' teaching. H. Richard rejects the idea of "the absolutism and perfectionism of Jesus' love ethic." Rather, the commitment to love is a case of the "extremism of devotion to the one God, uncompromised by love of any other absolute good. This virtue in him is disproportionate only in the poly-theistic–monotheistic sense, not in the sense that it is unaccompanied by other vir-tues perhaps equally great."[23] Justice is very prominent in these "other virtues" which are part of devotion to the God of Israel.

By love the harsh classical concept of justice becomes imaginative and sensitive to diverse needs. What is due to every person is theirs by virtue of their humanity and in accordance with their needs. Justice is the servant of love[24] but is not love itself, particularly as love appears when unexpressed in justice.

One of the greatest failures of the church is that it often has not applied love into the realm of justice. Christian love is incomplete when it is not fulfilled in justice. A love ethic that does not include an ethic of justice lacks the full power of love.

Love is the basis of justice. Love is the fulfillment of the Law, and justice is a major part of the demand of the Law.[25] Justice specifies the meaning of love in perennial situations of human conflict over the goods of social life. It also protects life from violations of the standards of society. Justice carries out the implications of the dignity bestowed on each person by God and the corresponding commitment to the well-being of each that love seeks. Accordingly, the basic Hebrew words for justice have within them a sense of gift (in $ṣ^e dāqāh$) and relief (in $mišpāṭ$). We saw in the last chapter that justice is closely associated in biblical passages with steadfast love. It is not a contrasting principle (cf. p. 87).

Justice is sometimes pictured as differing from love because it excludes emotion in order to be impartial. Arthur Dyck, however, demonstrates that true impartiality comes from both the discernment of the good found in one's own self-love (as in the golden rule) as well as the emotional contact with the suffering of others. Distant government officials and bombers from the air tended to be less impartial in under-standing the questions of justice when Vietnamese and Cambodian civilians were killed than the soldiers who had closer contact with the victims. Impartial justice is not emotionless; rather, its passion is refined by love for a diversity of individuals and involvement with their groups.[26]

Figure 6.1 suggests a way of conceiving the relationship of love and justice.

Figure 6.1.

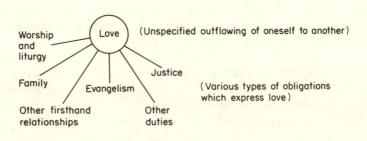

Justice and Sin

The depth and pervasiveness of sin require love to be expressed in justice. Sin produces conflict and conflict results in domination. The control of conflict requires more than the simple unarticulated self-subordination of love. Love needs its expression in justice as the intervening power performing the work of love. It needs justice to determine the limits and applications of power. The influences of groups on their members and their interactions with other groups are crucial shapers of society. Groups cannot love, but groups can be controlled by justice.

It is idle to expect spontaneous and gracious relations to take the place of just law. Such an expectation often simply begs the question posed by human reality by building a social policy with the premise, "*if* people only loved each other."[27]

Two different kinds of Christians are found among those engaging in this form of social thought. On the one hand are romantic liberals who deny the depth and permanence of sin. On the other hand are evangelicals who in the midst of the conflicting cries for justice respond by saying that the only answer to our social problems is Jesus. The latter folk present a special form of the condition, "*if* all people only loved each other." They add an important premise: "If all people only would be saved" (then they would love each other, etc.). They are equally utopian, however. There are no Scriptural grounds that such a victorious global revival will occur.

In the meantime there must be a struggle for justice that cannot be simply left to others. To allow that abandonment would be to take a contradictory position that God's concerns for justice can be left to the fallen people who are being called to repentance. The Christian must instead be obedient in response to God's command to seek justice while proclaiming the reconciliation to God provided through Jesus Christ. Many bumper stickers seem to ignore the former part of this obedience.

Jesus is the answer to social problems in two ways. First, justice is incomplete in itself. While there is need to work on the social and political environment, there surely is also need for the internal renewal and control by God that conversion to Christ provides. One does not have the whole answer without a personal relationship to Christ. Further, only Christ will bring complete justice at the return of Christ at the end of history.

Jesus is also the answer to social problems because commitment to Jesus means surrender to the will of God and thus commitment to the struggle for justice. Conversion provides a deeper and more permanent commitment to justice. Nevertheless, in a semi-Christian society individuals may hold a view of justice that approaches the biblical understanding without themselves knowing the Bible or Christ.

A lack of commitment to justice may instead reflect a pessimism due to a realization of the continuance of sin. This is in contrast to the preceding situations in which the sin factor is neglected. The evil of society may be understood so fully that no possible connections are seen between society and the purity of love. Slavery, capitalism, war, and discrimination are all conceded as invariable factors of this life.

Love is elevated to heaven or reserved for the sanctuary of intimate groups and person to person contacts. There is no bridging of the gulf between private love and public ethics in the form of principles of justice as applications of love.

In the history of the church this viewpoint has been expressed in the "relative natural law" theory that unjust institutions, such as inequitable property distribution and war, are necessities of the fallen world. The "absolute natural law" of God's original and higher intentions for human life is reserved for the monastery. It also may be reserved for one's personal relations as in a two kingdoms theory, which sharply distinguishes the kingdom of the grace from the kingdom of secular justice. The comprehensive distinction between benevolence as "universal justice," which is voluntary, in contrast to "particular justice," which applies to the state, functions similarly in withdrawing love.[28]

The guiding political principle of the Christian then becomes one of maintaining the present order. Change is either impossible or can lead only to greater anarchy and sinfulness. Any ministry for change must be confined to individuals. Alongside this type of conservatism regarding change is a complacency toward the organs that maintain the present order, such as the government, because they are given divine sanction as barriers against an eruption of evil.

This attitude makes more sense for individuals who are already materially and socially comfortable in life. Those with an upper-class social orientation, for example, have more to lose from change. If change means a loss of one's own social power, it is easier to withdraw love from its applications to social order. One is often unaware of such social reasoning affecting one's outlook. Morality has already been defeated on a lower level.

Karl Mannheim notes that Christian love for the human family can be a genuine subjective motive. If society is not organized on that basis, however, this love will be distorted when actually embodied in practice. Such love is thus ideological. For Mannheim *ideology* refers to ideals that are not in accord with present social reality but which are used to support the status quo. *Utopia* refers to these ideals when they are used to critique it. Love will veil the injustice in the present order unless the Christian also takes action to transform the existing structure, such as Christian love in a society built on serfdom.[29]

Ideology shields the incongruity between value and reality, thus shoring up the status quo. Justice exposes the conflict between alleged value and reality, and motivates and guides efforts to overcome it. If the concept of justice is recognized as being different from what is expressed in the status quo, then it produces an impulse for change. If the concept of justice is the same as the status quo, then it is a support for the status quo. Since all societies are unjust, however, they are continually confronted by the biblical concept of justice.

Tavard states that justice is a precondition to a more intimate love. It makes oneself a neighbor to others so that they may respond in love.[30] Unjust arrangements that elevate some groups of people over others make reciprocal love difficult. As Boesak argues, in a paternalistic love, such as apartheid love, one is willing to be neighbor to someone in a subordinate social position. One does not allow the other to be neighbor to oneself and to have the happiness of giving as well as receiving.[31] When we identify with the robbery victim in Jesus' parable, we learn, not that we must be neighbor to the Samaritan, but that the Samaritan has been neighbor to us. "[We are] placed in the position of meeting and receiving mercy from another, not dispensing it."[32] Martin Luther King understood the dynamic relationship between love and justice: "Justice at its best is love correcting everything that stands against love."[33]

Biblical justice relates to both power and love so that the false separation of love from justice is overcome. On one hand is justice is linked with benevolence,[34] yet on the other hand it is associated with power (cf. Ps. 71.18–19).

Power carries out justice and is legitimate when used for justice. In Deuteronomy 32.41 whetting the glittering sword is parallel to taking hold on justice *(mišpaṭ)*. The deliverance from Egypt was carried out by power ("outstretched arm") with great acts of justice (*šᵉpāṭîm*, Exod. 6.7; 7.4). As in the stories of the judges, so in the exodus God "is acting in history as the one who uses his power to see that justice is done."[35] Power is used against power.[36] In Isaiah 41.2 the human warrior's power brings the triumph of justice: "Justice *(ṣedeq)* meets him at every step." "The warrior is Yahweh's agent in restoring the right of his oppressed by the victories he wins."[37] God thus upholds the poor and needy (41.17) by God's "just power" (v. 10, cf. v. 20). Earlier we noted Ps. 10.15–18 where "justice to the fatherless and oppressed" is accomplished by breaking the arm (power) of the evildoer to eliminate the source of oppression.

Political and economic relief is accomplished by power. Power is not restricted to preserving order among the deprived and the depriving, it also is dynamic in producing change to guarantee basic human needs and to resist the forces that deny them. To turn again to the same passage from Martin Luther King cited earlier, " . . . Power without love is reckless and abusive and . . . love without power is sentimental and anemic. Power at its best is love implementing the demands of justice."[38]

The Singleness of Love

Another weakness of love when it is separated from its social expressions is its "singleness." The basic love relation is one to one, a self-giving to the other. What happens when there is more than one "other" claiming one's love at the same time? What criterion does one use then? The quest for guiding principles in this situation is where justice arises. We always have multiple and often contradicting claims on us; thus, we cannot avoid doing some things that have wrong characteristics, due to the claims that cannot be met.

The artificial simplicity placed upon love by its isolation becomes increasingly dangerous and unhelpful as our responsibilities increase. I can subordinate myself in love, but should I make choices that also subordinate those dependent upon me in ways that would be oppressive to them? I am then caught in the conflict between the demand of the enemy and the demand of those who are under my responsibility. I may decline resistance to an opponent when I would be the only one victimized, but I would not if that would mean that my spouse, child, or parent would be attacked. I must choose between the claims of love for the enemy and the claims of love for those depending upon me. Making a choice between claims on the basis of the weight of one's obligations to dependents is a consideration of justice.

In politics the politician also needs more than love. Lives other than one's own may be destroyed or defrauded by one's loving deed.[39] Likewise a leader of a group of disadvantaged people fighting for justice cannot be condemned for not turning the other cheek. One has a responsibility to one's contemporaries and one's descendents as well as to one's oppressors. Justice, not a undefined love, determines how the claims of the contending groups of society for the goods of society should be settled.

The insertion of an ethic of love, lacking an articulation in terms of justice and power, into the storm of political conflict will result in that love being broken up, and the calm that will eventuate will be that of the subordination of the weak to the tyranny of the strong.[40]

7

The Politics of Time

The understanding of time and history have a direct bearing on politics. Optimism or pessimism about the course of history is an important component of a political stance. The weight given to the past, present, and future varies significantly from one political ideology to another. Applying a theological interpretation of history to politics is significant not only because of its bearing on those factors. It also unavoidably discloses the relationship that the saving work of Christ has to political thought since the life, death, and resurrection of Jesus Christ form the center of history.

Exposing to the light of history the values and criticisms that Christianity brings to politics forces us to relate the political enterprise to our understanding of God's purposes in history. This relationship confronts the charge that Christian political activism is really secular humanism with a new face. Simultaneously, it disputes those who seek to separate salvation from responsible activity within the course of history, which invariably includes public life. It distinguishes Christianity as a historical religion, emersed in history and challenging history, from all mystical, gnostic, natural, and rationalistic faiths.

Examining politics in light of history, however, also reveals the severe limits of human politics. Politics is an activity of history, and in history, and history does not solve its own enigma.

The Dilemma of History

Limitations in Human Nature

In the second part of his Gifford Lectures, given in 1939, Reinhold Niebuhr presented a Christian understanding of his history that carefully holds in tension the predicament and the hope of humankind in history. Those lectures form his most systematic theological writing. We will enter our discussion of the theology of time by restating his argument with modifications and additions.

Human social activity, whether as a society, as a civilization, or as a totality stretching across time, is limited in its ability to overcome its basic problems. Despite utopian visions, the conditions of the temporal process cannot be overcome by politics or any other human activity.

The limitations of "the changes and chances of this mortal life" (*Book of Com-*

mon Prayer) correspond to the limitations in human nature. We are finite. We do not understand the depths of our own being or the intricacies of our common life. We are too limited in our knowledge to understand the full meaning of life, and we are too limited in our power to carry out the meaning.[1] Our personal lives are shadowed by the crisis of meaning that death brings for "the wise man dies just like the fool."

Our political achievements like the rest of our culture derive their ultimate meaning from a basis far transcending their own historical existence. Without this higher meaning, they too become "vanity and a great evil." The apocalyptic writers saw that the truth and justice after which we strive transcend us and are only partially incorporated into history.[2] As our cultural enterprise slides toward meaninglessness, however, truth and justice are thought to be easily within our reach. Then we lose sight of the spiritual struggle that must be part of the cultural struggle. We overvalue ourselves and our resources. As Eduard Heimann wrote, "The consciousness of the supremacy and sublimity of Truth and Justice wanes when they appear not as values that transcend the natural world, but as naturally or historically present."[3] Our most precious values and aspirations become tarnished and diminished when grasped by our hands alone.

Our created capacities of transcending historical causation do not extend to the point of overcoming the ambiguities of history. The prophets warned of the finite character of all human achievement.[4]

> Do not let the wise boast in their wisdom, do not let the mighty boast in their might, do not let the wealthy boast in their wealth; but let those who boast boast in this, that they understand and know me, that I am the Lord; I act with steadfast love, justice and righteousness in the earth, for in these things I delight, says the Lord. (Jer. 9.23–24, *NRSV*)

Technological and organizational developments also have not solved the basic problems of human existence; rather, they have disclosed our dilemma on progressively new levels.[5]

Perception into the incapabilities of the historical process points beyond it to the judgment and mercy of God. Such a wisdom is dependent upon a humble recognition of the limits of our own knowledge and power.[6]

Sin

The dilemma of history goes much deeper than our created limitations, however. It reflects our attempts to throw off those limitations placed upon us by our Creator. Freedom is essential to being human, but finite freedom creates the opportunity for sin. Because we have been created as beings who are dependent and yet free, even culture that effectively expresses the meaning of life continually faces the chaos of meaninglessness. No advancement in justice or in education is safe from corruption.[7] Even civilizations do not die from natural causes. Niebuhr argues that even more true for civilizations than for persons is Augustine's dictum that "it is by sin that we die, and not by death that we sin."[8]

To the end of the age there is a growth and intensification of evil as well as of good—rather than an expansion of only good or evil.[9] Despite the introduction of the Reign of God into history with Christ, not only God's Reign but also evil increase to the time of Christ's Return. Regardless of their misuse, the concepts of the antichrist and the tribulation belong to a biblical perspective of history. The consummation of history comes in the midst of a desperate conflict between good and evil. As we face the future, we have no guarantee of increasing security or virtue although we also need not dread an unmitigated plunge into disorder. Within history the essential problems of human existence come to a culmination rather than to a solution.[10]

Two cities are disclosed in the Revelation of John, according to Paul Minear. Through them history is viewed in the light of two interlocking mysteries—God's and the Devil's.

One great city has fully historical identities as Babylon, Sodom, Egypt, Jerusalem, and Rome, yet it reveals a unitary, universal, and eschatological pattern of hostility to God. It is the "great city" of the crucifixion and of universal audience to the suffering of the church. There the church is also vindicated. This great city is Jerusalem.

Jerusalem is also the other city. Jerusalem is the holy city and inner sanctuary of true worship. The witnesses stand in the streets of this city and in the inner sanctuary of true worship.

The cities of the world are faced with the simultaneous presence of both cities and the choice that they present before the end of history. The death and resurrection of Christ disclose the great city wherever people reject the word of God and the testimony of Christ. They disclose the holy city wherever people are faithful to that word and testimony. The institutions of our society are not to be divided up, however, into categories according to these two cities. (This was the mistake of the post-Augustinian church.) Rather their coexistence is nearly universal. They are in all and in each, but often in sharply varying degrees.[11]

Against a history that is such a battlefield between the demonic and the divine,[12] all programmatic, political, educational, and scientific schemes to build a final just city are placed under strict limits.

The images of John's Apocalypse do not strike the terror in us that they did in former generations. The technology of modern communications, however, provides sufficient terror in the accounts of the demonic inhumanities in our generation. Those who spiritually as well as cognitively perceive the dimensions of the struggle of human existence continue to find comfort and refuge as well as strength in the work of Christ in history and to end history. The basic solution to history lies in the atonement of Jesus Christ. Only at the end of history is this work brought to completion in the reconciliation of all things with the second coming of Christ.

The Need for Divine Atonement

The Savior who entered historical existence as a human also had to be God. God vicariously suffered and died for human iniquity. No human power could provide a solution for the condition of finiteness and freedom that is at the basis of historical existence. Every life and every portion of history stand in rebellious contradiction to God's purpose for creation. Only a divine wielding of power within history, therefore, could purge and complete it. Only a transcendent mercy could or would. Only God knew how to destroy and transmute evil by in mercy taking it into God's own self. Even in the highest reaches of its transcendent freedom humankind is too limited to comprehend the eternal will and purpose. Even in the most advanced cultural applications of justice it is too weak to apply this will and purpose.[13]

The victory of the cross was God's. Its victory does not belong to any principle, force, or norm of history, such as love, which progresses and triumphs on its own.[14] "For our sake God made him sin who knew no sin in order that in him we might become the righteousness of God" (2 Cor. 5:21). A sacrifice for sin without a blemish had to come from outside of history.

The resurrection of our bodies is God's final victory through Christ in taking up, completing, and transforming history. It is accomplished only by God's power apart from history. In contrast, in the Greek conception of the immortality of souls, history itself contains an autonomous spark of eternal substance.[15]

The manner of the final solution to the dilemma of history did not negate the meaning of history although it came and is coming from outside of history. It activates hope in history.

Hope Within History

Self-Transcendence

Within history there are elements of hope alongside the quandary of finiteness and sin. We have noted the freedom that is inherent in history. Despite the fall and the dilemma of history, we have retained an individual selfhood from creation that rises above the strict causative forces of the created world and history.

The human being is caught in the flux of time; yet only human beings are conscious of that fact. We are aware of the brevity of our years and can reflect upon it in anxiety or serenity.[16] "The days of our years are three-score years and ten" (Ps. 90.10, *KJV*). "It is appointed for mortals to die once, and after that the judgment" (Heb. 9.27, *NRSV*). In this very knowledge, we transcend the temporal. We escape history to some degree by our ability to know it. Recognizing the usual sequence of the created world, we can then, to some extent, change, reorder, or transmute the sequence and thus alter history.[17]

We also transcend history by our ability in any given circumstance to imagine a more ultimate possibility, whether it is to relieve our woes or to improve our achievements. We do not take the turmoil and conflicts of history as being right. We receive a vision of a greater order of peace and justice. We seek to eliminate within the flux of history what is contradictory and out of keeping with that vision. Further, we transcend the orderings of the created world through the "unnaturalness" of self-sacrificial love. Because of these capacities our creative tasks are never completed. No attainment of community life or cultural achievement is serene against criticism from the perspective of new possibilities of good and the obligation to pursue them.[18]

Recognition of our dilemma in history should prevent any misunderstandings of pride or optimism in these recognitions. Our realism about human nature and history, however, does not reduce the wonder of God's human creation to the level of a beast, nor should it be food for the cynic, fatalist, or the misanthrope. Cynicism is especially destructive when it removes our motivation to raise our manner of life to a higher level that is yet within our reach.

History in Salvation History

The dilemma of history does not remove the meaningfulness of history. Religions that present salvation as an escape from history may view history as incapable of receiving ultimate meaning. Similarly, activity in history may be regarded as incapable of expressing ultimate meaning. This is true of both some non-Christian religions as well as perversions of Christianity that view history at the most as neutral ground from which souls are rescued for eternal destiny. From such perspectives political action is irrelevant at best.

The sense of history is striking in Scripture, where the primary form of rhetoric is narrative. The Bible is declarative before it is imperative. Even admonitions are generally related to events in the past, present, or future. A characteristic biblical phrase is, "it came to pass." "Events follow one another, ever unfolding something new, something unexpected."[19]

The importance of history in the Bible can be illustrated by contrast. The non-canonical Gospel of Thomas is a collection of sayings of Jesus that has been compared with the "Q" sayings source hypothesized as common to Luke and Matthew. The Gospel of Thomas, however, provides no context for the sayings of Jesus, thus removing Jesus to a timeless, immaterial world. Matthew and Luke provide a narrative context for the "Q" sayings, anchoring them in time and space. It is for this reason that "Q" survived at all. In addition, "Q" contains an eschatological outlook totally lacking in the Gospel of Thomas. Consequently, the response called forth in "Q" is one of action and readiness. In the Gospel of Thomas the response is self-recognition and repose.[20]

The capacity of history to have meaning is reflected in all the events of salvation-history. The different acts of God leading to our final salvation weave into the fabric of history, yet they have transcending significance as belonging to the Reign of God. The pattern of promise and fulfillment that creates the expectation of salvation and facilitates its recognition is clearly part of the temporal sequence. History is thus capable of receiving meaning while we wait for the ultimate disclosure and realization of meaning now only partially seen. Our emancipation and enlightenment do not consist in being delivered from history.[21]

God's identity does not lie in God's absoluteness over and beyond history. God is known in the constancy of God's elective mercy and faithfulness in historic actions.[22] In the Incarnation the eternal life that had been "with the Father" was accessible to mortals who were fully involved in process and the created world. They could see it with their eyes, look upon it, and touch it with their hands (1 John 1.1–2). There can be no deeper relationship of the eternal to history than that the

Logos became flesh. Further, as Niebuhr states, in the utter historicity of the cross God destroyed evil without destroying history.

> The eternal and the divine which destroys evil is not some undifferentiated eternity which effaces both the good and evil of history by destroying history itself. God's mercy must make itself known in history, so that man in history may become fully conscious of his guilt and his redemption. The Messiah must give his life "a ransom for many."[23]

"It is an act rather than a thought which sets the Christ above history . . . "[24]

The anticipated return of Christ to historical existence in the Parousia again discloses God as acting and involved in the temporal while transcending it. History then will receive its waited meaning and completeness. God's sovereignty will be seen as sufficient over the world and history. Existence will no longer defy its own norm.[25]

The resurrection of our bodies is the very genius of the Christian idea of history. God fulfills rather than annuls the richness and variety of the temporal process. In contrast, only the immortal soul was preserved in the ancient Greek understanding of the afterlife. Nothing significant of the particular, historical human life remained; the historical unity of body and soul was thus denied. In the Christian hope, the body that is resurrected represents the person in its interaction with the historical environment. The body includes all which that environment contributed to human individuality. This individual life is of such value that the fulfillment of history would be incomplete without it. Nevertheless, the individual life does not receive its fulfillment until the whole course of history, with which it lived in mutual dependence, also receives its fulfillment. The resurrection of the body comes only at the end of history.[26]

Finally, the Great Judgment shows the seriousness of life within history. The distinction between good and evil has ultimate significance so that the historical realization of the good must be taken seriously.[27]

The modern world opened under the influence of a different understanding of history—the classical understanding of history as fortune. As understood by the sixteenth-century humanists, best illustrated by Machiavelli, fortune was irrational and unpredictable divergencies from a norm. Accordingly, it was uncontrollable and subversive of order. Through the Renaissance into the modern age fortune increasingly took on the character of corruption. The purpose of politics, indeed of human life, was to control fortune with virtue for the sake of the common good. Politics existed apart from grace, however, since the Christian alternative appeared to be only the total, apocalyptic redemption of history. The appearance of the Christian approach in the politics of this world consequently was associated with an irrational utopian character, as in the wild behavior of the medieval millennial movements.[28]

This interpretation of history, however, did not reflect the biblical heritage well. God is the creator of time and always present in it working for God's purposes. Heimann states, "It is the teaching of the Bible, and of the Bible alone among all the religious documents of [humankind], that history has a purpose and that all actions and events are positively or negatively related to that purpose."[29] The corrupting impulse is not history as an independent force. The source of corruption comes from personal beings because of their freedom in time to reject God's purposes. There is more potential for positive good and for evil than envisaged in the republican vision of history.[30]

The Christian resources for the life of the citizen provide more than a powerful vision of the future. They include both special revelation of God's purpose and will, and reason since God is also the creator. As we shall see, there also is an awareness of being between the times. The fullness of the future is not here.

The biblical sense of God's purposes in history leading to a final goal broke the cyclical view of time that has dominated many of the world's cultures. The classical and Hellenistic world included this outlook although there was a genuine sense of progress in history within and alongside it.[31] The cyclical view was in tune with the agricultural life with the rhythms of nature and agricultural work. Time was characterized by growth and decay, regularity and repetition. The Aristotelian and humanist tradition continued the cyclical view although influenced more by astronomy and physics. Fortune moves yet has no purpose.[32]

In Christianity history is transformed into a drama of deliverance.[33] As Simon De Vries notes, the future can be affected by two factors in interrelationship: God's will and the human response to God's will.[34] Political energy has been energized and citizenship encouraged when human problems have been separated from the traditional understanding of nature.[35]

Yesterday, Today, and Tomorrow

De Vries shows in his study of the adverbial uses of day *(yôm)* in the Old Testament that like many other peoples the Hebrews had a fixed idea of what was suitable activity for the day. References with *day* often refer to what makes that day memorable, rather than merely to one time period in contradistinction to another. "That day the Lord saved Israel from the hands of the Egyptians and Israel saw the Egyptians lying dead on the shore" (Exod. 14.30). *Day* thus is revealing about the attitudes regarding the dimensions of history as it is used to describe events past, present, and future. De Vries argues that in the Hebrew Bible the day past is "a moment of revelatory confrontation," the day present "a moment of crucial decision," and the day future is "a new opportunity for decisive action."[36]

Political orientation and ideologies differ sharply according to their attitude to the dimensions of time. A reactionary politics may give value only to the events of the past while a revolutionary political faith may look only to the future. A materialist culture looks only to the present. Biblical theology places significance on all three dimensions of time.

The Past

The past has high significance for all faith in historical revelation. For Israel and the church, the past provided the evidence of God's purpose in history in mighty acts and the knowledge of God's will in the reception of the Law. Hans Walter Wolff notes the striking perspective, found in Psalm 143.5 and Jeremiah 29.11, which describes the past as reality before, rather than behind, and the future as behind. People "proceed through time like a rower who moves into the future backwards: he reaches his goal by taking his bearings from what is visibly in front of him; it is in this revealed history that for [them] the Lord of the future is attested."[37] Direction in life comes from the past. Accordingly, the Hebrews were the first to produce any extensive historiography.[38]

Awareness of one's past is necessary for forming a self-identity for both individuals and communities. Jim Wayne Miller speaks through the voice of a mountain preacher:

> My own house, heired to me by my foreparents,
> was right there all the time
> yours is too
> but I wasn't living in it. Well, I went home.
> And when I stepped out of my own front door
> when I knew where I was starting from
> I knew then where I was going.
> The only road I could go was the road
> that started from my own front door.[39]

Kierkegaard saw marriage as a paradigm of the ethical obligation that binds us despite our current preferences and feelings. In the words of Alasdair MacIntyre, it is "a state of commitment and obligation through time, in which the present is bound by the past and to the future."[40] One reason why modern marriage is so hard is that many people have lost their sense of identity with themselves as the person in the past who made the vows.

The sense of history is also crucial for a sense of community. Clarity on what one has been provides a basis to build on the past and to transcend it so that the future can be faced with a sense of individual and group purpose. From this sense of purpose policies can be made for the present. As Augustine described it, memory recoils upon itself like a spring that gives momentum for driving forward. "To pounce, one must crouch."[41]

"The most reliable principle of authority in public life has been the idea of foundations."[42] The testimony of the forebears about their struggles, sacrifices, and goals instructs a people in a self-conscious way of life. It provides a lodestar for where the citizens belong, for what they are living, and for their hierarchy of values. Such self-identity from the past furnishes a basis for resisting that which would deny the values of the people. Machiavelli wrote that a more vibrant and politically active people is found where there are recollections of ancient memories. A society that has a beginning in freedom possesses a knowledge by which it can preserve its freedom. "He who becomes master of a city used to being free and does not destroy her can expect to be destroyed by her."[43]

The past provides a deposit of meaning and obligations that is ignored only at great peril, yet the past does not hold its listener to it. The past is the record of God's promises, which direct attention to the present and to the future.

The Present

"Today, if you hear his voice" (Heb. 3.13). "As long as it is today" (Ps. 95.7). The phrase, *this day,* in the Hebrew Bible shows the central significance of the present. It epitomizes every aspect of public life. It always involves something with a decisive effect for time to come. "This day" is a call for decision, not a comparison to another time. "I have set before you, this day, life and good . . . if you obey . . ." (Deut. 30.15–16). The present is the time of responsibility and action.[44] The urgency of the moment was heightened in the ministry of Jesus and his followers.

The present is tightly related to the past and future. There is significant continuity through time. The past and future exist in the present and impinge upon it. The people are punished for their own iniquity and for the iniquity of their forebears, whose sins they are also to confess (Lev. 26.40).[45] With such continuity, the present is a response to the past while correcting and transcending it. At the same time there is a grasp of future possibilities that the past has made available. In turn these can correct and transcend the present.[46]

The present is rich as the fulfillment of the promises of the past, yet one waits for further fulfillment in the future. Responsibility is based on the past gracious acts of God motivated by the present power of the Spirit. What I am doing now matters because of God's past actions of redemption and because of God's purposes for the future.

Christianity contributed a linear conception of time from its Scriptures.[47] Time has a definite beginning and a definite ending with a meaningful succession of events in between. It has been said that the most definitive characteristic of time in the New Testament is its closure.[48] The Christian view of time, however, is not linear in the sense of a straight line of steady and inevitable progress nor as a splintered series of successive moments. Friedrich Kümmel's image of time is helpful in understanding the biblical perception. Time is a whole consisting in both a succession of historical events and in an actual past and an actual future coexisting and in interrelationship with the present.[49]

Jesus, who suffered and died in history as a sacrifice for sin, is also living in the present and the future. "Jesus Christ, yesterday and today is the same, and forever" (Heb. 13.8). He was the inspiration of the leaders of the people of the God in the past (v. 7). His once-for-all sacrifice governs the nature of their worship and lives in the present (vv. 9–16). Those for whom Christ is present today have substance to their hope because of Christ's victory in the past sealed with his resurrection.[50] As James Cone has described the experience of his people,

> How could black slaves know that they were human beings when they were treated like cattle? How could they know that they were somebody when everything in their environment said that they were nobody? How could they know that they had a value that could not be defined by dollars and cents, when the symbol of the auction block was an ever present reality? Only because they knew that Christ was present with them and that his presence included the divine promise to come again and to take them to the "New Jerusalem."[51]

The presence of Christ also means that today is the time of responsibility and action. The indicative–imperative ethical pattern in the New Testament challenges our ethical life in the present to be that which corresponds to what God is enabling us to be through Christ's (past) death and resurrection (e.g., 1 Cor. 5.7). The present response is critical. Robert Coles observed that the inner city teachers who were the most excited and committed did not dwell on the handicaps of the past of their students nor on the long future years of overcoming them. For them it was all now. "We've got these kids here; we're going to do something."[52]

The response to the opportunities that God is opening up in the present is urgent. The Bible developed a Greek distinction in terms for time. *Kairos* as a significant moment of time, as "opportunity," was differentiated from *chronos*, time as duration. Christ's work is the great *kairos*, occurring in the fullness of time. Because of it, however, God has opened for us smaller *kairoi*. These are significant occasions for decisive actions in accord with God's purposes.[53]

Certain opportunities for mission and service are not recoverable. When a great number of patients were released from the large mental institutions in the 1970s, the community centers that were supposed to receive them were not established. This failure contributed significantly to homelessness in the 1980s since the former patients were among the most vulnerable participants in the housing market. Michael Harrington commented, "Perhaps society's inability to seize a precious moment when things might have turned out otherwise is irreversible."[54] In Esther there is a powerful sense of the working of God's political will in the present. The present was the day of decision to participate in that will through a political protest of injustice:

> For if you keep silence at such a time as this, relief and deliverance will rise for the Jews from another quarter, but you and your father's house will perish. Who knows? Perhaps you have come to royal dignity for such a time [*kairos*, LXX] as this? (Esther 4.14, *NRSV*)

The past, while of great import, cannot be the center of one's existence. The past is the record of God's promises and directs us to the future and to our present responses to them. In contrast, the people in the wilderness in rebellion murmured for the past when they had sat by the fleshpots of Egypt and ate to the fill (Exod. 16.3). A glorification of the past, which also distorts it, can be the basis of resistance to opportunities in the present.

The future with its indeterminate possibilities can also be used as an excuse to neglect difficult responsibilities in the present. The civil rights demonstrations in the 1960s were criticized for not allowing more time for the local governments to respond. Christian teachings take time to be implemented, it was said. Martin Luther King responded,

> Human progress never rolls in on wheels of inevitability; it comes through the tireless efforts of [human beings] willing to be co-workers with God, and without this hard work, time itself becomes an ally of the forces of social stagnation. We must use time creatively, in the knowledge that the time is always ripe to do right.[55]

A faith that delivers over the here and now by portraying a God who offers nothing which affects the course of the present, who is not present in history with power, is condemned to be degraded to an appearance of being empty of actuality.[56] Political theories may also attempt to absorb the present into the past or to ignore it for utopian dreams that do not affect present history, ignoring the day of decision. A proper understanding of the future, however, gives urgency to the decisions of the present.

The Future

The view of the future provides new reasons for decisive action in the present. Looking to God's future interventions, the prophet Isaiah declares that "on that day" human arrogance will be brought low and the Lord alone exalted (Isa. 2.17). This view of the future, summarizing the previous verses, is the basis of the appeal to present behavior: "O house of Jacob, come let us walk in the light of the Lord!" (v. 6, *NRSV*). "Always the future day that awaited them was predicted in terms that were calculated to influence their present behavior."[57]

The future as a form of sensitivity for history arose for the first time with the God of promise of the Old Testament. Since the promise has not yet found its fulfillment, it draws the mind to the future in creative and obedient expectation.[58]

The promise also affects most significantly the attitude toward the present, so that by comparison the present loses its aura of truth to the hope. A different and superior future devaluates the present as the automatic product of the past. Present existence can be changed only when it is viewed as in need of completion. Rather than being final, present conditions with their woes are capable of being surpassed. The present is confronted not merely with a superior idea as it was for Plato, for whom it made no difference whether the true city exists "or will come into being."[59] The present will be transformed into "a new heaven and a new earth in which justice dwells" (2 Pet. 3.13). That expectation conditions the manner of conduct in the present. "Therefore, beloved, because you wait for these things, make every effort to be found by him to be at peace, blameless and without spot" (v. 14; cf. v. 11).

The Christian hope is in Christ, whose past resurrection is the basis for anticipating his final victory, which will bring into being a world in which the peril of death has been overcome (I Cor. 15.20–28, 54–57; Rom. 8.11, 23–25).

For much of its history the church has lost its powerful vision of the future.

> God promises a new creation of all things in righteousness, but [humanity] acts as if everything were as before and remained as before. . . . The loss of eschatology—not merely as an appendix to dogmatics, but as the medium of theological thinking as such—has always been the condition that makes possible the adaption of Christianity to its environment and, as a result of this, the self-surrender of faith.[60]

However, when the future Reign of God is taken seriously as a reality confronting the present, human energies are stimulated for efforts to bring about change in the certainty of the abiding meaning of such labor.

The future can be stifled through preoccupation with the past or the present.

Donald Shriver, as pastor in Gastonia, North Carolina, noted that violent and community-wrenching events in the past, particularly the Loray labor strike, seemed to be feared but seldom mentioned. He said that Christianity can provide repentance and forgiveness that "contributes to social change by making the past genuinely past, the future a genuinely new possibility," which one is freed to explore.[61]

The selfish preoccupation with the present in a consumer, throw-away culture marked by triviality in all one's personal relations can prevent an interest in anything that will come after one's death. The ecological consequences present a threat to future generations.[62] The rapid destruction of the tropical forests illustrates the preoccupation with the present. When the jungles are cleared in Brazil, the soil is hardly suitable for agriculture. As a result, there are only a few seasons of crops. The soil then will support one decade of grazing before it is abandoned, yet the synchronized biological meshings that support more than 1 million species is lost.[63] A significant factor of rural poverty in the American South has also been the depletion of the soil.

The call for a new way of measuring progress in agriculture corresponds to this sense of neglect of the future. The current philosophy of industrial agriculture emphasizes short-term measurements, such as yield per acre and farm productivity. By contrast, long-term concerns would also count as progress such matters as preservation and enhancement of soil needs, quality of food, and the continuity of farm communities, skills, and culture.[64]

The future belongs to those of low status whose sense of dignity refers to a future lying beyond the present.[65] The present belongs to the privileged groups whose dignity is tied to comforts of things as they are. A bankrupt farmer said, "They wrecked our dreams. . . . Once they get you out of dreaming, they take away your self-worth and get you depressed."[66] The political ideologies favoring each group will contain similar time orientations.

The Judaeo-Christian idea of time encourages rational planning for the future. Since time is linear and contains purpose, preparation for the future is worthwhile. Moral response to God's historical actions and disclosure of will has an impact in the framework of a genuine contingency in history. The nonhuman created world itself is shown to be nonmoral.[67] We are not helpless or passive before it. Its processes guarantee neither happiness or corruption. Such an expectation of a changeable future is discouraged when time is viewed as irrational, corrupting, and cyclical.

Nevertheless, the future is divine not human. It does not lie in the grasp of human calculation. The dignity of the present can be preserved by an awe of the future with all its vagaries. Then basic human needs of the present are not sacrificed to a calculated projection of greater future good.

The forces for positive change are not inherent in history. Constructive change must be in tune with God's purposes. Evil is present until the end of history. Optimism based on a false assumption regarding inherent tendencies in history can fail to anticipate the permanence of evil. The result can be a disillusionment that stifles efforts for legitimate change. As Tillich stated, "A kingdom of God that is nothing but the historical progress produces that utopia of progress or revolution whose catastrophic collapse brings about metaphysical disillusionment."[68] Instead, a realistic activism that waits for opportunities that God opens up has similarities to that described by Arthur Koestler.

> What we need is an active fraternity of pessimists. They will not aim at immediate radical solutions because they know these cannot be achieved in the hollow of the historical wave. They will not brandish the surgeon's knife at the body politic because they know that their own instruments are polluted. They will watch with open eyes and without sectarian blinkers for the first sign of the new horizontal movement; when it comes they will assist its birth; but if it does not come in their lifetime, they will not despair and meantime, their chief aim will be to create oases in the interregnum desert.[69]

"Idealist without illusion," a description of John F. Kennedy, may be a better description of the activist we seek than "pessimist." Koestler, while alert to the pervasiveness of evil, is perhaps too negative regarding the divine force, new with Christ, that has entered history.

The Reign Breaking In

The New Testament view of the future was not merely one of a contrasting stage lying ahead in history. This future was now breaking into the present. The death and resurrection of Christ in this perspective are not events of the past. Rather, they occurred as the central events of the future Reign that is already arriving. The resurrection of Christ is the first fruit of the glorious future (1 Cor. 15.23–27).

This Reign that is challenging present life is also comprehensive. "Every rule and every authority and power" will be destroyed and every enemy placed under Christ's feet (1 Cor. 15.24–25).

That the Reign of God was breaking into history with Jesus and his ministry was the dominant theme of Jesus' earthly ministry and was crucial to the self-understanding of the early church.[70] A mark of a Christian philosophy of history must be that there is a new dynamic in human affairs with Christ and his church. Tolkien catches this change in history well. The hobbits notice a wind from the west, providing a remarkable change in the weather, and driving back the billowing clouds of the evil kingdom, Mordor. "'Look at it, Mr. Frodo!' said Sam. 'Look at it! The wind's changed. Something's happening. He's not having it all his own way. His darkness is breaking up out in the world there. I wish I could see what is going on!'"[71]

The Reign of God means that the future orientation is not only that of expectation and knowledge of the end. Aspects of the salvation of the end time are also presently available. There is an eruption of the new into the present.[72] The Reign of God is the new and updated force in history which makes the injustices and exploitations inherited from the past outdated as remnants of a past which is already being destroyed. Humankind is presented with a choice either to open itself up to the force of the future or to cling to the increasingly outmoded past in selfish fear. The Reign is the universal rule of the eternal God. In the face of its immediacy, old habits and institutions lose their sanction as representing the universal and eternal.[73]

The breaking in of the Reign means that access to divine transcendence is not to an everlasting world of ideas that is abstract, intangible, and above the concrete realm of history. The transcendent demand confronting humankind is instead a Reign—a new society, concrete and coming. The Christian hope in God is not a "pure hope"—a hope without concrete content. The promise of the Reign of God is of God's lordship, justice, and peace as dreamed in Israel. It is a public hope, not merely personal. It is political, not only psychological.

The Reign of God thus creates a different public posture and conduct. It produces a critical attitude to the institutions inherited from the past as one is forced to discern what is in conformity with God's new age. Uncritical loyalty is withdrawn from the present in favor of allegiance to the new future. Such an intrusion even more "undermines a traditionalist view of society where everything is expected to be always the same."[74] The oppressions of the present age that have been taken for granted do not have the last word.[75] As a result there is a sense of catastrophe and newness, giving urgency to mission.

H. R. Niebuhr wrote of how by living in expectation of coming judgment and restoration, the seventeenth-century English Protestants found it necessary to press into the Reign of God. "The time was short; the great revolution which would make all things new was no longer a dim dream and a mere culmination of ordinary life, but it was near and it was threat as much as promise."[76] From this ferment came reformation of the church, the birth of English democracy, overturning of the monarchy, and planting of colonies.

Such expectation produces a conduct of life that conforms life to the imminent hope. "Thus says the Lord: 'Maintain justice, and do what is right, for soon my salvation will come, and my deliverance be revealed'" (Isa. 56.1, *NRSV*). John the Baptist, the prophet of the imminent Reign, was sent to prepare a people for the Lord by turning them from disobedience to justice (Luke 1.17). In face of the coming King, human conduct was to be put into conformity with the way of life that God would be putting into force (Luke 3.4–14).[77] The theme was continued by Jesus. Now is the time (*kairos*) in which the fruits of God's Reign are demanded of the vinekeepers (Matt. 21.41, 43; cf. Isa. 5.7; Luke 3.8, 10). The coming of the Reign gives fresh substance, motivation, and power to the political task of changing the world in the direction of God's promises.

In responding to a future that is only partially present, the emphasis may lie on the power of the past that remains. One of the criticisms of Reinhold Niebuhr is that he failed to do justice, at least in his working theology, to God's power among believers in terms of the presence of the Holy Spirit, sanctification, or the present power of the Reign.[78] In Niebuhr's defense is the tragic contradiction between the promise of Christian theology and the actuality of Christian conduct. Langdon Gilkey compares Niebuhr's view to optimistic political eschatologies that see the present being molded by the promised future. Niebuhr correctly saw that the nature of humankind remains the same. The human failure to relate creatureliness to transcendence remains to the end. The center of the gospel for Niebuhr is the atonement, not the resurrection.[79]

Along with the power of the future, there is also an eschatological reserve. While voicing a powerful expression of Christian freedom (1 Cor. 3.21b–22), Paul also warns that the eschatological time is not yet: Judge not before the final judgment (4.5).[80] The powers of the future are already available. It is a time for responsibility and mission in response to them. It is not a time for blind celebration.

The Meaningfulness of Political Struggle

That God finds history capable of carrying meaning for redemptive activity lends meaning to political activity. God's involvement and redemption within history indicate its deep significance. Politics is in turn a form of molding history as it changes from past to present to future.[81] If history is meaningful, then politics is meaningful. Realization that God was involved in their historical striving to the very point of suffering with them and for them can prompt people to accept their historical responsibilities gladly.[82]

Even historical change outside of the church and outside of the church's influence upon its culture relates to the presence of the Reign of God. The scope of God's "kingdom work" is not confined to church. The problem then is identifying such activity of God's Reign where the sacred signs of God's presence are not visible and where God is not named.

Míguez Bonino correctly rejects the dualistic and monistic solutions to the relationship of God's redemptive work and secular history.[83] The dualistic solution of two separate histories—one of Israel and the church and the other secular—removes the Lordship of God from general history. In the monistic solution, on the other hand, there is but one history. The history of salvation is identical with the historical struggle for justice, an accusation made (often falsely) of liberation theology. This approach removes the independent significance of Jesus Christ and the church and renders a dangerous ultimacy to particular political struggles.

History is fundamentally one, but its unity will be fully established only at the final reconciliation at the end of history. Nevertheless, glimpses of that unity appear in the present time. The forces of redemption are at work in the midst of both the groaning creation and the children of God (Rom. 8.19–23). All of created life is involved in the struggle between God and Satan for control of life.

Within the church, however, Satan has been defeated in a decisive way not found beyond it. This victory gives a distinction to the church although God's conquest of "every rule and every authority and power" (1 Cor. 15.24) is not limited to the church. The victory in the church provides unique visibility for God's Reign. Where God is named in truth, there is an assurance and visibility of God's presence not found elsewhere.

The Reign is in creation itself in the measure that the creation follows the sovereign's orders, even in subconscious conformity.[84] Luther argued that if a prince rules well, then "it is learned through the inspiration of the Holy Spirit with experience."[85] Everything that occurs in conformity with God's rule is done through the guidance of the Holy Spirit.[86] Where this conformity reflects an advance in justice, it participates from afar in the Reign of Christ.

The activity of God outside the presence of the church must be discerned by the eyes of faith. God is at work in events which lack the normal visible signs of grace by which God's presence is acknowledged. Tillich is very helpful here when he speaks of the hidden forms of grace in secular life which can only be discerned by prophetic awareness.[87] The marks of God's presence on human history are recognized from God's revealed attributes of justice and truth. Thus God's active Reign can be detected where God's form of justice is overcoming the destructive powers of existence. The church has been created and chosen by God as the camp for the struggle with the demonic, but God's armies are not limited to the camp.

The church has a unique role in light of history's dilemma. Only the presence of the Reign provides the radical transformation of the created world underlying history. Such transformation will be completed only at the end of history; however this dying of the roots of human sin takes place in the present age in the church as Christ is named. The presence of the Reign in the form of public justice does occur outside the church, often at the instigation of the church. The transforming of human nature, however, a vital and central form of the Reign, is present only in the church. The Reign of God, therefore, must be much more partial in its realization where it is not named.

History will be unified and its dilemma overcome only when the presence of public justice and the creation of a new humanity are completed and united at the end of history. In the present time, participation in the tasks of the Reign of God is accomplished through evangelistic proclamation of the future that God is providing and through actions, including political actions, which correspond to that future.

II

OBSERVING THE VISIONS

8

The Grace of the Common Life:
Traditional Conservatism

The key concerns that a Christian brings to political thought have now been developed. We have articulated criteria by which various political viewpoints can be critically analyzed from the standpoint of Christian theology. Now we will use these categories to evaluate major options in contempory political ideologies.

Conservatism as a Political Theory

The first vision of politics that we will observe is in some ways the oldest. Our focus is upon conservatism as a political theory, not as a mood or disposition. Our interest is in not a temperament, based in the individual's personality or class position, to oppose any substantial change in one's manner of life, work, and enjoyment. Any uncritical defense or rejection of the status quo is wisely dismissed[1]; that is not the type of theoretically worked out position about which we are concerned.

The political vision most commonly described in America as "conservatism" is an expression of classical liberalism. It centers around personal freedom and limited government. We will turn to it after our discussion of liberalism.

Traditional conservatism is our concern. Its name reflects the central place that tradition has in its argument. It also draws upon traditions that precede liberalism and the conservatism developed within liberalism. It brings values from the Renaissance, ancient England and the Middle Ages, as well as the classical world into the modern world.

Traditional conservatism has not been a prevalent political philosophy in the United States. Russell Kirk, perhaps the best known twentieth-century American exponent of this approach, explains that it was a victim of capitalism and industrialism. "Industrialism was a harder knock to conservatism than the books of the French equalitarians." Personal loyalties gave way to financial relationships. The wealthy forsook their responsibilities in the community and came to hold no purpose in life but aggrandizement. The poor ceased to feel that they had a decent place in the community and were starved for most emotions except for ennui and envy. "To complete the rout of traditionalists, in America an impression had begun to arise that the new industrial and acquisitive interests are the conservative interest, that conservatism is simply a political argument in defense of large accumulations of private property. . . ."[2]

Accordingly, to some people traditional conservatism may appear anachronistic. Its appeal continues, however, and not only in studies in stone churches and private libraries lined with ancient books. Many thoughtful persons distraught with the failures of democratic structures and the crass materialism of modern culture look to it for a practical wisdom that may have been lost. It is found among reflective people who respect the mysteries of life, the power of tradition, and the tempered relevance of ancient ideas, and who believe that the gift of leadership is found among those with rare qualities of virtue, piety, and wisdom. Recent advocacy of narrative theology, the ethical virtues, and the community as the center for ethical and theological reflection echo familiar chords of this approach. Those convinced that secure wealth and leisure are pertinent to leadership and the defense of traditional values are also attracted to it.

Traditional conservatives prefer living out their philosophy over articulating it. The theory has been spelled out most forcefully in times when that style of life has been threatened by cultural or political developments. Kirk states that conscious conservatism did not manifest itself until 1790 with the publication by Edmund Burke of *Reflections on the Revolution in France*.[3] Samuel Huntington describes the French Revolution as the greatest threat to existing institutions in Western civilization up to that time and leading to the greatest outpouring of conservative thought.[4] Burke stated that his chief concern in those reflections was to keep that conflagration from disturbing the peace of his own country.[5]

The Vision

> Providence has taught humanity, through thousands of year's experience and meditation, a collective wisdom: tradition, tempered by expedience. A man should be governed in his necessary decisions by a decent respect for the customs of mankind; and he should apply that custom or principle to his particular circumstances by a cautious expediency.[6]

Traditional conservatism is not highly cohesive as an ideology. There is a great amount of diversity among those identified as its proponents so that any representative is apt to differ markedly on some aspects of any ideal type that may be proposed. Huntington argues that it is essentially a defense of established institutions, whatever they be, rather than a common intellectual tradition.[7]

There are, however, considerable common elements among thinkers in varied situations across time and place, who feared a disruption to traditional values posed by developments of individualism, democracy, equality, materialism, or capitalism. Their commonality has been due in part to the broad influence of Edmund Burke and to the classical and republican traditions that influenced him. Both exponents and students of traditional conservatism frequently identify Burke as its father.[8] He had great influence on Continental conservatism as well as on the English and American forms.

This conservatism is committed to the preservation of the ancient moral traditions of humanity. The stress is on traditions, not moral values in themselves, for it sees values as embedded in traditional patterns of life. The values are incarnated in the tradition so that to cut off the tradition is to cut off the values.

Thus traditional conservatism has a great respect for the variety and mysteries of traditional life.[9] The past is colorful, rich, and not completely submissive to rational analysis and control. Accordingly, there is a distaste for uniformity and reductionistic tendencies.

Civilized society needs orders and classes. People are unequal in most qualities of mind, body, and spirit. If a people destroy natural distinctions, despair will be the result. Democracy is given but grudging acceptance.[10] Freedom is based on personal property rights.

Change must be worked out in slow and careful stages because society is a living organism. Society must alter, but the change must be in tune with the order that is already in things rather than an order imposed upon them.[11] Conservatism at its best is not opposed to change; rather, it seeks continuity or identity within development.[12] Careful consideration must be given to long-term consequences of proposed changes. Conservatism is cautious not to fall into worse forms of injustice in the effort to eliminate old ones.[13]

The greater whole that gives meaning to things and which justifies them is from the past rather than from above or beyond.[14] A practice long in existence presents the "prescriptive" claim of prior usage; its already having been found to work well provides a "presumptive claim." Such usage rests on the experience of countless others across many generations.[15]

The organism of society is not an agglomeration of lonely individuals; rather, it is a unity of groups and institutions. The church is a very important member of these institutions. "Religion is the basis of civil society and the source of all good and of all comfort."[16] The groups and institutions are held in great endearment. The groups and social classes also serve as a check on one another, and with their diverse interests provide limits upon the power of the state. Effective government is but an extension of the other groups of the society, which contribute their essential values and affections. These groups, particularly religious, keep the practice of government from degenerating into the control of selfish interest and wanton caprice.[17]

For many of these reasons, industrial, commercial capitalism was often opposed. Capitalism was criticized from the right before it was from the left.[18] The French conservative, Louis de Bonald, wrote,

> Commerce has become the only concern of their [modern republics'] governments, the only religion of their people, the only subject of their quarrels. . . . The egoism, the factitious and immoderate wants, the extreme inequality of riches, like a devouring ulcer, have attacked the conservative principles of society.[19]

Historically, the most significant power behind this conservatism was cultivated, landed or hereditary wealth, rather than the business nouveau riche.

The opposition to modern capitalism was more ambiguous among the English conservatives. Burke denied the ability of the government to operate against the laws of consumption and production of the market, which alone can settle price and wages. The laws of commerce are laws of nature and thus laws of God.[20] On the other hand, Coleridge and some other Romanticists critiqued the capitalist market economy and the individualism in liberal political theories. Coleridge denounced the materialistic reductionism in the understanding of human beings and society, the loss of concern for the general good, and the failure of an adequate distribution of the abundance of England.[21]

A final component of the vision is the realistic view of human nature. Human beings have a capacity for both good and evil. They have an immutable strain of deep-seated wickedness and are governed more by emotion than by reason.

Pondering the Vision

Traditional conservatism often consciously seeks to justify the established order of its society. At the same time it expresses a deep commitment to humane community. How should its interpretation of society be evaluated from a Christian perspective?

Realism and Human Nature

A most valuable contribution of this form of conservatism has been its realistic appraisal of human nature. The source of evil lies in our nature rather than in any particular social institution. Burke wrote that human beings "are full as inclined to Vice as to Virtue."[22]

For this reason government must be constitutional; it should have a constitution to limit its power. Its powers must be diffused and balanced in order to limit change that is too rapid and to restrain abuses of authority. A social harmony is not possible. The ideal of statecraft is prudence, the wise application of the principles of justice to the limiting factors of power and social interests.[23]

Traditional conservatism in its realism recognizes the necessity of coercion and of dealing with the factors of interest and power.[24] Government protects people from the violence that they do to one another. Intervening and defensive power are required. Society needs powerful institutions, which have their own past and mystery. Government is one of these, and it provides significant functions for the community. Unlike the liberal tradition, the best government is not the least.[25]

This view of human nature is accompanied by a caution about human reason, particularly in the form of abstract speculation. Francis Canavan demonstrates, however, that there is not in Burke the anti-intellectualism or clear ordering of emotions over reason of which he sometimes has been accused.[26] Even without the greater corrupting presence of false principles, a person ruled by passions is "a wild beast."[27] Emotions do motivate human beings for both good and evil much more powerfully than do their mental ideas. We have been created with emotions that provide the basis for moral habits and virtues, as well as human relationships. These in turn provide the basis of received opinion, a fixed and settled faith, held in common by a large number of people. Truth and right are found in the flow of social life as it works for human benefit.

Burke presupposes a rational universe, the basic order of which is intelligible to the human mind. While the materials produced by emotion, experience, and received opinion precede logic, they must be corroborated by reason that reflects upon proven practice. "A constant vigilance and attention to the train of things as they successively emerge, and to act on what they direct, are the only sure courses."[28] It is not merely age that justifies ancient practices. People should not suffer evil merely because their ancestors have suffered worse. Received patterns of behavior are justified by the effectiveness of the results that they have produced. What is beneficial for human good is in accord with the universal order and is that which lasts. Rational activity is required to note that which is indeed the beneficial experience that has been passed on through the ages.

At the same time, while acknowledging the role that Burke does give to reason, it must be stated that for him the thinker apprehends history rather than analyzes it.[29] Burke is confident that the most crucial principles of government and liberty can be discerned as "inbred sentiments" understood long before we were born.[30] Such principles, however, need to be clearly articulated for the concerns of justice to be given their full weight and for a more adequate separation of that which is true and abiding from that to which we are merely habituated.[31] The avoidance of conceptualizing the normative character of the tradition significantly hinders the ability to evaluate the tradition ethically. In that way conservatism limits our rational capacity to transcend ourselves and our tradition.

Conservative thinkers have observed the iconoclastic use of reason to overturn valued elements of culture and religion. As a result there is a pragmatic tendency to trust instead those emotional drives that express our communal nature, such as love for the motherland, respect for authority, religious awe, loyalty and mutuality, and the cohesive feelings in ritual and ceremony. The Christian view of sin, however, should also lead us to distrust these emotions. Since sin couches before every aspect of our being, we must also have a proper respect for the tendency for sin to lurk in our positive emotions. These emotions are closely related to collective egoism, the destructive potential of which we have previously noted.

The Diversity of Groups

We should also appreciate in traditional conservatism its recognition of the basic social nature of human life. Individuals are historical and social beings whose well-being in a large measure is a gift of the community. Values and truth are borne by the community.[32] This understanding of life "looks to the cohesion and continuity of society—what makes people band together and remain together with some satisfaction." In this it realizes the importance to a group of sharing in language, history, and a concrete set of loyalties.[33]

Because human beings are social beings in a developed sense, attempts to understand them by reference to a simple "natural" state are not viewed as helpful. Conservatism criticizes the individualism of social contract theory. The requirement that individuals need to consent to their own political and social arrangements seems to divide the individual from society.[34] Civil society is the true natural state of humanity.[35] The purpose of statecraft is understanding, tending, and improving living, historical communities.[36] Urban renewal that destroyed communities but transplanted individuals could have learned from this understanding of the importance of community.

The conservative commitment to diversity is distinctive in that it is group life and the variety of groups that is the ground of diversity. For liberal thought diversity instead arises out of the development of individuality.[37] Chesterton writes how in the Middle Ages the variety of dress and color had significance in representing one's family, trade, or religion. The colors showed everyone who the person was. Today we dress with a great variety of colors, but the colors "are without a reason."[38]

A genuine diversity is one that "mattered morally, rather being simply a trivial matter of personal taste and self-expression." It is grounded in a moral and intellectual order, without which it collapses into mere randomness. Ultimately, diversity is supported by belief in the bounty and manifold potentiality of the creator God, which maintain the value and relationship of each part.[39]

Class divisions that form a hierarchy in the sense of the "rewards, degrees, and everything that comes with a frank recognition of superiority" are regarded by traditional conservatives as an essential basis for cultural diversity and vocation.[40] The upper class has a special significance. Digby Baltzell describes how the upper class can be "a translator of talent, power, and accomplishment, over the generations, into a system of traditional moral standards." This happens when the upper class has a pride in leadership that commands respect. This pride in authority can be lacking, however, and replaced by resting upon privileges and inherited wealth. When class standards of honor or duty are absent, the door is opened for ambitious individuals, often with few scruples, to engage in power struggles, guided only by the standards of success and self-interest.[41]

The conservative case for social hierarchy is often presented as if the only alternative were a radical egalitarianism that does not recognize any role for ability. The valuable function that they see in the upper class can be met, however, through more inclusive communities, institutions, and groups that also translate values, pride, and honor from the past to the present. These groups may be bound together by ethnic, religious, geographic, or professional traditions and present less potential for domination and abuse of power.

There is insufficient perception of the self-interest of the aristocracy. Because of the dilemma of human nature, the fellow-feeling of the great for law and the general good cannot be relied upon, even as Baltzell discovered. When one's own interests are at stake, the altruistic commitment is abandoned or distorted. The opposition of traditional conservatism to efforts of the lower classes to obtain effective power serves as an illustration. Labor unions were opposed as part of the general aversion to pressure groups rising out of the lower classes.

Traditional conservatism thus has been characterized by opposition to reforms to extend political participation. Burke was restrictive in his view of participative political rights. It was a matter of nature, not of prejudice, that ordinary people in trades lacking in social distinction should not rule.[42] An example is the constitutional crisis into which England was thrown by the public outrage at the initial defeat by the Tories of the Reform Bill of 1832, a bill that only extended voting franchise to owners or renters of homes of an annual rent of £10, over and above taxes. This protection of the political privileges of the elite was true also for some of the great Evangelical social activists in England, such as Shaftesbury. They were benevolent and led important reforms of social conditions. They also were paternalistic and antidemocratic. They shared their wealth and time with the poor, but not their political power.

The confidence that educated men can set aside their own self-interests to represent those who have no power over them represents a breakdown in realism about human nature. Because of sin there is a delusion of wisdom, and the wise as a human group cannot be trusted with power over others. As Machiavelli held, the ruling passions of the aristocrats were to dominate other groups, and no social arrangement could contain them long.[43]

Burke stated that "the individual is foolish . . . , but the species is wise, and when time is given to it, as a species it always acts right."[44] This understanding is countered by the biblical sense of the fallen cosmos and the pervasiveness of evil in human culture. Insufficient room is left for the transcending individual—the one who is inspired—the prophet. The Bible reflects many situations where the species is foolish but the individual is wise. Ethical and devotional demands challenge reliance on institutions from the past. The prophetic warning is that there is no security in the land or the temple (Jer. 5). The prophet may appeal to true origins in the far past or to a different future, both of which stand in criticism of the present as an inheritance of the recent past. Such leaps in time beyond mere development of current ways provide a basis for a change-oriented politics.[45] Traditional conservatism makes a powerful contribution to political thought in its recognition of the contribution of social groups, but there are gaps in the conception of group egoism and social evil.

One way in which conservatives reconciled this optimism toward the social order and their realistic view of human nature was to posit a divine sanction and operation in human institutions. James Russell Lowell identified the status quo with the order of the universe: "One of the strongest cements of society is the conviction that the state of things into which they are born is a part of the order of the universe, as natural, let us say, as that the sun should go round the earth."[46]

When one views the great variety of institutions among humankind, however, it is difficult to maintain divine preference for those that happen to be in England or America. The varieties of institutions are due to humanity and to history, not to God. Scripture presents the world as created by God, but it also teaches that the world is ruled by the prince of the power of the air. Conservatism's optimism toward the status quo tends to reduce the tension between the two. Such optimism veils the power plays, the pillaging, and the violence upon which the structure of society is built—historically and presently—in origin and in practice. The breakdown in the realism remains.

Justice and Inequality

While not denying an equality of worth of all persons as members of the human race and creatures of God, traditional conservatism draws serious implications from a factual inequality among human beings. John Adams, who was an American exponent of this form of conservatism, stated,

> They are all of the same species; and this is the most that the equality of nature amounts to. But man differs by nature from man, almost as much as man from beast. The equality of man is moral and political only, and means that all men are independent. But a physical inequality, an intellectual inequality, of the most serious kind, is established unchangeably by the Author of nature; and society has a right to establish any other inequalities it may judge necessary for its good.[47]

Instead of an abstract definition of natural rights and universal human nature, the traditional conservatives stress diversity.[48] Unity does not derive from humanity as a whole. It is found in a social group—in the family, estate, religion, nation. For Burke there are natural rights, but they are found in usage as what is advantageous for human well-being. History is not contrary to nature. History expresses and actualizes nature.[49] Accordingly, the rights that Burke recognized were rights of the English people, not human rights.[50]

Burke also felt that the attempt to transform society by reference to abstract rights simplifies the complicated task of effective government, which involves experiential understanding of human behavior and social change. It thus raises empty expectations that only aggravate and embitter the real inequalities that cannot be removed.[51] The commitment to diversity also comes to play here. For Burke the ancient is complex and thus diverse, while the new is simple—a thin slice of life. Attempting to conform life to an abstract principle removed from life fails to take into account "the peculiar and characteristic situation of a people . . . their opinions, prejudices, habits, and all the circumstances that diversify and colour life."[52]

Based on the attention to inequality, the customary English privileges and rights, and the commitment to diversity, the fruits of justice are not uniform. People are free to develop without hindrance up to their potentiality and limitations.[53] Those with greater potential should have more freedom and opportunity. Privileges and freedom are achieved by cultural and intellectual excellence. Appropriate privileges allow a cultivated person to enjoy life and to pursue his or her interests.

This is also the classical understanding of justice, which as we have seen in distribution does take into account degrees of personal ability. Nature assigns differing tasks for service to the city to those in the various classes. In turn each class receives the appropriate share of happiness that nature assigns.[54] It is proportional according to the distributive criterion of social contribution. As Thomas Aquinas expressed the Aristotelian tradition, more of the whole belongs to the part in accordance with the importance of the part to the whole (in terms of the part's responsibility in the community).[55]

Those with less ability to contribute also benefit from this arrangement. The advantages that persons with "greater natural endowments" possess present a corresponding noblesse oblige to help the poor. In the republican tradition freedom of choice was to be exercised with the common good in view.[56] This responsibility, however, must be voluntary. From his conversations with the families of the well to do, Robert Coles restates their sense of social responsibility combined with the need for the diversity of life, which means that wealth and power should be retained. "One tries to do good works, but there is a life to be lived, a way of life to preserve."[57]

In this perspective the poor are equally happy in the benefits that they receive from the inherent inequality. This beneficial ordering is accepted in "the unbought grace of the common life" in which there is a love of honor, generous loyalty to rank and gender, and dignified obedience.[58]

Because of the importance of groups to the traditional conservative, this conception of degrees of social access also applies to groups. Groups have different potentials and limitations; thus, they are granted different powers and privileges. Freedom can be defined in relationship to the differing expectations of the grouping to which one belongs. A woman's freedom and opportunity, for example, might then be found in terms of traditional expectations for women. One estate could be subordinated to another, or for some, the whole society could be subordinated to the state (although this was not characteristic of the British version).[59] T. S. Eliot held that society needed a hierarchal church, established by the state, with final say in matters of doctrine, faith, and morals.[60]

Burke argued that when people act like a mob without measure or foresight, it is necessary to raise an aristocratic principle—an interest of property and education—and to use every proper means to strengthen the authority and influence of such persons.[61] In the republican tradition this is a natural aristocracy, not one based on heredity or power. It is an elite of persons distinguished by a natural superiority in quality of mind and accompanied by contingent material advantages, such as property, leisure, and learning.[62] Burke's ideal structure was open to advancement by men of genuine ability, but the type of training that he describes as providing that ability is that by received by the English upper classes, by a structure which intentionally favored men of birth and wealth.[63] For Aristotle it had been clear that citizenship required leisure, which artisans did not have. Virtue is essential for the citizen, and the development of virtue requires time freed from toil (*Pol.* 1328b–1329a).

The concern for social diversity in this theory is commendable, particularly the vision of a social order that can encourage the development of the varying individual and group contributions. There is a utopian element to it in that one cannot locate the individual truly superior in wisdom and virtue by favoring any particular social group. The connection between a favorable social environment and individual ability is also slighted. Unless checked by transcending concerns of right, the commitment to diversity has a perilous tendency toward the naturalization of differences, such as those attributed to race and gender.

The special advantages given to a few is an inconsistency in the realism, as we have noted. If we have a permanent and great disposition for evil, then such evil will not be overcome by education, experience, birth, or wealth.

The conception is likely to produce social injustice if it is not accompanied by a thorough process of establishing each member in community. Those who seemingly have little potential for social contribution must not be denied, intentionally or consequentially, what is basic for political, economic, and social inclusion in community.

Burke, however, had more to say about such basic justice. He admitted in principle a broad scope for rights: "If civil society be made for the advantage of man, all the advantages for which it is made become his right. It is an institution of beneficence." Each person has "a right to a fair portion of all that society, with all its combinations of skill and force, can do in [one's] favor." This included "nourishment and improvement of their offspring," and instruction. "In this partnership all [people] have equal rights but not to equal things."[64] Providing for the "public prosperity" is part of the proper function of the state.[65] Individual interests in that sense are public interests in contrast to impersonal approach in laissez-faire conservatism.[66]

Burke, however, is hardly arguing for a welfare state arrangement. The preventive role of government is minimal and infrequent in comparison to its "great use" as a restraint. Government cannot help the poor by raising the wages of the laboring poor. Such matters have to be left to the laws of supply and demand. In addition, direct feeding of the poor creates dependency.[67]

Rights of benefit are thus to be understood as not met directly by the government, especially by the central government; rather, they are met by society in "all its combinations." It is the total workings of the society including economic operations that provide these "necessities." In contrast to Adam Smith, however, the general good is a conscious social purpose. The contribution of private interests to public interests is a social responsibility rather than impersonal and automatic.[68] The government's role is primarily providing the security, order, and information which allow the other aspects of society to perform their given roles.

There is a strong commitment to liberty in the writings of Burke.[69] He defended the inhabitants of Ireland and India against oppression. Original rights, however, do not include a share of power, authority, and direction for the management of the state.[70] Consequently, his conception of justice is incomplete since some members are thus cut off from the political aspect of community.

Traditional conservatives have bravely confronted injustice when it derives from new social forces (e.g., industrialism or technology), but less so as it derives from the old social order. There is not a commitment to advocate the cause of the weak to its conclusion. Social peace is considered to be more the task of government than social justice. "Keeping society alive, at peace with itself to the degree that it remains one society, is the first thing necessary." Thus, politics is placatory and minimalizing rather than revelatory.[71] Justice only works in the terms of the present unequal structures. People are obliged to accept the convention constituting the society in which they find themselves.

Abuses, however, must be politically challenged.[72] Recognition of social justice needs to be included in the statements of first principles or metaphysical rights. Fulfillment of social and political rights should be discussed in terms of alternatives other than the spector of a complete leveling of society and in conjunction with the conservative's proper concern for the recognition of duties. While there can be significant compassion in this approach, there is insufficient dynamism to make basic changes in society.

Burke did recognize a true natural right of participation in the common activities and consolations of society.[73] When all that is truly implied in that statement is recognized and made a public commitment, there will be little disagreement with his view of justice. Even as it is, there is a commendable affirmation that in a healthy society the total social network must contribute to meeting basic rights. Government, however, is too removed from its basic tasks of assuring the fulfillment of the basic rights of its people.

We share many central concerns of conservatism, such as the importance for politics of human weakness, the recognition of the social reality of group life, and the need of checks on power. A dynamic biblical view of justice makes a different use of those concepts. It changes the view of government. The state no longer serves primarily to hold the lid down on human wickedness, which threatens the traditional harmony of society. In the perspective of biblical justice, government also has a constructive purpose—to secure greater justice.

The Value of Private Property

Conservatism stresses private property rights to an exceptional degree. Property rights go hand in hand with other human rights. To destroy the former is to destroy the latter. Property gives physical sustenance to the protester and furnishes opportunity for training in virtue, which flourishes where choices are made possible.[74] At the core of this concern for property rights is a significant appreciation of defensive power. The particular conception of private property rights, however, reflects failure of the realism to penetrate the entire system.

Property is important in biblical values, but not in the form of the Western conception of private property. The command, "Thou shalt not steal," does not guarantee any particular form of property distribution, although it has often been cited to this effect. In itself, the injunction is relevant to the particular form of property distribution in a culture. Even a thoroughly collectivistic society has the vice and crime of stealing. The victim of the theft is the community as a whole rather than a certain individual.

Furthermore, property in the Mosaic system is not strictly private ownership. The standard economic definition includes the freedom to sell in what is essential to the cluster of rights that make up private property.[75] Rather, biblical property has characteristics of what comparative economics has called the cooperative property of the traditional village community. In that arrangement all livestock, crops, and tools belong to private peasants, but a family may not sell its land. The purpose is that no family shall impoverish its heirs by improvidence and that there shall always be some land available for everyone.[76] In accordance with the institution of the Jubilee, land could not be permanently sold. By the standard economic definition it was not strictly private.[77]

Because of the significant arguments that the conservative presents for the value of property, such a crucial right and privilege should be sought for everyone. Private property rights, however, differ from other basic human freedoms, such as freedom of speech and freedom of assembly. These other freedoms are basically nonmonopolistic. The amount of freedom of speech that I have does not subtract from the amount that another person has. If everyone in society has this freedom, my freedom of speech is not lessened; in fact, that universality protects my freedom. The separation of church and state that limits us when we belong to a majority religion would protect us if we came into a minority position.

Property, however, is relative. Although the total amount of property is often expanding, only a certain amount is available at one time. The poor compete with the well-to-do for scarce housing, and the homeless lose out. Burke states that "the characteristic essence of property, formed out of the combined principles of its acquisition and conservation, is to be *unequal*."[78] An increase in the amount of my property, and ways in which I use it, often affects others in society.

In contrast, another material right—the right to food—is a right to the amount of food necessary for nutritional health, not to as much food as I can get; therefore, that right is not monopolistic. The total amount of available resources on the earth is restricted but is not insufficient for meeting basic human needs.

Unlike the freedom of speech, which is a right for all to have, the conservative doctrine of the freedom of private property is a right only if one possesses property; it increases in value according to how much property a person has. It is a right for the one who possess property to protect it from interference. It is a right of property, rather than a right to property. The biblical provision is the right of all members of the community to have basic productive property "so that everyone of the people of Israel may possess the landed inheritance of one's forebears" (Num. 36.8).

The importance of property that the conservative demonstrates should lead one to oppose concentrations of property. Property as a right is acceptable only in a framework that guarantees such basics of life to all members of the society. R. H. Tawney said,

> Burke remarks that all men have equal rights, but not to equal things, and there is a truth in the distinction which is justly applauded. But, unfortunately, Nature, with her lamentable indifference to the maxims of philosophers, has arranged that certain things, such as light, fresh air, warmth, rest, and food, shall be equally necessary to all her children, with the result that, unless they have equal access to them, they can hardly be said to have equal rights, since some of them will die before the rights can be exercised, and others will be too enfeebled to exercise them effectively.[79]

As a right of humanity, everyone should possess it. That claim can be made for private property, but not for a right for some to have it in substantial quantities while others are without. Thus there is truth that access to material things is a basis of other rights, but not this does not apply to a right to have significantly more than other people. Where there are limited resources, the latter view becomes a denial of the rights of others. "Big property is a form of domination and stands side by side with personal and social serfdom of the masses in many countries of the world—the liberty of the strong side by side with the serfdom of the weak. . . . Private property is far from guaranteeing the personal liberty of nonowners . . ."[80]

These concerns from the standpoint of Christian realism also apply to a society in which there is abundance and excessive material resources (even apart from its obligations in the total human community). Concentrations of property lead to concentrations of power, producing a threat to the rights of those with deficits of power. The contribution that an individual's property makes to her or his participation within the community is less effective when others have appreciably more. Property is defensive only as long as the individual possesses so little of it that one is not tempted to use it to dominate others.[81] As the amount of property controlled by one person increases, the number of ways in which it limits the actions of others becomes more extensive.[82] As we have seen (cf. p. 19), the biblical writers perceived the explosive destruction inherent in the combination of human lust and unequal power (e.g., Mic. 2.1–2). Since it belongs to the fallen human nature, the lust does not decline with affluence. In fact, its tendency is to increase.

At times this concern has risen from within traditional conservatism. Richard Weaver states that what he calls the metaphysical right to property is not the abstract property of finance capitalism, which breaks the connection between the person and one's substance, is useful for exploitation, and makes the sanctification of work impossible. Rather, the solution is "the distributive ownership of small properties" in the form of independent farms, local businesses, and homes owned by the occupants.[83]

Recent papal thought has also stressed the value of property ownership for all families. Paul VI stated that the world is made to furnish each individual with the means of livelihood and the instruments for his or her growth and progress. "All other rights whatever, including those of property and of free commerce, are to be subordinated to this principle" (*Popularum Progressio*).[84] Such is the position of the ancient church. Augustine, for example, saw property as the common provision of creation giving a right to both the poor and the rich that restricted one person's private claims.[85]

A right of access by all to at least a minimum of material things is a more direct support of the other rights than is a right that is simply the protection of existing private property. Such a right, reflecting the importance of property will demand some process of at least modifying concentrations of property, while protecting the total range of human rights for all including the large property owner. A system of relatively equal private property may provide this protection.

Our theology, however, cannot reject a priori any other cultural variation in property arrangements that has more public or shared forms of ownership while also providing for all essential access to material goods and other human rights. Okun argues that freedom was enhanced by collectivization of roads, bridges, ferries, and civil, judicial, and clerical offices, which once were private property; however, collectivization of toothbrushes, clothes, and one-family homes would impair freedom.[86]

In less culturally relative terms we will describe a universal conception that private property attempts to express along with its other legitimate concerns. It is what James Luther Adams calls "the creation of a space" in relation to the rest of society:

> Freedom of the individual in relation to society . . . requires its own turf, its own toe hold, its own *terra firma* in face of dominating powers in the surrounding territory. In our day this means that it must have the economic resources and the political and economic rights—a dwelling, a job, freedom to move and to associate— enabling it to occupy space in which he or she can make choices, choices that concern not only the individual's privacy but also a concrete relationship to society.[87]

Adams goes on to mention those who fight to prevent others from sharing their freedom. "Private property" often has functioned as a code for that. The important concerns for one's own property must be given cultural expressions that secure them for all.

Embracing the Past

The sense of organic community in traditional conservatism provides a sense of social responsibility that transcends the present. Richard Hooker wrote, "We were then alive in our predecessors, and they in their successors do live still."[88] Memories, public and private, keep this connection alive. Through them we transcend our immediate situation and are "initiated into membership in the community."[89] Burke held that since the purposes of the partnership that society forms "cannot be obtained in many generations, it becomes a partnership not only between those who are living, but between those who are living, those who are dead, and those who are to be born."[90]

The sense of continuity through time provides accountability to the past and to the future. Bruce Smith notes that members of the aristocracy found motivation to sacrifice personal gratification in their identification with forebears and descendents. Knowledge of the past and care for the future is able to overcome love of "present convenience."[91] ". . . No people willingly moves into future unless accompanied by the past."[92]

Such accountability to the past leads to acceptance of "historic guilt" for social wrongs. "Guilt for the past is the other side of gratitude for the past."[93] If others are disadvantaged by what has benefited us, then this organic sense of unity and responsibility in time provides affirmative action or reparations to aid others in "leaning against the wind" of the burdens of race, gender, or poverty that they carry from the past.

There are similar important implications for an ecological responsibility for future. Tocqueville warned that when "the woof of time" is broken, "those who have gone before are easily forgotten, and no one gives a thought to those who will follow."[94] We have roots in human community that have been means of grace for our lives. Gratitude may move us to be gracious to others in our own present and future. As Burke put it, if they are "unmindful of what they have received from their ancestors or what is due to their posterity," the "temporary possessors and life-renters" of the commonwealth might act as if they were its complete masters and waste the whole fabric of their society, leaving a ruin for those who come after.[95]

The challenge and power of the future, however, can be neglected by a preoccupation with the past. One can be so satisfied with the present as if the all-surpassing future were not now breaking in by God's power.

There is, therefore, a loss of the beneficial functions of utopia. According to Mannheim, the conservative has drawn utopia into the status quo.[96] Utopia for Mannheim is a picture of society that is both incongruent with social reality as well as critical of present society; it is an activistic principle. By drawing utopia into the present, the conservative has lost an important tension for change. Christian eschatology loses its present social value. The future is no longer the critic of the present. With its confinement to the immediate and concrete in preference to what is based on speculation or hypothesis, the consciousness of the possible upon which all "progressive" activity feeds is lost.[97] Moltmann suggests that the utopia of the status quo is the worst of all utopias.[98] The maximum of freedom for the society is held to be already present. Burke was thus resolved to keep the establishments of church, monarchy, aristocracy, and democracy "each in the degree it exists and no more."[99] For some, clinging to the present as it is presented from the past can be an expression of our sinful nature. Tillich writes that anxiety seeks "in the past, which, after all, it has survived, securities that are unthreatened."[100]

A conservative sense of the present as only a result of the past, not a possibility for the future, which Mannheim portrays, makes sense within the ethos of the upper classes. They have been favored by the present arrangements of society. They naturally regard them as the best. In the midst of economic hardship, Burke argued that only a few of the poor had died, there were no great epidemics of disease, and they were better off than they had been even in times of plenty in the previous generation.[101] The optimism toward the present and the lack of a concept of the future is expressed in this description of Europe in 1848.

> Toryism regarded social distress and economic depression as evils entirely divorced from politics—as afflictions that any society must from time to time suffer because of bad harvest or disturbances of trade. Political agitation that played upon conditions of social distress and held out hopes of betterment through political reform seemed, therefore, both irresponsible (since it might endanger public order) and hypocritical (since it raised false hopes).[102]

Robert Coles observed the different attitudes toward time in children of the privileged and migrant worker children. For the privileged children, time is a "benefactor, a source of wonder, amusement, excitement, and mysteries that soon become casually amassed memories." For migrant children, the working day stretches on indefinitely. They express a fear that the sun will stop so there will be "no time but sun-time." For them time is "a demanding, insistent tireless task master whose power is never to be questioned."[103] A different attitude toward change and the continuity with the past will emerge.

Where there is a heavy orientation to the past, responding to the normality of change can be problematic. Christine Gudorf argues that the popes before John XXIII had difficulty dealing with change and so the teaching of the church was restricted in meeting mundane reality. Change was not regarded as integral to the world nor was it of theological importance. For Pius XI, for example, movements away from the social order of the Middle Ages were equated with evil.[104]

A reactionary is a conservative who has lost, or is losing, one's favorable position in the status quo. For this person there is no possibility for the future except to return to the past. The past is the judge, as well as the producer, of the present. It is a fossilized conservatism, still resisting what was the future to a conservatism of a previous generation.

> Do not say, "Why were the former days better than these?" For it is not from wisdom that you ask this. (Eccles. 7.10, *NRSV*)[105]

Conservatism presents an invaluable lesson for politics and society regarding the need for continuity with the past. It fails, however, to maintain this contribution in sufficient balance with the other necessary recognition regarding the past, the evil of the past. There is a crucial distinction between a critical retrieval of the wisdom of the past and an uncritical subjection to the authority of the past.[106]

Societies differ markedly in how they appropriate the past. Some are grounded in aspects of their history that are viewed as being in discontinuity with other aspects. Thus there is a dialogue or dialectic, rather than simply flow and continuity, in their tradition. Most societies have heroes or founding ancestors, whose creative power broke with or challenged any antecedent tradition. A radical critique may depict the tradition as a departure from its own beginnings. The Protestant Reformation included an intensive scholarly and critical endeavor to reconstruct the practices of the ancient church, which provided for the present the authority that had departed from the tradition.[107] In this different understanding of time and action, there is more room for understanding the fallenness of tradition. There are also is a place for special divine revelation in a particular period in the past that challenges both tradition and the present.

Memory and custom present a similar distinction. Memory recalls foundations and origins and the noble deeds and actions of great virtue of the past. Custom admires something because it is from the past. For a customary society, time is a series of repetitions.[108] Custom levels out history. It thus differs sharply from biblical time, which prepared for the critical history of the early modern republican tradition. Bruce Smith, who develops this distinction, argues that conservatism obliterates memories that make people realize that the present is not like the past, which also contains great innovations. For Burke custom provided an escape from the fears, horrors, and dangerous innovations hidden in memory.[109]

The traditional conservative does helpfully remind us that biblically significant time is not only time ahead, it is also time behind. The God of the future is also the God of the past covenants. These covenants were with a community, with a people. One has roots—roots in human community—roots that have been a means of grace. The individualism of success in our culture looks to the present and to the future, but one does not look back lest one be found not standing on one's own.

Yet the past is mixed. It records a struggle of God with history. What is old and traditional, therefore, is not necessarily Providential. Rather, our posture must be one of looking also to what can be new from the future. We look forward while also embracing the good from the past.

Summary

We can learn from traditional conservatism in its demonstration of the need for government and the need for checks in and on government in the face of the wickedness of human nature. Its perception of the importance of group life is valuable in the face of Western individualism. It cautions against wholesale changes that are based on abstract speculation rather than upon experience and a respect for continuity in group life.[110] It correctly discerns that there is a social and psychological need for ritual and tradition. It often fails, however, to place tradition sufficiently under judgment or to recognize the impact of other forces in the rapidly changing contemporary world which, without significant change in response, destroy tradition and continuity. Reformers desirous of incorporating this insight of conservatism into a more dynamic attitude toward social change can adopt the following principle: Retain as much continuity with the past as justice will allow.

9

Flourish in Freedom: Liberalism

Liberalism is the vision that has captured American political thought. That does not mean that conservative thought is insignificant. The dominant form of American conservatism lays claim to be the true interpreter of the classical liberal tradition. In reality it is a form of liberalism. The basic conflict in American political thought is between two developments upon earlier liberal thought.

The Original Aspirations

The seventeenth and eighteenth centuries in western Europe were a time of a rising middle class. People, such as merchants, bureaucrats, and lawyers, who were not noble or seminoble, had aspirations for goals that earlier had been restricted to the elite of birth and wealth.[1] The barriers to reaching their aspirations were the privileges and power in the hands of the aristocratic classes, who also controlled the government. Furthermore, the favored position of the upper classes was based upon tradition and religion.

Obtaining freedom from government and from tradition was very much in the interest of the middle classes. One path was to open government up to broader influence. Another path was to decrease the role of the aristocratically based government in the economy. In this context, liberalism was expressed as a commitment to freedom for the individual.

There were two basic intellectual sources for liberal ideology. One was the Protestant tradition, particularly as it was expressed in Puritanism. The Reformation was a crucial aspect of the trend toward individualism in sixteenth century society. The church was in decline as the dominating normative authority; bourgeois power, self-consciousness, and aspirations were increasing. The Protestant ethos itself had a powerful individualizing effect. Protestantism taught the direct communication of the individual believer with God in the priesthood of all believers.[2] This tendency received permanent formulation in the Puritan religious dissent in the seventeenth century. Religious conflict made clear the need for individual freedom of religious expression versus tradition and government.[3]

The second conceptual bank for middle-class aspirations was the secular Enlightenment. Here reason was lifted up as a weapon against tradition. The framework of thought centered upon the individual, as in the social contract theory. Reason, the determinant of society, was a possession of each person.[4] Both Puritanism and the Enlightenment contributed to the concept of equality as they described individuals as having equal access to reason and by creation to God. (There was also equal access to the Spirit of God within the community of the elect for the Puritans.)

Basic Characteristics of Classical Liberal Thought

The freedom of the individual from arbitrary external authority is perhaps the firmest tenet of liberalism as it developed in the seventeenth and eighteenth century, prior to the full development of the industrial revolution. Freedom is the central social motif. Arbitrary authority was opposed. Authority was to be provisional, restricted to the service of its limited tasks.

John Locke, the most influential thinker in this stage of liberalism, argued in the late seventeenth century that political authority must be resisted when its claims are incompatible with the discharge of Christian duties or when it explicitly denies the religious equality of all. The freedoms to be preserved at all costs are those that provide the necessary conditions for executing the responsibilities of the call that each person receives from God.[5]

The early liberals thus sought more equal distribution of liberty, free conscience, the right of opposition, religious tolerance, and freedom of the press. All of these ideals were secured in the American Bill of Rights and expressed in the American Declaration of Independence and were similarly gained in England starting with the Restoration of 1688.[6]

Liberals sought a regulation of social life by universal and impersonal laws. A crucial characteristic of liberal thought is that society should be self-regulated as much as possible so as to reduce dependence upon human decisions. In reaction against arbitrary authority, which meant dependence upon persons, there was a search for impersonal social and political controls. To be in touch with the reality that undergirds life, one must move from dependence upon the power of individuals to reliance "on some impersonal force—call it 'history,' 'necessity,' 'World-Spirit,' 'laws of nature,' or 'society'. . . ."[7] Politically, the rule and guarantee of law was to replace the favor of ruling personalities. Economically, impersonal control was to be left in the rule of the market.[8] Governmental noninterference in the economy, therefore, was a dominant objective. The liberals sought the abolition of monopolies and freedom of contract.

The concept of the public life became more restricted. The classical conception of political life as the promotion of the person's internal life no longer prevailed. Politics was significant only as it impinged on people's self-interest. In this change public participation as having meaning in itself declined. The traditional control mechanisms of the church, class, and political order were held to be unnatural. People could carry out their social activities without knowledge of principles of authority. Instead, society was seen as a spontaneous and self-adjusting order.[9]

The important tenet of the dignity of each individual expressed the liberal view of the person as the possessor of reason and a creature of God with callings from God in the world. Liberalism continued "the proud and heroic sense" of the ethical and aesthetic dignity of the individual of Christian humanism in the Renaissance.[10]

Every individual had equal dignity.[11] All people have a basic legal equality from God. Government rests on their consent.[12] The liberals correspondingly sought to overturn aristocratic privileges.

Reason had an important role within liberalism, reflecting the rationalism of both the Enlightenment and the Puritans. The concept of individuality that emerged at the close of the Middle Ages presented each individual as possessing reason from God and living in a universal, rational order established by God. The freedom of each is under law. This law is not established by arbitrary and capricious human wills. It is a natural law consisting of eternal truths and values. It transcends individuals and cultures, but it is attuned with human nature and human society. The civil laws and customs of the various societies give expression to it.[13] Individuals have the intellectual capacity to know the relevant moral truths of this natural order.[14] A rational, enlightened treatment of duties, needs, or desires will lead to morality and social harmony.

The view of reason varies, however. There is a restrained view of reason in the utilitarian strand developed from Thomas Hobbes to Jeremy Bentham. It did affirm the broader view of the rational character of the world, and the ability to know its inherent laws. Reason, however, is limited in its ability to know the sublime; therefore, philosophy turns to practicality and action.[15] The individual is rational in the sense of calculating which are the best means for reaching ends, but the ends are chosen by desire, not by reason. Emotions provide the ends of actions; reason finds and determines the means.[16] Each person is sufficiently well endowed with this capacity to pursue one's own interests effectively. A wise and prudent selfishness knows how to relate the interests of the self to the rest of society so that those who are wise in serving their own pleasure will know that this pleasure will only come by serving the greatest good of the greatest number.[17]

Another strain of liberalism associated with the Enlightenment believed formal general principles could be formulated, which would apply universally and which would be most conducive to the progress and happiness of humankind. Through reason one is liberated from the tyranny of desire and lives according to general principles.[18] Such optimistic expressions of liberal thought appeared in French Revolution and in America, where its optimistic nature was augmented later by theological liberalism. Reinhold Niebuhr was responding particularly to this romantic liberalism as he encountered it coming out of the 1920s.

In contrast to external control, importance is placed on internal control in the individual. Education is stressed. The more individuals that can be educated to rule themselves, the less need there will be of political authority. This outlook led to greater reliance on human gregariousness and cooperativeness. Moral teaching is effective, and appeals to love, justice, good-will, and the family of humanity can be relied upon.[19] One can calculate from human desires to rational moral and political positions.

An optimism regarding history arose out of the confidence in reason and the self-regulating laws of nature. The liberal had a hope and cheerfulness regarding the positive prosperity and happiness that would be achieved by individual freedom and democracy. Our essential goodness is seen in our capacity to subdue the forces of the created world and in advances in science and technology.[20] There is a belief in progress. The previous period in history was viewed as the *Dark Ages* (a term first used in 1730), "the dark of ages past"; but humanity and history are getting better. Humankind is achieving more and more inclusive loyalties, and this development lies in the nature of things, even in the structure of laws of nature at work in human history.[21] In religious expressions, the optimism is based on a gradual spiritualization of humanity.[22] German liberalism gave its own metaphysical grounding to this faith: Human destiny is tied with the universal spirit overcoming nature.

Self-interest and desire are taken very seriously in liberalism, particularly in the strands reflecting utilitarianism and the republican tradition. They are the driving forces in society. As Newtonian physics disclosed in the nonhuman world, however, a harmony among the forces would keep evil in check and produce social good. Capitalism expressed this viewpoint in economic theory and in a political perspective.

The Puritan Contribution

The Puritan outlook would seem incompatible with the optimistic thread in liberalism, including its confidence that the pursuit of self-interests and desires would be self-regulated into social harmony. The Puritans' judgment of desires had brought them into conflict with aristocratic life with its willful indulgence of desires.

K. R. Minogue describes the place of the Puritans in the consideration of desire in political thought. The Puritans distrusted desires. For the Puritan absorption in desires was a sign of being damned. Those who exercised self-denial of desires would be most successful.[23]

The Puritans, however, were positive toward one form of desire—that based on need. A Puritan contribution to liberalism was that their asceticism crystallized need out of desire. A need is a legitimate or morally sanctioned demand. "I *need* bread" is acceptable where "I *desire* bread" is not. Need thus is a legitimate desire based on what is essential versus what is superfluous.

The attention to need was part of the emphasis on the individual as human that started to develop in the seventeenth century. For the Puritans our needs were to eat, drink, procreate, be sheltered, and be saved. A defense of society had to show that human needs were met. Our duty derives from a rational recognition of our own needs and thus a recognition of the needs of our neighbors. I am to treat their legitimate desires as my own; I am not to threaten their lives, impair their health, or obstruct their own use of their property. The Puritan recognition of legitimate desires and needs, therefore, was a basis for the allowance of individual freedom.[24]

Many Puritans fought strongly for equality, liberty of the individual, freedom of conscience, and the importance of reason. The active Puritans of the seventeenth century

> by their open civil disobedience to English law laid the foundation for the English and American law of civil rights and civil liberties as expressed in our respective Constitutions: freedom of speech and press, free exercise of religion, the privilege against self-incrimination, the independence of the jury from judicial dictation, the right not to be imprisoned without cause, and many other such rights and freedoms.[25]

The doctrine of election produced an enormous emphasis on the importance of the individual, chosen by God before time was. Analogy from the equality of the believer and democracy in the church provided grounds for accepting the concepts of the rights of the individual and democracy in the state. The concept of Christian covenant, which supported democratic thought, was extremely important in American constitutional history, leading to the principle of government by consent. The explicit statements of the terms that God required for the covenant lent themselves to an extensive definition of rights of the subjects.

The emphasis in reform was on negative reforms, removing restrictions upon individual activity. Regarding the concept of the state, both the Independents and the Levellers among the Puritans had a tendency to circumscribe the activity of the government as such, providing guarantees against interference with the individual.[26]

The Puritan was often characterized by an experimental spirit. The Bible was believed to be a complete revelation, but room was granted for progressive comprehension and progressive interpretation of it. There was a quest for truth and a confidence in truth's ability to guard itself.

Puritanism was moved by an iconoclastic spirit resulting from the destruction of religious institutions of 1,000 years. To John Milton custom is a tyrant in religion and the state that has an ally in fallen human nature. "Custom countenances error,"[27] but God intervenes freshly on behalf of truth and righteousness. In a fashion quite opposite to Burke, Milton saw history as a wandering from the way.[28] Thus in the Puritans there is a shift from precedence as the basis for social validation to Scripture and the laws of nature, permitting an extension of rights versus a defense of rights already won.[29]

The Puritan contribution to liberalism requires a more critical examination of liberalism than a facile dismissal as "secular humanism," as some are wont to do.

Modern Liberalism

Much in this picture of liberalism will seem incongruent with how the term *liberal* is used in contemporary American society. The liberalism that has *expanded* external authority in the direction of the welfare state may seem to be of a different species than classical liberalism with its tenet of the freedom of the individual from arbitrary external authority. It served to *limit* governmental activity.

Liberalism arose in the middle class. The concessions and liberties that were gained by early liberalism were those suited for the middle class. They had the skill, property, and power to profit from them.

Because of liberalism's success, there was a diminution of governmental authority. At the same time great economic powers emerged with the technological explosion of the industrial revolution for those able to take full advantage of the new resources. Since the regulative and distributive power of government was weakened, the disproportionment of economic power was accentuated rather than mitigated.[30] The lower classes, in addition to not sharing in the benefits gained by the middle class, were also disadvantaged by the freedom that the middle class gained.

Middle-class freedom provided middle-class power, but it also led to a decline in power and care for those below the middle class. Where the middle classes of the seventeenth and eighteenth centuries had been held down by the collusion of aristocracy and government, the lower classes of the nineteenth century were held down by the passivity of government before the economic power of individuals and corporations out of the middle class. The middle class came between the poor and workers and the former masters who also had exploited them but who had a more paternalistic and organic unity with them. Industrial slums, long hours of work, low wages, disease, and cyclical work and unemployment all were signs of the new situation.

A question then confronted those who accepted the liberal dream of humanity and individual freedom. How can this freedom be provided for the lower classes? Patricia Hollis describes the change in radical social criticism between 1819 and 1830, the middle of the Industrial Revolution in England. The writers in the unstamped press in 1819 saw the people as being oppressed by aristocratic privileges, landed monopoly, taxes, and the established church. Writers in these papers in the 1830s saw the exploitation as also coming from capitalists and merchants and the low wages, unemployment, and business cycles of the system of political economy.[31]

Liberal values were articulated in terms of all humanity. The golden rule of Christianity demanded equal consideration of others. The situation required that the liberties sought for oneself and one's class should just as aggressively be sought for others. Robert Browning wrote:

> . . . . If fetters, not a few,
> Of prejudice, convention, fall from me,
> These shall I bid men—each in his degree
> Also God-guided—bear, and, gayly, too?[32]

The solution seemed to be to expand the authority of government over the new economic power. A second great tenet of liberalism developed. The emphasis of classical liberalism had been freedom from arbitrary authority. The new liberalism had another core emphasis: achieving free expression of the individual personality by upholding those *institutions* that foster and protect free expression.[33] The central such institution appeared to be the government if the peasant and the worker were to achieve such freedom.

The principle of subsidiarity changed. This principle states that government should not do what individuals and private groups can do for themselves. What had been a negative principle against state regulation now became a positive mandate for the government to deal with problems of injustice that could be tackled by no one else.[34]

Ramsay Muir defines liberalism in the following way:

> A readiness to use *the power of the State* for the purposes of creating the conditions in which *individual energy can thrive,* of *preventing all abuses of power,* of affording to every citizen the means of acquiring *mastery of his* [*or her*] *own capabilities,* and of establishing a real *equality of opportunity* for all. These aims are compatible with

a very active policy of social reorganization, involving a great *enlargement of the functions of the State.*[35]

Two aspects of this definition stand out. The first is the use of governmental power for social reorganization, the development of modern liberalism. The second is continuation of the traditional liberal concerns: provision for the individual to thrive by mastering one's own capabilities, and equality of opportunity for all.

This later development in liberalism laid greater importance on the social environment. Coercion and obstacles to individual development were perceived as coming from society itself and not only from government officials.[36] Nevertheless, the traditional liberal end of the autonomous individual was retained; thus, there continued the objectives of extending the scope of individual liberty, equalizing the distribution of liberty, and enriching the liberty.[37]

Another liberalism continued alongside that rejected the new expanded role of government. It is popularly described as *conservatism* ("laissez-faire conservatism"), and it is; however, it is a conservative liberalism. We will discuss it in our treatment of the capitalist vision.

A pivotal figure in the turning point from classical to modern liberalism was John Stuart Mill. Marx described Mill as the best representative of the effort to "harmonize the political economy of capital with the claim, no longer to be ignored, of the proletariat."[38] In his essay, *On Liberty,* in 1859, Mill opposes the tendency to stretch the powers of society over the individual unduly. He manifests the classical liberal concern to protect freedom of conscience, liberty of tastes and pursuits, and freedom to unite.

Mill, however, makes an important distinction between private and public activity. On the one hand he distinguishes all that portion of a person's life and conduct that affects only that person. Here the individual is sovereign.

On the other hand he identifies the conduct of a person that affects others. It is legitimate to use power to prevent harm to others. The person can also be compelled to perform positive acts for the benefit of others in the society because society provides that person with protection. For example, there is a positive, enforceable duty to protect the defenseless against ill-usage. The principle of liberty from government involvement is not involved in the doctrine of free trade because trade is a social act affecting the interests of others, Mill states. Also the principle of liberty is not involved in employers' responsibility to provide sanitary conditions and arrangements for the protection of their workers. The state has vigilant control over the exercise of any power that it allows one individual to possess over others.[39] This distinction is not original to Mill,[40] but he marks the most influential introduction of such a distinction into the individualistic thought of the nineteenth century.

The new role of government required fleshing out aspects dormant in the earlier conception of rights. The Puritan understanding of needs, which we have already discussed, is closer to the concept of welfare, so important in modern liberal thought, than is the idea of happiness, which dominated utilitarian thought. Welfare is more precisely calculable in terms of a hierarchy of needs than in the vagueness of the concept of happiness.[41] For example, Harvey Seifert writes, "The genuine needs of [human beings] give content to social definitions of rights. Each

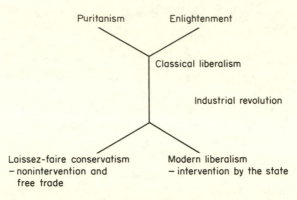

Figure 9.1.

person has a right to the opportunity to satisfy his [or her] needs to the fullest extent possible under the existing outputs of production."[42]

In modern liberal thought the basic needs of each individual are related to human freedoms or rights, and the meeting of them may require the role of welfare. The Four Freedoms of Franklin Roosevelt were freedom of speech, freedom of worship, freedom from *want,* and freedom from *fear.*[43] Similarly, Pope John XXIII, in his encyclical, *Pacem in Terris,* stated that each person has the right "to the means necessary for the proper development of life, particularly food, clothing, shelter, medical care, rest, and finally, the necessary social services."[44]

The Puritans, with their emphasis on needs, can thus be seen as contributing to both the old liberalism as well as the tendency that becomes the new liberalism. In addition, their quest for holy community and their inner-worldly asceticism provided an impulse for positive reform.

Figure 9.1 provides a diagram of the important split that occurs in liberalism.

David Smith argues that it was laissez-faire conservatism that made the change: It made the means of liberalism—the limitation of government—into an end in itself and transformed liberalism into a conservative ideology.[45] In a similar manner, Rossiter speaks of "The Great Train Robbery of American Intellectual History" to describe the way Thomas Jefferson's suspicion of centralized government, a concern to protect the common person against vested intersts, was later used to protect powerful vested commercial and industrial interests at the expense of the common person.[46]

Human Dignity and Human Woes

In many ways liberalism has given decisive historical expression to the Christian view of human nature as created by God and of human dignity as possessed by all. Every person has capacities to determine what is good for oneself, to reason, to create, to cooperate. Each individual has an ultimate value and dignity to be protected against intrusions of groups, governments, and other social and environmental forces.

Liberalism gives more weight to the human propensity for good than it does to the propensity for evil. This statement is harder to make of the strands that de-emphasize reason and rely more heavily upon the balancing of self-oriented drives of individuals and groups. Self-interest is the basic human drive.[47] Such recognition of sin, however, is not Sin in the Pauline sense of the powerful force of evil that makes even the Law impotent. Sin is not merely self-preservation in contrast to the interests of others. It also is greed and lust.[48] Self-regulating laws of nature and the countering of interest against interest cannot be relied upon to contain it.

View of Reason

The weakness of liberal optimism appears more in its view of reason than its view of human nature in general although we have seen that the manner of the confidence in reason varies among the various strands of liberalism. There is confidence that self-interest will be expressed with rational prudence and that injustice can be eliminated by education or reform.

In the modern form of liberalism the central government is understood as capable of rationally directing and shaping the public aspects of society by subjecting it to human reason.[49] The liberal confidence in reason, the search for objective controls through impersonal law, and middle-class appreciation of efficiency is an encouragement of bureaucratization, with its positive and necessary aspects, as well as its problems.

Education is highly regarded because it is the means of developing the human consciousness that shapes its environment; that consciousness does not come immediately.[50] The weakness of the reliance upon education is both the lack of penetration of education in the learner as well as the share of the educator and of the educational system in the fallenness of the human order. Personal and social biases enter the very fabric of learning and communication. The contribution of, and need for, tradition and religious change can be neglected by the educational strategy.

Confidence in reason is combined with confidence in the laws and progress of history. If reason and research are allowed to run their course, the most rational will prevail. The results will work out for the good in the end. Garry Wills describes this trust as the intellectual counterpart of the market and intellectual Darwinism.[51] With great insight he gives recognition to the many marvelous regulating devices that liberalism has provided. The pretense that they are self-regulating must nevertheless be abandoned.[52] The problems exposed in the development of technology and social organization must be directly confronted and latent consequences must be unveiled with the use of explicit moral criteria.

The confidence in reason and the commitment to education has had many positive consequences that must not be slighted. The facilities of reason, social science, and technology have been applied to social problems in ways not likely under traditional conservatism. The vast extension of education within society and globally has been a factor in the improved well-being of the laboring classes and the expansion of the middle class.

The confidence in reason, however, has also led to significant misreadings of social reality. For example, German liberals tended to dismiss the Nazis as psychopaths and to trust the high quality of German education to serve as a reliable check upon them.[53] Rational discussion is overvalued. The assumption is made that conflicts can be solved through discussion. The problems of racism would be solved if only people would talk to each other. Similarly, the social role of the church is to be that of a reconciler. Its purpose is to bring about dialogue among conflicting parties. The problem is not that there is not a necessary place for dialogue, reconciliation, and education. The problem is what is neglected.

The deficiency in this approach is the failure to come to terms with the reality of power. The impact made upon the rational processes by the possession of power or its lack is not perceived. The need to apply power to change the distribution of power is slighted. The responsibility of the church to take the side of victims in struggles for justice is ignored or opposed.

Reinhold Niebuhr, with his perception of group egoism, correctly saw that the individualistic analysis of liberalism failed to perceive adequately the compounding of evil on the social level and the need for social controls. "The drives of society require management just as much as the impulses of the individual."[54] Saul Alinsky described the failure to use adequate measures to carry out social objectives: "Every issue involving power and its use has always carried in its wake the liberal backwash of agreeing with the objective but disagreeing with the tactics."[55] Piecemeal and shallow reforms, with a lack of enforcing machinery, are the result. Controls eventually come under the influence of the very groups being regulated, as is the case in the life cycle of regulatory commissions.

The optimism also leads to shoddy planning. We previously referred to the lost opportunity in the failure to provide community centers for the massive deinstitutionalization of patients from mental hospitals in the 1970s (cf. p. 106). The intention stated in several acts of Congress had been to create a whole continuum of support institutions in the communities to receive these discharged patients. In the optimism of the 1960s when the effort began, the local financing of community centers was left to the undefined future. When the time came to act, all levels of government were under financial restraints. By the end of the 1970s, only 725 community centers had been built and 800 catchment areas around the country were without coverage at all. Given the housing crunch of the 1980s, many of the deinstitutionalized patients were now on the streets.[56]

The Progress of History

Liberalism has confidence that inherent self-regulating laws of nature work for good in the long run if they are not subject to interference. In the older liberalism an invisible hand worked within society bringing harmony out of the conflicting individual interests.

In the pluralism in modern liberalism similar reliance may be placed upon a natural harmony produced out of the interests of the major groups in society.[57] We have seen that a pluralism of groups provides cultural vitality for a society. The equilibrium within the network of interacting groups replaces undue reliance upon the wisdom and power of the state. There can be, however, a misplaced faith that a system built upon the confrontation and bargaining of groups is self-correcting. One harmful consequence is a failure to give explicit attention to questions of justice and other values in the formation of public policy.[58]

The ongoing necessity of a role for the state may also be neglected in this optimism. The private ends of the members and groups of society do not coincide on all major counts. "The fact of the matter is that the interests, far from always coinciding, cross and oppose one another, that they pit [individual] against [individual] and group against group. . . .Exploitation and oppression are possible only in society."[59]

Any view that assumes that there is a force within history producing a progressive advance toward the solution of evil is inadequate in light of the Christian view of history. In addition, the liberal commitment is made to a progress that is autonomous of both divine transcendence and basic human values. It is based instead on the mutually reinforcing factors of economic growth, technological innovation, and scientific aggrandizement.[60]

The liberal optimism regarding history has had valuable political consequences in that it encourages openness to change and willingness to experiment. People have confidence and trust for saving, investment, and family continuity.[61] We have also seen in our discussion of the Puritan experimental spirit the ability to be critical of the evil that comes from the past. Utopia remains functional; it can influence the present.

Utopia, however, is demystified. The tension that separates ideal imperatives from distorted reality is lost. According to Mannheim utopia becomes a theoretical tool for evaluation rather than a rivaling, threatening order. Utopia is farther down the same road of history and evolution.[62]

The orientation to time within liberalism is thus too oriented to the present. This orientation to the present is related to individualism within liberalism, about which we will comment further. Alexis de Tocqueville, in observing early nineteenth-century America, wrote:

> Such folk owe no man anything and hardly expect anything from anybody. They form the habit of thinking of themselves in isolation and imagine that their whole destiny is in their own hands. Thus, not only does democracy make men forget their ancestors, but also clouds their view of their descendants and isolates them from their contemporaries. Each man is forever thrown back on himself alone.[63]

The confidence about the future obfuscates the need for and possibilities of radical political change. It veils the hard struggle that justice requires. The progress to racial justice in America did not appear through the progressive unfolding of history but "through the blood of martyrs and the wrath of God," as Lincoln and Martin Luther King understood.[64]

The confidence in natural harmonies, reason, and education also neglects the fact that social transformation is not possible without a transformation of human beings.[65] The liberal optimism regarding reason and history often neutralizes the liberal commitment to justice.

Justice in Context

Liberalism made an invaluable contribution to history in establishing decisively the equality of all people and the civil rights that are implied. It has produced the basic concepts of much of what is admirable in the Western forms of government, such as the rights of the individual and democracy.

Special attention to the weak, so critical to biblical justice, has been present within modern liberalism. It asserted in the face of the disproportion of power from the Industrial Revolution that the machinery of the state is to be used on behalf of the working class and the poor. In becoming president of Americans for Democratic Action, Robert Drinan, the priest and former member of Congress, stated, "Fundamentally, an American liberal believes in government as an entity by which the last and the lowest and the least should in fact be assisted."[66] There is a degree of imaginative justice in liberalism, a consideration of social handicaps in evaluating justice.

The best-known articulation of justice for modern liberalism is *A Theory of Justice* by John Rawls. Rawls articulates justice in two principles. The first is most attuned with classical liberalism. "Each person is to have an equal right to the most extensive total system of equal basic liberties compatible with a similar system of liberty for all."[67] The second is a far-reaching statement of the concerns of modern liberalism: "Social and economic inequalities are to be arranged so that they are both (a) to the greatest benefit of the least advantage and (b) attached to offices and positions open to all under conditions of fair equality of opportunity" (p. 83).

Rawls' theory shows the commendable concern within modern liberalism to hold firmly on to liberties while addressing distributive inequalities. Greater economic and social advantages cannot justify compromises of the first principle of assuring basic liberties (p. 61). At the same it perceives that justice must give special weight to the predicament of the least advantaged persons. It is from their perspective that a society is to judged, and the bias of the basic conditions that have contributed to their predicament must be redressed in the direction of equality (pp. 91, 100).

The thoroughness of this approach to justice will depend on how one defines its basic categories. Those who interpret it within the confines of modern liberalism may magnify the liberties in the first principle, such as rights of private property, to an extent that hinders the application of the second, distributive principle. The greatest benefit to the weaker members may be defined in a paternalistic way that justifies too easily the inequalities of the society.

Reliance upon the provision of equal opportunity to obtain advantageous positions may not sufficiently take into account barriers resulting from present inequalities. A clearer statement of the priority and standards of minimal participation of all persons in all essential areas of society would strengthen Rawls' redistributive concerns while necessarily retaining his concerns for freedom. This statement of justice is commendable provided that it is interpreted within an adequate interpretation of the relationship of the individual to the community.[68] The weakness, then, is less in the statement of justice than in its context in liberalism.

   In liberalism the strategy for change often is weighted heavily toward equality of opportunity. Arbitrary barriers of discrimination are to be removed, and at least an elementary and secondary education provided for all, as well as benefits of subsistence for the most needy. Individuals are freed to seek their own well-being within the competitive market. Actual inequalities, however, often prevent one from using the opportunities that are provided. Equality of opportunity bears too heavily upon the weak. The biblical demand for assuring the well-being of each individual is left uncompleted within the inadequacies of the competitive economic world. The principle of rendering according to basic needs thus is fulfilled only in part. The prevailing form of distribution instead is according to ability through the impersonal market mechanism.[69] Only with reluctance is oversight of distribution returned to the political sphere. The ability to succeed in the market varies markedly, however, for reasons of natural endowments and historical circumstances.[70]

The Limitations of Freedom as the Dominant Motif

Freedom, the central theme of liberalism, indeed has biblical roots. There, having "an iron yoke on your neck" is placed on the same level as being "in hunger and thirst, in nakedness and in want of everything" (Deut. 28.48, *NRSV*). The life of freedom is one of dignity. "I have broken the bars of your yoke and made you walk erect" (Lev. 26.13, *NRSV*).

   The freedom is not a negative freedom, however. Their freedom does not bring them into emptiness, struggle, or freewheeling opportunity. They are brought into an abundance of goodness, which provides genuine endowment. The Lord brought them *out* of Egypt *and into* a land flowing with milk and honey (Deut. 26.7–9). The Lord "brought us out from there in order to bring us in" (Deut. 6.23, *NRSV*).

   The concerns of freedom center around slavery and subjugation to other peoples, represented especially by Egypt and Babylon. Members of the community may serve others only for a limited period of time and may not be sold as slaves (Lev. 25.39, 42). Runaway slaves may not be returned to their masters (Deut. 23.15–16). Hans Walter Wolff argues that the Old Testament sees the people as "on the road to freedom," and in this context there is a critique of the monarchy and of slavery.[71] The warning against accepting a Canaanite type of kingship was that such a figure would not only violate many of their economic rights, it would also make them slaves (1 Sam. 8.11–17 [cf. pp. 68–69).

   Freedom rights occur in the form of mandating due process for all claimants of justice. Legal judgments are not to go beyond the just claims that are presented. On the one hand, bribes are not to be accepted from the rich; on the other hand, the poor are not to be favored beyond the merits of their cause (Exod. 23.1–3, 6–8).

   There are deficiencies, however, in freedom (or liberation) as the leading motif for political thought despite its inseparability from other demands of justice. It is satisfactory for criticism of the old social order, but it is limited in building up a new one. Freedom is a vague, abstract idea. Freedom is essentially "freedom from"; it is a negative and transitional concept.[72] Since "freedom from" is a limited concept, those who speak of "freedom for" need to use separate, positive concepts and criteria to provide the content of the objective of freedom. Freedom thus is not as basic as is assumed. Rather than being the lead motif, freedom is better treated as one tablet of the basic demands of justice.

Because freedom is granted to the sphere of conscience that does no harm to others, liberals have sought to allow others to be free to live out their own beliefs rather than to impose their view on them.[73] This has led to the compartmentalization of life under liberalism: the separation of faith from the public square, and the secularization in confining religion to one sphere and role in life.[74] This situation also in part reflects the absence of a positive unifying core for its social philosophy.

The Liberal Achievement

Liberalism in the past two centuries has made definite contributions toward "Christianizing the Social Order." Slavery was abolished, and the franchise and eduation universalized. Liberal theory and ideals have been behind a whole series of reforms from the guarantee of the human rights in the nineteenth century to the protection of the labor movement to the attack on racism in the twentieth century. The gains have spread globally.

Through economic growth and reform the average American worker has been pulled farther from the subsistence level. Up to the early 1970s the real wages of the average production worker increased more than four times from the beginnings of twentieth century. Before World War I such workers did not own a home, provided their own medical care, and their vacations were confined to the reaches of the local trolley company. The worker then also put in almost ten more hours a week for those wages. Liberalism thus contributed to a bulging middle class. The liberal ideals still have not been provided for many who do not have home ownership, adequate medical care, and who are experiencing declining wages and, for many, continuing racial discrimination. A cause for suspicion of liberalism is the failures of our society despite the fact that liberalism has been our dominant political philosophy. The persistence of poverty in such a wealthy nation is a case in point.[75]

Liberalism posits an ideal of equality and freedom that is incongruent with reality for many people but which, because it is accepted as a description of society, justifies the distribution of property and power. For some, such as victims of racial discrimination, the ideology of freedom veils the civil liberties that they do not share. For others the contrast is between the provision of political freedoms and deficiencies in their actual freedom due to their unmet economic needs. As Marx described the situation, liberalism provides political emancipation, which is a great progress. Here the individual seems to be a communal being, but this political community is an abstraction and obscures the fact that in real social and economic life the individual continues as an egoistic being, treating others as means and being degraded to the role of mere means.[76]

Our society can be accused as being hypocritical, but the standard of that critique continues to be liberal ideal. Hypocrisy at least provides a tension for change. It is better to live in a society that has equality and freedom in its ideology than one that does not. What liberties there are in the status quo are protected: When the incongruence is discerned, the ideal can then function in a critical manner.[77] Gunnar Myrdal's introduction to his classic treatment of race, *An American Dilemma,* accordingly contrasts the American dream of the common person with our failure to observe it.[78]

Individuality and Community

The severest criticism of liberalism from the left and from the right is its lack of community. In this regard liberalism does not adequately reflect the biblical doctrine of humanity in community.

Robert Paul Wolff offers an intelligent criticism of liberalism in this area.[79] In the split within liberalism, modern liberalism seeks to make a place for the *communitarian* features of social life. The difficulty is putting a communitarian sociology together with an individualistic liberal philosophy.

Liberalism in its individualistic base tends to be blind to evils that affect the entire body politic. It may see how the individual hurts, but not how the system hurts. For example, in ecological concern one might be aware of the harmfulness of polluted air, but miss the relevant materialism and competitive motivation in the value system of society that leads to the exploitation of the created world. Providing job training for the unemployed may help the particular trainees, but it does not produce more jobs to decrease unemployment overall. Shelters for the homeless do not increase the supply of low-cost housing.

Our public enterprises are social in nature, but the public–private/interference–noninterference model of human relationships provides an inadequate guide for our responsibilities. Our society is not so neatly divided. Criteria of a good community are needed.

Liberalism deals with private values. *Simple private values,* according to Wolff, refer to a state of consciousness in exactly one person, such as taking a sip of cider. *Compound private values* refer to the multiplication of private values to any number. The group is drinking cider. I close the window to create a feeling of warmth in Jones and a feeling of warmth in Smith, et cetera. Liberalism's social harmony is the sum and mediation of all the particular interests in society.

There also is social value, however. This is Wolff's point. Jones hates Smith and wants him to suffer. Essential here is the thought about the state of consciousness in another. There can be reciprocal consciousness. Smith may want to know that Jones is suffering and for Jones to know that he knows. The important emphasis is the relationship rather than the state of one unit in it.

Social values of community can be expanded to large groups. One then asks what makes a good community, not just what makes a good individual. The definition of property in a community is a definition of a social relationship, not the characteristic of an individual which is then secondarily modified when one brings in the community context. The barriers and opportunities of a black, Native American, or a woman cannot be understood adequately in terms of discrete individuals or a generality about equality of opportunity. They must be interpreted in terms of groups that have their own significant historical and current relationship to other groups in the society.[80] Peaceful unity is valued both because it protects individual rights and because without it communal life is a burden. Where there is not a commitment to brotherhood and sisterhood, equality is subverted by the competitive individualism of liberty.[81]

John Locke, although drawing upon the Puritan conception, removed duty and calling from its covenantal and community context because the individual can and must know for oneself. The church no longer has meaning as a source of knowledge or a source for the recognition and affirmation of duty. Locke thus represents a significant step in the secularization of Puritan thought. The calling loses the moral status that external definition gives to it, and the institutions lose their independent and necessary place. In the words of John Dunn, "The complete individualization of religious duty evacuates human social organization and its hierarchy of all value except its contingent convenience."[82]

In liberalism the autonomous individual becomes social through contracts that are freely entered into when seen as advantageous. As Heimann points out, society then is only derived, a means, and a matter of expediency.[83] This individualism affects political life as well as every other institution in society. Even where there is commitment to a pluralism of groups, the ideology of individualism undercuts it with the conception that members are free to leave at any time.[84] The family is frequently affected. A provisional and instrumental view of authority and loyalty or the ideal of individual fulfillment contests values of family strength.[85]

Rosalind Petchesky attempts to provide a more satisfactory case for abortion than its grounding in the liberal dichotomy between autonomy and social interdependence. There a woman's right to choose an abortion is based in privacy or individual liberty. Such liberal individualism and exclusivity fails to perceive that reproduction and child birth are part of a social network involving fathers, children, the medical profession, employers, the church, and the state. The privacy argument "lets men and society neatly off the hook." Fathers should share in the decision on the grounds of their actual social relationship to the pregnancy and actual demonstration of care and responsibility in the decision. The society has a responsibility to ameliorate the conditions that make either abortion or childbearing a difficult decision for many.[86]

Institutions have rights in addition to those of individuals. There is an obligation to prevent harm to institutions and systems that serve the public interest and support the essential spheres of life. Family, church, and marriage are obvious examples.[87] There are also legitimate concerns for beauty, recreation, ecology, and public morality that victimize the community when violated, not necessarily a particular individual; yet what is violated is the common good, which is essential for the thriving of individuals.

Liberty as the power to do everything that does not harm others assumes the human being to be a self-sufficient monad, "withdrawn into himself, wholly preoccupied with his private interst and acting in accordance with his private caprice."[88]

The restricted perception of the social nature of the individual can be illustrated from Kantian liberalism.[89] Here loving your neighbor as yourself means respecting every human being as a rational creature.[90] Since rationality is a given already present in humanness, rather than something to be produced, this respect acts negatively: Rationality is something against which one should never act. The first principle of human relationships, then, is a freedom concept—noninterference. The understanding of human dignity as being an end in itself is to exist in itself. One is to be undetermined and self-legislating.

The positive obligation to promote the well-being of others is secondary and is always qualified. Their well-being is to be sought as long as such promotion does not unduly injure or coerce others or create disproportionate injury to oneself.

Human beings, however, also express their genuine humanness by knowledge and love. An understanding of the relationship of the individual and society is derived that is significantly different from that which starts with rationality. Margaret Farley writes:

> Freedom can do anything so long as it does not violate itself or the freedom of another. But knowledge and love must deal with a reality in persons that is structurally complex, essentially interpersonal and social, existing in correlation with a world that is historical and that is constituted not only by other persons but by things and other living beings and institutions.[91]

The basic mutuality found in the definition of human dignity is expanded when we take this valid insight, which is biblical, to its ultimate foundation in the love of God, who calls us to others just as God calls us to God's own self. The agency that is to be secured for each individual is not that of autonomy; it is the ability to share actively in the life of society.[92]

Out of the autonomous context of liberalism comes its conception of private property. In American Puritan writings one finds the view of the Creator, who had created the earth for all persons, along side a view of private property, which allowed many to have no share in that creation. This is puzzling. Elisha Williams, as one example, wrote of a natural equality that meant an equal right "to such things as nature affords for their subsistence." He also described a right of each person to "his property" and to all the necessary means of defense of his property. The logical connection is the principle that each person has the right to the product of one's own hands: "the labour of his body and the work of his hands are properly his own."[93] Williams and others, according to their understanding of Locke, assumed a natural state where prior to the social contract each individual existed by and to oneself. They correspondingly saw one's labor as prior to social help or responsibility.

From a sociological or theological perspective, however, production is not an isolated task without dependence upon the social systems in which one lives. They provide not only the economic framework but also the essential security, language, and culture. In light of both divine and social grace one cannot speak so privately of "my own labour." The consequences of ownership then do not follow.

For an illustration of the lack of community in the liberal conception one can compare natural law in Thomas Jefferson and in Thomas Aquinas. To the liberal[94] Jefferson, "these truths are self-evident, that all men are created equal, that they are endowed by their Creator with certain inalienable rights, that among them are life, liberty, and the pursuit of happiness." Rights are related to the individual.

In Thomas Aquinas the focus is on the common good, not on the single individual. The emphasis is on duties, not rights. Natural law provides general principles of an order not created by us. It is from God, known through our reason. We have no inalienable rights—neither of thought, nor of association, nor of property. The individuals are not free nor equal in the state, although they share a common humanity.[95] The concern is for the whole, for the good of the whole community. Here is a level of thought and categories that deal with the whole that liberalism misses.

The application to the concept of property is significant. On one hand, in liberalism, private rights which had been considered to be relative to some public purpose in the past are now "thought to be absolute and indefeasible, and to stand by their own virtue."[96] Aquinas, on the other hand, held that the distribution of property is a matter of human agreement, not of natural law. The arrangements for property may not detract from natural law, and God has arranged the natural order so that material goods are provided for the satisfaction of human needs. Therefore, right to private property must not detract from the general welfare. The duties of property take precedence over its private rights. Owners should not consider property as only their own. Whatever a person has in excess "is owed, of natural right, to the poor for their sustenance." A poor person who because of dire necessity takes from another's superabundance does not commit robbery.[97] Here conditions are laid down for sweeping interventions of the state in the control and regulation of economic life.[98]

By pointing to the community context of right in the traditions associated with Aquinas we do not mean that one should choose Thomas Aquinas over Thomas Jefferson. We need the protection of the individual that liberalism contributes. It has formulated a view of human dignity that must never be lost, anywhere, or any time.

We perceive, however, a lack in liberalism that must be supplied. The orientation to the whole community and its conditions, not only to the abstracted individual, is missing.

We need a political philosophy that has both elements. The result would be closer to the Puritan roots of liberalism, where the starting point in the understanding of the individual was in definite mutual covenantal responsibilities.

For the Puritans in the making of a covenant, unique men and women pledged themselves to values that previously had existed for them as abstractions, even though established by the Creator. Covenant transforms static and general ethical responsibilities into bonds of community with a particular set of people. Political liberalism is in need of a restored sense of the human as a social being with attending responsibilities and potential fulfillments. Liberty and equality also require the previous experience of "intense interpersonal" familial community in which personal identity is secured and in which one's education in the virtues of constraint, honor, obligation, and authority have had their beginnings.[99]

Eduard Heimann, V. A. Demant, and earlier Max Weber saw that the destructive force of liberal thought appeared when it had sloughed off its religious grounding, losing the realism of a transcendental reference and the integration of a concern for community.[100] Liberalism could become a powerful and effective social force if the old perspective were recovered through the re-Christianization that Heimann envisaged.[101] Christianity would provide a transcending basis for cultural values in which social distribution and personal freedom are held together and in balance by a commitment to a community of persons, whose dignity, worth, and calling rests outside of the social and material process. The contemporary Western forms of Christianity—whether liberal or Evangelical—however, must be reformed themselves before they can provide the needed spiritual base because they too have been permeated with the individualism of the conquering middle class.

10

A Space in the Public Place: Democracy

And this multitude, appearing for the first time in broad daylight, was actually the multitude of the poor and the downtrodden, whom every century before had hidden in darkness and shame. What from then on has been irrevocable . . . was that the public realm—reserved, as far as memory could reach, to those who *were* free, namely carefree of all the worries that are connected with life's necessity, with bodily needs—should offer its space and its light to the immense majority who are not free because they are driven by daily needs. (Hannah Arendt[1])

Modern democracy developed in the liberal quest for freedom in the seventeenth and eighteenth centuries. Democracy had already appeared in earlier forms in prehistoric and early historical societies[2] and in ancient Greece. The latter appearance of democracy was democracy only in a qualified sense since in reality it included only a small portion[3] of the civil community, the sons of citizens of the city–state who married women of the city–state.

These earlier forms of democracy were characterized by direct involvement in the assembly of the citizens. In the developed postmedieval society, direct democracy was no longer an option for the state. The democracy that developed was self-rule of the people through their representatives.

Democracy was an integral part of the liberty sought and obtained by the rising middle class. It developed as part of the transfer of power from the few to the many.[4] Although its modern foundations lie within the greater liberal political ideology, democracy poses a question of international significance today that transcends liberalism. We will consider political democracy in this chapter; subsequent chapters will ponder its economic manifestations.

Christian Contributions to Democracy

Democracy not only gives expression to the Judaeo-Christian concept of the dignity and capacity of the individual, it also reflects the Judaeo-Christian warning of the individual's capacity for evil. Furthermore, monotheism provides a source of authority in God from the standpoint of which the individual may defy the authorities of the world.[5] Democracy follows an iconoclasm of political idolatry as people are activated from apathy before the masters they had worshipped.[6] Yet the experience of encountering God's majesty also imparts a sense of humility in intellect

150

that opens the individual to the limitations of one's own expression of truth and information. The contributions of other people, even one's adversaries, are needed for community decisions.[7]

The Judaeo-Christian contribution to democracy goes back to the assemblies in ancient Israel, where rudiments of democracy can be found. They belong to the structure of the covenantal community although for the most part they were not actually commanded. They have provided an influential example for government throughout Western history.

At the village level, the adult males participated in the judicial and policy decisions made at the gate of the town.[8] In the wilderness those who were to help Moses rule the people were to be chosen by the people (Deut. 1.13).[9] Even in the monarchy, in addition to checks on the power of the monarch (cf. Deut. 17), there was participation by the people. Fohrer calls it a "covenantal kingship."[10] Two elements were involved in the choice of the monarch. In addition to the oracle of God, revealing God's choice, there was an acclamation of the people connected with a covenant between the monarch and the people.[11] Representatives of the people participated in this civil legitimation. Gordis argues that the terms for assembly, *'ēdāh* and *qāhāl*, have a technical usage meaning an assembly of the people. It was originally a tribal assembly that had an extensive role in the early history of Israel as the supreme arbiter in all phases of national life. After the establishment of the centralized monarchy, its judicial function was abandoned; however, the assembly still appears in times of crisis affecting the entire people.[12] It was such an assembly that participated in the civil legitimation. "And all the assembly made a covenant with king . . ." (2 Chron. 23.3). This type of covenant bound the king as the more powerful party to the duties of kingship and expressed commitment to the king by the people as the weaker party.[13]

At least in the ideal, the assembly continued to have periodic major responsibilities like redistribution of land (Mic. 2.5).[14] David consulted with the assembly about bringing back the ark of the covenant. They agreed, so he did it (1 Chron. 13.4, 5). David did not return after Absalom's rebellion until invited by the elders of Judah (2 Sam. 19.11, 14–15). What characterizes Israel in contrast to other Semitic peoples is that this assembly continued to function in the later agriculture and urban state, even if only in times of national crisis.[15] Thus in these ways the Israelite people were subjects as well as participants in rule.[16]

In the New Testament leaders share decision making with the local community. Rudolf Schnackenburg states, "Important decisions were never taken without the consent of the community." In Acts the whole community shares in the election of leaders and major decisions.[17] For the local community of believers Paul explicated the doctrine of the body of Christ. The different responsibilities manifest the distribution of Spirit-given abilities to each member. They are interdependent for service to the community as a whole.[18] In 1 Corinthians 5 Paul wants a consensus between himself and the community and leaves it to them to make the formal decision to expel an offender.[19] Matthew reflects a community of brothers and sisters, subject to the same Lord and mutual service. The community acts by consent in an important decision about a fellow member (18.15–17). This idea of community was predominant in the early church.[20]

We have commented earlier on social revolution in the early church in its giving the common person opportunity to learn skills for social organization and participation in social decisions in response to a transcendent purpose. Freedom of association is essential to democracy, and voluntary association is the "distinctive and indispensable institution of democratic society." It provides the training ground for the skills required for viable democratic society. This trend was reversed in the concentration of power in the medieval church.[21] The Protestant Reformation, however, again placed great emphasis upon the maturity of the ordinary, nonordained member, who is guided by the Word in responsibilities in the church, family, and civil community.[22]

Other periods of history provide further evidence of the leveling that occurs in Christian movements driven by a strong sense of a common sharing in the Holy Spirit. In his Pulitzer Prize–winning history, *The Transformation of Virginia,* Rhys Isaac describes the impact evangelicals had upon a hierarchical society, legitimated by religion yet prone to competitiveness and aggression. In mid-eighteenth century Virginia, the Baptists particularly, but also the Presbyterians and Methodists, provided escape from these harsh values. Their revivals produced "a congregation of faithful persons, called out of the world by divine grace, who mutually agree to live together and to execute gospel discipline among them." No matter how humble, each person's personal experiences would be heard with respect. "A concomitant of fellowship in deep emotions was comparative equality." Important church elections required unanimity and might be held up by the doubts of a few. The movement was composed of the poor and unlearned, and many converts came from among the slaves.[23]

To the north, Charles Chauncy, pastor of the First Church of Boston, was complaining that the lay "exhorters" of the Great Awakening included "babes," "chiefly indeed young persons, sometimes lads, or rather boys: nay, women and girls; yea, Negroes, have taken upon them to do the business of preachers."[24] In the Great Awakening there was "an emerging popular culture asserting itself against a paternalistic social ethic." Itinerant preachers and lay exhorters outside the institutional channels derived their social authority from the consent of their audience. The audiences themselves were self-initiated associations "meeting outside of regularly constituted religious or political meetings and, in so doing, creating new models of organizations and authority premised on the sovereignty of the people."[25]

The Puritans were also communities of the Holy Spirit and they contributed the most to the Christian formulation of the concepts of democracy. As part of the liberal vision, democracy likewise emerged from both Puritan thought and secular rationalism. Because we are analyzing democracy from a Christian perspective, we are particularly interested in its Puritan roots. We nevertheless acknowledge the creative importance of secular Enlightenment thought. The Puritans' political conceptions indeed were not developed in isolation from it. The Puritans in their religious and political struggles in England in the seventeenth century formulated most of the principles upon which democratic institutions are based.

The Puritans built upon developments in the late Middle Ages and in earlier Calvinism. The concept of the normative will of the people was expressed in late medieval Christian writings.[26] The democratic impulse in Calvinism was grounded in the doctrine of the sovereignty of God and human sinfulness. God is truly sovereign, and human power must and can be limited in the Kingdom of God.[27] Calvin had argued that because of human moral frailty, government is safer and more tolerable when held by many (*plures*) for the sake of mutual support and restraint of individual wilfulness. For him the many would be the lower magistrates.[28] Ezra Stiles, a New England–ordained minister, later argued for popular elections on the grounds that it was easier to corrupt a few than many.[29] The Puritan Levellers such as John Wildman had argued that the magistrate is more likely to err than the people because of his access to power.[30]

Calvin also held that the privilege of peoples to choose "people who would govern," was a liberty that protected against tyranny. In Geneva the citizens had the right to choose their governors.[31] The Calvinist preachers appealed to public opinion and the electorate through the sermon.[32] Calvin's followers established a Calvinist republic in Holland and active republican parties in England and in Scotland.[33]

The first major Puritan contribution to democratic thought was the concept of freedom of conscience and individual decision. John Wise of Massachusetts stated that the human being is by nature a free-born subject who owes homage only to God. Since no particular form of government is prescribed in Scripture, government is a product of human compacts under the guidance of reason.[34] The Leveller, Thomas Rainborough, earlier found it to be clear that "every man that is to live under a government ought first by his own consent to put himself under that government; and I do think that the poorest man in England is not at all bound in a strict sense to that government that he hath not had a voice to put himself under." The poorest person "hath a life to live" as much as the greatest.[35] Another Leveller, John Lilburne, argued that all persons, spiritual or temporal, who assume power to rule "over any sort of men in the world without their free consent . . . endeavour to appropriate and assume unto themselves the office and sovereignty of God . . . and to be like their Creator."[36]

The second major Puritan contribution was the concept of setting goals through democratic discussion and that goals can be reset according to the needs of the group. John Saltmarsh wrote, "The interest of the people in Christ's kingdom is not only an interest of compliancy and obedience and submission, but of consultation, of debating, counseling, prophesying, voting, etc."[37] Explicit analogy was made from the mutual free covenant and active participation in the church to the proper form of association outside the church (cf. p. 135).[38] John Cotton, for example, wrote that the commonwealth should be "fashioned to the setting forth of Gods house"[39] (see Figure 10.1).

The contribution of the church life of other groups whom Weber includes with the Calvinists as ascetic Protestants should also be noted. Such a group was the Quakers. Their influence upon democracy can be seen in the leading role that Pennsylvanians had in the Jeffersonian period. They and other sectarians who contributed to the "Pennsylvania spirit" recognized the need for curbing unregenerate power. Since the exercise of power tended to corrupt and make its possessors usurpers of the sovereignty of God, however, the desire for power needed to be eliminated at its source.[40]

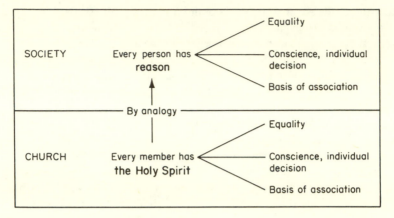

Figure 10.1. Democracy in Church and Society in the Puritans.

Congregational polity (Congregationalists, Unitarians, Baptists, Disciples) also contributed the conception of dispersion of power both in participation by the lay members and in power placed in local government. This polity also contributed to the concept of separation of powers in the Baptist and Independent demand for separation of church and state.[41]

Because of the combination of freedom of conscience, individual decision making, and voluntary associations based on covenantal cooperation, individuals highly motivated with a sense of calling and purpose through cooperative social action could remake the social order in which they found themselves.

Finally, the ideas of the Puritans and related groups about democracy contributed significantly because of the penetration of their churches throughout the society. In the words of H. Richard Niebuhr, "In America as in England the Christian enlightenment stood beside the rational enlightenment in the battle for democracy, and it furnished ten soldiers to the cause where the latter furnished one, for it dealt with the common [people] about whom the rationalists wrote books."[42]

In God's Image

The best theological support for democracy draws upon a balanced Christian view of human nature. Reinhold Niebuhr's famous statement of the justification of democracy is "man's capacity for justice makes democracy possible; but man's inclination to injustice makes democracy necessary."[43]

First, "humanity's capacity for justice makes democracy possible." Democracy depends on a conviction of the unique dignity and worth of the individual, based upon God's love for all persons regardless of their status in society.[44] Because of their value in God's eyes they are not to be mere instruments of any political program, nor are they to be manipulated for some community good.[45]

Democracy is based upon the intended and created freedom of every person. The freedom is one of members of a community. Each of these members, however, is of transcendent worth directly related to God as a unique creature; as such each is of equal transcendent worth.

Responsibility for their own life is an attribute of all people.[46] The right of equal vote is granted to all regardless of factual inequalities. "Every person capable of determining his own acts and in that much of shaping his own fate has a right to make use of this capacity to the widest possible extent."[47]

In the liberal democratic vision each individual is the earthly source of the authority to which each subjects herself or himself. The actual and concrete exercise of this power is transferred to representative governmental officials, but it is subject to recall. Governmental officials and the technological elite are functionaries without a special depth of meaning of their own. The source of the authority possessed by every individual is the universal human reason in which every individual participates.[48]

This perspective correctly perceives that because of humanity's place within creation, each individual has an irreducible authority and responsibility. Christian natural law also affirms the significance of the universal possession of reason. The exercise of this authority, however, is carried out in concert with others in the communities to which one inherently belongs. The basic communities also are intrinsic to created life. Not to have a government is not a human option, but the nature of that government and to whom its offices are entrusted are within the prerogatives of human decision.

Democracy is an expression of self-government by free choice within and by the community to which one belongs. Each member contributes equally to that choice. Because the individual is a communal being, his or her individual power is expressed through community. Because of the freedom and authority possessed by the individual, his or her communities must be democratic themselves. Democracy reflects the people's power to control every aspect of their lives and also to change the way in which they live together.[49]

The Christian view of the person as made in God's image and preserved by God's general grace provides sufficient basis for expecting individuals to have some capacity to act rationally about their own interests. Democracy requires faith in people since power and opportunities are to be entrusted to them. It depends upon some confidence in the individual's ability to tell right from wrong[50] and to make rational choices about one's own destiny. It demands that individuals make their own decisions, contribute to the structuring of their own environments, and see causal links between "rational" ends and means.

The value of all people may be depreciated because of an exaggerated view of depravity, a lack of transcendent support for human worth, or a rejection of human equality. There is danger that individuals or groups in society will then be subjected to the tyranny of others who are viewed as having a superior moral or rational capacity. They may be subject to a scientific and technical manipulation. That only a preponderant power can coerce the various forces in the society into a working harmony may be assumed.[51]

Democracy not only requires that elites be convinced of the dignity of all people, it demands unshakeable respect by all toward adversary, fellow creature, and minorities.[52] Democracy assures each member a place in the political community.

That alone makes effective democracy an essential instrument of justice. Participation in formal debate and decisions is an essential prerogative of membership in community. In addition, the community requires the contribution of all members for its own good so that its decisions can be appropriate and effective. Discussion is fundamental to democracy. Criticism is demanded, and opposition, even official opposition, is essential for representative government.[53]

Large communities, however, cannot be "one enormous discussion," nor can the discussion that democracy requires be met merely by the election of representatives. Democracy calls for a spontaneous and diverse society composed of voluntary associations in which its members discuss and express the aims and purposes of their lives and communities.[54] Effective political democracy depends on democratic processes existing in the other associations throughout the society. So Tocqueville in his examination of democracy in the United States found "Americans of all ages, all stations in life, and all types of disposition . . . forever forming associations." Where in France you would find the government, "in the United States you are sure to find an association."[55] The nonpolitical institutions train the citizenry in the habits of democratic behavior.[56] Accordingly, there can be no compromise between the totalitarian state and democracy.[57]

In turn democratic participation in government spreads a general habit and taste for association throughout the society. "So one may think of political associations as great free schools to which all citizens come to be taught the general theory of association," Tocqueville stated.[58] John Stuart Mill considered the benefit that most showed the superiority of democracy to be the "education of the intelligence and the sentiments which is carried down to the very lowest ranks of the people" through responsible participation and choice in decisions on great issues affecting one's country. Mill wrote that even if one granted that there could be an eminent despot who would provide good laws and elicit virtuous performance, the moral character of the citizens still would be stunted in the qualities of an active and "uncontented" outlook on life. In contrast democratic participation provides development and moral growth by exposing ordinary people to impartial conduct in conflict, a cosmopolitan perspective, and the practical application of principles of the general good.[59]

Power Against Inordinate Power

Niebuhr also stated that "humanity's inclination to injustice makes democracy necessary." Democracy basically deals with the question of power. Grounding democracy in concerns about power in light of human nature provides even stronger support than the natural capacity argument. It is less vulnerable to overly optimistic assumptions. The essential fervor for human equality must be channeled through measures of government that take into account human evil and the complexity of organized life.

Because of our universal propensity toward evil, no one is good enough to be trusted with control over the destiny of someone else. Abraham Lincoln proclaimed it clearly: "What I do say is, that no man is good enough to govern another man *without that other's consent*."[60] In Christian humility we realize that because of our proneness to sin we should reject a paternalistic relationship in which we serve the interests of less privileged people through the use of power over them.[61] We have seen that this applies to ideal groups as well as to individuals (cf. Chap. 2).

The only reliable and permanent source of human interest in oneself is one's own self-interest. This principle is sometimes called "the protective argument" for democracy. That public decision making will be exercised for the benefit of the individual, or his or her group, and not be oppressive can most assuredly be determined by the representation of the individual's own concern. As James Madison stated in *The Federalist*, "The private interest of every individual [must] be a sentinel over the public rights."[62] Saul Alinsky put it this way: "No clique, or caste, power group or benevolent administration can have the people's interest at heart as much as the people themselves."[63]

The groups of society are not only spontaneous centers of diverse vitality, they also express destructive egoism. A. D. Lindsay, however, states that a healthy democracy cannot exist where there are economic, racial, and religious cleavages and where permanent social minorities exist.[64] The problem is that these are permanent marks of human life in groups. The democratic dream is dimmed accordingly, yet in the very midst of social conflict democracy still presents less evil than do its alternatives.

Democracy provides a form of defensive power. Individual democracy brings the equilibrium of power of society down to smallest units. The interests of one individual balance off the interest of another.

In pluralistic democracy, more accurate to actual decision making, individuals associate with other individuals in order to advance their interests against other social combinations. Democracy diffuses power amid the various units of society. Not all power is granted in an open society to the proponents of one view. All claims to truth are under critical view.[65] The power of the government is also checked by this dispersion of power. Democracy does not eliminate elites, but elites are restricted by one another so that they must compete for leadership and the votes of the people.[66] Moreover, democracy demands that these larger units be internally democratic themselves.

The iron law of oligarchy described by Robert Michels presents a problem for democracy in that in any organization "eager beavers" can take advantage of the indolence of the average member and gain control.[67] If this development is inevitable, the most effective counter to the problem is to insure that the eager beavers of vested interest groups are outworked and outmotivated by eager beavers in associations pressuring the course of decision making in the interest of general welfare.

The liberal search for impersonal controls and confidence in natural harmonies comes to play in the conception of a satisfactory equilibrium arising among contending units within political democracy. Out of the arbitrariness of all individuals and groups a power is to emerge that achieves what is reasonable.[68] The liberal optimism about natural harmonies, however, is as false when applied to democracy as it is in its other applications. Society must be structured to constrict the contention of forces to the channels of justice. Constitutional liberty requires safeguards against a destructive use of democratic processes by any group.

A constitution specifies for the political arena the minimal requirements of justice for any equilibrium among democratic forces. Constitutional checks and balances are intended to protect rights and the common good from a dangerous advantage that any group or individual may achieve through the democratic political process. At this point democracy goes beyond being merely an expression of individualism. There is an order to community that transcends individual choice. There are designs for institutional life that precede social contract.

Since a majority may be wrong, Karl Popper argued that the fundamental requirement for an open society is not that the will of the majority should prevail. Rather, it is that institutions be free so that bad and incompetent rulers may be criticized and peacefully removed from office.[69]

Genuine popular participation in political rule requires much more of democracy than the mere existence of fair elections. Other essential aspects of democracy can be illustrated from Central America, whose elections in the 1980s were widely cited as evidence of a new democracy in the region. For example, in 1985 Guatemala had a national election for congress and the presidency that observers judged to be fair and accurately counted.

One characteristic of democratic government is that the government is broadly responsible and responsive to the popular will. In the 1985 Guatemalan election, however, real power continued in the hands of the military without any control over it by the elected officials. In rural areas, for example, the military coordinated and regulated all normal civil governmental functions under its direct supervision.[70]

Democratic participation also means that such participation has the potential of influencing public decision.[71] It is meaningful. The issues are not framed by elites outside the electoral process. In Guatemala concerns crucial to the well-being of the majority of the people were not legislated. Any agrarian reform policies beyond the most superficial were successfully blocked, and overall social legislation protecting the working class was absent. Human rights violations remained unprosecuted.[72] The failure to affect real issues is related to the violation by the preponderant power of the military of the next characteristic of genuine democracy.[73]

Democratic participation is autonomous.[74] Participation is not manipulated or controlled by others not participating. The people are able to make choices freely, without fear, in terms of their self-interest and vision of social good. The context in which the 1985 Guatemalan election occurred was quite different from the formal correctness of the election itself. The murders of 150 party organizers of the centrist Christian Democrat party only four years earlier had silenced all but a handful of party activists; its grass-roots leadership was decimated. Three years prior to that the leaders of the two centrist-reformist parties had been assassinated. Other activists, especially union leaders, had also been killed in the early 1980s. The massacres in rural Guatemala since 1978 had been almost indiscriminate. The election was "conducted in an atmosphere of crushing fear of political repression," and only a tame "opposition" participated.[75] The reality of that terror is indicated in continuing human rights abuses since the election, even if at rates much lower than the worst levels of the preceding few years. While significant inequality is present in all existing democracies, "the Central American cases illustrate the limits of inequality and unresponsiveness beyond which no meaningful democracy can be established."[76]

The Limits of Democracy

The principle of self-government has been the hope of the oppressed: They need not and must not be governed by those superior to them in power, esteem, and knowledge.[77] Henry Maine, a late-nincteenth-century English traditional conservative, argued that democracy is simply a form of government and nothing more; the test is whether it carries out the necessary and natural duties of government effectively.[78] To state this in a liberationist perspective, "the procedure of democracy must go hand in hand with the end result the process seeks." In a country in which the poor form the majority of the society, then the poor will fully participate in political rule, and that political rule will be fully for the poor.[79] We have seen that procedures of democracy can be present, even free elections, without there being a situation even approaching rule of the people. Political democracy that is genuine should not be discounted as a good in itself, however, even when it exists in a society that otherwise falls short of being a just society.

If democracy brings the members of the community into participation in the political life of that community, that it is certainly worthy in itself. Political participation is an aspect of what is essential for life in community. Democracy is a partial expression of justice. One can then agree that democracy is to be valued for preventing totalitarianism and for preventing a strong minority from encroaching upon the basic rights of the other citizens.[80]

Each aspect of justice, however, is designed to reinforce, not to undermine, the other aspects of what is essential for human well-being. A reason for political participation, or for economic empowerment, is defensive power for oneself and for others. If political participation is used to undercut other basic rights in the community, then something has gone wrong. If democracy is used to vote justice, equality, freedom, or the preciousness of human life out of existence, then, according to Alinsky, "the process prostitutes the purpose of an open society and democracy is dead." "These values are not even debatable in a free society; they are the reasons for democratic society."[81]

To put the question in more positive terms, one participates in the community to see that the purposes that one envisages for the community are fulfilled. Such a view of the common good must include freedom and participation, but we do not engage in the community merely to be engaged. We also seek to bring Christian values to bear for "the substantive goals to which a democratic society should be moving."[82] At the same time those goals are not to be imposed in an undemocratic fashion that removes one's opponents from their own just share in the full life of the community.[83]

The problem of democracy also involves the relationship of the majority to the minority, in addition to the relationship of the majority to the government.[84] The principle of the will of the majority is capable of being used to deny the basic values of a democratic society in the treatment of a minority. Democracy itself as a political procedure provides no guarantee against the tyranny of the majority.

The false idea of a "general will" that is supposedly the final harmony of conflicting individual wills offers inadequate safeguards for the minority.[85] As correct as the democratic process may be, it provides no automatic assurance of truth. James Fenimore Cooper compared "resisting the wishes of the many" to "resisting the sovereign, in his caprices."[86]

The major way to protect minorities has been to provide a constitution that puts restraints upon self-government. The basic rights of the people are placed higher than whatever the majority can legislate through positive law. A separation of powers limits hasty actions by a majority or a dominating minority. Establishing the independence of the judiciary and granting it immense power through the authority to judge law by that constitution allows the constitution to be a living force. The separation of powers also occurs vertically as local units of government limit the extent of the central government.[87] Limits on terms for members of government provide opportunity for regular replacement of those entrusted with the tasks of leadership.[88]

Proportional representation is a further method of moderating majority rule. Through this method the number of representatives is assigned according to the proportion of votes which each party's candidates received. A party receiving only 20 percent of the votes could have two out of a total of ten representatives from the region. When the representatives are only those receiving the most votes in the various subdistricts, this party might have no representatives and possibly little chance of ever getting any.

In a proportional system, groups with different principles and programs, or those representing the interests of racial, economic, or religious minorities can have spokespersons in the deliberating bodies (provided only that they receive a certain minimum of votes). The decisions of the deliberating body itself are still by majority vote, but in this method minorities can participate in the debate and have the opportunity to form coalitions. The diversity of social groups throughout the society is encouraged.[89]

Even constitutions can be changed if the majority is large enough. Constitutional guarantees can be undercut. Democracy depends even more fundamentally upon restraint in the use of liberty through compliance by minorities and respectful toleration by majorities. "Restraint in the use of liberty is the prerequisite of liberty, the alternative to authority."[90] That is an ideal prerequisite, however. Plato's criticism of democracy was that it gave "authority to do whatever one wanted"; free vent was given to unnecessary pleasures.[91] What prevents a majority from simply following its immediate self-interest, without regard for right or for those who will consequently suffer now or in the future? A contented majority can always outvote its economically deprived and discriminated against minorities.[92] For example, in times of government deficits and economic recession, will the cost of balancing the government budget be borne by needy minorities through reduced programs and increased costs? Or will the cost be borne by a tax increase spread across the general populace?

The assurance for the moderation of government must come from outside the sphere of law from the values and customs of the people themselves.[93] Since restraint is voluntaristic, democracy needs a cultural commitment to the human family and the welfare of the public. To prevent a subversion of the process by the majority, democracy depends upon a supporting cultural system which will uphold the ends of justice. People require a sense of belonging, of nationhood, to ready them to submit individual difference to the common good. They need a pervading notion of the moral life for which their country stands.[94]

Accordingly, democracy depends upon the vitality of religion in the society. Religion provides the surest foundation and driving force for the values of a culture. Thomas Jefferson stated that our rights are grounded in faith in God. "Can the liberties of a nation be thought secure when we have removed their only firm basis, a conviction in the minds of the people that these liberties are of the gift of God? That they are not to be violated but with [God's] wrath? Indeed I tremble for my country when I reflect that God is just; that [God's] justice cannot sleep forever. . . . "[95] Tocqueville saw that the drive of self-interest that threatened every democracy was restrained in America by the supernatural goals to which religion directs: "While the law allows the American people to do everything, there are things which religion prevents them from imagining and forbids them to dare."[96] The ethic of restraint will be understood for many in the modern age in autonomous secular terms; however, for even the secular ethic to endure, it needs the foundations of a contemporaneous living religion.[97]

Freedom is also rooted in a sense of selfhood that gives capacity for moral judgment, self-regulation, capacity for self-sacrifice, and a willingness to accept the consequences of one's actions. It requires an awareness of the substance and importance of one's environment. Christopher Lasch, noting the decline in these areas in modern consumer culture, states that the greatest danger that we face is not so much the decline or collapse of political freedom as the gradual weakening of its cultural and psychological foundation.[98]

Democracy is a process that more effectively reflects the values of its people than do the alternatives. For this reason it is at the mercy of the culture's state of health. Dengerink is correct, the Sword of the Spirit (the Word) must precede the sword of the state.[99]

11

Prosperity Through Unfettered Competition: Laissez-Faire Conservatism

> The natural effort of every individual to better his own condition, when suffered to exert itself with freedom and security, is so powerful a principle, that it is alone, and without any assistance, not only capable of carrying on the society to wealth and prosperity, but of surmounting a hundred impertinent obstructions with which the folly of human laws too often incumbers its operations; though the effect of these obstructions is always more or less either to encroach upon its freedom, or to diminish its security. (Adam Smith[1])

Laissez-faire conservatism and capitalism are related historically. They are not synonymous.[2] Laissez-faire conservatism is a theory of government adopted for capitalism, which is an economic theory. For laissez-faire political philosophy, the self-regulating interplay of price values in the market solely determines the allocation of prices and productive resources as well as the distribution of social goods for the needs of people and the environment. This is to proceed without governmental assistance.[3]

Capitalism can be associated with other understandings of the state. This is partially the case even in the mixed economy of the United States, which is not strictly capitalist and is not laissez-faire. Our approach is to evaluate laissez-faire conservatism in its historical form in order to understand its basic idea. It should be acknowledged that changes have occurred in capitalism that have modified many features most open to criticism. A Russian scholar notes that even modern Marxists recognize that regulations have been introduced to make capitalism more manageable and flexible. "Socialist" economies can now benefit from the tremendous accumulation of practical experience in the long, historical development of capitalism.[4]

These changes have modified the laissez-faire aspects of capitalism.[5] The new developments also have been influenced by ideas from visions other than the original laissez-faire and capitalist dream; however, some thinkers today, including some religious scholars, remain laissez-faire in theory. Other scholars and businesspersons, while making significant concessions to governmental roles in the economy and in distribution, still regard those arrangements as at best lesser evils. They regret the spoiling of the basic underlying dream of a society free from the interventions of government. Underneath there is a sense that the original laissez-faire vision was fundamentally right and would work if it were finally fully implemented. The continuing opposition to governmental distributional programs and the shabby public programs for the disadvantaged in American society reflect the continuing influence of that dream.

The New Economic Freedom

Capitalism originated in the middle-class quest for liberty from tradition and aristocratic control. Capitalism was the economic expression of classical liberalism.

There was a notable lack of economic freedom previous to the rise of capitalism. Lending money at interest was condemned as usury in violation of the Old Testament. Excessive profits were restricted. For example, in Boston in 1644 a man was charged with making more than sixpence profit on the shilling. A pastor preaching on this contemporary event condemned the false principle of trade that an individual can sell as dear as one can or buy as cheap as one can.

Order, continuity, and current advantage were protected in many ways. Even propriety constrained economic activity. The Merchant Adventures Company in its articles of incorporation stated that no one was to carry unseemly bundles in the streets. Uniformity and security were jealously guarded. The number of threads in a fabric was controlled. In France one town could produce one number, another town another number. If the cloth was found objectionable three times, the merchant was to be put in stocks. On one occasion in the seventeenth century, in Valence, France, with the old order now under threat of economic change and new freedoms, seventy-seven persons were sentenced to be hanged, fifty-eight to be broken on the wheel, and 631 to be sent to the galleys. The crime was dealing in forbidden calico goods. Expansion was also controlled. No master hatter in England or its colonies could have more than two apprentices.[6]

The theory of national economy was mercantilism. Wealth equalled money. It provided status rather than goods to be consumed. There was close supervision of the economy by the government to achieve a balance of trade in order to heap up gold and silver. Favor was given to the particular sector of society that was considered to be most effective in accumulating that hoard. Privileged groups of merchants, manufacturers, country gentry, or working guilds received such patronage.[7]

The Puritans made contributions to support new freedom in the economic realm as they did in the political. Like liberalism in general, capitalism should not be dismissed a priori by Christians as the product of the secular enlightenment. John Calvin contributed significantly by giving legitimation to lending money at interest, a cornerstone of capitalism. In contrast, hostility toward usury was a constant theme throughout Luther's life.[8] Calvin, however, provided strict moral boundaries for lending.[9]

The Puritans provided further foundations for economic freedom and expansion. They provided a motivational basis for diligent and rational economic enterprise. The Christian disciplined oneself to carry out God's will in all one's activities including the economic. The success produced by such discipline and achievement orientation was interpreted as divine blessing or a sign of election.

The favor that the Calvinists gave to economic activity, however, was in the context of responsibility to the community. The world of the Puritans was diverse. While the English Puritan Levellers appealed to Parliament for removal of restrictions on trade, there were regulations and price controls in New England. The concept of the Reign of God led John Cotton and John Winthrop to seek economic limitations lest power and pride lead to rebellion against God's Kingdom.[10] To the early American Puritans the statement that could summarize the capitalist approach, "every man for himself and God for us all," was "wicked." Callings were profaned if pursued for profit. Temporal blessings were a recompense, not the purpose of our vocations, which is to serve God, in serving humanity.[11] Max Weber, who made the case for the Calvinist contribution to economic motivation in capitalist society in his classic, *The Protestant Ethic and the Spirit of Capitalism*, stressed that the disturbing aspects of capitalism appeared as the Puritan influence subsided:

> Today the spirit of religious asceticism . . . has escaped the cage. But victorious capitalism, since it rests on mechanical foundations, needs its support no longer. . . .
> The individual generally abandons the attempt to justify it. In the field of its highest development, in the United States, the pursuit of wealth, stripped of its religious and ethical meaning, tends to become associated with purely mundane passions.[12]

Capitalism and liberal society have suffered from the loss of the Puritan moral and social framework. Weber considered the ascendancy of materialistic concerns in capitalism to be one of many forms of inner-worldly asceticism's dissolution into pure utilitarianism (p. 183). In America by the time of the founding of national independence there was a conflict between two currents of thought about political community. The New England Puritan approach placed the individual within the covenantal context, which provided a transcending moral order that defined individual and corporate responsibilities. The other strand centered upon the individual. Social good came through the ultimately positive effects of the individual's pursuit of either one's own economic self-interest (utilitarian individualism), or of one's own self-enhancement (expressive individualism). While the tension remains, the balance has tilted in favor of the individualistic strands. Even those committed to the public good often do not perceive an objective moral basis for the public good.[13] V. A. Demant made the striking suggestion that when Christianity fails to inform the culture it largely made possible, humanity is in a more risky predicament than if it had remained pagan.[14] The dynamic emancipation and activism in history that Christianity produces then loses the discipline and check of the transcendental stance.

The dynamic character of capitalism is indisputable. The theory of economic independence was most convincingly stated by Adam Smith in his *Wealth of Nations* in 1776. Smith, summarizing thought over the preceding century, argues that the wealth of a nation is not the treasury of gold derived through trade, dear to mercantilist theory. Rather the real wealth is "the annual produce of its land and labor." "Consumption is the sole end and purpose of all production." Wealth is produced from domestic consumption. It emerges from the flow of goods and services consumed by *everyone*. This is a democratic conception of wealth. The poor, too, had drives that would lead to their personal improvement and spur the economy.[15]

Smith built his theory around capitalism. The surplus accumulation remaining after the cost of the laborers' subsistence, the machinery, and the rent of the land is received by the bourgeois class, who employ workers for wages.[16] What the owners receive is not only revenue for consumption, it is also most importantly capital for further production. Smith used *capital* to describe the property stored up for financing further production. Economic growth comes when capital is rendered active and productive. Industry cannot exceed what the capital of society can employ. In capitalism this perspective governs those who engage in free markets, rationally calculating the pursuit of profit. The machinery and land for production is private, and the workers are free.[17]

Ownership and control of the productive resources lies in a different class than that of the laborers. The greater the capital needed to stay in the market, the less possible it is for people with a small amount of property to stay in independent production.[18] The corporation, which became prevalent later, allows the cost of capital to be more widely shared, but its actual effect is to expand the class of capital ownership rather than to eliminate the significant class division with respect to ownership.

Smith argued that the market should be controlled by the basic law of supply and demand rather than the traditional external controls. This was another expression of the liberal search for the rule of universal law. Consistent with the Newtonian world, society was to be self-maintained through inherent natural laws.[19] For the material aspect of social life these laws were the laws of supply and demand of the market. Smith was a Deist. The invisible hand, which through natural laws wrought equitable distribution out of the competition of the market, was a deistic version of providence.[20] Social authority was transformed from the person to reliance on universal impersonal laws.[21]

By accurately measuring what is desired for purchase and what resources are available for sale, the interworking of supply and demand in the market takes care of the social goods needed by the society. Individuals have only to pursue their own self-interest without intention or awareness of the public interest; yet, the good of society will be produced, frequently more effectively than when one actually plans to contribute to it. "He intends only his own security; and by directing that industry in such a manner as its produce may be of the greatest value, he intends only his own gain, and he is in this, as in many other cases, led by an invisible hand to promote an end which was not part of his intention."[22]

Smith thus recognized the drives of self-interest among people but viewed them as socially useful if treated properly. The drives of self-interest produce competition within the market. Competition provides the type of goods that society wants, the quantity of goods that society wants, and the price of goods that society wants to pay. It restrains self-interest and over the total society produces harmony. "It is not from the benevolence of the butcher, the brewer, or the baker, that we expect our dinner, but from their regard to their own self-interest."[23] The rich only intend to provide for their own convenience. To secure it they must hire the poor and divide the produce with them in payment. Without knowledge or intention, "they are led by an invisible hand to make nearly the same distribution of the necessaries of life, which would have been made, if the earth had been divided into equal portions among its inhabitants," thus advancing the interests of society and the plan of providence.[24]

There is a bifurcation of means and ends within this capitalist world view.[25] Society is intentional about the means—the free market—but the ends are left to the private world as it expresses itself through the means. The difficult task in a pluralistic society of achieving a consensus about values in order to make political decisions on the ends is avoided.[26]

Smith saw in history progress over the long haul in terms of an ascending spiral. The overall trend would be good for all the people. Division of labor and specialization would increase the capacity to produce and eventually bring wealth to the lowest workers. Capital would produce more machinery, which in turn would act in a multiplying fashion in the market. The market would continue to harness people's creative powers and competition would force them to invent. Tradition and monopolies, on the other hand, had often discouraged invention as a threat to stability and control.[27]

The self-regulating quality of the economy must be respected, Smith wrote. There should be no government meddling with the market mechanism. Smith was laissez-faire regarding the economy. The government should not interfere with trade nor provide shelter from competition. The government is limited in its knowledge. Individuals know their own needs and abilities best, and in their own situation can judge the type of domestic production their capital can employ and what produce is likely to be of greatest value much better than the public administrator or legislator. A government official who

> should attempt to direct private people in what manner they ought to employ their capitals, would not only load himself with a most unnecessary attention, but assume an authority which could safely be trusted, not only to no single person, but to no council or senate whatever, and which would nowhere be so dangerous as in the hands of a man who had folly and presumption enough to fancy himself fit to exercise it.[28]

Preventing people from making all they could out of their produce or employing their capital in whatever way that they consider most advantageous violates "the most sacred rights" of humanity.[29]

Laissez-faire advocates later opposed any humanitarian legislation that could be interpreted as hampering the free operation of the market, including the whitewashing of factories or the prevention of the shackling of children to machines. They misquoted Smith, however. For him the government did have responsibilities for negative effects of mass production on the individual and for education.[30]

Dealing with Inequality

The growth in economic power that the Industrial Revolution and the new economic theory produced led to extreme class distinctions. For example, a study of wills in Lille, France, in the latter half of the nineteenth century, showed that the estate of an industrial owner exceeded that of a worker by a ratio of 20,541 to 1. Of the wealth available to be passed on to the next generation, 9 percent received 90 percent.[31] The point is not that capitalism is unique in producing or allowing great inequalities,[32] but rather that they do occur, particularly in its laissez-faire mode. Adam Smith, writing in 1776, was only at the beginning of the Industrial Revolution (often dated in England from 1790 on). This was a relatively more equal time between the dissolution of the feudal estates and before the rise of the classes of capitalism. His more egalitarian vision was inadequate for the later period.[33] Those benefiting from the new economic freedom and power now needed a rationale, both of liberty, and of such gross differences among human beings.

This rationale was required because of the avowed egalitarian ideals of post-Puritan and post-Enlightenment society. It is striking that at this same time the American South became the only slave society to justify slavery on grounds of race. Because of the emphasis in the United States upon the equality and freedom of all people, the time-honored defense of slavery as but one of several forms of subordination within economically necessary social orders would no longer do. Black slaves had to be portrayed as not truly human by reason of biological inferiority to whites.[34]

The Social Darwinism of Herbert Spencer helped to provide the needed arguments. Spencer wielded tremendous influence, including a great impact in America.[35] Charles Darwin contributed a scientific view of how evolution worked in *nature.* Spencer provided a "scientific" description of how "nature" worked in *society;* thus, his philosophy is called "Social Darwinism." Darwin went to nature for evidence; Spencer went to nature for analogies.[36]

Darwin had spoken about the struggle for existence in nature, a natural process by which all species of organic life adapted themselves to their environment. The strong live on and the weak perish, thus assuring the strongest characteristics for those that survive.

Spencer applied these concepts to human beings, developing the terminology of "the survival of the fittest." Nature working through the nineteenth-century economic world will secure the human race if it understands the conditions of its existence and is able to act upon them. Nature provides this security by weeding out those of lowest development and by subjecting those who remain to the never-ceasing discipline of experience. The selection process depends upon unrestricted competition. Those who were best adapted to the social environment of that time were regarded as those who were fittest biologically.

Since corporations rather than individuals were now the major economic actors, the competitive struggle for survival included business enterprises. John D. Rockefeller, Jr., is reported as declaring in a Sunday School address, "The growth of a large business is merely a survival of the fittest" just as a rose develops its beauty "only by sacrificing the early buds which grow up around it. This is not an evil tendency in business. It is merely the working out of a law of nature and a law of God."[37]

As the ideas of Spencer, himself an agnostic, became popularized in America, members of the clergy gave them theological support. Henry Ward Beecher declared that "God has intended the great to be great and the little to be little." Governmental paternalism in taking care of the welfare of its subjects and giving them work was against natural law.[38] William Graham Sumner of Yale, an early American sociologist and a former pastor, was Spencer's prophet in this country. He saw the current social order as built on eternal verities: "God and nature have ordained the chances on earth once and for all. The case cannot be opened. We cannot get a revision of the laws of human life."[39]

The natural laws of sorting and selection that occur in the economy should be allowed to work freely without interference. Spencer saw social evolution as so predetermined in its course that it cannot be speeded up, "yet it is quite possible to perturb, retard, or disorder the process."[40] Interference with natural selection by restricting the industrialists or by legislating social welfare for the masses would bring the unfit up into society, threatening all. It would be an obstruction to nature's course of eliminating and removing the unfit. This is a stern discipline, but it is one that is beneficent to the human race. "The poverty of the incapable, the distresses that come upon the imprudent, the starvation of the idle and those shoulderings aside of the weak by the strong, which leave so many 'in shallows and in miseries,' are the decrees of a large, far-seeing benevolence." It is this highest benevolence for the interests of universal humanity by which incapacitated laborers suffer, widows and orphans struggle for life, and the children of diseased parents are brought to early graves.[41]

Since the fertility of the race exceeds the rate of death, there is a pressure of subsistence that motivates a sharpening of skill, intelligence, and self-control, particularly in science, technology, and commerce. The government's interference through care of the poor, as in the English poors laws, hampers these reactions and may retard evolution. Thus there should be no "forcible burdening of the superior for the support of the inferior." The money used for government welfare through taxes comes out of funds that would have gone to superfluities or to savings, in either case providing jobs, which really help the poor.

There can be a mitigation through voluntary charity, however, since the amount given usually not would encourage "the unworthy" to have more offspring. Sympathy is indeed the human faculty that needs to be used more than all others. Charity is appropriate when it helps people to help themselves. Its proper recipients are the poor who have adequate skills yet have been set back by accidents, dishonesty of others, or discouragement.[42]

A role of government on behalf of the poor is accordingly both useless and destructive. Nicholas Murray Butler, president of Columbia University, said in 1907 that "nature's cure for most social and political diseases is better than [humanity's]."[43] Spencer rejected the idea that the state has a duty to protect the health of the people. He stated, "If to be ignorant were as safe as to be wise, no one would become wise." In the context of this remark, Spencer is opposing governmental licensing of the medical profession, as elsewhere in the chapter he disputes other regulations such as requiring landlords to provide ventilation and water and to clean dwellings after each tenant. Market exchanges will correct such problems. Further, the government cannot fulfill this duty without universal regimentation of the numerous details of private life. The principle of the state's being responsible for the people's health is analogous to its being responsible for moral or spiritual health. Spencer also raises the utilitarian argument that such protection of the weak is harmful to society as a whole. The ordination of life is that suffering and death are penalties and remedies for ignorance. As with physical disease those who are not sufficiently complete to live, die, so it is with incompleteness of strength, effort, agility, perception, or self-control.[44] "The whole effort of nature is to get rid of such to clear the world of them, and make room for better. Nature demands that every being shall be self-sufficient."[45]

Government is limited to a police role. If life is to be a competitive race, "the referee should not be benevolent, but neutral."[46] Although used frequently, *race* may not be the best metaphor for this vision. There is not an equal start and there is not one, unified goal. Rather, as was also affirmed in traditional conservatism, the projects pursued "are infinitely various." *Game* provides a better metaphor. The government is still to be neutral to enforce the rules. It is not to act like another player or even to be an arbiter as to who should get what at the end.[47]

Spencer saw the function of government as solely that of protector (not provider). It protects the liberty of using one's capacities in any way that is compatible with the equal freedom of the others in the society. In the economy the state is to enforce contracts and prevent cheating. Accordingly, he opposed state operation of the post office, public works, education, and the mint.[48]

A contemporary conservative such as Milton Friedman would agree with Spencer in defining the major functions of government. These are to protect freedom from external enemies and from citizens, preserve law and order, enforce private contracts, and foster competitive markets. Friedman makes some utilitarian adjustments, however. Additional responsibilities are fraught with danger; however, where there is a large advantage, government should be used to help the citizens do jointly what it would be more difficult and expensive to do separately.[49]

Social Darwinism is still with us, although it is rarely articulated as an explicit philosophy. The ideas have become thoroughly absorbed into the thought of American individualism,[50] particularly in attitudes toward the poor and people of color. Most of Spencer's ideas continue apart from the biological evolutionary context although even this has not been completely abandoned.[51] The individualistic philosophy of society requires some rationale to do what evolution did for Spencer. The weaker members must be shown to bear their own blame if there is no just reason for the community as a whole to intervene for their well being. Although they are less frequently considered to be inferior biologically, they are regarded as inferior morally, culturally, or spiritually.

We live in a success-oriented culture, and success is most apparent in material measures. A constant task is to find one's self to be strong, and the free arena of competition is a way of proving oneself to *oneself.*[52] To the association of success with self-worth corresponds the "blame the victim" attitude toward those in society who stand out by their lack of success. Welfare is hated because if the undeserving rise, what happens to the whole scoring system upon which one's self-worth depends?

Growth for the Sake of Social Justice

Capitalism brought rationalization to the market. Max Weber uses *rationalization* to describe the situation where decisions are made critically with reference to conscious goals, in contrast to tradition, superstition, or authority. Freedom from the tradition did stimulate growth and creativity.

The previous control of economic matters by traditional patterns had value in providing stability and protecting the weak, but it also provided little promise of improving the situation of the weak whose only hope was in the next world. As Peter Berger notes, the great mass of human beings eked out their existence in a subsistence economy without growth with remarkable continuity throughout history. Their lives were characterized by high rates of infant mortality, low life expectancy, inadequate nutrition, frequent starvation and disease, and high vulnerability to the ravages of nature.[53] Marxists agree that there is no going back to the preindustrial world.[54]

Capitalism led to a more efficient use of nature. Natural resources were freed for human use. In a world of hunger, one cannot discount a system that is superior in getting the greatest amount of productivity possible out the resources that God has given to us.[55] Hunger, however, does not arise from a general scarcity of resources, but from blocked or withheld access to resources.[56] Growth in itself then is not a basic solution. A world that continues to be characterized by injustice will nevertheless tend to have more available for the poor when there is more for all.

It was free enterprise that discovered a path to productivity higher than ever found before. Capitalism allowed for the first time the application of improved technology to large scale production. Entrepreneurial investors assumed the risk for mercantile ventures or the introduction of new technologies. They drew upon the aggregation of capital by others so that it was invested rather than consumed. Individuals were free to undertake the production of any product or service where profit appeared attainable.[57]

This freedom has a positive effect on the individual, similar to the impact of democratic participation, especially on those who did gain the actual freedom to vie competitively in the market. De Tocqueville described how "Americans put something heroic into their way of trading."[58] Erich Fromm comments on how capitalism "contributed tremendously to the increase of positive freedom and to the growth of an active, critical, responsible self." The individual was on one's own feet; whether one succeeded or failed was one's own affair.[59]

As new products and procedures are developed society reaps the benefit of setting free the creative aspects of the individual. The reliance upon the market recognizes the virtue of trial and error. Creativity lies with the many, not with an elite of economic experts.[60]

There are elements within capitalism, however, that are contradictory to these dynamic forces of growth. One of these lies in the pull of the market toward a time perspective overly oriented to the present. The market responds to factors of supply and demand that are present and not future. Further, management personnel as they frequently move from job to job are not concerned for the long term, by the end of which they could well have moved on to another company.[61]

Researchers at the Massachusetts Institute of Technology concluded in 1989 that the United States was losing its dominant economic position in the world because of profound defects in its culture. Among the factors that they disclosed is the tendency for American business to be preoccupied with short-term results. Several of the reasons for this orientation relate to American industry's being governed more closely by the market and a laissez-faire climate than are its rivals, particularly Japan. Because of a reliance on the profits provided by the market on the short-term, American business executives are less willing to live through a period of low cash returns that could last for decades while heavy investment is put into product development. The executives fear that such investment policies would be under-valued by the market so that their companies would be vulnerable to takeovers. The focus on short-term profits also stems from a primary commitment to shareholders versus the wider commitments made by Japanese and European firms, including the continuity and growth of the firm itself.

The active economic role of the Japanese government is also significant in pro-viding confidence for risks in product development. The governmentally coordi-nated strategy encourages exports, rewards investments in future productive growth, protects the domestic market, subsidizes research and development, and discourages conflict between firms. The result is that spending on research and development by United States firms (as a fraction of total economic output) has grown more slowly in recent years in comparison to Japan and (then) West Ger-many.[62]

An unusual advertisement by a prominent American corporation, calling for closer interaction of government, business, labor, and educators for the sake of long-range goals, strikingly anticipated the MIT conclusions. It stated, "The next quarter . . . towers over American business; a monument to short-term thinking." "In business, the future is always less than ninety days away." This has meant a decline in spending upon research and development and investment in tools and equipment. "America can no longer sacrifice its future on the altar of short-term thinking."[63]

Harnessing Self-Interest

Since laissez-faire conservatism is an expression of the liberal tradition, its under-standing of human nature has the same general characteristics. We will not repeat the evaluation made regarding human nature (and other areas held in common) in Chapter 9, but focus on more distinctive developments within the tradition.

Capitalism clearly gives a prominent role to the driving force of self-interest in society. The function of the market is to restrain self-interest through competition and channel it so that it achieves the proper ends of society. Self-interest is granted a certain free play because "there is no one in society good or wise enough finally to determine how the individual's capacities had best be used for the common good," to decide how one should be rewarded, or to anticipate efforts that one might make on his or her own initiative.[64] The social system envisaged is not dependent upon finding good people to run it.[65]

Capitalism has brought a legitimate realism to the attention of the modern world. A workable system will indeed need to channel our selfish drives for the economy. It must preserve whatever self-regulatory forces that exist in the economic process, such as in market mechanisms and in the relationship between self-interest and productivity. As a Nigerian businessman told Andrew Young, "No one stays up all night with the government's pig."[66]

The task of rational control through a central command system is too complicated and slow to be efficient and demands such extensive control as to endanger basic liberties.[67] Even before the collapse of the Soviet type of economy at the end of the 1980s, it was clear that capitalism had won a tremendous victory in establishing the necessity of the market mechanism for the allocation of productive resources and prices. If that function is what one means by *capitalism,* then capitalism needs to be universally embraced in modern society.

Such market allocation of prices and resources is only one aspect, however, of the vision that we are examining. The mechanism so effective at that level is insufficient to harness selfish drives as they affect deeper questions of ownership, inclusion in decision making, and just distribution of the basic requirements for life in community so that the interests of the weak and the strong are expressed.

This philosophy reflects the liberal lack of recognition of the radical and irrational nature of sin. A satisfactory equilibrium is perceived as possible with only a very external role for the state. As Goudzwaard put it, it is "rather foolish to expect a mechanism to permanently check and channel the impulses of human desire, will, and faith."[68] Assurances based on the valid perception that most people act with decency[69] can lead to confidence that selfishness is easily countered by the exercise of the market in the context of reason and sympathy.

Prevailing social evils in decent societies, however, cannot be contained in this mold, nor can the dynamics of exploitive power when one element in the social harmony attains more power than another. The harmony is manageable when the conflicting interests are fairly evenly matched. When they are not, the contrast of power ends in injustice.[70] Apart from its due concern about governmental power, there is a lack of realism about other forms of power in society and about the need for a corresponding application of intervening power.[71] Reinhold Niebuhr rightly states that we must be equally impatient with those who persuade people "to fear economic power but not political power, and those who teach that political power is dangerous but economic power is not."[72]

Economic life requires both moral discipline and political restraint. In addition to competition, "the guarantor against injustice in capitalism," the power of conversion and religion must internally shape individual's lives to temper selfish pursuits. Institutional requirements and restraints must provide external control.[73] "The political community must have the ultimate authority in handling economic power relationships."[74] Where the concerns of justice are involved, a sufficient subordination of economic power to political power is required.

Recent proponents of capitalism have pointed out that self-interest, which is to be pursued freely in the economy, is not identical to selfishness. Self-interest includes genuine responsibilities toward our own welfare and those of our own groups along with selfishness.[75] The opportunity to pursue legitimate interests freely and creatively belongs to the attractiveness of the laissez-faire approach.

Unfortunately, the market cannot distinguish between legitimate interest and greed. By opening the gate to so-called enlightened self-interest or rational self-interest, it loses the ability to restrain our deeper destructive self-interest. At the same time the freedom for our noble interests is an opening for drives that are destructive to human well-being and community. While a particular self-interest that is pursued may be legitimate, the drive to make the best exchange possible that is possible in the market contains no regard as to whether a particular exchange may be harmful for the other party. The impulse is still "to seek one's own interest at the expense of others." Some of the goals may be proper, but it is still a "war of all against all."[76]

Because we are so inherently interconnected and because of the destructive nature of many of our choices, more structure is needed. The ideal to allow the individual to be free from the judgments of others as to what he or she should be doing for the sake of society[77] must be balanced by intentionality in conforming the social order to the basic values appropriate to it.

Because of the human propensity for evil, all of individual and social life needs to be under some form of authority. The equilibrium that is one of basic forms of preserving social order itself requires the government's function of molding the process and modifying it. This maintains and humanizes the interplay of the social forces. Laissez-faire thought to a large degree removes the economic aspects of social force out from under this superintendence. The control of property, the most important nonpolitical form of power, which is vital to all else in society, is then only partially under authority. The ability of the whole of society to be kept just and in order is endangered.

Private economic forces in this situation can gain power with respect to the other elements of society. This power of economic power is seen not only in the buying of a legislative vote or driving a smaller competitor out of business. The savings and loan crisis in the early 1990s showed how social systems become intertwined with the advantages of the economic elite. The crisis followed a deregulation of the industry a decade earlier. The direct beneficiaries of several hundred billions of tax dollars from the general public were those who made millions in speculative ventures (some of which were fraudulent) and those with large deposits. Nevertheless, this payment was required for the common good to support the faltering savings institutions in which many diverse persons had a stake as well to maintain confidence in savings bank industry. James Madison was rightly concerned about the threat to democracy in the inordinate power of a single faction (cf. p. 45).[78]

The Historical Impact of Laissez-Faire Policy Upon Social Well-Being

Because of the removal of governmental authority from much social and economic life, the negative impact of capitalism upon society was most pronounced during the period in which laissez-faire policies were most prevalent.[79] The growing economic power of the industrial revolution was freed from governmental controls and state intervention was restricted in ameliorating the negative social forces.

Capitalism is associated with economic growth. Most people generally benefit from the improvements in the standard of living; however, the growth stretches the populace out. People stand in different relations to the market so that deeper divisions occur among them.[80] At times some sectors, even massive sectors, even have a declining standard of living. The problem at this point is when the economic model is linked to the laissez-faire model with respect to the government and the broader society. The government is hamstrung in its ability to help those who are hurting from the economic changes.

Much of the impact upon the personality, the social suffering, and environmental damage that has occurred under capitalism can be said to be a part of modern life that is much broader than capitalism. Blame cannot simply be laid at its door. The impact of technology and urbanization must be considered. Many of the symptoms also occur under command economies. Capitalism, however, still shares blame as a system. It is anemic in values to resist those factors. A characteristic of modern capitalism is "unobstructed admission to the forces of economic growth and technological development."[81] Our focus is not on the important economic debate regarding capitalism's contribution to the problems; rather it is on the political restrictions that the laissez-faire framework provided so that there was not more intentional institutional responses to the problems that arose.

Eric Hobsbawm, in commenting upon the pessimistic observations that contemporaries gave to the social situation of the early Industrial Revolution in England, between 1790 and 1850, states that there was no effective mechanism for making the distribution of the national income more equal and several for making it less so because of the prevailing laissez-faire climate.[82] The same could be said for American society during the industrial expansion from the nineteenth century to the time of the New Deal, which to a large extent ended laissez-faire capitalism.

A small fraction of the society held a great proportion of the aggregate wealth.[83] Workers experienced powerlessness in light of expanding machinery and significant unemployment in bargaining with corporations. The workers were caught at the butt end of cyclic depressions. Unemployment was substantial even in good times.[84] In times of depression some received drastic wage cuts while executive salaries and dividends were maintained.[85] Many lived in company textile towns, and some mining areas had almost feudal conditions of servility. Workers were without provisions for retirement or sickness. They labored for long working days and working weeks. Industrial accidents and deaths abounded, and there was no worker's compensation.[86] One-third of the workers were children in Southern textile mills.[87]

Workers also lived in packed tenements for which they often paid a large portion of their wages.[88] Disease and epidemics were a problem and infant mortality rose drastically in some urban centers.[89]

Among business enterprises, monopolies were formed because of the severe competition. For example, Rockefeller cornered transportation facilities against his rivals and won rebates on his rates from railroads and drawbacks from rates on his competition. He owned all kinds of industries that contributed supplies for his major enterprises. He controlled 90 percent of America's refinery industry by 1879.[90]

The capitalistic model was breaking down because of its own forces. Competition was reduced by the destruction of rivals. As Pope Pius XI later observed, domination had replaced competition in the capitalist system.[91]

These negative developments under laissez-faire capitalism were reduced only by a compromise of the theory sought not only by labor and social reformers but also by business interests.[92] Legislation was passed to provide governmental interference on behalf of the poor, the worker, and smaller businesses. The subsequent improvement across the board in health, safety, and welfare gives added evidence of the severe social liability of the laissez-faire restriction on the government's social role. The history gives evidence of what would be expected from a theological consideration of sin and power.

Business Enterprise as Voluntary Association

Capitalism has made a significant contribution to the group formations of democratic societies. One further Puritan contribution must now be mentioned. The drive for the small, free congregation and for the small, free business enterprise appeared at the same time, both rejecting centralized establishment control.[93]

The social form that eventually prevailed was the corporation. The limited liability commercial corporation is a significant voluntary association contributing to pluralism. It gives the economic enterprise an autonomy from the domination of the government and the favoritism and parochialism of the family. Accordingly, it breaks through the social and geographical boundaries that separate people. At its best, the corporation provides individuals with the opportunity to produce in association with others, engendering greater cooperation. It provides a discipline of rational control and stewardship of wealth that is not one's own. It can be a stimulating social, moral, and intellectual engagement, provoking broader loyalties and purposes.[94]

Association is not identical with community, however, and the degree to which the individual benefits from the group life of the corporation will vary according to the corporation, the part of the world in which one lives, and the position that she or he has within it. Corporations within the capitalist tradition historically have been hierarchical with forms of domination within similar to those exercised without. The South African businessman in André Brink's novel, *Rumors of Rain*, articulates this other side of capitalist relationships: "But in my sort of work there isn't any room for sentiment. Kill or be killed. And if one is forced, from time to time, to step over corpses, well, then it is simply part of the game."[95]

Such negative relationships, however, are not inherent to the idea of the corporation itself.[96] With further political visions, we will consider proposals to reshape the corporation. Already corporations within our mixed economies are becoming more participatory under the influence of some of these ideas. Marx himself recognized the social and economic contribution that capitalism made in socializing production. What remained, he stated, was to socialize property.[97]

The Market as Democracy

A significant argument for capitalism is to understand the free market as a democracy. Market democracy portrays a realistic way for all persons to look out for their interests through their own exchange. Each consumer's purchases are votes. What goods are to be supplied, in what quantity, and at what price is decided by this consumer sovereignty. In this arena only the voters decide; it is a direct democracy. The greatest amount of distribution goes on all the time in exchanges freely chosen for one's own benefit.[98]

The theory of democracy holds that the best policies result from a discussion that is inclusive of the great variety of pertinent opinion. The concept of equality of opportunity in the market also gives recognition to the God-given contributions that all members of the community have to make. The society that encourages and receives such universal contributions will be enriched the most.[99]

The type of political democracy closest to market choice is proportional representation. Majority choices of buyers are not only the ones successfully met. All sorts of minority consumer interests are able to influence sellers. The market produces an enormous variety of products in response to the demands of the public. It provides marvelous flexibility where there are significant variations in desires, tastes, and choices.[100]

There are large blocks of voters, however, whose dollar ballots are so meager that they have only partial success in affecting the market for their basic needs. If low-income housing is not profitable to build or maintain, its supply will continue to deteriorate even though the need for it increases. Democratic market choice works best when the financial means of the buyers is relatively equal. Its distributive system does not serve well those who are significantly disadvantaged. A notable illustration comes from the great famine in the Sahel of Africa in the early 1970s. While a massive amount of grain was sent as relief into the region to prevent starvation, a greater amount in cash crops was being exported by farmers of the region to wealthy nations.[101]

There are other weaknesses in the analogy of the market to political democracy. The concept of one person, one vote is easier to maintain politically than in the economic market because in the latter sphere one person can more easily multiply effective "voting" power. Not all people have equal votes. Market balloting is not one person, one dollar; the differentials become enormous. Effective self-protection and self-regulation is lost. Though everyone does participate, it cannot be described accurately as democracy.

Discussion is essential to democracy (cf. p. 156). In political democracy the process of decision making and resolving conflicts is considerably more intentional, conscious, and rational than it is in the invisible process of the economic market. ". . . political power can, at its best, express the will of a total community while economic power is by its nature private and partial."[102] In the democracy of the market, each decision is made in isolation from the decisions of other voters. It is more akin to government by plebiscite, which A. D. Lindsay declares to be "successful Caesarism."[103] The reasoning within capitalism is that of "private piecemeal considerations in the conduct of essentially collective large-scale productions."[104] In this "curious referendum," "consumers cannot initiate or participate in an effective campaign prior to the voting. All the effective speaking is done in one direction, directed at the consumers from the advertisers."[105]

More central, intentional, and publicly responsive rationalization is needed if human priorities will be met or preserved. There are aspects of social life that require more considered reflection and common discussion than do aggregate individual choices in the market. Some economic decisions that affect the whole community must be included. The market cannot efficiently deal with the diverse factors and values that go into decisions for the organization of health care or the planning of cities. It does not adequately reflect the benefits of clean air.[106] The laissez-faire process of the market, however, is the most appropriate form for private decisions for private consumption.[107]

Needs and desires are not efficiently distinguished by the market system. The market responds to wants; whether or not they are genuine needs is not reflected and does not matter.[108] The result is insufficient control of greed and unmet genuine needs. What is required for the welfare of the poor may not offer the most available profit, if any, to the sellers. As Marx pointed out, in this system because a person has no money, one's needs effectively do not exist.[109]

The consumer can vote in the market only for those options that private enterprise presents. This initiative by the seller is such that the significant costs of modern business include maintaining demand through advertising. (For example, nearly twenty cents of every retail dollar spent on breakfast cereals goes for advertising.[110]) Consumer demand is both planned and modified.[111] When the number of producers is small, as when a few corporations control at least half of the production of an item, competition in prices is the exception and low demand or high supply seldom functions to reduce prices. As a result, the consumer is less sovereign than he or she was at the beginning of the industrial revolution.[112]

The market, like political democracy, is a sensitive reflector of the values of the culture. The choices that people make in the economic sector will manifest their basic scale of values.[113] As in political democracy the choices of the majority may be destructive to the interests of the minority. Political democracy protects minority interests through a constitution. What "constitutional" framework will the economic system provide to protect such minority interests? The laissez-faire approach is hesitant to provide any checks beyond the fairness of the process. Rights, including benefit rights, however, must be part of the checks and balances on the market.[114]

Justice as Merit in the Market

Laissez-faire conservatism has a deep commitment to equality of opportunity. This arises from the liberal belief in subjective versus objective equality. One is to be equal before the law, in political rights or in freedom of association, but not in things or in economic power. Liberalism produces the ideal of equality of opportunity while its capitalistic expression produces the reality of economic inequality. Its advocates and critics disagree on the justice of the latter.

Adam Smith expressed considerable concern for the fate of the workers in the society of his day. He commented upon those who would import yarn to keep down the wages of their workers: "It is the industry which is carried on for the benefit of the rich and the powerful, that is principally encouraged by our mercantile system."[115] Favoring the interest of any one order of citizens over another was not only bad economics, it also was contrary to "justice and equality of treatment."[116] All should be able to start at the same starting line for the economic race, perhaps not with equal wealth, but under the same procedures that are open to everyone and apply to everyone from start to finish. A fundamental object of society is "to establish, so far as is humanly possible, equality before the law."[117]

The ethical principle of the market, therefore, is procedural fairness. No matter what the participants' race, creed, gender, or origins might be, exchanges are made at a fair price, and there are no tricks. No force interferes with the fairness of the bargain.[118] Fairness has become such an inherent part of our cultural values that we fail to appreciate its historical and comparative moral achievement. True equality of opportunity eliminates procedural advantages given on the basis of worth. It also eliminates political favoritism and political power as a factor in determining economic status.[119]

Capitalistic thought has a democratic emphasis on ability versus privilege of birth and rank. All individuals should be free to make full use of their knowledge and skill to pursue the particular things that they know and for which they care.[120] In a capitalist society a person with ability who was born into an environment rich in cultural attitudes, even though poor and of low status, has a possibility of significant advancement. Adam Smith emphasized the violation of "sacred natural justice" when some restriction on mobility or employment prevented workers from living and working in the places and occupations for which their strength and dexterity were most suited.[121]

Equality of opportunity, restrictive as it is, is harder to achieve without more substantive justice than conservative thinkers suggest. Markets operate effectively only when complete information is available on both sides. Sellers can then locate unsatisfied demands and buyers can detect excess supplies of goods. Even theoretically, however, people do not start with the same wealth of knowledge.

The type of justice that deals with exchange is called *commutative justice.* Capitalism receives its powerful dynamic from its ability to save a great amount of resources from consumption in order to fund further productions. The consequence is that there can be a great distance in time and space and a whole series of exchanges between the source of these funds and their final application to production. That the social meaning of the goods involved in the exchange is adequately shared by all becomes more difficult. For example, labor may be completely ignorant about a decision to move a plant. Consumers, particularly minors, may receive inadequate information about a product through advertising. Because the market is so socially important, the government has a significant responsibility to see that the exchanges are fair. In exchange its role in establishing the conditions for mutual competence will be much more involved than that envisaged for simpler forms of the market. Where these conditions do not exist, market solutions "always favor the stronger party in the exchange" while the weaker party bears the costs.[122] Commutative justice is accordingly pertinent to distributive justice.

The worker is not free to provide adequately for the security of his or her family because that security depends not only on diligence in the workplace but also on an anonymous process that dictates even whether the job exists. People do not enter an economic contract with equal freedom; rather, they differ in the degree of necessity that is upon them. Okun pointed out that a poor person who cannot afford to wait will *rationally* take a $3.50 job without opportunity for advancement over a $2.50 job with opportunity for a $5 job after apprenticeship.[123]

Once the race begins the conflict with biblical justice becomes increasingly apparent. The outcome, how distribution of society's advantages is to take place, according to laissez-faire thought is rendering to each according to each one's economic *ability*.[124] This is not the biblical conception of justice to each according to each one's *needs*. As Herbert Spencer put it, "Each adult gets benefits in proportion to merit—reward in proportion to desert."[125] According to Henry Ward Beecher, people should be ranked by their productive powers. The more brains, skills, and knowledge, the higher should be the wages.[126] Spencer draws upon traditional liberal individualism. People do not have a right to have something done for them, but only a right to do. To exercise freedom that does not take away from the freedom of others is inherent to humanity and "antecedent to society." Benefit rights, such as a "right to maintenance" or to have work provided, however, assume that a person is a member "of a community." They are, therefore, not natural rights. Such claims emerge after the "natural" condition has been replaced by organized society.[127]

The advantage of distributing justice according to this kind of merit is that the market automatically does the assignment. The distribution through the market comes from reciprocal relationships and without overt coercion in contrast to the more conscious and usually more forceful discipline of large-scale organization.[128] Justice according to needs, on the other hand, at some points requires governmental authority. Taxpayers then provide assistance against the wills of at least some. Recipients also usually have some limitations placed upon their freedom to do as they choose.[129]

The comparison of just distribution according to merit and according to needs can be stated in another way. Laissez-faire conservatives are correct in seeing the market as a great and valuable distributor of goods. Many of the basic needs and legitimate wants of a great many people are provided for in this way.

There are some matters, however, that must not be left solely to the processes of the market. The concept of human rights points to such matters. Freedom rights should not be decided by the market at all. For example, the right to a jury trial is not to be sold, nor are ballots for voting.[130] Benefit rights, in contrast, are adequately provided for many by the market.[131] This is the market's proper and most essential function. Where they are not provided, however, the community as a whole has a responsibility to modify the market process or to supplement it. The government has an ultimate responsibility for the benefit rights of those who are left deficient. The clearly defined basic requirements for life in community are to be secured. They are the first priority. Subsequent market distribution according to merit is not excluded. The goal of justice is not complete leveling, nor is it to be motivated by resentment at elitism[132] (although we have seen other theological reasons for concern about great concentrations of power).

One takes out of the competitive market what one puts in when the exchanges are fair.[133] The input is not a measure of individual merit or effort, however. The effectiveness of effort differs according to its accompaniment by ownership of productive property or specialized knowledge.[134] The liberal individualism of laissez-

faire thought fails to perceive accurately environmental factors that provide fortu-
nate circumstances to some and prevent them for others through no fault of their
own. As Victor Hugo commented, in such thought "prosperity supposes capacity.
Win in the lottery, and you are an able [person]."[135]

Economic efficacy expresses differences in family background, privileges, and
status so that one reaps what others have sown.[136] P.J.D. Wiles observes that the
distribution of wealth is a matter of "economic and political history—three long
words for which the single shorter one, 'chance,' might be substituted without great
loss." He states that there have been no truer words than those of Irving Fisher, who
said that the distribution of wealth is due to the "unequal forces of thrift, ability,
industry, luck, and fraud." Where one is born makes a great difference on how
much income one can expect.[137] Studies have shown that the wealth of one's parents
has a significant impact upon one's own wealth and earnings, even apart from how
much education one receives.[138] *Fortune* is an astute term for wealth, and lottery
expresses a significant aspect of economic life missed in the imagery of race.

Production in the market also is part of a complex, interdependent system. It
cannot be neatly attributed to individual contributors.[139] Moreover, the competition is also between groups, often differing sharply in their size and command of
resources.[140]

The justice of the market is presented by some thinkers in terms of distribution
according to worth (proportional equity).[141] The market distributes according to
one's contribution to the economy. Since the contribution is specifically to the
economy and not to society,[142] and since it is not asserted that market value is the
same as true or ethical value, this form of worth appears in reality to be another way
of stating ability in the market.

The capitalist's wealth and power is said to reflect the importance of capital to
the modern economy.[143] The argument for a reward to those with modest incomes
who sacrifice the immediate pleasures of spending in order that society might have
productive capital has merit. The concept of risk becomes stretched, however, when
those who make the largest investments "do so without any diminution of even the
most luxurious living standards."[144] The modern corporation does not need millionaires, who perform no unique economical function.[145] Sufficient capital can be
obtained through more equitable means.

Conservatism has provided a helpful reminder of the importance of production.
Those who emphasize the self-reliant individual perceive that more is required than
caring for minimal sustenance needs in the form of a safety net. Long-term community participation calls for the individual to have productive power. Laissez-faire
restrictions, however, prevent the conservative from drawing out the full implications for justice. The provision of the basic need for productive resources and
empowerment belongs to distributive justice. The distributive functions of justice
must include productive resources, including access to, control over, and economic
ownership of the means of production.[146]

The original definition of capitalism includes the means of production being possessed by a different class than that of the workers.[147] This integral dimension of
capitalism is incompatible with the biblical conception of productive property possessed by all as part of what is basic to life in community.[148] As we are using the term

capitalism has by definition an inherent injustice. If one defines *capitalists* as those who receive at least half of their income from capital ownership, then less than 5 percent of Americans are capitalists. Well over half own no capital at all.[149] Capitalism as understood by those who do not include this concept of ownership in their definition obviously does not come under this critique to the degree that the system that they have in mind supplies this need to all.

Cultural Implications

The strength of the laissez-faire approach to justice is the secure place it provides for freedom rights. The ends for which production is to be used are left to the choice of the individual, as we have seen.[150] An aspect of being a human person is being one who pursues "projects"—ends that a person pursues for long stretches throughout one's life, which motivate one's actions, and which are a part of one's self-identity. Part of being a member of the community is having the moral space in which to select freely these ends and not to have someone else, especially the state, decide them for oneself. Rather, the state's function is to protect that moral space for each person. Basic freedom rights are constraints ensuring that "individuals can pursue projects amidst a world of similar beings, each with his own life to lead, and each owing the same measure of respect to others that they owe to him."[151]

Eduard Heimann, however, notes a cultural cost. In reality the competitive and materialistic struggle, which is supposed to be only the means, psychologically becomes the end despite the human quality of many projects because it is pursued through great effort and peril.[152] The absence of socially stated ends and the emphasis on material pursuit impacts the character of its people, who reflect the materialism, competition, and self-orientation that the system teaches in theory and in practice. The substance of one's day is governed by the principle of giving as little to the other person as possible while getting as much as possible from her or him. This sharply contrasts the principle of demanding little for oneself while giving much service.[153]

Superfluous acquisition is encouraged as ultimately contributing to the good of society, yet such pursuit is contrary to Scripture. John McCulloch, an early nineteenth-century exponent of classical economics, made recommendations for economic growth: "The first and grand object ought always to be to excite a taste for superfluities; for, when once this taste has been excited, it is comparatively easy to give it any particular bias or direction; and until it has been excited, society can make no progress."[154] Scripture, however, specifically condemns devotion to the acquisition of wealth: "Do not toil to become rich."[155] John Wesley drew upon the ancient Christian tradition going back to such biblical texts. "If a man pursues his business that he may raise himself to a state of honour and riches in the world, he is no longer serving God in his employment. . . . For vain and earthly designs are no more allowable in our employments than in our alms and devotions."[156]

The negative impact upon character undercuts capitalism's historical strength in its attitude toward time. This is another cultural contradiction within capitalism. We noted earlier the present orientation encouraged by the market perspective. Historically, capitalism was nevertheless driven by the positive orientation to the future characteristic of liberalism (cf. p. 141). The act of saving, which is necessary for the increase of capital, always involves thinking beyond the present and some degree of self-denial in the present.[157] Adam Smith stated that "parsimony, and not industry, is the immediate cause of the increase of capital." What is saved from revenue is added to capital and puts an additional quantity of productive resources into motion.[158]

Business in advertising, however, has stimulated a contradictory character of self-indulgence and orientation to the present, undercutting the Protestant virtues of thrift, industry, and self-discipline for production, capital formation, and organizational commitment that has motivated the economy.[159] Rosalind Wells, the chief economist for the National Retailer Marketing Association, described the generation of "baby boomers" (a third of the American population in the early 1990s), "They have a lifestyle characterized by wanting." "They want everything. They don't want to postpone. They're big spenders, not savers, and they have a lot of needs at this time of their lives."[160] In Smith's terms, although the economy needs frugal persons, who thus are "public benefactors," it is instead encouraging a society of prodigals, its own "public enemies."[161]

Another problem with leaving the ends for society in the hands of isolated individual choices rises from the perspective of the Reign of God over all of life. One cannot dismiss the tension between biblical justice and consequences of the market in situations where those who do physical work have basic human needs unfulfilled while managers and owners enjoy a significantly higher well-being and social status.[162] Aristotle criticized Sparta for seeking the common good through pursuit of one particular virtue. For Sparta it was courage in war and conquest; for capitalism it is economic freedom. The virtues rather need to be pursued directly and intentionally.[163]

Paul Tillich diagnosed the self-sufficient view of the world that is presupposed. The world is calculable and manageable by science and business. Value concerns need not enter in. "Since the beginning of the eighteenth century God has been removed from the power field of [human] activities. [God] has been put alongside the world without permission to interfere with it because every interference would disturb [humanity's] technical and business calculations."[164] There is a conflict between the perception of a divinely based order for life and a process that must be left alone for selection through unobstructed competition.[165] In this way, laissez-faire conservatism is a significant expression of and contributor to secularization.

12

Unfolding the Possibilities of Humanness: Marxist Socialism

"They determined to send support to the brothers and sisters living in Judea *each according to each one's ability*" (*Acts* 11:29).
They gave the proceeds of selling their lands and houses *"to each as any had need"* (*Acts* 4:35).

Karl Marx in his *Critique of the Gotha Program* in describing the standard of justice [*das Recht*] states that the goal is to bring society to a point where "the narrow horizon of bourgeois right [can] be crossed in its entirety and society [can] inscribe on its banners: 'From each according to his ability, to each according to his needs!'"[1] This central theme of Marxism is taken from the New Testament.[2] In both contexts the concern is the highest standard for human relationships in material things.

This New Testament stem of a key Marxist principle is tantalizing, and it should stimulate us to a more thorough evaluation of Marx's thought from a Christian perspective. Marxists would be the first to note the very different context in the early church for the Christian standard. It is more important to examine carefully Marx's vision in light of Christian foundational concerns for political thought.

Pessimism in Classic Economics

Adam Smith did his writing in the more gentle period at the beginning of the Industrial Revolution. The succeeding classical economists were pessimistic, reflecting the social crises of the half century following Smith.

Thomas Malthus worked with a theory that centered on population and wages. It is food that regulates the number of people. Population increases geometrically while food increases only arithmetically. Famine is the last resource of nature to preserve the race. From the perspective of David Ricardo some classes rise to the top, but some go to the bottom. In contrast to Smith, society is not a great family, but a bitter contest for supremacy. The pressure in the increasing demand for land forces prices to rise. John Stuart Mill sought to temper the laissez-faire helplessness before the impending crisis by restricting the domain controlled by economic laws to that of production; society can make intentional changes in distribution.[3]

The most pessimistic of the classical economists was Karl Marx. His *Das Kapital* is the necessary sequel to the teachings of Smith and Ricardo. He noted that Ricardo and Mill had seen that the market is indifferent to the fate of the workers. Production goals do not take into consideration the number of workers that a given amount of capital maintains, but the amount of interest that it earns. Marx sensed the imminence of even deeper problems. The economic crisis is not caused by the increase of population; this is a libel on the intelligence of the human race. The crisis is from the pressure of unemployment on wages. When the economy expands, there is more demand for workers. With the greater demand the employer must give higher wages. To counteract this pressure on the overhead of labor, the employer introduces labor-saving machines, which produce unemployment. Machines, however, are worth only what they can produce; the employer receives back only what was paid for the machines. One's profit is from the time in which workers labor beyond earning their own wages for their sustenance. With increased unemployment, market consumption dwindles, and the economy is thrown into a series of crises, each one bigger than the previous one, until there is a collapse of the whole system.[4]

Making the World Attuned to Human Needs

While Marx shared in the pessimism of the other economists of his time, he refused to leave the matter as one only to be described. The situation had to be changed. In light of his conception of history he saw that it would be changed. Nevertheless, human action was also called for as a vehicle of that turn of events. Ideas only change ideas. Activity is necessary to change reality. "The philosophers have only *interpreted* the world in various ways; the point is to *change* it."[5]

Marx was concerned to put justice into the universal structure, not into an experiment in the woods that could influence only by example. Justice is to be world-forming and world-transforming. Justice is activistic. It delivers and restores, and is also like biblical justice in being patterned by the expectation of a new society that compels one's actions in the present.

The most significant thing about Marx is his passion for a justice that is compatible in several ways with biblical justice. Many scholars have been uncomfortable with describing Marx's thought in terms of values and ethics because of his criticism of bourgeois ethics, as well as the scientific atmosphere of his writings. Underlying this thought, however, is a firm assumption of values, indeed a passionate devotion to them. The values of justice and truth are grounded in his conception of what it is to be human.[6]

Marx's attention was directed to the weak and oppressed element in industrial society, the proletariat. Such an orientation to the disadvantaged is biblical. Marx's view of justice was that of equality and beyond equality. In the *Critique of the Gotha Program* he states that "right instead of being equal would have to be unequal" because some workers have more needs than others. They may be married or have more children. Justice requires distribution to each according to each one's needs.[7]

In his application of justice Marx resisted any *right* of inequality that one should receive more because of greater productive ability. Liberal theory made natural inequalities a principle of justice. The just distribution to workers in accordance with their contribution of labor, the basis of the socialist critique, was to be modified by distribution according to basic needs. A human being is not simply a producer when distribution is considered, but is also a person with needs.[8] Distribution according to needs is a higher principle of justice, held back only by the present condition of society.[9]

Marx demonstrated that among such needs there is one that has been neglected in other modern theories of justice. We are reminded that access to "the objective conditions of property" (i.e., to the means of production) is a key component of life in community and thus a demand of justice.[10]

Marx's Support of Political Freedom

Marx held that rights can never be higher than the economic inclusiveness of society and the cultural development conditioned by it. Formal, political democracy without economic and social empowerment imperfectly tries to abolish alienation within the sphere of alienation. He is writing of those who have political liberties but are so consumed by the struggle to provide for the needs of their families that they do not have time to use them. They are then but "imaginary member[s] of an imaginary sovereignty." The everyday life that they experience in society and in the economy is instead one of isolated individuals who treat others as means. They experience their own selves as mere instruments and playthings of alien powers.[11] Their freedoms are on the books, but in their exhausted lives they cannot avail themselves of them.

His point is profound, though overdone. Political relations also are concrete, and political rights have some protective value even for the economically oppressed. Marx shows correctly, however, their artificiality with respect to relations left untouched by political emancipation.

Marx does not deny the importance of freedom rights. He struggled for them throughout his career. Political emancipation "represents a great progress," but it is not the final step of progress.[12] Taking the full range of rights seriously requires producing social and economic institutions that allow people the leisure and energy to follow the possibilities that freedom provides. They can then pursue the development of their own selves and contribute to the development of others.

Marx's support of freedom rights is reflected in his devotion to democracy. Originally a young liberal journalist who championed political democracy, Marx, according to Hal Draper, was "the first socialist figure to come to an acceptance of the socialist idea *through* the battle for the consistent extension of democratic control from below."[13] "The party of the red republic" was characterized by "adherence to democratic–republican institutions."[14] Marx argued for freedom of assembly, freedom of the press, minimization of executive power, and maximization of the representative system. Pushing democratic forms to the point of genuine popular control from below would eventually extend into the organization of the whole society, including the economy. The fight for democratization in the state was a leading edge of the socialist effort.[15] Marx also saw that genuine democracy does not exist as long as there are gross inequalities and dominating elitist interests—a democracy that does not abolish class differences and class property.

Marx stated that universal suffrage would be a far more socialistic measure than anything favored by the name of socialism on the Continent. It is not compatible with the state controlled by the capitalist classes. When universal suffrage is incorporated into the bourgeois state, a tension is produced between the constitution and the social forces in the society.[16] The result is either the perversion of universal suffrage by the bourgeoisie to protect their advantage or the victory of the proletariat. Marx felt that in developed countries—England, America, Holland—the victory of the proletariat majority would be synonymous with "winning the battle of democracy"; the capitalist state would be changed by legislation rather than by violence.[17] Revolution for Marx means "forcible," not necessarily armed, radical change. He appears to advocate the use of arms to subdue capitalists only as a defense.

"The *class dictatorship* of the proletariat" meant class rule by the proletariat just as the bourgeois class had ruled in previous democracies.[18] *Dictatorship* did not have the pejorative associations that it has for us. It meant the direction of society by the proletariat, who were the majority. The proletariat would become the ruling class by winning the battle of democracy. The coercive agency of the state would be employed for the first and last time in history by "the immense majority, in the interests of the immense majority."[19] Moreover, the forces of history would increasingly make the interests of society in general that of the proletarian class.[20]

Richard Hunt shows from the context of Marx's first extensive use of *dictatorship* around 1848 that it connoted measures that were unavoidably outside the established legal framework although representing the will of the majority.[21] When Marx later applied the term to the rule of the proletariat, he was borrowing the Blanquists' terminology in trying to persuade them to accept the inclusiveness of class, rather than clique, rule. Louis Blanqui and his followers were using the term for their conception of revolutionary government by an elite.[22]

Friedrich Engels, Marx's long-standing colleague, stated, "Do you want to know what this dictatorship looks like? Look at the Paris Commune." All offices there were filled by the "infallible means" of "election on the basis of universal suffrage of all concerned, subject to the right of recall at any time by the same electors."[23] The Paris Commune, which was to serve as a model, was "the self-government of the producers" when every person was a producer—"a government of the people by the people."[24]

The selection of the term *dictatorship,* however, was careless—a part of Marx's general carelessness about the potentiality of abuse of proletarian power. It easily could be taken as the rule of the few, which is what happened.[25]

The higher phase of communism would be a true democracy. This society would no longer have a sphere of state power nor a sphere of private interest differentiated from that of society. State power would be reabsorbed by society and would operate largely in local social units rather than in hierarchic forces of a central government controlling and subduing society.[26] The goal is the control of people over all of their life—a basic democratic impulse.

Marx was mistaken in his expectation. Twentieth-century communists found no countries with a proletarian majority. The communists ignored this contradiction to their theory. Although operating in the name of democracy, they forsook it for a uniform one-party rule based on a denial of freedom rights.[27]

The Central Core of Justice

Carol Gould demonstrates that the key principle in Marx's thought for identifying what validly belongs to justice is that which provides the conditions for individual self-realization.[28] This positive freedom as the key may seem more individualistic and Aristotelian than the biblical rule of thumb of that which is essential for life in community. The approaches are not incompatible, however, since individual self-realization for Marx requires full participation in community, and a biblically just community provides the freedoms that enhance the opportunities for the individual to be saved, worship God, and pursue perfection.

Marx had a strong sense of commutative justice, the justice that pertains to exchange, in addition to the distributive justice that we have been following. Marx held that exchange must be reciprocal so that the interests of each party are met.[29] In the capitalistic market, however, the equality and liberty that seem apparent in the positing of prices and their circulation disappear beneath the surface.[30]

Labor, which the worker offers in capitalistic exchange, is for Marx a productive activity that creates new value. What capital receives, then, is not a mere commodity, as the terms of the exchange would indicate. Rather, it receives a creative, value-producing activity. In the exchange of one's labor capacity, the laborer "surrenders its *creative power,* like Esau his birthright for a mess of pottage."[31] Although the exchange was for labor as a commodity, the capitalist in fact receives the value-producing capacity of the labor without giving equivalent return. The laborer exchanges labor for subsistence. The rest of the time, in which labor is used to produce capital, the laborer is unpaid; it is a "theft of alien labor time."[32]

Contrary to commutative justice, the exchange is not of benefit to both parties. It in fact harms the participants who offer their labor. Labor's quality of producing new value is removed from the worker as it is alienated. We will discuss later the importance that the product of labor has for self-realization as the individual discovers in it her or his capacities. This is also lost. In addition, the exchange is not one of freedom since the worker is not free *not* to sell her or his labor because the wages go for subsistence.[33]

Gould sees Marx's view of justice in exchange to be more than reciprocity in which the interests of both parties are met. Justice requires mutuality in which the self-realization of the other party is sought.[34] She is correct that this is a principle of justice for Marx, not merely an additional social value. Society and its institutions are formed around it. The principle of mutuality ensures individual participation in communal control over the processes of social life and over social production.[35]

Commutative justice contributes to distributive justice. This mutuality in social exchange is one of the conditions of positive freedom, which is central to justice.[36] Perhaps Marx's most distinctive contribution to our understanding of justice is that participation in social processes that enhance the growth of all members of the community is essential to membership in community.

Marx's significance for social justice also lies in the fact that he saw that the vision of social right had to be combined with a strategy based on a thorough understanding of history and society, including the nature of power in the present society. No one else has so comprehensively and explicitly incarnated this passion for justice into an analysis of society. Marx's originality is seen in his immense effort to synthesize the entire legacy of social knowledge since Aristotle in a critical way. (He did not complete this project.) Heilbroner notes that although unnecessarily laborious, cumbersome, and at times oblique, Marx's economic model did accurately disclose hidden tendencies in the economic and social world that he described. Heilbroner calls it "the gravest, most penetrating" examination that was ever made of the capitalistic system. "For all its passion, it is a dispassionate appraisal. . . ." Nevertheless, Marx did not perceive the remedies that rose up within liberal society. That society changed into a social atmosphere different from what he knew.[37]

The development within people of their true potential as human beings, however, was an even more central concern for Marx than was social justice.[38]

Human Growth and Creativity

Marx seeks to free our full individual potentials so that they may be expressed in various forms not found in a uniform, state-ridden society. The proletariat values its self-respect and independence more than bread.[39] Marx criticized proposals to increase wages, or even to equalize incomes, because this type of change does not extend the needed "human significance and worth" "to the worker or to the work." It only universalizes private property with its attendant vices of envy and materialism.[40] The variety of life is as much an aim of true communism as equality of condition, and nothing but a union of these two would bring about real freedom. Marx criticized "crude communism" for negating the human personality in every sphere and wishing to eliminate talent by force.[41]

Fromm rightly links Marx with the humanist socialists of the nineteenth century.[42] From Marx's viewpoint the life of those in the society around him was alienated from their essence as creative beings and as social beings. The creator had become subject to his or her creation. A person's self-consciousness was thwarted by a perversion in the relationship to his or her own activity, to others, and to nature.

The goal is the emancipation of the individual from five forms of alienation within capitalistic society. The human being is alienated from nature, from one's own self, from one's labor, from the products of one's labor, and from others. Alienation means that human distinctions are lost. Human life takes on the qualities of animal life.

The concept of alienation is important in understanding the assumptions Marx held about what it is to be truly human. His conception of the human essence functions as an ideal form in Marx. It reveals many positive components of his understanding of human nature that a Christian analysis can affirm. It forms the basis for an eros or mythos of technology. If its true ontological grounding were perceived, it could serve to overcome the domination of technology.[43] In contrast to alienated existence, a person is to have freedom, self-direction, creativity, and mutuality with other human beings.

Each of the forms of alienation expressed the person's alienation from one's own self. The self includes within it an effective relationship with nature, with creative labor, and with others. In alienation, "*my* means of life belong to *someone else . . . , my* desires are the unattainable possession of *someone else . . .*" The capitalists also suffer alienation as they see humankind and their own selves as a sacrificial and superfluous being, caught in the same inhuman power that rules over everything.[44]

In emancipation, the human world and human relationships would be restored to the individual. All of one's "inner wealth" would then be born. A person would develop her or his own true gifts, abilities, and interests.[45] In the higher phase of communist society the value of labor would be elevated, and "the all-round development of the individual" would emerge.[46]

The human being, Marx wrote, has also been alienated from nature, which is one's inorganic body. One must live in continuous interchange with nature in order not to die. Nature, however, was progressively becoming less the means of existence for one's labor and one's physical subsistence in industrial life. It no longer formed a bond with other people as the basis of their existence for each other.[47]

The human being is also alienated from labor. The workers no longer fulfill themselves in their work. Their mental and physical energies are not developed freely. Instead they are physically exhausted and mentally debased. "The worker feels himself at home only during his leisure time, whereas at work he feels homeless." The workers feel themselves to be freely acting only in their animal functions—in eating, drinking, sexual relationships, or at the most in their own dwelling and in personal adornment. At the same time, in the person's uniquely human function as a worker, he or she is "reduced to an animal." The human being becomes "abstract activity plus a belly." The tasks produce stupidity and cretinism for the workers; for some, they are barbarous. The stimulating scientific and technical knowledge of production is absorbed by the capitalist class.[48]

Labor does not in itself satisfy a need; rather, "it is only a *means* for satisfying other needs." Instead of being free and self-directed, labor is compelled only by a physical need, as it is for the animals. The work is not one's own. In it one does not belong to oneself but to another person.[49]

The worker also is alienated from the products of labor, from one's own creation. One's labor is appropriated by the employers as capital, which adds to their power over the worker. The result is that the more the workers produce, the more they fall under the domination of their own product. "The worker puts his life into the object, and his life no longer belongs to himself but to the object." The means of the worker's existence are in the hands of the capitalist. "The more objects the worker produces the fewer he can possess." The products of the labor produce beauty and luxurious mansions for the rich, but hovels and deformity for the laborer.[50]

This alienation is particularly significant because of Marx's extremely high evaluation of creative labor and its place in his psychology. Individuals discover their mature identity by recognizing their capacities in their work. They are changed by this. From among the different capacities reflected in the product, a person is free

to choose the aspects that she or he wishes to develop and to be. In alienation, however, individuals no longer recognize themselves in their labor. It has become a
removed object in its new form as capital.[51]

Alienation, Marx states, is first expressed in the alienation between each individual and every other individual. A person becomes separated from the community,
drawn into oneself, and preoccupied with one's own private interests.[52] Being successful in competition meant that one was able to convert more of the powers of
others to one's own use than they are able to convert from oneself.[53] In the economic system the worker is an object, valued only as a producer of capital. One
"exists only as worker, not as a human being." The worker's social significance is
parallel to that of any other productive instrument. In contrast, emancipation is a
return of the individual to oneself "as a *social*, i.e., as a really human, being."[54]

All social relations are affected; the alienation is not only between classes. In the
relations of the market, the relations are that of things. Everyone seeks to use others
only as a means for one's own egoistic needs.[55] The inner wealth of a plentitude of
physical and intellectual senses has been replaced simply with the sense of personal
possession.[56] One has lost the human consciousness of oneself as a person for others,
rising above animal isolation.

Capitalism does neglect the noneconomic aspects of human beings, such as creativity and meaning in labor. For Smith "the sole end of production is consumption." Production, however, should also be a vocation of service so that income and
consumption might be sacrificed for a productive technology that is more humane
and more joyful. Economic development needs to be attuned to broader norms.
For the classical economists, particularly Mill, labor is a disutility, a drain on profit
rather than a satisfaction of need. Economic rationality means that the primary
concern for labor is to keep expenses down.[57] Capitalistic theory fails to support
adequately the value of human producers and their creative abilities.

Marx argued rigorously that to be really human is to be a social being. He
describes the human being as a "species being."[58] The individual is conscious of
being part of the whole human race, with corresponding ties, social longings, and
responsibilities. The other person becomes one of my needs. He or she is our greatest wealth. Association with others is a sufficient end in itself.[59] In contrast, the problem with political rights unaccompanied by the creation of community through the
economic empowerment of all is that the rights then serve the private interests of
isolated beings, who are withdrawn into themselves.[60]

Marx's critique of alienation assumes a positive freedom that stresses the self-
development and self-determination of the individual that can occur only within
harmonious relations with others. As one recognizes oneself in the products of one's
labor, one also finds self-recognition and self-creation in relating to other individuals.[61]

Individuality must be preserved within this recognition of community. Marx saw
communism as the solution of the conflict between the individual and the species.
He attempts to avoid a polarization to either individualism or to collectivism,
where society in general is the final subject.[62] A person is both an individual and at
the same time a social being.[63] He or she is "a unique individual," "a really *individ-*

ual communal being"; and Marx underlined *individual.*[64] The individual is the fundamental entity of society.[65]

Society is not to be a new excuse for crushing individuality. There is not a social being independent of individuals that has needs that must be met before theirs. Social life is not an abstraction, but other individuals with whom I am linked. "The individual *is* the *social being.*"[66] Marx resists the argument that the product of labor belongs to society since useful labor is possible only through society. Such reasoning has been twisted as desired by the champions of whatever state of society is prevailing at a given time.[67] The claims of society are really claims of individuals, and they are to be accepted or rejected as such. Throughout history, whenever it seems that society prevails over individuals, it is really the domination of some individuals by other individuals. Marx's vision is a "community of free individuals" freely agreeing to their enterprise.[68] It means democratic equality.

In this connection we should make the additional observation that Marx rejects dogmatic materialism. The human being is the instrumental actor in the movement of material history. History significantly limits and conditions what can be done, but individual responsibility and initiative lie within those boundaries. "[People] make their own history, but they do not make it just as they please."[69] "The materialist doctrine that men are products of circumstances and upbringing, and that therefore, changed men are products of other circumstances and changed upbringing, forgets that it is men that change circumstances, and that the educator himself needs educating."[70] The proletariat's recognition of the positive consequences of uniting to transform society is an expression and an advancement of the historical process.[71] There is a tension between individual free will and historical determination.

In summary, there is a strong strand of individualism in Marx's thought, reflecting the powerful individualism of the nineteenth century. Marx's individualism is not antisocial, however, because for him true individuality is defined to include consciousness of responsibility for others. Marx departed from liberal individualism in his achievement of strongly affirming the social nature of humanity while retaining individual identity.

Individualism and the Major Institutions of Society

Marx perceived powerful social forces that both positively and negatively condition individual life. Marx's social criticism makes one of its most significant contributions in the recognition of the difference between institutional life and individual life. The destructive effects of the capitalist society were not due to the ill will of individual capitalists, but to the structural forces of the economic process. The institution of capitalism rather than the individual capitalist is to blame.[72] The social conflict is to not to be explained in terms of individual antagonisms, but in terms of tensions rising from the conditions of society.[73] One of Marx's greatest influences upon subsequent intellectual history lies in his contributions to the conception of institutional causation for sociology and of structural evil for social ethics.

The deficiency of Marx's individualism is found in his neglect of essentiality of groups for human life. This individualism is apparent in the informal networks of social reciprocity to which the power of the state will be returned. Its detrimental aspect appears in a lack of appreciation for the permanent need for formal, large group institutions. This optimism opens the door to renewed exploitation. It does not provide institutional controls on oppression emerging from new concretions of private egoism. It does not formulate an institutional theory to provide checks on oppression arising from within the institutions that inevitably must emerge.

The simple and unstructured form of institutions in the final phase of society indicates a point of view that links institutions primarily with our alienation. Marx is close here to relative natural law theory in Christianity that sees institutions as a result of the fall and necessary only as a restraint on sin. As in Christianity, the utopian final phase reverses the fall.

Marx frequently wrote of the eventual abolition[74] of the state. Richard Hunt demonstrates that the end of the state meant two things for Marx. First, there are no longer professional rulers distinct from the rest of the people. This political development is connected to important general characteristics of the eventual communist society. Many significant divisions are ended, including that between city and country, between manual and mental labor, and exclusive gender roles in employment. Most important for our discussion, the division of labor is transcended (*Aufhebung*[75]).

Transcending the division of labor for Marx is not a return to the simplicity of a craft and agrarian society. Marx and Engels are speaking about an economy of scientific agriculture and factory production, using all the advances of science and technology. Each individual, however, will then develop several skills, and there will be a rotation of positions. Public service, along with management in the economy, is included. As in the Paris Commune, professional soldiers, bureaucrats, and judges all will be gone. The Paris Commune was "a resumption by the people of its own social life," "the reabsorption of the State power by society, as its own living forces instead of forces controlling and subduing it."[76]

The second way in which the state would come to an end is that coercive power passes away. With the complete ending of bourgeois property and resistance, the "*forcible* means" of proletariat rule come to an end.[77] Engels notes that authority as the will to which others have to be subordinated is inherent in organization; it will always be present in large-scale industry—even if that authoritative will ideally is only embodied in a delegate, or a committee, charged with executing a majority resolution.[78] What will come to an end is the command by others against their will by the use and threat of force.

Marx held that the authority relationships within the workers' cooperative movement provided an organizational model of what would eventually occur societywide. In the "republican and beneficent association of free and equal producers," the worker members willingly subordinate themselves to the managers whom they elect, pay, supervise, and remove. "The distribution of general functions has become a routine matter which entails no domination."[79]

"Public power" remains, but it will have lost its "political character" by which one class oppresses another.[80] In this society there would be a continuing administrative role in direction and planning of the economy. A few but important legitimate functions for the central government continue. They are "discharged by Communal, and therefore strictly responsible agents."[81]

The institutions that remain will carry on the positive functions of institutions. These institutions would consist of the entire population involved in worker cooperative associations, which exist on a national scale. The delegates who are responsible for the national, central administration are responsible to the local units. In addition Marx's interest in the full development of arts and skills would suggest the probability of cultural associations. Religious associations could continue for any who might still take seriously what Marx regarded as the irrelevancy of religion. These institutions, with the continuing forms of the family, would ensure the accomplishment of the positive and necessary social functions of preserving traditional knowledge, imparting culture, seeing that the tasks essential to society get done, and determining the final good in the midst of varying individual interests. That they indeed would be sufficient is tied to the other aspect of the human condition that calls forth institutions, the more difficult problem for Marx of the continuation of human sinfulness.

Marx's anticipated social framework is not sufficient for the continuing occurrence of group and personal exploitation, materialism, and sloth that is inevitable because of the permanence of evil. Marx again appears as a classical economist, sharing both the minimalistic conception of the state and the lack of a penetrating view of human sinfulness with laissez-faire economic theory.[82] Alasdair MacIntyre has stated that Marxism has suffered "moral impoverishment as much because of what it has inherited from liberal individualism as because of its departures from liberalism."[83] To evaluate the fairness of this assessment, a more detailed look at Marx's view of human evil is called for.

In many respects Marx can be considered a realist—one who recognizes limits that resist ideals. Marx has been the most potent critic of liberal illusion and liberal optimism. He carried out rigorous attacks on the utopianism of other socialists. The socialist humanism of which Marx was a part was itself part of the Romantic reaction against the perceived utilitarianism and economic reductionism of the new economic order.[84] As Tillich saw, however, Marxism was also a countermovement against the resulting idealism.[85] Marx's critique of the utopian socialists was directed at their expectation of being able to mold history by personal innovative action and contrived organization. They relied on the force of example of their small experiments. They wanted to achieve their ideal in opposition to the reality of society, which for them had no shadows. They presented no program that would establish their social ends by restricting or eliminating the causes of oppression.[86] Others who proposed more just or equal pay for workers also neglected defensive power by concentrating on distribution and ignoring production.[87] Change must come in the form of far-reaching intervening power. ". . . Their ends can be attained only by the forcible overthrow of all existing social conditions."[88]

Reinhold Niebuhr claimed that Marx's greatest ethical contribution to the problem of social life was his demonstration that the destruction of power is prerequisite to its attainment and that the disproportion of power in society is the real root of social injustice.[89] The control of the dominant mode of economic production in a society leads to control of how the technology of the society will be used and how the resources will be utilized. Those who are in this position will then exercise power throughout the total society.[90]

Power in the ownership of the means of production will not be abated by any other means but the use of force against it. There will be no arrival to power as long as the bourgeoisie has the apparatus of power in its hands. Marx in this way applied realism to the group life of society. He saw social classes in terms of the conflict of power with power. The group egoism of the bourgeoisie must be countered by arousing the self-conscious egoism of the proletariat.

The realism of Marxism is based on historical factors—where humanity is presently in history—rather than on understanding its essence. Marx perceived the limits of humanity in its present destructive existence. He did not recognize the limitations that exist even within humanity's greatest potentialities. Marx vividly identified the inherent egoism and corruption of human relationships in historical societies. He attributed them, however, to the inadequacies in the productive relationships.[91]

Marx's conception of the minimal government in the future society is a reflection of this misunderstanding of the human essence. Insufficient structure is provided to restrict and channel forces of evil. "The irrationality of the abuse of power for its own defense and enhancement cannot be checked where it is considered impossible by definition."[92] Marx is realistic because he understood his present society so well, not because of his understanding of human nature.

With a deeper understanding of human nature, Marx would have provided more checks against perversion of the proletariat's anticipated new powers in the transition after their victory. As Karl Popper stated, ". . . Whatever class they may have belonged to, once they are rulers they belong to the ruling class."[93] Marx was not sufficiently critical of the failures of democracy and provided little check upon the legislative majority in his concern for the entrenched antipopular power in the executive.[94]

At this point Marx did not succeed in breaking clean from the Romantic individualism of the early nineteenth century. His concept of human nature is a product of the secular Enlightenment. Human nature is separated from a transcendental grounding. As laissez-faire conservatism was criticized earlier for removing God from the economy, even so must Marxism. The removal in Marxism is intentional, not only consequential. In demonstrating the priority of the individual in Marx's society, Carol Gould describes it as an "ontological" priority. The precedence of the individual is not merely a social and ethical matter. The individual is "the ultimately real being," who creates his or her own nature.[95]

One result is the loss of human nature as something universal and permanent.[96] This denial has a significant cost for ethical criticism within Marxism. The denial of a permanent human essence appears to contradict his own operational assumptions. The definition of humanity is the most fundamental ethical referent in Marx's thought. A human being must act consistently with what it is to be human and has an obligation to seek human possibilities.[97] His critique of alienation presupposes an ideal in his thought of a human essence which in that context he uses in a critical way, as we have seen. By not establishing this concept of humanity as a constant and recognizable standard available to challenge all that denies it, Marx's convictions about the human essence lose their ability to critique present practice in any society, including a culture that claims to be developing his tradition.

Eric Voegelin noted that since human nature is open-ended in Marxism, enlightened reason can operate on human substance through the instrumentality of the pragmatically planning will, producing the perfected humanity.[98] Marx shared in the broader European rationalism, including its faith in science. A consequence may have been the Bolsheviks' devaluation of worker self-activity and ideas both politically and economically in favor of the dominant role of the party, the rationally enlightened elite. Reliance was instead placed on the development of productive forces and the education of the people in economic activity and social administration.[99]

The second result is similar. Without the transcendental reference, the concept of basic human sinfulness and rebellion is also lost. If an ideal environment actually could be achieved, it would indeed have a significant positive effect on human behavior. Marx correctly saw the unity of the vital and the spiritual in the person. It would have an impact on sin.

Even if for the sake of argument, however, one should grant the impossible extreme of removing human sinfulness, the new society could still be no more than a new Eden. Sin and rebellion would crop out again. In the transcendental approach to human nature, sin is rooted in our goodness and nature as creatures; it is occasioned by our freedom and finitude.

Furthermore, it would be an Eden whose inhabitants were worn with time. They would still carry the burden of the history of the race; for example, sin is deep even in the patterns of parenthood. The parents repeat deficiencies in their own developmental stages and pass them on. Sin is immersed within social and psychological cycles so subtle and so intertwined with our frailties that it cannot be expunged.

New forms of inequality would emerge and tempt individuals and groups into actions destructive to the new ethos. In a society geared to individual development through pursuing several skills, even something as seemingly innocuous as some deciding to devote their energies to only one pursuit would create an advantage like that of a professional athlete over an amateur.[100]

The fallen inheritance of the human race cannot be removed in a couple of generations—or in many generations. It will not be removed in history. The only power to do so is Christ's, which non-Christians reject and Christians neglect.

With great insight Reinhold Niebuhr states, ". . . Marxism expected [human beings] to be as tame and social on the other side of the revolution as Adam Smith and Jeremy Bentham thought them to be tame and prudential on this side of the revolution." Their differences lay in contradicting estimates of particular social institutions rather than in the estimate of human nature.[101] "[Marxism's] program of the socialization of property is a proximate answer to the immediate problem of achieving justice in a technical age. The validity of this answer . . . would have been the sooner recognized had it not been falsely made . . . into an ultimate answer to the ultimate problem of human existence itself."[102]

As Míguez Bonino argues, since alienation does go back to the fundamental estrangement, one more fundamental than Marx discerned, the mediation must also be radical. The proletariat is insufficient. Christ as mediator does not replace human action, but does do what we cannot so that we may be restored to be "God's free and active agent in God's humanising purpose."[103]

The weaknesses of Marxism are thus revealed in the utopian scheme. They are present in both the description of the final phase of history as well as in the time perspective in which utopia is seen. The redemptive factors are inherent forces within history, which are subject to rational analysis.[104] Like liberalism, utopia is too much assured, too much calculated upon. The Marxist utopia is due at a sufficiently definite time so as to justify long and painful intervening imperfections and acts of injustice.[105] Its imminence and the certainty of its coming can discourage working for temporal social justice. It then becomes the opium of the socialist state. When Marxist theory is thus perverted, the presence of this utopia in history can lead to the holding on to one's expectations by every means available. As Tillich noted, this has led to the use of terror to defend the victorious revolution until the final phase shall come.[106]

Nevertheless, unlike liberalism, it is a genuine utopia. It does radically contrast and challenge present social existence. It provides hope and grounds for diligent action.

Can Secularized Christianity Be Desecularized?

In many of its aspects Marxism appears as a secularized Christianity. The concept of justice is one such aspect. The view of "history as a unique process with a unique goal" is another.[107] Alasdair MacIntyre wrote,

> Marxism is the only systematic doctrine in the modern world that has been able to translate to any important degree the hopes which [people] once expressed, and could not but express in religious terms, into the secular project of understanding societies and expressions of human possibility and history as a means of liberating the present from the burdens of the past, and so constructing the future.[108]

Marx appears to recognize this common ground as "the human basis of which Christianity is the transcendental expression" or as "the *human core* of the Christian religion which can realize itself in truly human creations."[109]

The weaknesses that we have noted in conceptions of human nature and history are due to the new secular framework. Humanity and history are now interpreted apart from the transcendental perspective, thus losing a deeper and universal basis for critique. One might wonder, therefore, if the secular framework could be removed so that the remaining ideas could be again apprehended in a religious framework. Such a transition could not be accomplished, however, without a radical reconstruction since the creativity of the thought occurred after the secularization. An extensive Christian use of Marx's social vision could not take place without considerable fracture.

The materials of Marxist creativity, however, do include ideas that are properly Christian. Those ideas could be wrestled out of the human-centered framework and reappropriated by Christianity along with Marxist perceptions. Christianity can supply the necessary ontological basis missing in Marx for what humanity is and why values of humanness must be pursued. This would remove the arbitrariness in Marx's normative case, which has difficulty persuading anyone who might lack the intuition that human potentiality is something that should be sought. A Christian framework would also provide more satisfactory barriers to the terror and oppression that contradicted Marx's humanism in the perversion by later claimants to the Marxist tradition.

Despite the fact that Marx's removal of God is more intentional than laissez-faire conservatism's, Marx provides windows for reentry in that he does not exclude values from the economy. The question then becomes one of which values and which foundation for values should guide the economic sphere.

The hidden elements of Christianity in Marxism make many of its concepts appropriate for an overtly Christian social philosophy. The importance of Marx is much more than Marx's further articulation of affinitive concepts: justice; exploitive and defensive power; social struggle; identity with the oppressed; the influence and independence of social structures, including structural evil; dedication to full democracy; the essential and creative status of work; and zeal for transforming action. The Christian also can profit from valid aspects of Marxist analysis and proposals, such as analysis of capitalistic society, the crucial place of economic power and categories used to describe it, class interests and struggle, the use of force, and socialism.[110] It is also conceivable for a Christian to interpret history by means of a dialectical historical analysis subsumed under the Reign of God, never fully in history.

In the more pessimistic Christian view of history the utopian scheme would be clearly identified as utopian (i.e., outside of history). It could then still serve as an ideal and as a critique without being the cause of disillusion or of artificial attempts to attain it or to wait for it. The more realistic Christian view of human nature would supply the democratic theory with far more checks to stand guard against the permanent possibilities of humanity's cruelty to humanity.

In the early 1990s with the collapse of the centralized societies that claimed to be erected on Marx's thoughts, Marxism appeared to many political theorists to be finished. If Marxist socialism should disappear as a significant vision gathering social movements in its beams, then that would have been because so many of Marx's insights have become absorbed into other systems of thought. As human social injustices, materialistic shallowness, and alienation persist, however, new social visionaries will attempt to be more faithful in translating Marx's vision out of its nineteenth-century confinement.

13

Participatory Ideals Encountering Human Nature: Socialism

Socialism has other faces besides Marxism, which has provided the dominant form of the vision. Socialism is indeed difficult to separate from Marx. Marx's own original ideas and effective articulation have had great influence upon later socialists, and many of the ideas of the socialists who influenced him have been best known through his writings.

Nevertheless, Marx is a part of a socialist tradition that began in the decades before he started writing. There are enough socialist traditions whose followers do not consider themselves as directly following Marx, and which may even be rejected by Marxists, to warrant a separate treatment of socialism from that of Marxism. When the democratic socialist parties reconstituted the Socialist International in 1951, they stated in the Frankfurt Declaration that socialism could build on methods other than Marxism for analyzing society.[1] In this chapter we consider the broader expressions of socialism. In keeping with reality, however, we will not exclude Marxist elements from this general treatment.

The first difference between socialism in general and Marxist socialism is that a socialist is not bound to the Marxist view of history, historical determinism. Christian socialists, and others, may seek to express socialist theory in a form different from the antireligious, materialistic character of Marxism.[2] The non-Marxian socialists also tend to be more evolutionary than revolutionary in their approach to change.[3] Other socialists can independently mine the wealth of older and broader traditions, including the Judaeo-Christian and the democratic heritage, upon which Marx himself drew. In doing so they can avoid tendencies appearing in the Marxist succession that are less attractive today, such as nationalization of industries and the classical economic theory of surplus labor value.[4]

Socialism is the conviction that the best society and the best environment for individual self-fulfillment is one where the means of production are both owned and controlled by the community. Both elements should be present to have socialism. Community refers to a democratic participation of all the members of the particular social unit involved.

The well-developed welfare state that lacks these elements is not socialist, although it commonly is called that. Developed systems of social insurance and social services provide participation in consumption. Socialism involves participation in production.[5] In the welfare state, community control is strong enough to insure a more egalitarian distribution of private property. This is seen in Western European countries, which are capitalistic in terms of the dominant form of ownership of productive property, but which have some centralized planning and extensive social insurance programs. The developed systems of social sharing are consistent with, and derive in part from, the socialist vision of community; however, without elementary economic sharing they belong to modern liberalism and mixed economies.

Extensive nationalization occurred in Western Europe immediately after World War II. In England this involved coal, gas, electricity, railways, air transport, steel, and the Bank of England. Nationalization often occurs when the government takes over industries failing under private ownership ("lemon socialism"). Nationalization by itself provides workers with insufficient control to change their work life. It is merely a switch in the unseen and distant owner, the contradiction of socialists administering capitalism.[6] It lacks the participatory character of vibrant socialism.

Societies in which state ownership dominates productive property are not socialist. Erich Fromm described the Stalinist system as closer to the early and purely exploitive forms of Western capitalism than to any conceivable idea of a socialist society.[7] In fact the state capitalism of czarist Russia bequeathed much to the former Soviet Union and Soviet-type economies generally.[8] This form of society is *statism* (or *etatism*). It is distinct from both capitalism and socialism although both its supporters and its critics have labeled it "socialism." In statism private property has been eliminated and the exploited classes emancipated, but the main pivot of society is a strong, centralized, authoritarian state.[9] The early socialists remembered too vividly the excesses of the monarchic state to look to the state for deliverance. Rather, they presented a third way between the opposites of control by the "all-controlling and uncontrolled political state" and control by the autonomous forces of economic life itself.[10]

Community ownership and control mean that each member participates in the ownership and control of the means of production. Each one shares in its planning, policy formation, production, and profit.

"A work community of living people" is the substance of an enterprise. As capitalism moves through an increasingly mixed economy, people begin to perceive that ownership pertains to the capital goods of the enterprise, not to the work community itself. The rights of investors are satisfied when account has been rendered of how their capital investment has been handled. In a similar manner church trustees have legal ownership of the building, but not of the church community. They also do not control the life and decision making of that community.[11] The question, therefore, is about how this community should conduct itself.

The socialist answer presupposes equality and democracy. It presupposes equality in that each individual has equal status in the total community, including the economic community. It presupposes democracy in that each person participates in the significant decisions that affect his or her life and community, including the economic decisions. In the economy as well the old maxim should be realized, "What touches all should be decided by all."

Democracy as a form of human liberation entails participation in the decision making of the major institutions that regulate a person's life. Economic production is one of these. Democracy should apply to economic power as well as to political power. In both areas the arbitrary power of human being over human being is to be eliminated. The very human activity of arguing and deciding about the common life on the grounds of basic human values must be sustained. This requires structures that foster it.[12]

Accordingly, socialism is an extension of the theory of democracy into the economy. "Socialism is a participatory, self-governing society." In the first century of socialist revolutions, all of them but two attempted to establish self-governing enterprises.[13] The right of participation in economic decision making is to be based upon contribution to production apart from the degree of financial ownership that the worker might or might not have. Democracy in the economic area means restoring control of production to those engaged in it.[14]

The making of economic decisions, like political decisions, is the task of the whole community through responsible representation. Michael Walzer tells a story that compares the founding of a town with the founding of an economic enterprise. Political community as well as economic community are characterized by power that seriously affects many people. They both require entrepreneurial vision, capital investment, and freedom to join or not to join. The only difference is that ordinary democracy organizes people where they live, while socialism organizes them where they work.[15] Every person is entitled to share in both economic power and political power as a necessary aspect of participation in community.

The arguments for political democracy are equally valid for economic democracy, and most arguments against socialism have been used against democracy as well.

The seventeenth-century Puritans, as we have seen, used normative analogies from the order of the church to justify democracy: As in the order of *grace* all *believers* are equal, so in the order of *nature* all *people* are equal. The Levellers applied this analogy only to participation in government. Their conservative opponents, however, pointed to the economic implications of such thought: The same argument for a right of elections would validate a right to land and any other goods necessary for sustenance.[16]

A group on the left fringe of the Puritans, the Diggers, also saw that the analogy extended to participation in property, but they approved it.[17] They went and dug up the town commons, planted their crops, and waited in anticipation for the Reign of God. Private property was to be left alone, but the time would come when all others would voluntarily leave their estates and join them.[18] The Diggers presented an early glimpse of how socialism would be an extension of the theory of democracy.

Equality is expressed in the understanding of ownership. Socialism means abolishing exclusive ownership of capital, the means of production. There is no longer a class, separate from the laborers, that owns the machinery. All share in the fruits of community-owned capital; therefore, what used to go into the pockets of the capitalists after reinvestment[19] is distributed among all the members of the work community. The means of production are to be shared by all, through corporate arrangements.

The form of community ownership of property can take several forms, including both cooperative and public forms, as the accompanying chart indicates (see Figure 13.1). Alec Nove, for example, commends a variety of forms of ownership. Centralized state corporations would be the norm in sectors where economies of scale and vertical integration greatly offset the cost of corporation bureaucracy. These are very large units that require hierarchical forms of control. This would include monopolies, such as rails and electric power generation. It also would include industries that require investment and production activities to be closely integrated and have a high cost of research and development. Petrochemical complexes provide an example. Their management is responsible to the state, users, and the work force.

There would be state- or socially owned organizations with full autonomy where competition is present and production decisions belong at the level of production. Representatives of the work force would have a major management role. Worker cooperatives would be the form of ownership where a smaller manufacturing scale is appropriate.

Many contemporary socialist theorists approve forms of small-scale private property. For Nove the three socialist forms described earlier would dominate, but private enterprise would also exist. It appears where an individual working entrepreneur is effective, such as a painter, dressmaker, or freelance writer. Nove is arguing for a mixed economy and would permit the employment of a few people in private enterprises. Such employment would have limits on the number of employees and value of capital assets. The limits could vary according to the sector of the economy.[20]

Figure 13.1. Property in Socialism.

	Production	**Consumption**
Nature	by whom?	for whom?
Means	raw materials, machines, investment funds, information	wages, shares, social insurance, individual market purchases
Ownership	social: worker owned: public: from municipal to autonomous commission to federal; family and small scale private	private, egalitarian in distribution for basic needs; collective in voluntary associations rising out of private; social administration for basic needs; public administration and security
Traits	association inclusion in power participation equality	basic needs first; variety and choice as much as possible in that context; variation in distribution as needed for motivation and recruitment

service → profits → egalitarian
in   consumption
production
→ investment →

Family production in the form of family farms or small-scale family businesses is consistent with a socialist form of economy. Informal or formal controls ensure relatively equal shares of all productive property to each basic economic unit. This occurs in the traditional village economy, and the biblical jubilee is such a control.[21] A full socialism, in contrast to the socialist mixed economy urged by Nove, would require that these small-scale productive units do not exclude employees from ownership and participation. Once employees are hired, a transition is made from private individual entrepreneur to worker cooperative.

Socialism, therefore, does not require that all private property be abolished. Marx and Engels stated that the intention was not to abolish personal appropriation of the products of labor, but rather the bourgeois form of property in which surplus property is used to command the lives of others. The focus in shared property was upon the means of production in order to make property for consumption, "individual property," a truth.[22] A Christian socialist, George Herron, wrote, "Liberty as a human fact means communism in natural resources, democracy in production, equality in use, private property in consumption, and responsibility of each for all and of all for each."[23] Walter Rauschenbusch suggested that "socialists are probably quite right in maintaining that the amount of private property *per capita* in a prosperous socialist community would be much larger than it is now."[24] Thus the argument that in socialism private funds would not be available for giving to missions is based on a misunderstanding. In describing the Paris Commune, Marx stated that the pay of the priest would "depend only on the spontaneous action of the parishioners' religious instincts."[25]

Historical Background

Primitive and tribal societies are often communitarian. Throughout Western history there have been small egalitarian and communitarian movements, such as the monasteries and some sects. Some sought to flesh out the radical counsels of the Gospels and the example of the early church. These movements were also under Greek influence, which spoke of a golden age at the beginning of history. In the Stoic tradition equality was based on possession of the Logos. Such concepts were readily combined with the biblical view of paradise, God as the common creator, and common possession of God's image and, at least among the elect, of God's Spirit. Hellenistic philosophical communities provided the model for the Qumran community and for the early Jerusalem church's attempt to express the Scriptural ideals of radical sharing as a community of the end time.

Ideas also came from Greek influence that were foreign to the Hebrew perspective—ideas of the contemplative philosopher and mystic who rises above the particularity and materiality of existence by reflection and religious vision.[26] In the Middle Ages, and even in the Reformation at Münster, there were millennial mystical sects that combined Greek and biblical egalitarian views and added claims of possession of the powers and privileges of the future. These medieval communitarian movements were elitist. The sects included the spiritual elect and lower classes dominated by charismatic and visionary leaders who at times made idolatrous self-claims.[27]

Modern socialism, however, comes from the same period of history in which liberalism and capitalism emerge. Like modern liberalism, it originated at the end of this formative period in reaction to classical liberalism. The term *socialism* came into usage in the 1830s at the height of laissez-faire dominance—before government intervention on behalf of the workers.

Socialism rose as an attack on the individualist alienation and exploitation perceived in the Industrial Revolution. The socialists saw individualism acting as a centrifugal force casting society apart in violation of the essence of human community. They sought to replace individualistic conflict with association, harmony, altruism, and socially held property.[28]

The socialists resembled the traditional conservatives in rejecting the lack of community, the individualism, and the conflict in classical liberalism. Traditional conservatives, therefore, have easily moved over to socialism—most notably, R. H. Tawney and Bishop Gore in Britain and George Grant in Canada. Pope John Paul II similarly applied traditional Roman Catholic organic social ideals to an orientation that emphasizes the empowerment of the poor and of the worker.[29] The socialists differed from traditional conservatives in their devotion to democracy, human rights, and equality. They thus have one of the strengths of traditional conservatism, the sense of community, but without basing it in aristocracy, nobility, and tradition. At the same time the socialists retained liberalism's values of democracy and the rights of the individual, yet placed them in a context of community.

The socialists approved the new industrial and technological growth, but they perceived that the climate of economic freedom had produced an economic oligarchy. It was absorbing a disproportionate amount of the new wealth and opportunities of culture. The socialists saw that bonds of community needed to be reestablished in order for liberty and individual growth to be a reality for the masses. Socialism was to achieve justice for those left out of the benefits of the new industrial society. Economic democracy would displace economic oligarchy and distribute broadly and equally the opportunities of modern society.

To emphasize only the obvious quest for justice in socialism, however, is to miss much of the meaning that for many socialists ranks higher than justice.[30] Socialism is also a quest for an ethical and spiritual quality of human life that its followers claimed had been reduced by the individual materialism of capitalism. Erich Fromm, speaking as an advocate, described socialism as one of the most "idealistic and moral movements of our age."[31]

This aspect of socialism is seen in the nineteenth-century visionaries whom Engels and others called the Utopian Socialists. Among them, Charles Fourier described a healthy society that would meet our basic passion of familial love. We also have a "butterfly passion," the human need for change. In this society work would be enjoyable as it would correspond to the diverse potentialities in every person. In free and voluntary associations individualism would combine spontaneously and harmoniously with collectivism.

Robert Owen spoke of a new society, the aim of which would be the improvement of people, not increased production. A person is "the creature of circumstances." In a new order with satisfactory conditions of life, the inherent virtues of human character would develop. People would be trained in principles that would enable them to act in union and to create genuine social bonds. The problem of the poor would be solved by making the poor productive in self-sustaining villages of cooperation.

Pierre Proudhon argued for the need to build a political order expressive of society; such an order would be characterized by reciprocity, rather than hierarchical authority. State-financed social solutions only produce the same economic fatalism as did capitalism. People would instead work for each other in free and spontaneous associations. Self-respect would be the first maxim of ethics, followed by respect for one's neighbor.[32]

This note continued in later socialism. Herbert Marcuse's *One Dimensional Man* in 1964 was an outcry for transcendence over the unthinking, undifferentiated mass technical society. We again see the left and the traditional right merge as Marcuse at times sounded like Bernard Iddings Bell's *Crowd Culture.* Marcuse's hope was that the individual would be free to organize and direct one's life toward the satisfaction of vital needs. Such freedom was not available in the domination mode of social relationships in capitalism.

The emphasis of socialism thus is not only upon the injustice of the domination and passivity of the worker in capitalistic society; it also is upon what such control does to the spirit. The socialist protest is against the lack of vocation in work, the insecurity, and the lack of creativity and self-affirmation in capitalistic production.

Justice and Human Fulfillment

Marxist socialism, which we have already examined, expresses many characteristics of socialism in general. We will not repeat the previous discussion in our theological analysis, but will instead concentrate on elements that do not have a particular Marxist flavor or which require further elaboration. To some extent this chapter is a sequel to the previous one. Our major concern is the workability of the socialist vision. First, however, we will note the important strengths of socialism in justice and in affirmation of the positive aspects of human nature.

Justice and Work

We have seen the high degree of correspondence to biblical justice in the socialist commitment to justice, which in its highest form is distributed according to needs. Socialist theory suggests that in practice adjustments be made in the ideal of justice and equality. The primary criterion of distribution according to needs is supplemented by the socialist criterion of distribution according to work. People are rewarded in accordance with the contribution of their labor.

The first criterion is the biblical emphasis although the latter is also assumed. An assigned portion of the social product is reserved for those basic economic benefits essential for minimal inclusion in community, as well as the funds required for public administration and security. Distribution according to needs may be provided through social insurance or social service networks. It also may occur in adjustments in remuneration: Workers with special needs because of many dependents or other requirements for basic needs receive additional funds. The remainder of the social product, the part not reinvested, is distributed according to work. Those who contribute more, receive more.

Socialist theorists are not in agreement on whether each worker should receive the same remuneration. Some call for this as an expression of equality and to ensure that the needs of all are met. More frequently, a socialist community is advised to allow some variance in the income that members receive so that requirements of the community can be met. Some monetary incentives are provided for jobs deemed most valuable for society. Work that is more difficult, dangerous, unpleasant, unhealthy, or which requires more training is more valuable.[33]

Income differentials, however, continue to be much less than in capitalism or statism. Among several existing production cooperatives whose pay differential has been described, the ratio varies from equality to 7:1. The standard for work organizations in the United States is generally about 100:1.[34]

Socialists also vary over the necessity of equality between members of different firms. There is agreement that in justice the basic needs of all members of the society have prior claim. Differences appear regarding the distribution of the social product beyond that. Horvat, working with a Marxist conception of social property (in contrast to state or private property), consistently seeks arrangements for egalitarian distribution across society. Those who would see ownership resting within the members of a particular firm would not be under the same compulsion. In seeking equality in distribution according to work Horvat relies upon processes of taxation or reinvestment to distribute broadly the value of products that is due to especially favorable resources or location, rather than to the work of the producers. Tax and investment policies thus supplement the distribution of the market.[35]

Human Capacity

Probably no major political alternative gives more recognition to the fullness of the human potential and ties it so closely with our social nature. The human being is seen as a vital physical and spiritual whole, with a complex relationship of needs. Impulses dealing with love (which is not cut off from the physical), aesthetics, and faith must have ascendance over those that merely preserve life.[36] Socialism searches for an arrangement that gives the best expression to the capacities of a person to participate in the decisions that affect her or him. It seeks to free creative abilities in normal vocation as well as to expand the concept of vocation to include creativity that is neglected in vocations determined solely by economic requirements.

The socialist seeks to construct a society that recognizes and encourages humanity's communal motivations and values. The concepts of property in conservatism and liberalism, rising out of the Roman heritage and the middle-class ethos are inadequate. They are atomistic and contrary to the biblical example. A concept of property is needed which gives due recognition to social interdependence and responsibility.

Socialism in Light of Christian Realism

Our consideration of socialism must dwell on the major theological and ethical question. In light of the fraility of human nature, the limitations of history, and the complexity of economic society, will socialism work? Socialists admit that there is no society that has been a socialist society as they envisage it.[37] The tradition also has been characterized by optimism. Many people admire the ideals in the vision but wonder if it is capable of even approximate historical expression on a society-wide basis. This question has become all the more central with the economic failures, in addition to the long-perceived political failures, of the societies that were called "socialist."

Since there are no full-fledged socialist societies to evaluate, our ethical analysis must include an understanding of how the forms of implementation proposed and empirical information on presently existing socialist enterprises. This section will accordingly have a pragmatic detail beyond that provided for most of the other visions. The key theological question about socialism involves social reality, not ideals.

Unsociable Human Nature

As socialism has been expressed historically, it has been heavily influenced by the Enlightenment and liberal optimism about human nature. This creates a significant problem for the dependability of the theory. Obstacles to the ideals may be discounted as merely temporal accidents. Too much confidence is often placed upon the communal and creative drives of the personality. As P.J.D. Wiles put it, "[Human beings] are bad and socialism is unnatural."[38] Albert Mollegen states, "Beneath all modern socialist theories, evolutionary or revolutionary, there lies the dogma of the goodness and the perfectibility of human nature."[39]

The weakness of viewing humankind too positively is seen in many Christian socialists. The late-nineteenth-century Christian socialists tended to be shallow and sentimental in their social descriptions. Key terms for social action selected from the Christian tradition often were those that stressed human altruism and harmony: God as Father, "brotherhood of man," love. These domestic metaphors are weak regarding social change because they do not point readily to the conflictive and political aspects of society. The optimism was also reflected in the view of history. American Christian socialists shared the liberal conviction of progress and evolution. Socialist society was a certainty because of the operation of natural laws.[40]

The neglect of the negative side of human nature produces weaknesses in the social strategy. Trust is placed in reason, education, persuasion, and voluntary progress.[41] Historically, piecemeal reform was encouraged because every slight improvement in working conditions or labor legislation was heralded as a step toward the Reign of God.[42]

A further question rising from the same concerns is whether adequate checks against our evil nature will be provided if a socialist system is installed. The fear is that a new concentration of political and economic power would emerge despite the socialist critique of capitalism and statism on these grounds.[43]

There are, however, other possible ways of framing socialism. The lack of unity in socialist thought provides opportunities for creativity and critique. The romantic optimism of socialism regarding human nature and history was critiqued from within socialism itself. This indicates that a more realistic framework for socialist theory is possible. We have seen the Marxist critique of utopian socialism: Socialist theory must give attention to contemporary factors of exploitive power and the strategic requirements of defensive and intervening power. We have also seen, however, the elements of optimism in Marxist theory itself.

The optimism of socialism has also been exposed by socialists who are Christian realists.[44] Their awareness of human corruption leads to grounding socialism on a realistic understanding of democratic theory. Democratic theory, as we have seen, is most satisfactory when it is based upon a realistic view of human nature. Socialism needs to be kept down to earth by a vigorous penetration of democratic realism. Human beings are attracted to shared production not only by altruism and communal longings. They also are motivated by self-interest in the profits of the firm in which they would have a share.

The scope of our inquiry in this book points us beyond voluntary socialist communities within a nonsocialistic society. Our ultimate interest is in what they demonstrate regarding the possibilities for the larger community. We are thus concerned with socialism as a philosophy regarding normative property arrangements and decision making in the larger economic and political community. Horvat suggested that the lesson of Yugoslavia was that the real problem of self-management is associated with macroeconomic and macropolitical organization. The most complete and direct self-management is possible only at the level of the business enterprise. How does one construct a whole society based upon worker-owned and -controlled enterprises?[45]

The Appearance of a Society That Is Democratic and Socialist

An awareness of the barriers which resist our ideals calls for socialists to move beyond their visions to describe the institutions that they propose. The approach of Christian realism requires the implementation of socialism to be accompanied by a careful arrangement of checks and balances. Building socialism on the protective argument of democratic theory is one measure. Power is dispersed throughout the populace. Heimann viewed socialism not as the alternative to liberalism but as the corrective of its institutional defects.[46] This perspective highlights a *tenacious* adherence to democracy and the bill of procedural human rights.

Almost all the socialist parties of Western Europe have relinquished the idea of nationalization or state ownership of the means of production as a "first principle."[47] Contemporary socialism looks to small, competing units.[48] The primary socialist economic unit is the worker-owned firm with the workers sharing in profits and control (industrial democracy). These firms compete with other worker-controlled firms within a free market.

We have seen that capitalism has won a significant victory over one historical component of socialism—democratic, yet centralized direction of the economy.[49] The free market is an efficient allocator of resources and prices and is compatible with localized social ownership or a more egalitarian distribution of income.

The free market is preferable for socialism because the removal of the bureaucracy needed for central planning gives more direct control to the producers.[50] The desired autonomy and self-government is obtainable in the market as it is not in a command economy. "Socialist economy implies a market and autonomous, self-managing productive units." Worker-owned and -controlled companies do not have an incentive to buy or own other companies since the workers would then have less control over the affairs of the expanded firm. A labor-managed economy is therefore likely to operate closer to the textbook model of a competitive market.[51] This concession to the market removes the most significant economic objections to socialism, such as those raised by Friedrich Hayek and Ludwig Mises.[52]

In addition, the common good requires some economic activity to be more directly accessible to the control of the whole community. As seen earlier in the example of the position of Alec Nove, there would be bodies alongside worker-managed companies that are municipally owned and controlled, such as the municipal power plants that already exist among us. Other federal or regional publicly owned companies would not be directly managed by the state, but by autonomous public corporations that would include worker and consumer representation.

For the situation of a developing country, Severyn Bruyn recommends that regional or national concerns in a particular industry be acted upon by a public corporation set up separate from the government. It is organized by representatives of government, church, labor, consumers, and industry. It would initially purchase land in combination with a local community development corporation. Community- and employee-owned and controlled companies would be developed upon this land.[53]

To evaluate the realism of the socialist vision it is important to identify more fully the internal makeup of the worker-owned firms, how a whole society of such firms would be constructed, and the possibilities that such economic institutions would become normative in current societies.

The basic decision-making unit in a worker-owned company is also its smallest functioning unit, probably having at least ten members. Such a work group deals with questions of job assignments, work conditions, employment, dismissal, and conflict resolution. Research indicates that these also are matters with which workers want to be involved in decision making.

When decisions substantially affect other work units, they are delegated to a body representative of all the units. Some matters are of such importance that they are treated by a plenary assembly of all the workers from the units, rather than by the delegated body. These are matters such as merger, radical reorganization, passage of the constitution, and heavy investment programs.

Additional organizations of the workers include a grievance committee and a committee to provide communication between workers and managers and to give the managers evaluation and support. Larger organizations would have additional levels of management and workers' councils, organized in the same fashion. The pattern would be simplified for smaller organizations.

Similar participatory structures would be present in nonbusiness associations in which individuals make their living. Where significant societal interests are involved, a board of trustees would be introduced into the structure and composed of representatives of the work community and the particular societal interests in question.[54]

The business theory of worker control needs further development. There continues to be considerable trial and error. Socialism recognizes that people are not equal in abilities and gifts. Individuals need a variety of available tasks, and communities need a variety of workers to fill them. Some people are cooks and some are managers of the funds set aside for industrial expansion. There also is affirmation of the interchangeability possible among jobs and provision for sharing menial tasks. For example, in the Israeli Kibbutz, the most radical form of currently existing self-management,[55] all members, even managers, take a turn in undesired jobs; managerial offices are rotated among those qualified in three- to five-year terms.[56]

Economic democracy does not mean that all workers have management skills. Economic enterprise continues to require individually gifted and trained managers and entrepreneurs. Executive and supervisory functions, however, no longer earn the privilege of ruling the life of others in some particular interest. Each wields that authority only to perform the duties of one's tasks.[57]

The theory of workers' self-management provides a distinction of two spheres of decision making. The first pertains to value judgments. Policies are made that reflect the ethical interests of the body. These decisions are based in political authority. Each member of the organization has an equal vote.

The second sphere of decision making deals with the execution and implementation of the policy decisions made in the first sphere. These are technical decisions based on professional authority arising out of skill and experience. This is a matter of technical competence, not of democracy. Those who make these decisions are identified in the division of labor expressing the differing skills of the various members of the enterprise.[58] Failures of worker-owned companies show that they need to be large enough to have several staff members who have mastered various business skills.[59] Where competence beyond that of the members is needed, external consultants are used. In addition, an annual external audit evaluates the business results.[60]

One of the problems faced by workplace democracy is maintaining the necessary boundaries between the legislative and administrative spheres.[61] Organizational incompetence and egoism, which confuse these boundaries, will be ongoing threats to efficiency. This problem is one of democracy in general and is not unique to worker control, as those scarred from ecclesiastical or university politics can testify. The distinction between the two spheres, however, should not be completely maintained in practice. For example, workers should provide input for the implementation process through advisory commissions working with professional managers.[62]

When working within a framework that is primarily capitalistic, worker-run enterprises have had difficulty retaining managers as they are bid higher salaries from companies with traditional hierarchies. "In the context of a society that grants highly unequal pay, the more or less equal compensation within collectives brings great differentials in relative sacrifice."[63] Few managers are willing to make the personal financial sacrifice to stay on.[64]

The higher salaries that managers with entrepreneurial skills receive to attract or retain them poses a threat to the worker democracy. Some argue that market socialism will tend to revert to capitalism through such salary differentials. In addition, companies who give these managers more autonomy would possibly have a competitive advantage that would undercut workers' control.[65] The reliance on governmental activity to compensate for such inegalitarian tendencies, such as through assigning investment to the government,[66] creates a centralizing tendency that is also unfavorable to market socialism. A resort to a value agreement that no individual or group shall expect extraordinary benefits[67] will not be dependable in light of human nature.

Another operational problem of workplace democracy is misplaced solidarity (ecclesiatically known as "cheap grace") that avoids necessary discipline of fellow workers, such as firing for gross irresponsibility or dishonesty. Conflicts also increase, rather than decrease, when power is more equally distributed. Effective designs for conflict resolution must be devised.[68] While alienation decreases in collectives, stress increases. Several factors contribute. The distinction between the decision-making authority of the individual and that of the group can be unclear. With a broader array of jobs, role ambiguity also can rise. The strong sense of purpose in the firm can increase the possibility of burn-out.[69]

Worker management thus is no panacea. It creates its own problems.[70] These problems are not insignificant. They are the substantial price of replacing hierarchical authority. They provide occasion for human sinfulness and finiteness. When not controlled, they can undermine the efficiency and even the continuity of the firm.

Worker-controlled firms, as much as investor-controlled firms, need the supervision of the government to protect the integrity of the market, individuals and other firms, and the common good. Government also provides central long-range planning and insures justice in distribution.

The commitment to free markets significantly modifies the degree of central planning. Planning and regulation would use the wisdom of the market, not override it.[71] Horvat distinguishes social planning from bureaucratic or "central" planning. Social planning is not an imperatival coordination that destroys autonomy. It provides the global proportions within which individual firms can make decisions with autonomy. It uses monetary, credit, fiscal, and income policies to ensure market equilibrium, full employment, price stabilization, balance of payment equilibrium, and develop policy against stagnation and inflation. A federal development fund provides capital for projects requiring large concentrations of capital and long periods of construction. It also deals with regional and other disproportions not successfully handled by the market.[72]

As more economic concerns become subject to public decision making, some separation of power is required between this process and other political processes to avoid over politicization and political abuse. The danger needs to be broadly perceived so that part of the public ethos is the preservation and encouragement of economic freedoms, pluralism of groups, and freedom of association. Horvat suggests a bicameral legislature in which a House of Producers, in addition to a House of Citizens, would represent business units. Each body would deal with its own specializations, but they would act jointly on common interests.[73]

In this political order, centralized units must not be allowed to make decisions that can be made by lower levels without adversely affecting those not involved in the decision or to protect minority rights.[74] Marx sought to localize decision making in smaller units with the central government dealing with general administrative tasks.

Present Seeds of Socialism

The theological concern about the actual possibilities of achieving a socialist society is met in part by noting the degree in which socialist elements already exist in our societies. Cooperative production and marketing historically have had a surprisingly significant place in American culture, and worker ownership and control is compatible with contemporary interests and trends. We already have a mixed economy. The separation between socialism and capitalism has become blurred.[75] Following the collapse of statist economies around 1990 and the convincing demonstration of the necessity of the market, there was considerable talk of triumphant capitalism. Yet surveying the increasing trends toward worker participation in management, Branko Horvat had written earlier, "There is little doubt that the world is moving toward a socialist, self-governing society at an accelerated pace."[76] The two developments are not irreconcilable.

Industrial democracy is not as alien to American values and economic development as some might expect. Certain forms of socialism have a long history in American tradition.

Rural cooperatives have been a producer-owned way of giving family farms economy of scale to compete with corporations in marketing, as well as meeting needs of specialized services and technology.[77] Customer-owned cooperatives are common in the wholesale business. Law and accounting firms are often worker-owned cooperatives among service professionals.[78]

A sign of the possibilities for industrial democracy appeared in the passage of the Small Business Employee Ownership Act in 1980. This act established worker ownership as a priority in the Small Business Administration and opened all loan and loan guarantee programs of that agency to workers who wish to buy an existing firm or start a new one. The bill passed unanimously. Conservatives voted for it on the valid principle that it provided the promise of local and voluntary solutions to problems versus governmental transfer payments. It would furnish empowerment rather than dependency.[79]

Socialism, properly understood as tied to democracy inherently and to the free market by experience, could be considered as the proper extension of the capitalist revolution. Traditional arguments for private property point to it. An example would be the conviction that ownership should not be separated from incentives.[80] Expanding access to economic power (defensive power) means less need for political power (intervening power).

Worker democracy also responds well to the concern for freedom in the liberal tradition. The search for worker control through participatory processes of decision making is a regard for procedural justice.[81] Cooperative production maximizes freedom in the workplace by giving the workers control over the conditions of their labor and over all the other decisions of the enterprise as a whole. As P.J.D. Wiles commented on cooperation or worker self-administration, "If ever the 'absence of human restraint over individual economic activity' had meaning, it is here."[82]

One of the valid arguments in Marx's concept of dialectical development was that capitalism has prepared the way for socialism by socializing production.[83] Part of this development is the economic idea of the corporation. In reality the joint stock corporation is a producer's cooperative by those who lend capital for an enterprise.[84] In modern capitalist societies the means of production are owned corporately, not privately. The individual stockowner does not have private ownership of a piece of the particular company to do with it what he or she wishes. This association, however, is not socialistic: It is elitist, held by a class separate from that of the workers. The form for industrial democracy is there; only the content would need to be altered, as workers replace, or are added to, investors.

Worker-owned enterprises are small in number but increasing.[85] There are considerably more employee stock ownership companies (ESOPs)[86] A significant number of American companies have profit-sharing programs.[87]

The most significant stock ownership sharing program was the Meidner Plan for Economic Democracy, instituted in Sweden in 1983. A tax on profits of large companies purchased stock in a series of mutual funds controlled by workers. The stocks remained in the company; individual shares could not be sold. Eventually, the organizations of wage-earners would have owned and controlled a majority of all company stocks.[88] Horvat sees such a method of investment for worker ownership through taxation of profits as the way socialism will arrive in economically advanced nations.[89]

Workers' share in control has advanced in Europe. Most of its countries require labor representation on the supervisory and management boards of major companies. This is called *co-determination* (decision making by both workers and management representing investors). This is minority representation as a rule, but strong pressure exists toward parity for workers and beyond.[90] In Germany, often considered a prize example of capitalism, large companies must give a significant proportion of the seats on their supervisory boards to worker representatives. All businesses with five or more employees must have work councils in which representatives of wage and salary workers work with middle management.[91] In 1972 workers rights were expanded to include being informed on planning and sharing in determining hiring, transfers, pay based on performance, and technical devices measuring worker performance. Labor courts, also "codetermined," are available to handle personnel issues which could not be settled by workers councils. Codeterminism had been a goal of Christian trade unions in Germany as far back as the imperial period.

Sweden, which like Germany has a capitalist form of ownership, has similar patterns of worker representation and issue negotiation.[92] The European Economic Community encourages participation on both worker councils and boards of directors. A similar step in the United States would be legislation requiring an employer above a certain size to set up a worker consulting and co-decision making system upon request of a majority of the workers of the firm. Public and consumer interests could also be represented. Codetermination measures represent the control rather than the ownership side of socialism.

Publicly owned utilities have been another socialist element in American life. A significant portion of Americans receive their electricity from public power systems. Almost half of these are consumer-owned cooperatives. The others are owned by municipalities. This development was part of the Progressive movement and reached its most significant advance in the New Deal.[93] Municipally owned utilities had been part of the socialist agenda.[94] Even free market economists have held that utilities, as natural monopolies, should be assumed by government so that the advantages of concentration would accrue to all rather than a few.

The Economic Viability of Socialism

A further question about socialism that rises out of a realistic posture regarding human nature is whether the economy would falter because of a lack of motivation. Aristotle observed that property common to the greatest number of owners receives the least attention. Passivity emerges from the assumption that someone else is taking care of it.[95] The theological concern is that with the solidarity provided in socialism, people will not work diligently.

A strictly egalitarian socialism does not provide the monetary incentives considered necessary to motivate efforts for advancement. We have seen that some socialist theories modify strict equality for recruitment for posts that are difficult to fill and other requirements for economic viability. Thus some monetary incentives are provided. The variation is still much less than in capitalism. Workers must also have a financial self-interest in the prosperity of the firm. This factor is crucial for the approach to socialism of democratic realism.

There are also more important motivations for work than monetary increments. According to Wiles one should not confuse the profit motive with the totality of economic self-interest. Alinsky wrote,

> We must recognize that one of the best ways to insure that [people] will assume obligations to their fellow human beings and to society is to make them feel they are definitely a part of society and that society means enough to them so that they actually feel obligated or have obligations.[96]

The challenge in the area of worker motivation demands the provision of units small enough for participation and a sense of belonging. On the other hand, the permanence of short-sighted, self-interest must be recognized.

Considerable studies of worker participation and control have been made in recent decades. The question is still open, however, about the variables that influence motivation and output. Paul Blumberg's *Industrial Democracy,* an important early synthesis of these studies, concluded that an increase in workers' decision-making power significantly enhances satisfaction and productivity. Blumberg's explanation of this correlation was that participation enhances the worker's senses of intelligence and competence. The basic human need for respect, appreciation, responsibility, and autonomy is gratified. In addition, the job becomes an extension of the person, increasing commitment and thus satisfaction. Democratic organization supports the maturity of the worker by stimulating activity, independence, and egalitarian relationships.[97]

Less supervision is required in cooperative settings. When people are motivated by the perception of working for themselves and identifying the company with themselves, the top-heavy supervisory structure of command in current capitalism, whose main job is to see the people immediately below them are doing the job they are supposed to be doing, can be decreased.[98] In the traditional plant there are enormous supervision costs.[99]

Employee share in profits and equity encourages employees who have been trained at considerable expense and whose knowledge is critical to the competitive nature of the firm to stay with the firm. Such employees also engage more fully in the training of new workers.[100]

Later studies have confirmed the increase of efficiency with participation.[101] The Quality of Work Life programs in a substantial number of the largest American corporations indicate recognition within the business establishment of the link between increased worker influence and improved productivity.[102] The relationship between productivity and the broader factor of job satisfaction is less clear than it is with participation.[103]

Worker-owned firms appear to be economically viable on the whole although superior profitability is not the prime purpose of industrial democracy. Socialists are moved more centrally by other values, such as vocation and individual fulfillment. Further empirical work on the economic significance of workplace democracy continues and is needed.[104] The empirical data to date, however, is encouraging that this is a viable economic alternative.

Initial studies show employee ownership companies to be 150 percent as profitable as conventional firms and to have a higher average increase in productivity.[105] There is considerable information on the Pacific Northwest plywood and the San Francisco garbages collection cooperatives that were established in the 1920s and are still in operation today. The plywood cooperatives average 20–30 percent higher productivity than do conventional plywood companies, and the refuse collection cooperatives provide higher-quality services at lower prices than do refuse collection firms in any other major city in the country. In some industries, however, cooperatives have performed worse.[106]

Studies of worker-owned firms that have emerged out of impending plant closures reveal a number of cases in which corporate earnings after the conversion are far higher than before. A survey of thirty worker-owned firms, controlled for size and industry, found that they had a level of profit higher than similar conventional firms. Another study found that the most important single determinant of profitability is the percentage of the company's equity owned by nonsalaried employees. When it goes up, so does the company's profits.[107]

Rothschild and Whitt conclude in light of the available evidence that worker ownership and democratic management produce levels of worker commitment and solidarity that can be turned into productivity and profitability advantage. The key is that worker ownership must be combined with democratic control.[108] On a separate note, based on what little data does exist, collectives have a better longevity record than do conventionally own small business, despite assumptions to the contrary.[109]

Two extensive networks of workers cooperatives are highly significant in that they give information about this phenomenon on a regional basis and as a vital and substantial part of a nation's economy. In the Basque region of Spain, the Mondragon network is significant for bringing eighty-two worker-owned cooperatives into an integrated regional economic system with its own banking system. Over 20,000 worker-owners are involved.[110]

The kibbutz movement, which has been in existence in Israel since 1910, comprises 4 percent of the Israeli population and 28.5 percent of its agricultural work force, yet it produces about 40 percent of the gross farm product of the nation. In manufacturing, with 5.5 percent of Israeli industrial employees, it produces 7.2 percent of the national industrial product.[111]

A countertype to the success of Mondragon and the kibbutz has been the Amana community. The decision of this Iowa community to move from collective production to capitalism has become part of the mythology of American political economy. The *Philadelphia Record*'s headline in 1933, "Nation's Only Communist Utopia turns Capitalistic and Prospers," is indicative of the use of the event at that time and since to reinforce the capitalist system.

Several aspects about its situation are not disclosed by the myth. Amana was a community of a separatistic pietist and mystical group, "The Society of True Inspiration." The communal structure was not part of its European experience, but it was adopted when it immigrated to America in the 1840s. It was an experiment to solve an economic problem rather than as a basic component of its faith. In contrast to the kibbutz, the community had an authoritarian decision-making structure in which much of the personal life, including whom one married and what work one did, was decided by elders. Amana thus does not belong to democratic socialism. The vote to leave the collective approach took place in 1931 in the Great Depression in a region pocketed by economic failures and foreclosures. When the community entered the Depression, it still had not recovered from the destruction of its main woolen and flour mills from a fire in 1923. That in turn had followed upon the collapse of the woolen market after World War I.

Amana did not abandon its solidaristic approach after the vote. It developed a corporation led by its former elite leadership. Church members who so desired became shareholders with a right to homes and a job. The famous Amana Refrigeration company, later taken over by Raytheon Corporation, was not the successor of the community enterprise. It was started by one member who took the option provided of going his own way.[112]

A society is not socialist until the member-owned and -controlled productive units have become legally and/or culturally normative for the entire society. The kibbutz and the Mondragon, despite their size, are not normative institutions for a whole society. A very different dynamic is involved. The Mondragon has the cohesive unity and tradition of a homogeneous geographic region. The kibbutz, while no longer drawing upon the same socialist and Zionist ideological commitment that it had in earlier decades, is still chosen by its members for both utilitarian and intrinsic reasons.[113] The element of choice and calling is missing when everybody must be involved. While not true of all cooperative organizations, many cooperative communities find their identity in a countercultural stance over against the majority society. This driving force is diminished when the dominant organizations reform or accommodate themselves to the cooperative stance.[114]

Unfortunately, the former Yugoslavia had been the only society-wide example that approaches socialism; however, it does not fit the model. As Branko Horvat, the economist and top government planner of the former Yugoslavia, indicates, political democracy had not sufficiently accompanied economic democracy. He claims, however, that in the period in which workers' self-management was given its fullest expression (1953–1965) its rates of growth were superior to that of capitalist and statist economies, as well as that of the previous capitalist and statist stages in Yugoslavia.[115]

Like political democracy to which it gives economic expression, socialism depends upon the cultural, and particularly the religious health of its people. Affluence poses a dilemma for socialism. The self-interest in solidaristic solutions can decline when a person feels more capable of making it on one's own. The common lot that supports one when weak can seem a hindrance when one appears capable of doing better separately. On the other hand, Michael Harrington states that poverty cannot be socialized. There must be enough for everyone. Competition for resources is linked with scarcity.[116] At the same time wealth transfers rather than removes human competitiveness since such strife is based on deeper insecurities than material necessity. Socialism would then seem to have motivational problems with either wealth or poverty.

Oscar Wilde commented that the problem with socialism is that it would take too many evenings.[117] Participation in decision making is time consuming, requiring substantial time given to the group. One of the challenges of workplace self-management is the extensive time that can be wasted in discussion. Competent leadership is crucial to provide adequate preparation, information, and previous discussion in advisory committees.[118]

Workers conditioned in a system in which they are accustomed to depend upon others may lack the desire for this responsibility. Even if they have the desire, they may not have the discipline and objectivity to operate effectively within democratic processes.

The American labor movement has focused upon wages. There has been some evidence that workers, in terms of their actual behavior and in contrast to self-descriptions of their values, are willing to sacrifice more skilled work and more self-determining situations for higher wages. An indication of this preference appeared in a frequently cited 1949 study of assembly line workers at an automobile plant. Well over a majority had left jobs in which the pace was mainly determined by the worker (rather than by the machine). They had had at least partial responsibility for planning the job and the tools and materials to be used. They had left jobs that were less repetitive and required longer training than their present jobs. These characteristics were true for only a minority of the jobs at the new plant. Higher or more secure income had drawn the large majority of them there.[119] Although these previous situations were far from positions of worker self-management, the study does point to the question of whether workers in American society sufficiently treasure the values of economic democracy to provide the grassroots basis for a successful movement to achieve it. This is a strategic question, not a normative one. As the apathy demonstrated by the voter participation in American elections is not grounds for dismantling political democracy, neither should apathy be an argument for not pursuing economic democracy.[120] The question of ideals and social reality, however, remains.

The only solution for socialism is the development of a self-management culture.[121] Socialism seeks to provide a structure that will sustain the values of individual responsibility and freedom, mutual respect, hard work, crafts skills, honesty, loyalty, authority, and property.[122] The nature of the workplace does influence the rest of one's life. One can universalize John Booth's observation for Central America that workplace and community participation offer greater potential for building democratic political culture than do sporadic voting, campaigning, and party activism.[123]

While encouraging them, however, socialism does not create these values. They come from the cultural heritage.[124] They sustain socialism and must be based on commitments transcending socialism. The positive influence of religion upon a culture is thus essential in providing voluntary sacrifice, elevating the family as a necessary microcosm of a genuine society, and liberating people from the "'iron cage' of loneliness, despair, materialism, and death."[125]

The Value of a Vision

Socialism has a significant utopian value apart from the question of its capacity to become the prevailing life of a society. Socialism provides a standard against which various options can be measured. When immediate adoption is not a possibility, socialism can be approached gradually as an ideal influencing decision making. Many of the ideas that Norman Thomas, an American socialist, expressed earlier in the twentieth century were eventually legislated.

Socialism as a vision of a better human community leads its followers to support policies that provide the disadvantaged with more control over their social and economic lives and which give them economic power so as not to be dominated by the selfish power of others. As a vision of community in democracy, the socialist vision lends support to the limited efforts to establish beauty, morality, tradition, health, the future of the environment, and spirituality against unrestrained pursuit of material wealth. In addition, its alternative organizations absorb the risks and costs of experimentation and innovation for the dominant society.[126]

Such piecemeal socialistic developments are correctly attacked by radical socialists as keeping the generally capitalistic system intact and preventing more decisive change. This strategy results in socialists focusing on the means of socialism rather than the ends. Such accommodation has been a problem for socialism throughout its history.[127] The purifying and motivating flame of the utopian fire dies down. When more revolutionary change does not appear as a present alternative, however, the reformist strategy does provide some improvement in the quality of life. In our world we should seize upon any genuine improvement, while holding the evil that remains before the light of our deepest visions. In addition and fundamentally, we must seek God and commit ourselves to a resurgence of the full Christianity that springs forth in commitment to the human family essential for the security of liberty and just community.

Epilogue

Are We Better Prepared?

On the day that I was born, as my father came to the hospital, he picked up the Cleveland *Plain Dealer*. The headlines blared the news that Hitler had marched on Denmark and Norway. My father used to comment in sermons that I had already outlived the thousand-year reign that Hitler had proclaimed; however, the lessons from this period live on. They provide a pertinent case study from which we can raise some final questions about political ideologies and the relationship of Christianity to them.

Fascism led to the most all-out war that the world has known. Although it no longer has a major following, fascism has adherents among extremist groups. Its geopolitical views have significantly influenced national security states in Latin America. Fascist movements could reemerge in developing countries that have conditions similar to those in which fascism first rose. In such situations, rapid change is desired; however, the current laws, cultural values and motivation, and self-regulating economic processes provide insufficient structure to support the change. This deficiency in economic and cultural authority leads to a dependence upon political authority. In fascism political authority is used autocratically to solve the conflict between groups whose economic power is changing in favor of traditional groups.[1]

It is debatable that fascism is a unified political tradition. Ralph Bowen warns that fascism was radically anti-intellectual and incoherent and should not be treated solemnly as a worldview with philosophical foundations.[2] By nature the fascist movements were intensely nationalistic; they neither ideologically nor politically recognized any overlapping international connections. The major expressions of fascism in Germany and Italy gave a sharply different emphasis to elements that they held in common. Nevertheless, the term can be used to describe the destructive use of bourgeois democracy by right-wing and anticommunist dictatorships in crisis-ridden parliamentary and capitalistic systems.[3] Our emphasis in these final reflections will be upon National Socialism in Germany, but with some reference to fascism in Italy.

Fascism reveals to us how political visions can be corrupted and how the Christian church can fail to act strongly against the regression. We must continue to ask how the systematic murder of a whole people occurred and for no other reason than that they were Jews in a modern society that developed under Christianity and which continued to have major Christian institutions.

Those who fully shared in the cultural advantages of modern civilization were deeply involved. The leaders of Hitler's Einsatz commandos, the mobile killing units with responsibility for the liquidation of civilian populations, were well educated. Six of the fourteen commanders had Ph.D.s.[4] Members from Germany's medical profession were essential instruments of the worst of National Socialism's policies. Physicians administered, and disguised, the programs of racial selection through sterilization and hospital murder of Jews and other unwanted peoples, including those with physical disorders, handicapping conditions, and mental disease. Medical doctors at Auschwitz had much of the responsibility for the genocide including choosing the victims, carrying out the physical and psychological mechanics of the killing, and balancing the killing with the needed supply of prisoner workers for the camp. They carried out their tasks not only out of obedience or fear, but also out of belief in the National Socialist ideals.[5]

The Corruptibility of Political Visions

National socialism absorbed elements of other visions. In many cases it incorporated their worst possibilities. Generally, the dangerous developments of these values had occurred earlier in German society. National socialism took these tendencies to their most perverse extreme and combined them in a system that heightened the social peril. Traditional conservatism, capitalism, and socialism were the ideologies played upon the most. Fascism thus provides a countertype to one hoped-for response to the great political visions. To draw upon the best and most helpful features of each and to work them into a new vision of society that enhances the contribution of each element.

Traditions associated with traditional conservatism provided fascism with many of its tendencies, although in a perverted form. Fascism arose in countries in which the democratic roots of the political ideas and institutions that circumscribed the political decision makers were frail.[6] There was a powerful traditional conservatism in Germany that was much more extreme than that in England. It was a potent antiliberal tradition, perhaps the dominant German tradition. Its conceptions of power—authoritarianism, nationalism, racism, the warrior hero, and imperialism—stood in opposition to the ideas of natural law, liberty, universalism, equality, and peace.[7] "There is not a single element in Nazi doctrine as developed by its leaders and apologists that does not have a long and frequently dominant tradition in the century and a half preceding the rise of Nazism."[8]

Karl Bracher, in his outstanding work, *The German Dictatorship,* presents National Socialism as an amalgam of two deeply rooted German traditions: the tradition of the bureaucratic authoritarian state standing above both society and the individual, and the *völkisch* ("People-based") community ideology based on race.[9] One specifically German element in German nationalism was the evocation of a unique Germanic prehistory whose heroic tradition was broken by Roman and Jewish and/or Christian influences.[10] German Romanticism was an organistic conception based on blood and community with the individual occupying a relatively minor role.[11] The nation was glorified over against the problems produced by individualism.[12] This tradition rejected the social contract theory in which the individ-ual had rational rights preceding the state. The free market was assaulted as "soul-less egoism," and a revival of the medieval closed and controlled economy was urged.[13] Liberalism and social democracy were regarded as expressions of selfish materialism that violated the vision of an organic society free of adversarial conflict. A new unity of people would provide a bond that would overcome class divisions without effecting any substantive change in property relations.[14]

National Socialism distorted and perverted traditional conservatism overthrow-ing the positive aspects of the Christian teaching about the nature of humanity. The revolutionary and conservative aspects of National Socialism were combined in its commitment to restore an allegedly lost unity of the people.[15] The perversion of traditional conservatism occurred as its delight in diversity was transformed into a disdain for other peoples and cultures as corrupt and inferior.[16] "Radical biological anti-Semitism" became the major tenet of National Socialism. The ideas of the superiority of German culture and the idea of a universal mission were already expressed in the nineteenth century. "Merely rational" Western political thought and the rationalist constitutional state were dismissed. The Jews were associated with the West and the problems attributed to progress and modernization.[17]

Racist doctrines articulated in England and France received more of a reception in Germany than they did in their home countries. This would include Thomas Carlyle of England and Joseph Arthur de Gobineau of France.[18] Gobineau, a nine-teenth-century essayist, argued that the purity of the Aryan race could be main-tained only by strengthening its Nordic strains. Houston Steward Chamberlain, an expatriate offspring of an aristocratic English family, became the foremost propa-gandist of *völkisch* ideas in Germany. His *Foundations of the Nineteenth Century,* written in German, was *the* literary fad of 1900. It was a synthesis of Germanic ideology and anti-Semitic and other racist ideas that resounded throughout the National Socialist era.[19]

"Antirationalism" was a self-chosen name of fascism.[20] Traditional conservatism was critical of rationalism, but National Socialism went on to reject not merely the excesses, but the very principles of Western rationalism. Alfred Rosenberg, a col-laborator with Hitler whose *Myth of the Twentieth Century* was the most widely read book in the movement after Hitler's *Mein Kampf,* stated that Socrates was the first Social Democrat in Europe and the originator of the disease of rationalism because he established the principle of settling vital issues through argument and debate.[21] "Action" was the highest ideal, exalted above reason and intellect.[22] Hans Barth notes in criticism that ideas are not "reducible to other forms or modes of being, such as economic activity, folk spirit, culture soul, race, or social power." Truth is the precondition of all rational agreement. Human association depends upon this agreement. In National Socialism, the loss of belief in truth undermines the foundation of social life.[23]

National Socialism also liked to define itself as antiliberalism, including both Christianity and Marxism as liberal. The primary goal of the National Socialist rev-olution was the eradication of liberalism and individualism. In 1933 Joseph Goeb-bels, Hitler's minister of propaganda, declared on the radio upon the National Socialist victory, "The year 1789 is hereby erdicated from history." The intellectual forerunners upon whom they drew were primarily ideologists fervently opposed to the ideas of democracy, human rights, freedom, and equality.[24]

Liberalism in National Socialism meant the recognition of a spiritual element in the human personality beyond the control of political force.[25] All Western moral and religious concepts about the individual and his or her inalienable dignity as a human personality were rejected. Fascism was the antithesis of the liberal state in Italy as well. Its specific nature there can be defined by its opposition to the existing system. It was antiliberal, antidemocratic, antisocialist, and anti-internationalist.[26]

Laissez-faire conservatism and capitalism were also perverted by fascism. Social Darwinism had provided laissez-faire conservatism with justification for replacing equality with competitive struggle. In Germany an extreme form of Social Darwinism was developed that was later incorporated into the ideology of National Socialism. The survival of the fittest was applied to all of life, including the nation, capturing the racist potentialities of Social Darwinism. The necessary triumph of one nation over another was determined by the quality and progress of the nation and its race.

Education and penal law were instruments of natural selection. The unfit cannot be educated and therefore must be eliminated. Vulgar biological theories applied the racist selective elitism to eugenics. The fittest were in danger of being decimated in the struggle. In democracy the fittest can be overwhelmed by the masses, and the weak are protected in Christianity. Even capitalism favors the unproductive businessman and speculator over the "honest workingman." There was one common theme, "a declaration of war on all those moral values stressing compassion, tolerance, and the protection and welfare of the individual." Social Darwinism simply gave National Socialism an ideology and political strategy based on the right of the stronger.[27]

Capitalism was separated from its democratic and liberal base. In Germany there was a resumption of the old ties of industry with a government that had antisocialist, antidemocratic, and imperialist policies. The fascists needed capitalism as an economic structure to control the proletariat, and the earlier anticapitalist rhetoric became absurd in the face of the requirements of powerful war economy, necessarily based on industry.[28]

As they campaigned for support, the National Socialists took advantage of laissez-faire inabilities to respond quickly and directly to human needs. They made great inroads in Protestant rural areas where, in the face of the most severe economic disaster in living memory, local notables defended laissez-faire strategies. When these officials opposed any suggestion of debt relief, the National Socialists promised it in particular. They also restricted dividends and increased corporate taxes.[29]

Finally, there was the corruption of socialism. The fascists differentiated themselves from orthodox socialists by calling themselves *nationalists.* "The National Socialist German Workers' Party" *(Nazionalsozialistische Deutsche Arbeiterpartei)* (*Nazi* for short) was the name of the party when it started in 1919. Nationalism rather than socialism was the main driving force.[30]

As they emerged and vied for public support, the National Socialists promised something for everyone. This included promises of socialist sharing in industry, but the method in which this would be implemented was said to be not under discussion.[31] What the National Socialists promised was control of capitalism and relief from its effects—not the socialist agenda of worker participation and ownership. Mussolini also at first presented a revolutionary program backing the occupation of factories by workers, and he intended to give workers the political role that they lacked. At the eve of the final collapse and his death in 1945, Mussolini again tried to appear as a genuine socialist, speaking of plants being turned over to the workers.[32]

Fascism gave expression to the statist aberration of socialism. Once in power the National Socialists reduced "socialism" to the vague invocation of a national, community-directed economic idea.[33] The work councils initiated in early developments of codeterminism, and the most socialist aspect of that society, were abolished.[34] *Socialism* was used in the sense that private economic decisions were abrogated or restricted and replaced with a strict regimentation; thus *socialism* for them meant the supremacy of political control over economic and social life. There are repeated references in National Socialism to the socialization of the military companies which originally had been the captain's private enterprise. The hired employees now are soldiers; the company is rented to political powers with a contract of sharing the loot.[35]

Economic forms of capitalism continued, but the laissez-faire theory of capitalism was abruptly abandoned. While capitalist ownership and private profits were still in place, capitalism was absorbed into the state bureaucracy. Business and finance were tightly controlled. Mussolini declared that the community alone had the right to determine what the national interest is; the conflicting interests of owners, workers, technicians, and the state were to be brought under the control of the state.[36] An atmosphere of fear hung over the world of business. While business and the fascist party joined for the suppression of labor and democracy, the party used suppressed labor as a threat against business.

Strict regimentation of capitalism by the state is not socialism. The crucial elements of socialism were missing. Capitalist ownership was retained. There was neither democratic ownership of the means of production, nor shared participation in productive decision making. The fascists divorced socialism from its democratic and humanist base.[37]

When in power, the fascists installed a totalitarian state, distorting both capitalism and socialism. The term, *totalitarian,* was used by Mussolini, who held that the state is absolute and individuals and groups relative.[38] The national–imperialist state formed the core of Italian fascism (in contrast to the racist core of German National Socialism).[39] In the National Socialist version of geopolitics the state is the vital organism that has to grow, struggle, expand, and defend itself. The individual exists only as part of the state, to serve it and defend it.[40] This doctrine was continued in the ideology of the national security state in Latin America.

Fascist statism was also a perversion of the elevation of the state that occurred in the conservative traditions of the national community. In Germany, even among many liberals, the idea of freedom was overwhelmed by "the idea of the state as a force above society assuring unity and efficiency, power and protection ..." Submission to the *völkisch*-national community was contrasted favorably to the "mere" personal freedom of the West. The state secured the wholeness of the people and was a bulwark against materialistic self-seeking.[41] Nationalism, communal solidarity, and the necessary place of state power were intensified into the glorification of the state. In National Socialism the "national community" was to be the panacea for economic and political ills, in place of the pluralism of democracy and class society.[42]

Three elements were included in the totalitarian framework of fascism: the central place of the leader, party rule, and terror.[43] In Germany, Hitler was the sole representative of the people on all levels of political and social life. He claimed to embody the total unity of the people, leaving no room for opposition or criticism. The norms of justice and law were but the façade for the unrestricted "measures" of the total powers of the leader. The tasks in which Hitler was really interested were carried out by the police and the "defense corps" ("SS" [*Schutzstaffel*] or "blackshirts"), the all-important instrument of internal policy.[44]

The body that controlled the state was not the people; it was the elite fascist party that energetically opposed democracy and maintained a militaristic, oligarchic hold on the state. Party rule reflected in part the primacy of the technician over the parliamentary politician in fascist theory; the technician's precision was counterposed to the bombastic rhetoric of the politician.[45] In Germany, the party was subordinate only to Hitler. It had its own sphere of legal jurisdiction, including the imposition of prison sentences.[46]

The terror built upon the racism, the quest for the super race, the elevation of the state, and the dissolving of liberal rights and democratic controls. The result was the classic example of what might follow. In addition to the genocide of 6 million Jews, the Nazis murdered millions of Slavs and members of other people groups that were excluded from the Aryan fiction. In Poland alone, in addition to the extermination of 3 million Jews, 3 million Gentile Poles also were destroyed.[47] Almost one-third of Europe's 1.5 million Gypsies were killed.[48] Of millions of captured Russian soldiers, the second largest group of victims of National Socialism, only a fraction were alive at the end of the war. Only 40 percent remained, compared to 95 percent at the end of World War I.[49] Large numbers of political opponents, handicapped children, and mental patients were also murdered.

The Readiness of the Church for Political Critique

Our experience with fascism points up a concern that is at the heart of these pages. The church was not prepared to resist the evils of the fascist regimes thoroughly and consistently. The corporate statements of church judgment, particularly those that explicitly and forthrightly condemned the Jewish policy, were few.[50] The failures were characteristic of both Protestants and Catholics. Cooperation and accommodation were an attraction accepted by many. Only a minority in Germany refused the loyalty oaths.

At the same time there was a significant resistance to the entry of the government into the domain of the church, and many individuals provided courageous resistance. We can learn from both the failure and the faithfulness of witness during this period of severe trial.

The National Socialists were vulnerable to opposition in the period in which they were gaining power. Where the press opposed them or where there was widespread opposition by local notables, such as in Catholic and working-class communities, the party made little headway. Catholic rural areas were heavily opposed to the National Socialists before they took power.[51]

Once the National Socialists became the rulers, much of the opposition shifted to reluctant respect for authority. Later with the outbreak of the war, opposition was further deflated as the churches largely fell back to their "patriotic duty" of supporting their government. The anticommunist policies of National Socialism also blunted much of the opposition of both Protestants and Catholics.

Negotiations after the National Socialist victory in 1933 led to the Vatican's giving official recognition to the Hitler regime and agreeing to restrictions on political and social Catholic organizations in Germany in exchange for protection and freedom of religion.[52] In France the papacy assured Marshall Pétain of Vichy France that it would not make trouble over the deportation of Jews.[53] The German Roman Catholic bishops were unprepared by their education and historical background to act in opposition to authority. Although they opposed the party before 1933 for its opposition to religious liberty and nationalistic claims of superiority, they ignored the antisemitism and threat to democracy. Once the National Socialists were in power the bishops urged support of the regime.[54] The church in Italy supported the regime as a step toward theocratic order.

It appears that the atrocities to the Jews were well known. Even in retirement, Curt Prüfer, an ill-informed and second-level diplomat, knew the worst and wrote in his diary in 1942, "Men, women and children have been slaughtered in large numbers by poison-gas, or by machine guns. . . . Today every child knows this in the smallest detail."[55] Marrus and Paxton claim that in Vichy France the intensity of the Jewish suffering by 1941 was apparent to anybody who would look.[56]

The failure of opposition included a shortcoming in theology. The Lutheran two-kingdoms teaching as it was interpreted from the nineteenth century on had engendered an attitude toward the state in which the primary Christian obligation was obedience. The two realms of the church and the state were but partners for the care of humanity. They left each other alone except to support the authority of each.

Christian citizenship in this thought was divorced from the transcendent absolutes of the Christian faith. It did not offer a criticism of justice in terms of love; love was reserved for the life of the church and personal relationships. There was no dynamic sense of justice and equality arising from religious understanding. The state and other institutions of secular life were autonomous. Obedience and respect for their authority were required. Christian theologians supporting the National Socialists explicity drew upon the two-kingdoms teaching as mandating grateful support for Hitler. As Wilhelm Stapel phrased it, "Everything concerning justice and morality belongs to the totalitarian state."[57] Such statements were the extreme. The more significant consequence was the general individual apathy to political questions.

The attitude of moral indifference toward the public domain was widespread in German culture. Albert Speer was Hitler's architect, later armaments minister, and finally director of the economy. He managed this so effectively that he has been credited with prolonging Germany's war effort by two years. He was highly educated and one of the most intelligent persons around Hitler. Looking back from prison in later years, he wondered how in good conscience he could have overlooked the destruction of the Jewish people. He saw how in a totalitarian regime everyone gets caught up in her or his own compartment of technical competency. There one felt responsibility, but the overall policies were being made by another and were too complex. Individuals felt no personal responsibility for them, or for their brutal implementation, if they themselves did not take part. As the events developed that were the beginning of the annihilation of a whole group in his society, Speer busied himself in his architectural work. He built vast stadiums for Hitler's storm troopers and other public buildings, including the chancellery for Hitler himself. "Political events did not concern me," he wrote. "My job was simply to provide impressive backdrops for such events." He later realized, however, that "in the final analysis I myself determined the degree of my isolation, the extremity of my evasions, and the extent of my ignorance."[58]

William Harlan Hale saw Speer as exemplary of a German upper middle class betrayed by its own culture. It had been taught that life and politics were things apart. Politics was fundamentally corrupt. The truly civilized, cultured, and highly educated person should be above it. Even Thomas Mann wrote that he was *unpolitisch*.[59] Tocqueville's warning was almost prophetic: "When the great mass of citizens does not want to bother about anything but private business, even the smallest party need not give up hope of becoming master of public affairs."[60]

The theological basis of resistance was based in Calvinism rather than in Lutheranism. Historically, Calvinism has seen a responsibility of the Christian for the social order to mold it toward the sovereignty of God in all things.

The Confessing Church was set up as a counterfront after a Christian arm of the National Socialist movement took over the Lutheran church hierarchy by fraud. The Barmen Declaration of the Confessing Church in 1934 rejected the two-kingdom matter as a false doctrine "as though there were areas of our life in which we would not belong to Jesus Christ, but to other lords."[61] The Confessing Church was not political resistance in itself. The formation of this body was not directed against National Socialist authority as such but on behalf of the preservation of religious autonomy and the freedom to teach.[62]

Opposition to the Jewish policy was largely limited to individual acts and assistance. Only a few took the path of political resistance.[63] This heroic resistance emerged in actions by both Protestants and Catholics, lay and clergy. Since it was presented on the grounds of the total demand of Christ, it preceded without suggestion of opportunism. Such an uncompromising attitude was translated into underground activities and political resistance. It created an atmosphere that permitted a conversion from nationalism to acknowledgment of the primacy of justice, suprarational humanity, and responsibility for the whole of humankind.[64] The criticism of the regime possessed a greater potential force within the church than in other sectors. The National Socialist policy of ideological coordination was limited here, and Hitler believed that he would not be able to break through those limits until after he had won the war.[65]

For the churches to resist the National Socialist appeal more effectively, they would have had to begin many decades earlier. Bracher observes that nothing basically new was evolving in National Socialism. Everything that was happening was inherent in the development in Germany of nationalism in the nineteenth century.[66] The churches needed to have critically encountered those ideas as they emerged. This would have required a fully developed theology of society and economy and the application of it to the political visions of that day. The engagement with the world of politics and economy would need to have been as much in thought as in action. Preparation for major overt challenges to the faithful witness of the church begins in continual critical evaluation of the political concepts of the present.

Too often the disengagement from political evaluation and critique has been characteristic of Christianity as we know it. The separation of love from justice and the consignment of these virtues to separate spheres has characterized many American Christians, including a great many who are not Lutheran. We often claim to be dealing with concerns that are so important that we cannot afford to spend time on something so meaningless, if not corrupt, as politics. Our individual efforts, much of which are genuine and essential in their own right—our evangelism, pastoral work, counseling, even much of our social ministry with an apolitical character—serve as an impressive backdrop to the political struggles of our own day. The uneasy conscience of modern Christianity too frequently stands as a backdrop for a society full of injustice and corruption because of misapplication, or neglect, of political and economic power. We consider that our ministries will be furthered if we have the friendship and respect of those in power rather than furnishing them with a critique based in concerns that transcend that which is present and visible. Like Speer we claim to be objective and living a life superior to politics while giving support by silence or by cooperation with the destructive forces of the status quo.

A view of the world will always have at least an implicit political dimension, and it is the world-life view that brings to politics direction for the distribution of power. A theology which makes no political application will leave this part of the world-view to be filled by its competitors.

Christianity must contribute its burden for liberty, justice, and participation. It must carry it out with special attention to the weak so that these essential pillars of life in community can be actual for them. Because we believe that humanity has a propensity for good, we must support the forces that encourage individual self-expression and control and responsibility. Because we believe that humanity has a propensity for evil, we must defeat all concentrations of power that deny the masses of the people representation and are not responsible to them. We must hold forth a vision of the common good that resists atomization and a denial of the person as a social being.

Revitalization of faith in God is an essential part of a political strategy. To have our deepest political dreams come true to any appreciable extent requires a strategy of politics that goes beyond the long and necessary process of political education, organization, and exertion of power. True evangelism and the creation of discipling communities are political acts as the Lordship of Christ becomes a reality in the personal lives of an appreciable number of the citizenry.

As we have observed of vision after vision, the fondest political hopes are dependent upon a culture that will sustain them. They cannot be produced merely by political action or economic organization. This is true whether we are thinking of democracy or laissez-faire conservatism or socialism. To nourish their strengths and guard against their proclivities for evil, they require virtues of love, communality, self-restraint, justice, and devotion to truth. Such values, in order to convict, to compel, and to last from generation to generation, depend upon a foundation in religious faith, a rootage found most deeply in a faith in the God made known through Jesus Christ.

Such faith requires humility in the political thinker and actor. We must engage in continuous soul searching to uproot the dimensions in our own political positions that serve us and our class and race to the detriment of the wretched of the earth.

NOTES

Introduction

1. Sheldon Wolin, *Politics and Vision. Continuity and Innovation in Western Political Thought* (Boston, Little, Brown, 1960), 6, 9–11.

2. Gary R. Orren, "Beyond Self Interest," in *The Power of Public Ideas,* ed. R. Reich (Cambridge, MA, Ballinger, 1988), 13–20, 25; Steven Kelman, "Why Public Ideas Matter," in idem., 31, 53; Philip B. Heymann, "How Government Expresses Public Ideas," in idem., 90, 92.

3. We are using *ideology* neutrally here, combining its visionary and conserving aspects. Later in the book we will also take up the critical, negative use of the term.

4. André Béteille, "Ideologies: Commitment and Partisanship," *L'Homme* 18, 3/4 (July/December, 1978), 53.

5. Guy Rocher, "Le Droit et l'imaginaire social," *Recherches sociographiques* 23 (1982), 68. Rocher stresses the symbolic and educative contribution of laws.

6. James Luther Adams, "Religion and the Ideologies," *Confluence* 4 (1955), 72.

7. Peter C. Lloyd, *Classes, Crises and Coups: Themes in the Sociology of Developing Countries* (London, MacGibbon, 1971), 76. An ideology in some sense is an argument (Béteille, "Ideologies," 65).

8. Béteille, 65–66.

9. Terry Eagleton, "What is Politics About? Terry Eagleton Replies to Bernard Bergonzi," *New Blackfriars* 47 (1966), 372.

10. Pierre Bourdieu, *Distinction: A Social Critique of the Judgement of Taste* (Cambridge, MA, Harvard U., 1984), 434, 454.

11. Kelman, "Why Public Ideas Matter," 44.

12. Cf. Jacques Le Goff, "Is Politics Still the Backbone of History? *Daedalus* 100 (Winter, 1971), 2.

13. Adams, "Religion and the Ideologies," 77.

14. A. P. D'Entreves, "Introduction," to *Aquinas. Selected Political Writings* (Oxford, Blackwell, 1948), xii. See also, Ronald Beiner, "The Classical Method of Political Science, and its Relation to the Study of Contemporary Politics," *Government and Opposition* 19 (1984), 472.

15. Carroll Kilpatrick, "Friends Say Nixon Deeply Worried, Upset by Watergate Affair," *Boston Globe,* August 12, 1973, 14.

16. Jürgen Habermas, *Theory and Practice* (Boston, Beacon, 1973⁴), 42; cf. Richard J. Bernstein, *The Restructuring of Social and Political Theory* (Philadelphia, U. of Pennsylvania, 1978), 185.

17. R. H. Tawney, *The Acquisitive Society* (London, Bell, 1922), 2. The image of the road is also from Tawney, loc. cit.

18. Paul Ramsey, *Who Speaks for the Church? A Critique of the 1966 Geneva Conference on Church and Society* (Nashville, Abingdon, 1967), 152–54. To restrict the church from recommending particular policy choices on the grounds that that is the function of the ruler is

incorrect, however. That is an undue segregation of functions; it also limits the possibilities of democracy.

19. S. C. Mott, "The Use of the New Testament for Social Ethics," *Journal of Religious Ethics* 15 (1987), 225–60; Mott, "How Should Christian Economists Use the Bible? A Study in Hermeneutics," *Bulletin of the Association of Christian Economists* 13 (Spring, 1989), 7–19.

20. Jacques Ellul, *The Political Illusion* (New York, Vintage, 1967), 200–201.

21. José Míguez Bonino, *Doing Theology in a Revolutionary Situation* (Philadelphia, Fortress, Confrontation Books, 1975), 148.

22. John V. Taylor, *Enough Is Enough* (Minneapolis, Augsburg, 1975), 41.

23. Míguez, 149.

24. Ralph Waldo Emerson, "The Conservative" (1841), in Emerson, *Works,* Concord ed., Vol. 1: *Nature: Addresses and Lectures* (Boston, Houghton, 1903), 299; cf. Clinton Rossiter, *Conservatism in America. The Thankless Persuasion* (New York, Vintage, 1962²), 56.

25. One of the sources which nourish an ideology is rival ideologies (Béteille, "Ideologies," 65). Such a range of alternative ways to respond to the critique of ideologies is consistent with what Béteille describes as the "intellectual restiveness" of our times (49). This results from the failure to find satisfying intellectual solutions to the problem of the distribution of power.

26. Le Goff, "Is Politics Still the Backbone of History?" 10–11.

Chapter 1

1. Herman Dooyeweerd, *Roots of Western Culture: Pagan, Secular and Christian Options* (Toronto, Wedge, 1979), 66–67.

2. James Luther Adams, "Theological Bases of Social Action," in Adams, *Taking Time Seriously* (Glencoe, IL, Free, 1957), 43 (originally in *Journal of Religious Thought* 8,1 [Autumn–Winter, 1950/51], 102–19; also reprinted in Adams, *On Being Human Religiously;* and Adams, *Voluntary Associations*).

3. Reinhold Niebuhr, *The Nature and Destiny of Man. A Christian Interpretation, Vol. 2: Human Destiny* (New York, Scribner's, 1964), 262.

4. Robert Bierstedt, "An Analysis of Social Power," *American Sociological Review* 15 (1950), 737.

5. Mary F. Rogers, "Instrumental and Infra-Resources," *American Journal of Sociology* 79 (1974), 1424.

6. Cf. Amitai Etzioni, *The Active Society. A Theory of Societal and Political Processes* (New York, Free, 1968), 320. Dennis Wrong notes that there can be a situation of equality in which different individuals hold advantage at different times or in different roles (*Power: Its Forms, Bases and Uses* (New York, Harper, Key Concepts in the Social Sciences, 1979), 10–11.

7. Bierstedt, 735. Wrong, however, would limit power to *intentional* influence in distinction to "diffuse controls" while recognizing that unintentional influence is likely to follow (*Power,* 4).

8. Amos H. Hawley, "Community Power and Urban Renewal Success," *American Journal of Sociology* 68 (1963), 422.

9. Bierstedt, "Analysis of Social Power," 731.

10. Richard M. Emerson, "Power-Dependence Relations," *American Sociological Review* 27 (1962), 32.

11. Literally, *hand. Hand (yād)* metaphorically means *power* (Hans Walter Wolff, *Anthro-*

pology of the Old Testament [Philadelphia, Fortress, 1974], 68; cf. Gen. 39.21–22; Deut. 8.17–18; Ps. 89.13). Used in this way, *yād* expresses several aspects of power, as seen in the following examples: oppression, often regarding deliverance from it (Judg. 6.9 [frequent]); total domination (Deut. 3.3); control, authority (Gen. 39. 6); agency (Gen. 39.22); capacity (Num. 6.21); possession (Num. 21.26); having at one's disposal (Gen. 9.2).

12. Max Weber, *Economy and Society. An Outline of Interpretative Sociology,* ed. G. Roth and C. Wittick (New York, Bedminster, 1968⁴), 2.926. (This treatment of power [pp. 926–40] appears also in *From Max Weber: Essays in Sociology,* ed. H. Gerth and C. W. Mills [New York, Oxford U., 1946], 180–95.)

13. Or power makes the options less attractive (Etzioni, *Active Society,* 320).

14. Bierstedt, 733.

15. Floyd Hunter, *Community Power Structure. A Study of Decision Makers* (Garden City, NY, Doubleday, 1963).

16. Hawley, 423.

17. Pierre Bourdieu's brilliant sociological study of class in France (*Distinction: A Social Critique of the Judgement of Taste* [Cambridge, MA, Harvard U., 1984]) uses "class" to describe the whole and the interaction of the phenomena that Max Weber described as "class" and "status" (Weber, *Economy and Society,* 2.926–40). Weber is helpful for the basic distinctions; but the understanding of the variables within class and status and their interrelationships became more sophisticated in the twentieth century. More recent studies should be consulted for specific application of the concepts.

18. Weber, *loc. cit.*

19. The significance of Bourdieu's work is showing how much a person's preferences in the ordinary matters of life, such as in ways of dressing, eating, speaking, and appearance, express and reinforce the basic social divisions of the society. He shows that lifestyle relates very much to Weber's "class" and how deeply rooted the divisions of society are in one's personal and group history.

20. Adams, "Theological Bases of Social Action," esp. 42, 50; "Blessed are the Powerful," *Christian Century* 86 (June 18, 1969), 838–41 (also in Adams, *The Prophethood of All Believers*). Paul Tillich, *Love, Power, and Justice. Ontological Analyses and Ethical Applications* (New York, Oxford U., 1954), esp. 35–53; "Shadow and Substance: A Theory of Power" (1965), in Tillich, *Political Expectation,* ed. J. L. Adams (New York, Harper, 1971), 115–24; Tillich's first essay on power (1931) has been as reprinted as "The Problem of Power," in Tillich, *The Interpretation of History* (New York, Scribner's, 1936), 179–202. For a fine summary of Tillich's position, cf. Théo Junker, "Paul Tillich: Une théorie du pouvoir pour le socialisme," *Studies in Religion* 12 (1983), 325–36.

21. Cyril H. Powell notes the open references to God's power in the great credos and doxological statements and designations throughout Scripture, e.g. 1 Chron. 29.11–12; 2 Chron. 20.6; Ps. 21.13; 68.34; 111.6; Matt. 6.13; Rev. 7.12; 4.11; 5.12; 19.1–2 (*The Biblical Concept of Power* [London, Epworth, Fernley-Hartley Lectures, 1963], 6, 71, 194–95).

22. Cf. Rudolf Schnackenburg's warning in "Macht, Gewalt und Friede nach dem Neuen Testament," in Schnackenburg, *Massstab des Glaubens* (Freiberg, Herder, 1978), 232. On the other hand, the usefulness for social ethics of many writings about power in the Bible is limited by the failure to discuss its language of power in terms of a sociological theory of power or to develop what the understanding of social power is in the biblical materials. The biblical cultures had a concept of social power; all cultures do.

23. Wrong, *Power,* 28–30.

24. Roderick Martin, *The Sociology of Power* (London, Routledge, International Library of Sociology, 1977), 35.

25. Tillich, "The Problem of Power," 193. Similarly, in *The Socialist Decision* (New York, Harper, 1977 [1933], 98), Tillich speaks of inner power with which an object "resists total absorption into the technological system."

26. Tillich, *Love, Power, and Justice,* 41–42.

27. Wrong, *Power,* 2, 129.

28. Economist Andrew Reschovsky, as quoted by Charles Stein, "The Trouble with Taxing the Rich," *Boston Globe,* July 10, 1990, p. 41.

29. Lyle E. Schaller, *The Change Agent* (Nashville, TN, Abingdon, 1972), 146.

30. Plato, *Soph.* 247d-e *(dynamin eit' eis to poiein . . . eit' eis to pathein)*; cf. Adams, "Theological Bases of Social Action," 44. Bernard Loomer describes "the ability to produce an effect and undergo an effect" as "relational power" ("Two Kinds of Power," *Criterion* 15,1 (Winter, 1976), 20–28). It "takes physical and psychic strength to endure an effect" (p. 20). We mutually make claims and permit others to make claims for sake of the enhancement of the relationships of all participating members, rather than focus on a particular side of the relationship (pp. 23–24, 26). Preferable is the term *communal power,* supplied by Peter J. Paris (*The Social Teachings of the Black Churches* [Philadelphia, Fortress, 1985], 107–27), who applies Loomer's relational power to the tradition of power in the black churches. Paris and Adams' treatments are helpful in that they do not see an either/or choice between "unilateral power" and "relational power." Intervening power, or unilateral power, often is necessary to create the relationship and is included within the broader context of communal power.

31. Cf. the helpful distinction between influence and power by Bierstedt ("Analysis of Social Power," 731) and Etzioni: Influence changes the recipient's preferences, but power does not. "Resistance is overcome not because the actor subjected to the use of power changes his 'will' but because resistance has been made more expensive, prohibitive, or impossible" (*Active Society,* 359–60).

32. Cf. Paris, 113, 121–23.

33. Allan Aubrey Boesak, *Farewell to Innocence. A Socio-Ethical Study on Black Theology and Black Power* (Maryknoll, NY, Orbis, 1977), 51.

34. Rollo May, *Power and Innocence. A Search for the Sources of Violence* (New York, Norton, 1972), 100.

35. Emerson, "Power-Dependence Relations," 36–38.

36. I discuss this power in more detail in relation to strategic noncooperation in *Biblical Ethics and Social Change* (New York, Oxford U., 1982), 143–45.

37. Elizabeth Janeway, *Powers of the Weak* (New York, Knopf, 1980), 115, 160, 162, 218. H. Miriam Ross suggested to me the appropriateness of Janeway, Gutman, and Antonovsky for understanding defensive power.

38. Frederick Douglass, *Life and Times of Frederick Douglass* (New York, Collier, 1962[2]), 79. Douglass commented, "In this Christian country men and women were obliged to hide in barns and woods and trees from professing Christians, in order to learn to read the *Holy Bible*" (p. 153).

39. Janeway, 169, 172.

40. Herbert G. Gutman, *The Black Family in Slavery and Freedom, 1750–1925* (New York, Pantheon, 1976), cf. 260, 433, 71–72, 274.

41. Aaron Antonovsky (*Health, Stress, and Coping* [San Francisco, Jossey-Bass, 1979], 99–122) analyzes the diverse resources that are characteristic of those who have been healthy in dealing with and overcoming significant stresses in their lives. A black grandmother related to Robert Coles: "We've had God; and He's something to have—Someone. And I'll tell you: we've had each other to turn to. I'd go down the road in Strawberry and sit with a friend and

we'd feel a lot better by the time we'd had a cup of coffee" (Robert Coles, *Children of Crisis, Vol. 3; The South Goes North* (Boston, Little, Brown, 1971), 129).

42. by *wāw* explicativum.

43. Tillich, "Shadow and Substance," 121.

44. Karl Rahner, "The Theology of Power," in Rahner, *Theological Investigations* (Baltimore, Helicon, 1966), 4.404.

45. Will and power work in tandem, cf. Acts 4.28. So Aristotle stated that all people do what they wish if they have the power (*Pol.* 1312b3, cf. 1313b32).

46. James H. Cone, *God of the Oppressed* (New York, Seabury, 1975), 228.

47. Coles, *South Goes North*, 55.

48. Coles, 102, 110.

49. "An Eye-Witness Account—Shatila Camp," Palestine Human Rights Campaign. *Special Report* (September/October, 1982), 4.

50. Adams, "Blessed are the Powerful," 838, 840. Edgar Z. Friedenberg was more explicit earlier: "All weakness tends to corrupt, and impotence corrupts absolutely" (*Coming of Age in America. Growth and Acquiescense* [New York, Vintage, 1965], pp. 47–48). The term *absolutely* in either form is an overstatement. Cf. May, *Power and Innocence,* 25: " . . . a common characteristic of all mental patients is their powerlessness." The statement of Lord Acton, a Roman Catholic liberal, is found in a letter by him to Mandell Creighton, April 5, 1887 (Lord John E. Acton, *Essays on Freedom and Power,* ed. Gertrude Himmelfarb [Gloucester, MA, Peter Smith, 1948], 335).

51. Tex S. Sample, "Toward a Christian Understanding of Power," in *Toward a Discipline of Social Ethics,* Walter Muelder Fest., ed. P. Deats (Boston, Boston U., 1972), 122.

52. Examples of the poor becoming poorer during economic expansion are Brazil during the 1960's (cf. Celso Furtado, *Economic Development of Latin America. Historical Background and Contemporary Problems* [Cambridge U., Cambridge Latin American Studies 8, 1976²], 87–88) and the United States in the unusually long economic recovery in the 1980s in which the top income quintile (fifth) had very significant income growth while the lowest fifth significantly declined, measured in constant dollars. The richest 1 percent of all families (those who made about $500,000 a year and up in 1990) more than doubled their after-tax income between 1977 and 1990; meanwhile, the average income of the poorest fifth of all families fell by about 6 percent. Real wages also declined in this period (cf. David Fasenfast and Stephen Rose, "A Growing Gap: Income Distribution in The 80s'," *Blueprint for Social Justice* 42, 10 [June, 1989], 2; Interfaith Action for Economic Justice, *Networker* [July/August, 1990]). This was probably the situation in Israel in the time of the eighth century (B.C.) prophets.

53. Rahner, "Theology of Power," 395.

54. Cf. Antonovsky, *Health, Stress, and Coping,* 116, on the health producing effects in resisting stress of networks of stable social relationships and belonging to a coherent and relatively integrated subculture.

55. This term was the suggestion of a former student, Richard O. Funk. The problem I have with my term *intervening* and with *substitute* is that they might imply that this form of power is not inherent in human life. The term which I used in previous writings on this topic was *creative power*. While creative power related well with the concept of "creative justice" and the creational aspects of God's Reign, it did not help the reader recall other distinctions of this form of power.

56. Powell, *Biblical Concept of Power,* 77, 81, 84.

57. Wolff, *Anthropology of Old Testament,* 163: *kibšūhā*—to apply force so as to have something at one's disposal. Tillich indicates that the "struggle of power of being with power

of being" involves "*all* relations of *all* beings" [italics added]—not necessarily out of hostility or neurosis, but as inherent in the structure of being (*Love, Power, and Justice,* 42–43). A nonromantic presentation of frontier life, such as O. E. Rölvaag's, *Giants in the Earth,* makes understandable this concept of struggle with power of being in nature, even without personifying it as happened in the neurosis described in this striking novel.

58. William J. Dumbrell, "Genesis 1–3, Ecology, and the Dominion of Man." *Crux* 21,4 (December, 1985), 21.

59. James E. Wood, Jr. "A Theology of Power," *Journal of Church and State* 14 (1972), 111.

60. Matt. 23.8–11; Luke 22.24–30; 2 Cor. 4.5, 7; 12.9–10; Jan Lambrecht, "Dienende Macht," *Erbe und Auftrag* 60 (1984), 434–41.

61. Cf. Reinhold Niebuhr, *The Children of Light and the Children of Darkness. A Vindication of Democracy and a Critique of Its Traditional Defence* (New York, Scribner's, 1972), 113. Every form of power is "both defensive and offensive; and no sharp line can be drawn between its two functions" (p. 109).

62. Tillich, "Shadow and Substance," 118.

63. Tillich, 123–24.

64. Wallace I. Wolverton, "The King's 'Justice' in Pre-Exilic Israel," *Anglical Theological Review* 41 (1959), 281.

65. Adams, "Blessed Are the Powerful," 840–41.

66. Reinhold Niebuhr, *Moral Man and Immoral Society* (New York, Scribner's, 1960), xii, xiv–xv, 21.

67. E.g. Craig M. Watts, "Dealing Responsibly with Power," *Cross Currents* 36 (1986), 74–84.

68. Boesak, *Farewell to Innocence,* 5–6, 29.

69. Lewis B. Smedes, *Love Within Limits. A Realist's View of 1 Corinthians 13* (Grand Rapids, MI, Eerdmans, 1978), 7–8.

Chapter 2

1. Eugene F. Miller, "Political Philosophy and Human Nature," *Personalist* 53 (1972), 215–16. Paul Tillich stated that the roots of political thought lie in human being itself, which is the "interrelation of drives and interests, of pressures and aspirations, which make up social reality" (*The Socialist Decision* [New York, Harper, 1977 (1933)], 2).

2. John Wesley, Sermon 129, "Heavenly Treasures in Earthen Vessels" [Preface] 1, in *The Works of John Wesley, Vol. 4: Sermons 4* (Bicentennial Ed.) (Nashville, Abingdon, 1987), 162.

3. Wolff, *Anthropology of the Old Testament,* 160–61.

4. On the image deformed but retained, cf. John Calvin, *Institutes of the Christian Religion,* ed. J. McNeill (Philadelphia, Westminster, Library of Christian Classics 20–21, 1960), I.5.5 (p. 57); I.15.4 (p. 189). Wesley includes in the remains of the image of God, an immaterial principle, a spiritual nature, understanding, affections, a degree of liberty and of a self-moving and self-governing power, some discernment of good and evil ("Heavenly Treasures in Earthen Vessels" 1.1, p. 163).

5. Niebuhr, *Moral Man and Immoral Society,* xxiv–xxv.

6. Calvin held that by the grace of God there is a natural and universal apprehension of reason implanted in human beings that provides them with knowledge of "earthly things," including government. This includes a natural instinct to foster and preserve society and a

universal impression of "a certain civic fair dealing and order" although there is great dispute about the specific meaning of this conception of equity and hatred of it because of lust (*Institutes,* 2.2.13–14 [pp. 272–73]; cf. Sheldon Wolin, *Politics and Vision. Continuity and Innovation in Western Political Thought* [Boston, Little, Brown, 1960], 184–85).

7. Paul Tillich, "The Political Meaning of Utopia" (1951), in Tillich, *Political Expectation,* 137.

8. The attention shifts from developing the rights of the governed and the prerequisites for living together to the character and ethics of the rulers (Elizabeth Janeway, *Powers of the Weak,* 85). In addition, human beings "suppose those below them to be worse than themselves" and in need of the whip (Robert G. Wesson, *The Imperial Order* (Berkeley, CA, U. of California, 1967), 506.

9. Bob Spencer as interviewed by Ed Wojcicki, "Good Citizens Can't Be Cynics," *Salt* 11, 4 (April, 1991), 19.

10. Blaise Pascal, *Pensées* 358 (Paris, Garnier, Classiques Garnier, 1958), 164: ". . . *le malheur veut que qui veut faire l'ange fait la bête.*"

11. John Cotton, "An Exposition upon the Thirteenth Chapter of Revelation" (1658), in *Puritan Political Ideas,* ed. E. Morgan (Indianapolis, IN, Bobbs-Merrill, American Heritage Series, 1965), 174–75.

12. Reinhold Niebuhr, *Christian Realism and Political Problems* (New York, Scribner's, 1953), 119.

13. Niebuhr, *Moral Man and Immoral Society,* 232–34; cf. Niebuhr, *The Irony of American History* (New York, Scribner's 1952), 148; "Our Moral and Spiritual Resources for International Cooperation," *Social Action* 22 (February, 1956), 18–20.

14. Reinhold Niebuhr, *The Nature and Destiny of Man. A Christian Interpretation, Vol. 1; Human Nature* (New York, Scribner's, 1964), 180.

15. Tillich, "Political Meaning of Utopia," 126. Cf. this entire section, 126–40 ("The Root of Utopia in Man's Being"), which correlates well with Niebuhr's perspective.

16. Tillich, 128.

17. Niebuhr, *Human Nature* 16, 179.

18. Cf. Niebuhr, *Human Nature,* 167, 16.

19. Niebuhr, *Human Nature,* 182, 185.

20. June 27, 1766, in John Wesley, *The Letters of the Rev. John Wesley, A.M.* ed. J. Telford (London, Epworth, 1931), 5.16.

21. Tillich, 128–30.

22. Niebuhr, *Human Nature,* 184.

23. Niebuhr, *Human Nature,* 183, 16.

24. Augustine, *City of God,* 14.13 (trans. M. Dods; New York, Modern Library, 1950), 461. John Wesley identifies the roots of wickedness as "self-will, pride, and independence from God" (Sermon 128, "The Deceitfulness of the Human Heart" 2.3, in Wesley, *Works 4: Sermons 4,* 156; cf. 1.3, p. 154).

25. Cf. Richard J. Mouw, *Politics and the Biblical Drama* (Grand Rapids, MI, Eerdmans, 1976), 48. Mouw correctly criticizes Fromm's interpretation of the rebellion in Genesis as a positive act of freedom from God (Erich Fromm, *The Fear of Freedom* [London, Kegan Paul, International Library of Sociology and Social Reconstruction, 1942], 27–28. [American title: *Escape from Freedom*],). God is not presented there as a despot but as one affectionately seeking relationship (Mouw, 39–41). It is in loving and obedient relationship to God that one's power of being is restored so that one can secure the spontaneous relationship with humanity, nature, and one's self that Fromm presents as the proper response to the unbearable isolation of freedom rather than escaping into new dependencies (*Fear of Freedom,* x, 24).

26. Mouw, 39–45).

27. R. Niebuhr, *Children of Light,* 19–20.

28. Augustine stated that the rich "abuse the poor as their dependents, to minister to their pride" and estimate their prosperity . . . by the servility of their subjects" (*City of God,* 2.2, p. 59).

29. Helmut Schoeck. *Envy: A Theory of Social Behaviour* (New York, Harcourt, 1969). Schoeck demonstrates the universality and social importance of envy. He perceptively distinguishes envy from genuine relative deprivation, conflict, or movements for social justice that may indeed require structural intervention. Envy rather instead relates to structural aggression motivated, not by a firm commitment to a standard of right, but by the intent for the destruction of the happiness of others (cf. pp. 8, 93, 103, 226). To miss his affirmation of social justice in distinction to envy by attributing to envy valid movements for social justice is to engage in what Schoeck called "the envy of aloofness"—envy from the top down, resenting those who appear to be advancing up to our level (p. 163). For the power of envy, cf. Eccles. 4.4 *(NRSV):* "Then I saw that all toil and all skill in work come from one person's envy of another. This also is vanity and a chasing after wind."

30. Niebuhr, *Children of Light,* 20; *Human Nature,* 189–90.

31. R. Niebuhr, *Human Nature,* 192.

32. Augustine, *City of God,* 18.2, p. 610.

33. Fromm, *Fear of Freedom.*

34. Cf. Søren Kierkegaard, *Kierkegaard's Writings. Vol. 19: The Sickness unto Death. A Christian Psychological Exposition for Upbuilding and Awakening,* ed. H. Hong and E. Hong (Princeton, Princeton U., 1980), 82.

35. Cf. Mouw, *Politics and the Biblical Drama,* 49.

36. Fromm, 149–52.

37. Judith Plaskow, *Sex, Sin and Grace: Women's Experience and the Theologies of Reinhold Niebuhr and Paul Tillich* (Washington, D.C., University Press of America, 1980), cf. 35, 64–65, 90, 151–52. She speaks of the self which cannot meet others as a subject because it has not become a subject itself (p. 154). The exertion of responsibility is exchanged for love and care (Carol Gilligan, *In a Different Voice. Psychological Theory and Women's Development* [Cambridge, MA, Harvard U., 1982], 67; cf. 54, 61, 88). I am by no means generalizing that this condition to applies to all women who find themselves in a situation in which they are unfairly treated as subordinates. For example, despite appearances, in a man-centered family the mother and wife is often the strong one who with great skill is holding together many lives and relationships. Tillich describes self-protection as a form of courage—saying "Yes" to being "despite the threat of nonbeing and the loss of security provided by the past" ("The Political Meaning of Utopia," 132).

38. Kierkegaard, *Sickness unto Death,* 34. For his description of "feminine despair," cf. pp. 47, 51.

39. John C. Raines, "Sin as Pride and Sin as Sloth," *Christianity and Crisis* 29, 1 (February 3, 1969), 5. Raines' criticism of Marx that he restricted this slothfulness of being to the disinherited must be qualified. Marx included "the capitalist" in this form of alienation ("Economic and Philosophical Manuscripts" 3.20 in Marx, *Early Writings,* ed. T. B. Bottomore [New York, McGraw-Hill, 1963], 178); and he described in a similar way those under the power of money (*idem.* 3.63, pp. 193–94 [see p. 189]). Raines is correct, however, about Marx's utopian failure in not seeing this behavior as a universal and permanent aspect of human existence.

40. R. Niebuhr, *Human Nature,* 192.

41. Reinhold Niebuhr, "The Age between the Ages," in Niebuhr, *Discerning the Signs of the Times* (London, SCM, 1946), 43.

42. R. Niebuhr, *Human Destiny,* 272–73; Augustine, *City of God,* 2.21, p. 63; 19.24, p. 706.

43. Cf. S. N. Dubey, "Powerlessness and Orientations towards Family and Children: A Study in Deviance," *Indian Journal of Social Work* 32 [1971], 35–43. One must be sensitive, however, to the influence of the authoritarian patterns in the father's own family of origin which vary along cultural lines.

44. Augustine, *De Musica* 6.41, in Augustine, *Opera Omnia,* ed. Migne (Paris, Montrouge, 1841), 1.1186. (An English translation is found in *Fathers of the Church Vol 4: Writings of Saint Augustine 2* [New York, Cima, 1947], 365.) Augustine cites pride as the source.

45. For this reason they are called "noble, good, and notable" (Aristotle, *Pol.* 1293b38).

46. John Calvin, *Commentary on the Book of Prophet Isaiah* (Edinburgh, Calvin Translation Society, 1851), at Isa. 19.4, 2.53; cf. Harro Höpfl, *The Christian Polity of John Calvin* (Cambridge, Cambridge U., Studies in the History and Theory of Politics, 1982), 166.

47. Paul Lehmann, *Transformation of Politics* (New York, Harper, 1975), 122. Machiavelli argued against fortresses in times of peace because they give princes a false sense of security and ultimately undercut their rule, which must rest in the will of the people. He warned that the illusion of security releases springs of ambition and domination, tempting the ruler into cruel and extreme acts (Niccolo Machiavelli, *Discourses* 2.24, in Machiavelli, *The Chief Works and Others,* trans. A. Gilbert (Durham, NC, Duke U., 1989), 1.393; cf. Wolin, *Politics and Vision,* 213.

48. Christine Bolt, *Victorian Attitudes to Race* (Toronto, U. of Toronto, Studies in Social History, 1971), cf. 181, 185, 211, 213, 217.

49. The passage also states, "Give me not poverty . . . or I shall be poor, and steal . . ." Similarly, Aristotle wrote that because of *hybris* the wealthy do not follow reason, while the poor envy the rich; both are sources of wickedness (*Pol.* 1295b9).

50. Marx, "Economic and Philosophical Manuscripts" 3.41, 43, pp. 191, 193. Marx is following an older tradition. Cf. Wesley's quotation from an unknown source: "A thousand pound [sic] supplies the want of twenty thousand qualities" (John Wesley, Sermon 108, "On Riches" 2.4, in Wesley, *Works 3: Sermons 3,* 525).

51. Julius K. Nyerere, "The Economic Challenge: Dialogue or Confrontation?" *International Development Review* 18,1 (January, 1976), 5. Plato similarly saw a natural limit that is set by our necessary wants. Going beyond that, there is no limit for those who abandon themselves to the acquisition of wealth (*Rep.* 373d, e). For Aristotle, desire is insatiable and human baseness insatiable. The greatest injustices are done on behalf of superfluities, not necessities (*Pol.* 1267a4–9; 1267b1,4). For Machiavelli, since craving always exceeds the power of attainment, people get slight satisfaction from their acquirements. "Some strive to get more, and others fear losing what they have gained," producing enmity and war (*Discourses* 1.37, p. 272; cf. Wolin, *Politics and Vision,* 218).

52. Plato, *Rep.* 416c–417; cf. Ezek. 45.7–9; 46.16–18.

53. John Woolman, "A Plea for the Poor," in *The Journal and Major Essays of John Woolman,* ed. P. Moulton (New York, Oxford U., Library of Christian Thought, 1971), 255, 262.

54. E. F. Schumacher, *Small is Beautiful: Economics as If People Mattered* (New York, Harper, 1973), 21.

55. Cf. also Fromm, *Fear of Freedom,* 139.

56. Niebuhr, *Human Nature,* 193–94.

57. Joseph Conrad, *Nostromo* (New York, Signet, 1904), 119.

58. I expand Reinhold Niebuhr's discussion of these three groups in *Human Nature,* 194–203.

59. J. R. Tolkien, *The Lord of the Rings* (Boston, Houghton Mifflin, 1965²), Pt. 1: *The Fellowship of the Ring,* 281, 414; Pt. 3: *The Return of the King,* 177.

60. John Wesley, Sermon 128, "The Deceitfulness of the Human Heart" 3.3, p. 159.

61. William V. Shannon, "Congress and Irangate," *Boston Globe,* December 17, 1986, 17.

62. As John Wesley noted, "The disorder of the will again disorders the understanding, and perverseness of affection will again cause an equal perverseness of judgment. For whatever inclination is contrary to reason is likewise destructive of it" (Wesley, Sermon 142, "The Wisdom of Winning Souls" 2, in Wesley, *Works 4: Sermons 4,* 313).

63. R. Niebuhr, *Moral Man and Immoral Society,* xiv–xv, 40–41; *Human Destiny,* 151.

64. Lionel S. Lewis, *Cold War on Campus: A Study of the Policies of Organizational Control* (New Brunswick, NJ, Transaction, 1988). This is a study of 126 faculty members in fifty eight institutions for 1947–1956. Lewis comments, "There are great risk, of course, when men who do not seem to have any special gift of morality become its guardians" (p. 272).

65. Langdon Gilkey, *Shantung Compound. The Story of Men and Women under Pressure* (New York, Harper, 1966), 232.

66. Cf. articles by John Garcia, Jane R. Mercer, and Peter Watson, *Psychology Today* 6 (September, 1972), 39–56, 90–99; Allan Chase, *The Legacy of Malthus. The Social Costs of the New Scientific Racism* (Urbana, IL, U. of Illinois, 1980), 432–509.

67. Cf. National Commission on Testing and Public Policy. *From Gatekeeper to Gateway: Transforming Testing in America* (Chestnut Hill, MA, National Commission on Testing and Public Policy, 1990), esp. 13, 32–33.

68. Bolt, *Victorian Attitudes to Race,* 208; cf. esp. ch. 1.

69. Cf. the summary by Peter DeJong in DeJong and Donald Wilson, *Husband & Wife. The Sexes in Scripture and Society* (Grand Rapids, MI, Zondervan, 1979), ch. 2. Particularly significant has been the research of John Money of Johns Hopkins University. Goldberg's work is *The Inevitability of Patriarchy* (1973).

70. T. S. Eliot, "Choruses from 'The Rock'" I, in Eliot, *Collected Poems 1909–1962* (San Diego, CA, Harcourt, 1970), 147.

71. Billy Graham, Letter to Senator Mark Hatfield, February 9, 1973, quoted in Hatfield, *Between a Rock and a Hard Place* (Waco, TX, Word, 1976), 99–100.

72. Aristotle, *Eth. Nic.* 1130a1.

73. Thomas Aquinas, "On Princely Government" 1.9, in Aquinas, *Selected Political Writings,* ed. A. D'Entrèves (Oxford, Blackwell, Blackwell's Political Texts, 1959), 51.

74. Plato, *Rep.* 489d, 491, 494b–c, 495b.

75. Gilkey, *Shantung Compound,* 193.

76. For example, Richard McBrien, chair of the theology department of the University of Notre Dame, who agrees with the position of the Roman Catholic church that abortion is morally wrong, received letters in which the writers expressed desire for his punishment in hell. He had opposed the excommunication of Catholics who support abortion rights on national television (Paul Galloway, "McBrien of Notre Dame," *Chicago Tribune,* July 19, 1990, Section 5, p. 1). On the other side are those who treat all opponents of abortion rights as if they had no interest in other ethical issues for the securing of life.

77. Cf. Niebuhr, *Human Destiny,* 129.

78. Cited by Charles V. Bergstrom, "When the Self-Righteous Rule, Watch Out!" *FOCUS on Governmental Affairs* 13, 12 (December, 1979), 3.

79. Robert Levey, "'I expect more of this,' says cults scholar at Tufts," *Boston Globe,* November 23, 1978, 16.

80. Jonathan Edwards, "Some Thoughts Concerning the Revival," in Edwards, *Works of Jonathan Edwards, Vol. 4: The Great Awakening.* ed. C. Goen (New Haven, CT, Yale U.,

1972), 414, 416; cf. Richard F. Lovelace, *Dynamics of Spiritual Life. An Evangelical Theology of Renewal* (Downers Grove, IL, Inter-Varsity, 1979), 246–49, 103–4.

81. Reinhold Niebuhr, "The Christian Perspective on the World Crisis," *Christianity and Crisis* 4, 7 (May 1, 1944), 4; cf. Niebuhr, "Age between the Ages," 47–48; cf. Niebuhr, "Ten Fateful Years," *Christianity and Crisis,* 11, 1 (February 5, 1951), 4.

82. Victor Hugo, *Les Misérables,* Fantine 1.2 (London, Dent, 1909), 1.10.

Chapter 3

1. Larry May, *The Morality of Groups: Collective Responsibility, Group-Based Harm, and Corporate Rights* (Notre Dame, IN, U. of Notre Dame, Soundings, 1987), 10.

2. Kurt Lewin, "The Background of Conflict in Marriage" (1940), in Lewin, *Resolving Social Conflicts. Selected Papers on Group Dynamics,* ed. Gertrud Weiss Lewin (New York, Harper, 1948), 84. Lewin also states that a group is a "dynamic whole" in that a change in the state of one part changes the state of another part. Lewin agrees with May's stress on groups as relationships. The essence of a group is not the similarity of its members but their interdependence.

3. Eph. 1.4; cf. 1 Pet. 2.9 ("a chosen people" [quoting Isa. 43.20] because built upon Christ, the elect one [1.20; 2.4–5]); Paul S. Minear, "Church, Idea of," *Interpreter's Dictionary of the Bible* (1962), 1.609.

4. Walter Rauschenbusch, *The Righteousness of the Kingdom,* ed. Max L. Stackhouse (Nashville, Abingdon, 1968), 103.

5. Rauschenbusch, 100–101.

6. Christopher J. H. Wright, *An Eye for An Eye. The Place of Old Testament Ethics Today* (Downers Grove, IL, InterVarsity, 1983), 106.

7. Robert A. Horn, *Groups and the Constitution* (Stanford, Stanford U., 1956), 2.

8. Thomas Aquinas, "On Princely Government" 1.1, p. 5.

9. Eduard Heimann, *Reason and Faith in Modern Society, Liberalism, Marxism, and Democracy* (Middletown, CT, Wesleyan U., 1961), 230.

10. Ibid.

11. Friedrich von Hügel, "On the Place and Function, within Religion, of the Body, of History, and of Institutions," (1913) in Hügel, *Essays and Addresses on the Philosophy of Religion* (London, Dent, 1926), 2.76, 87.

12. R. M. MacIver, *The Web of Government* (New York, Macmillan, 1947), 411. Even in tribal societies there are varied groupings according to family, kin, totem, cult, or tribe.

13. Yoel Yinon et al. "Escape from Responsibility and Help in Emergencies among Persons Alone or Within Groups," *European Journal of Social Psychology* 12 (1982), 301–5.

14. Frederick S. Carney, "Associational Thought in Early Calvinism," in *Voluntary Associations,* James Luther Adams Fest., ed. D. B. Robertson (Richmond, VA, John Knox, 1966), 41–43, 52. The attention to associations reflected the commitment of Calvinists to purpose and high calling in life under God and their concern that the associations be ordered so that their rule would be neither too weak or tyrannical, expressing here their conviction of human finitude and sin (Carney, 46). This tradition continues in neo-Calvinism in the sphere sovereignty of Abraham Kuyper and Herman Dooyeweerd.

15. Johannes Althusius, *The Politics of Johannes Althusius,* 3rd ed. (1614), ed. Frederick S. Carney (Boston, Beacon, Beacon Series in the Sociology of Politics and Religion, ed. J. L. Adams, 1964), 22.

16. Horn, *Groups and the Constitution,* 10–13; William Kornhauser, *The Politics of Mass Society* (New York, Free, 1959), 78, 81.

17. Even that complete replacement by the state of all other groups independent from itself probably never is completely accomplished. Group life is too endemic to the human scene. Cf. Kornhauser, 41.

18. Aristotle noted that one of the ways tyrannies were preserved was by limiting as much as possible occasions for people to know each other, particularly by prohibiting intellectual clubs, gatherings, and common meals (*Pol.* 1313b1–7). For examples of the antipathy that despotic rule has toward unofficial associations, cf. Robert G. Wesson, *The Imperial Order* (Berkely, CA, U. of California, 1967), 154–55.

19. James Luther Adams, "Mediating Structures and the Separation of Powers," in *Democracy and Mediating Structures,* ed. Michael Novak (Washington, American Enterprise Institute, AEI Symposia 80A, 1980), 1.

20. Adams, 2–3. As was noted earlier, this was perceived also by the early Calvinists.

21. Kornhauser, 83.

22. MacIver, *Web of Government,* 421–30; cf. Karl Hertz, "The Nature of Voluntary Associations," in *Voluntary Associations,* ed. Robertson, 17–19. Augustine wrote that the state is merely a unified group of people (Letter 155 [to Macedonius], in *The Political Writings of St. Augustine,* ed. H. Paolucci [Chicago, Gateway, 1962], 269).

23. R. M. MacIver, *Society. A Textbook of Sociology* (New York, Farrar, 1937), 11–12. The confusion of the state with the nation creates the danger of totalitarianism (Jacques Maritain, *Man and the State* [Chicago, U. of Chicago, 1962], 7).

24. James Madison, *Federalist,* No. 51; cf. No. 10 (Alexander Hamilton, James Madison, and John Jay, *The Federalist* [New York, Everyman's Library, 1970], 266, 264; cf. 47).

25. MacIver, *Web of Government,* 423.

26. William Temple, *Christianity and the State* (London, Macmillan, 1928), 124–25; cf. John C. Bennett, *Christians and the State* (New York, Scribner's, 1958), 75–77.

27. Adams, "Mediating Structures," 10–11.

28. Robert Cooke, "A Warning on Scientists' Ties to Firms," *Boston Globe,* April 3, 1984, 1, reporting on an address by Sheldon Krimsky. Krimsky also raised concern about similar ties by medical doctors.

29. James Luther Adams, "Freedom and Association," in Adams, *On Being Human Religiously,* ed. Max L. Stackhouse (Boston, Beacon, 1976), 63–64, 66–67; Adams, "The Indispensable Discipline of Social Responsibility: Voluntary Associations" (1966), in Adams, *The Prophethood of All Believers,* ed. G. Beach (Boston, Beacon, 1986), 259 (also in Adams, *Voluntary Associations*).

30. Max L. Stackhouse, *Public Theology and Political Economy, Christian Stewardship in Modern Society* (Grand Rapids, MI, Eerdmans, Library of Christian Stewardship, 1987), 165–66.

31. Adams, "Freedom and Association," 57.

32. Seymour Martin Lipset, Martin A. Trow, and James S. Coleman, "Union Democracy and Secondary Organization," in *American Social Patterns,* ed. W. Petersen (Garden City, NY, Doubleday Anchor, 1956), 171–218.

33. Adams, "Mediating Structures," 3.

34. Lane Kirkland, President, American Federation of Labor and Congress of Industrial Organizations.

35. Edmund Burke, *Thoughts on the Cause of the Present Discontents* (1770), in *Works* (London, Bohn [vols. 1–7; vol. 8: Bell], 1855–1894), 1.372. He later described the "force which a few, united in a good cause, have over a multitude of the profligate and ferocious" (*Speech on a Bill for Repeal of the Marriage Act* [1781], in *Works,* 6.171).

36. Kornhauser, *Politics of Mass Society*, 33, 41, 107–12. The totalitarian appeal is strongest not to those involved in class organization and class struggle, but to those with the weakest attachment to class organizations, or to any other kind of social group (p. 49).

37. Niebuhr, *Human Nature*, 213.

38. Niebuhr, *Moral Man and Immoral Society*, xi, xxiv, 49, 107; *Human Nature*, 208. This observation is important against a simplistic misunderstanding of Niebuhr.

39. Niebuhr, *Human Nature*, 212–13.

40. Coles, *South Goes North*, 333.

41. Seneca, *Epistulae Morales* 66.26, trans. R. Gummere (Cambridge, Harvard U., Loeb Classical Library, 1962), 2.19.

42. Alan Richman, "Take Your Anger Out on Injustice," *Boston Globe*, January 28, 1981, op-ed.

43. Eric S. Fife and Arthur F. Glasser, *Missions in Crisis* (Chicago, Inter-Varsity, 1962), 41.

44. Niebuhr, *Moral Man and Immoral Society*, xi, 48, 88.

45. May, *Morality of Groups*, 64.

46. Cf. Garry Wills, *Nixon Agonistes: The Crisis of the Self-Made Man* (New York, American Library, 1970), 421–26.

47. Tillich, *Love, Power, and Justice*, 92–94; "Shadow and Substance," 116–17.

48. Maritain, *Man and the State*, 14.

49. Niebuhr, *Moral Man and Immoral Society*, xi, 88–89.

50. Wills, *Nixon Agonistes*, 432–40. (The quotation is from pp. 439–40.)

51. "An American Tragedy," *Boston Globe*, February 25, 1973, 6-A.

52. Niebuhr, *Moral Man and Immoral Society*, xi, 85.

53. Robert Jay Lifton, "Existential Evil," in Nevitt Sanford and Craig Comstock et al., *Sanctions for Evil: Sources of Social Destructiveness* (San Francisco, Jossey-Bass, Behavioral Science Series, 1971), 40.

54. Sanford and Comstock, *Sanctions for Evil*, 3.

55. May, *Morality of Groups*, 138.

56. May, 116–17.

57. Irving L. Janis, "Groupthink Among Policy Makers," in *Sanctions for Evil*, 71–84. He examines the Korean Crisis decision in the Truman administration, the Bay of Pigs invasion plan in the Kennedy administration, and the decisions for Vietnam escalation in the Johnson administration.

58. May, *Morality of Groups*, 40.

59. Cf. Niebuhr, *Moral Man and Immoral Society*, 96.

60. Irving Lewis Allen, "A Retrospective Note on Urban 'Neighborhood School' Ideology," *Urban Education* 12 (1977), 205–12.

61. Michael Banton, *Racial and Ethnic Competition* (Cambridge, Cambridge U., Comparative Ethnic and Race Relations Series, 1983). (These examples are on pp. 244, 387). Thus if a descriminated against minority can be empowered so as to be able to compete economically without drawing attention to its race, it does not face the racial consequences of a high profile strategy in which the racial group identity is foremost. Thus a high profile strategy is particularly effective where the benefit is overcoming exclusion, rather than merely discrimination (pp. 406–7). The problem in implementation is overcoming the group based barriers which block the empowerment that would allow individual competition.

62. Niebuhr, *Moral Man and Immoral Society*, 48. Its greater power itself makes social restraints less effective.

63. Niebuhr, *Human Nature*, 209–12. Cf. Robert Wesson on the universal empire: "With the prestige of mystery, distance, and vast resources, it bedazzles and overawes" (*Imperial*

Order, 190–91, 79). Those empires that were not inhibited from spending freely for uneconomic magnificence, making incredible displays of their ability to arise above the ordinary had an advantage (142).

64. Max Weber, "Religious Rejections of the World and Their Directions," in *From Max Weber,* 335.

65. Cited in Donald W. Shriver, Jr., et al., *Spindles and Spires: A Re-Study of Religion and Social Change in Gastonia* (Atlanta, John Knox, 1976), 60–61.

66. It later became *Sojourners.*

67. President Ford, however, could not have known then that in the sixteen-year rule of the military junta of Gen. Augusto Pinochet, which replaced Allende, an estimated 4,000 Chileans would become victims of disappearances, summary executions, torture, and terrorism (*Boston Globe,* Editorial: "Chile's 'Heart of Horror,' " September 10, 1990, 4).

68. Troy Druster, "Conditions for Guilt-Free Massacre," in *Sanctions for Evil,* 29, 31.

69. *In These Times* (June 1–14, 1983), 19.

70. Tillich, *Love, Power, and Justice,* 99.

71. Niebuhr, *Moral Man and Immoral Society,* 91.

72. Kurt Lewin, "Self-Hatred among Jews" (1941), in Lewin, *Resolving Social Conflicts,* 199–200; cf. Lewis A. Coser, *The Functions of Social Conflict* (New York, Free, 1956), 114.

73. Coser, 116. In that framework, combatants become more forceful and intransigent.

74. Niebuhr, *Moral Man and Immoral Society,* 46–47.

75. Michael Harrington, *The Long-Distance Runner. An Autobiography* (New York, Holt, 1988), 85.

76. Adams, "Freedom and Association, 83.

77. Gilkey, *Shantung Compound,* 143.

78. Niebuhr, *Moral Man and Immoral Society,* 19

79. Niebuhr, xxiii.

80. May, *Morality of Groups,* 117.

81. *In These Times* (February 17–23, 1982), 11.

82. Alfred W. Blumrosen, "Quotas, Common Sense, and Law in Labor Relations: Three Dimensions of Equal Opportunity," *Rutgers University Law Review* 27 (1974), 679–84 (quotation is from p. 681); cf. Daniel C. Maguire, *A New American Justice. Ending the White Male Monopolies* (Garden City, NY, Doubleday, 1980), 106.

83. Morton Sosna, *In Search of the Silent South: Southern Liberals and the Race Issue* (New York, Columbia U., Contemporary American History Series, 1977), 163; and the review of Sosna by Numan V. Bartley, *American Historical Review* 83 (1978), 840. In reaction to its stance, the membership of the liberal Southern Regional Council declined from 3,400 to 1,800 from 1950 to 1954 (Sosna, 166).

84. Cf. S. C. Mott, "Where Is the Cross? A Political Reflection on Hebrews 13," *The Other Side* 10,2 (March/April, 1974), 39–42; and Helmut Koester, "Outside the Camp: Hebrews 13:9–14," *Harvard Theological Review* 55 (1962), 299–315.

Chapter 4

1. *ho anthrōpos physei politikon zōon, Pol.* 1253a3; cf. *Pol.* 1278b20.

2. Calvin, *Institutes,* 2.2.13 *(homo animal est natura sociale).* Calvin apparently received this through Seneca, who had great influence upon his early political thought; cf. n. 56 by McNeil at this passage (p. 272).

3. The Puritans continued this thought in their covenantal view of justice. William Perkins stated that "the common good of men stands in this, not only that they live, but that they live well, in righteousness and holines, and consequently in true happinesse" ("A Treatise of the Vocations or Callings of Men," in *Puritan Political Ideas 1558–1794,* ed. E. Morgan [Indianapolis, IN, Bobbs-Merrill, American Heritage Series, 1965], 39; cf. E. Clinton Gardner, "Justice in the Puritan Covenant Tradition," in *Annual of the Society of Christian Ethics,* 1988, ed. D. M. Yeager [Knoxville, TN, Society of Christian Ethics, 1988], 99).

4. Aristotle, *Pol.* 1253a33, 37; 1278b20–26.

5. William Temple, *Christianity and Social Order* (New York, Penguin, 1942), 47, commenting on his own statement, "Man is naturally and incurably social."

6. Cf. Niebuhr, *Moral Man and Immoral Society,* 2.

7. Augustine, *City of God* 14.1, p. 441.

8. Wolff, *Anthropology of the Old Testament,* 29.

9. Cf. Meredith G. Kline, *Kingdom Prologue* (Hamilton, MA, Meredith G. Kline, 1983), 2.25–26.

10. Jacques Ellul assumes the latter in *The Meaning of the City* (Grand Rapids, MI, Eerdmans, 1970), 5–7.

11. Kline, 23.

12. Reinhold Niebuhr, *The Self and the Dramas of History* (New York, Scribner's, 1955), 103.

13. Bronislaw Malinowski, "Culture," *Encyclopaedia of the Social Sciences* (1931), 4.621.

14. Niebuhr, *Children of Light,* 50.

15. Plato, *The Republic* 369b, trans. P. Shorey (Cambridge, Harvard U., Loeb Classical Library, 1935), 2.149

16. Contributed by a former student, Sunday B. G. Olasehinde.

17. Rollo May, *The Art of Counseling* (New York, Abingdon, 1939), 62–63, 66–67.

18. Leszek Kolakowski, "The Priest and the Jester," in Kolakowski, *Toward a Marxist Humanism. Essays on the Left Today* (New York, Grove, 1968), 23.

19. Juan Luis Segundo, *A Theology for Artisans of a New Humanity,* Vol. 2: *Grace and the Human Condition* (New York, Orbis, 1973), 38.

20. William Ernest Hocking, *Man and the State* (Hamden, CT, Archon, 1968 [1954]), 143–46. Forming a social contract assumes a previous condition of society, which provides the common agreement of what constitutes a contract and belief that contracts are binding (John O. Nelson, "The Function of Government," *Personalist* 52 [1971], 164).

21. While its modern exponents articulated a middle class outlook, the theory itself is ancient. Glaucon expresses it in Plato, *Rep.* 395.

22. Nelson attempts to retain the logic of social contract thought to affirm a laissez-faire view of the state while asserting the social nature of the individual. What the individual presents that makes society imperative, however, is reduced to a Kantian rational judgment-making capacity combined with manifold desires. The resulting conflicting practical conclusions must be mediated, requiring government ("Function of Government," 161–85).

23. Niebuhr, *Moral Man and Immoral Society,* 3; Niebuhr, *The Structure of Nations and Empires. A Study of the Recurring Patterns and Problems of the Political Order in Relation to the Unique Problems of the Nuclear Age* (New York, Scribner's, 1959), 33; Hocking, *Man and the State,* 140.

24. Meredith G. Kline, "Oracular Origin of the State," in *Biblical and Near Eastern Studies,* ed. G. Tuttle (Grand Rapids, Eerdmans, 1976), 132–41. The law form is that in which the offense is expressed with a participle and the penalty with the third person imperfect (e.g., Exod 21.15, 17). Kline (136) cites G. E. Mendenhall (*The Tenth Generation,* 75) that vengeance *(nāqām)* is not an act of one's own hands in a blood feud but "the very foundations

of political legitimacy and authority." J. P. M. Walsh states that *nāqām* is a term for uphold-ing *ṣedeq* (justice) (*The Mighty From Their Thrones* [Philadelphia, Fortress, Overtures to Biblical Theology 21 (1987)], 185, n.12).

25. Richard J. Mouw, *Political Evangelism* (Grand Rapids, MI, Eerdmans, 1973), 45.

26. Hocking, *Man and the State*, 147–50. *Man and the State* explores the psychological basis of the state. Since this instinct of self-conscious social control is peculiar to human beings, animal studies are correspondingly limited in their application to political behavior.

27. Walter G. Muelder, *Foundations of the Responsible Society* (New York, Abingdon, 1959), 87.

28. Etzioni, *Active Society*, 361.

29. Cf. Tillich, *Love, Power, and Justice*, 97. Note that the power of being of the com-munity is not the state; the state expresses what is delegated to it.

30. J. Philip Wogaman, *Christian Perspectives on Politics* (Philadelphia, Fortress, 1988), 13.

31. Ibid., 13, 16.

32. Bennett, *Christians and the State*, 86.

33. Harvey Seifert, *Ethical Resources for Political and Economic Decision* (Philadelphia, Westminster, 1972), 99.

34. Augustine, *City of God*, 22.22, pp. 846–47. The only escape, however, is the life pro-vided by the grace of the Saviour Christ (p. 848).

35. Malcolm Feeley, "Coercion and Compliance. A New Look at an Old Problem," *Law and Society Review* 4 (1970), 512.

36. Seifert, *Ethical Resources*, 100.

37. Muelder, *Foundations of Responsible Society*, 90; Niebuhr, *Self and Dramas of His-tory*, 166, 190–92; Jan Dengerink, *The Idea of Justice in Christian Perspective* (Toronto, Wedge, 1978), 57 (also in *Westminster Theological Journal* 39 [1977], 1–59).

38. Henry P. Lundsgaarde, *Murder in Space City: A Cultural Analysis of Houston Homi-cide Patterns* (New York, Oxford U., 1977), 141.

39. Ibid., 16, 92. The average prison sentence for those who killed a relative was eight years, for those who killed a friend ten years; but it was twenty-eight years for those who killed a stranger.

40. Heimann, *Reason and Faith in Modern Society*, 180.

41. Patrick Devlin, *The Enforcement of Morals* (London, Oxford U., 1965), 10, 25. Dev-lin's analysis, however, on the whole appears less helpful for societies that are highly multi-cultural.

42. Cf. Niebuhr, *Children of Light*, 44; Niebuhr, "A Dark Light on Human Nature," *Mes-senger* 13 (April 27, 1948), 7.

43. Niebuhr, *Human Destiny*, 258.

44. Niebuhr, *Moral Man and Immoral Society*, 262.

45. Niebuhr, *Human Destiny*, 266.

46. Interview by Scott Simon with Herbert Sandler and Marion Sandler, co-executives of Golden West Financial Corporation, "Weekend Edition," National Public Radio, Oct. 6, 1990.

47. Adams, "Freedom and Association," 80–81; cf. Maguire, *New American Justice*, 25, 104.

48. A. D. Lindsay, *The Essentials of Democracy* (London, Oxford U., William J. Cooper Foundation Lectures, 1935^2), 71; cf. Maguire, *New American Justice*, 80. For the develop-ment of these ideas in papal social teachings, such as in the encyclicals, *Rerum novarum* and *Quadragesimo anno*, cf. John Courtney Murray, "Leo XII: Two Concepts of Government," *Theological Studies* 14 (1953), 552–56.

49. Maritain, *Man and the State,* 12. It should be limited to those public services closely connected to the public good (21).

50. Niebuhr, *Human Destiny,* 266.

51. Ibid.

52. Maguire, *New American Justice,* 92–93.

53. Niebuhr, *Self and Dramas of History,* 166.

54. Reinhold Niebuhr, "Pacifism and Sanctions: A Symposium" [with John Nevin Sayre], *Radical Religion* 1, 2 (Winter, 1936), 28.

55. Cf. S. C. Mott, *Biblical Ethics and Social Change* (New York, Oxford U., 1982), ch. 9.

56. Niebuhr, *Human Destiny,* 266.

57. Cf. José Porfirio Miranda, *Marx and the Bible. A Critique of the Philosophy of Oppression* (Maryknoll, NY, Orbis, 1974), 30.

58. Niebuhr, *Children of Light,* 174.

59. Cf. Paul Tillich, "The State as Expectation and Demand" (1930), in Tillich, *Political Expectation,* 99, 104.

60. Kline, *Kingdom Prologue,* 34, citing Dan. 4.27 in support. Professor Kline's position on this matter is significant because a mark of his scholarship is great care not to apply to civil governments the theocratic features of Israelite law that are distinctive to Israel "as a holy, confessional, redemptive kingdom" (19).

61. José Miguez Bonino, *Christians and Marxists. The Mutual Challenge to Revolution* (Grand Rapids, Eerdmans, 1976), 94–97.

62. Kline, *Kingdom Prologue,* 34. Cf. F. Charles Fensham, "Widow, Orphan, and the Poor in Ancient Near Eastern Legal and Wisdom Literature," *Journal of Near Eastern Studies* 21 (1962), 129–34.

63. Letter by Adad-Shumu-uṣur to king Assurbanipal, ABL no. 2, 10, cited in J. P. J. Olivier, "The Sceptre of Justice and Ps. 45:7b," *Journal of Northwest Semitic Languages* 7 (1979), 50.

64. CT 46 no. 45 (of Nebuchadnezzar), Olivier, 51.

65. Olivier, 52.

66. J. Robert Vannoy, *Covenant Renewal at Gilgal: A Study of I Samuel 11:14–12:25* (Cherry Hill, NJ, Mack, 1978), 228.

67. I. Mendelsohn, "Samuel's Denunciation of Kingship in the Light of the Akkadian Documents from Ugarit," *Bulletin of the American Schools of Oriental Research* 143 (1956), 17–22. Cf. the description of Canaanite society in Norman K. Gottwald, *The Tribes of Yahweh. A Sociology of the Religion of Liberated Israel 1250–1050 B.C.E.* (Maryknoll, NY, Orbis, 1979), 212–13, 391–400.

68. *mišpaṭ hammelek,* "the kind of justice of the king," v. 11.

69. *mišpaṭ hammelukāh,* "the kind of justice of the kingdom."

70. Vannoy, 231.

71. As we turn to Calvin in the next paragraph, we note here that Calvin's social and political thought is "shot through" with the concept of mutuality in service and in obedience. No one is exempt from subjection (John T. McNeill, "John Calvin on Civil Government," *Journal of Presbyterian History* 42 [1964], 80).

72. As phrased by Abraham Kuyper, *Lectures on Calvinism* (Grand Rapids, MI, Eerdmans, Stone Foundation Lectures [1898], 1931), 81. Without ruling authority we would have "a veritable hell on earth." Kuyper goes on to say, however, that in light of the same view of sin, we must constantly watch against the danger that the power of the state presents to personal liberty.

73. Calvin, *Institutes,* 4.20.9 (p. 1496), citing Jer. 22.3; Ps. 82.3–4. Calvin saw the Israelite

state as a model for other states since God had used the best conceivable means to lead God's people to peace and harmony. This application was distinguished from Israel's peculiar role as a type of the future rule of Christ (Gisbert Beyerhaus, *Studien zur Staatsanschauung Calvins* [Berlin, Trowitzsch, Neue Studien zur Geschichte der Theologie und der Kirche 7, 1910], 132, 140).

74. Calvin, *Institutes*, 4.20.9: *quibis* [magistrates] *studium unum sit, communi omnium saluti ac paci prospicere* (*Joannis Calvini opera selecta*, ed. P. Barth and W. Niesel [Munich, Kaiser, 1936], 4.481). *Salus* meaning "a sound and whole condition" (Lewis and Short) is close to the Hebrew *šālôm*.

75. Höpfl, *Christian Polity of John Calvin*, 195–96. The magistrates' power was also essential for public institutions for the relief of distress (191). Similarly, in Luther there is the government's, particularly the town council's, support of a common fund for the genuine needy and education for both sexes, cf. W.D.J. Cargill Thompson, *The Political Thought of Martin Luther*, ed. P. Broadhead (Sussex, Harvester, 1984), 167.

76. Calvin, *Sermons sur le Deuteronome*, in *Joannis Calvini opera quae supersunt omnia*, ed. G. Baum et al. (Brunswick, Schwetschke, 1863–1900), 27.568 (Sermon 114, on Deut. 19.14–15, 1555); cf. Höpfl, 167.

77. Ernst Troeltsch, *The Social Teaching of the Christian Churches* (New York, Harper, 1960 [1911]), 616. The purposeful and rational approach to the state reflects Calvin's stress on God's will and active working in history for purposes not yet achieved. Those who surrender to God's electing and renewing will become instruments of that active will (582–84).

78. Charles Finney, *Lectures on Systematic Theology*, ed. J. H. Fairchild (Oberlin, OH, Goodrich, 1878), 215, 218, 220.

79. Niebuhr, *Structure of Nations*, 3, 8, 34–48.

80. Kuyper, *Lectures on Calvinism*, 82.

81. Ronald H. Nash, *Freedom, Justice and the State* (Lanham, MD, University Press of America, 1980), 27. The state is "a *necessary* evil" rather than "a necessary *evil*."

82. Calvin, *Institutes* 4.20.3, 4, 22 (pp. 1488, 1490, 1510); cf. Höpfl, *Christian Polity of Calvin*, 44–46. Similarly for Luther, government is an inestimable blessing of God and one of God's best gifts, cf. Cargill Thompson, *Political Thought of Luther*, 66.

83. Augustine: "Justice being taken away, then, what are kingdoms but great robberies?" (*City of God* 4.4, p. 112).

84. Tillich, "State as Expectation and Demand," 104–5.

85. Mott, *Biblical Ethics and Social Change*, ch. 8.

86. G. H. Boobyer, "New Testament Perfectionism and Christian Citizenship," *Hibbert Journal* 51 (1952/53), 144.

87. E. R. Goodenough, *Introduction to Philo Judaeus* (Oxford, Blackwell, 1962²), 154–62.

88. Cf. Wisdom of Solomon 6.1–8 (possibly in early decades of first century A.D.). God grants power to the monarchs and will examine their actions. They will be punished because they did not carry justice out correctly (*ekrinate orthōs*, v. 4) as servants of God's reign.

89. George Foot Moore, *Judaism in the First Centuries of the Christian Era. The Age of the Tannaim* (Cambridge, Harvard U., 1927), 2.114.

90. Kuyper, *Lectures on Calvinism*, 90.

91. Martin Luther King, *Stride Toward Freedom* (New York, Harper, 1958), 188.

92. Eileen McNamara, "State to Offer Prenatal Care to Urban Poor," *Boston Globe* (September 20, 1990), 9, quoting Dr. Anthony Schlaff, medical director of the Codman Square Health Center in the Dorchester section of Boston.

93. Niebuhr, *Human Destiny*, 267.

94. Niebuhr, "Synthetic Barbarism," in Niebuhr, *Christianity and Power Politics* (New

York, Scribner's, 1940), 120; cf. Wesson, *Imperial Order,* 500. Augustine similarly noted that princes rule by "the love of ruling" and delight in their own strength (*City of God* 14.28, p. 477).

95. Niebuhr, *Children of Light,* 45–46.

96. Karl Marx, "The Class Struggles in France, 1848 to 1850" 1, in Karl Marx and Frederick Engles, *Collected Works* (New York, International, 1978), 10.65. Niebuhr, however, points out that Marx made the same error about the social class by failing to anticipate the rise of a ruling group which would create its own impulses rather than expressing a common class understanding (*Children of Light,* 46).

97. Madison, *Federalist,* No. 51, p. 264.

Chapter 5

1. Aristotle states that justice is an element of the society (polis) for the "regulation of the community *(koinōnia)*" (*Pol.* 1253a37–39). It is a "community virtue" (*koinōnikēn aretēn, Pol.* 1283a39).

2. Otto Bird describes them clearly in his work, *The Idea of Justice* (New York, Praeger, 1967), 163–80.

3. Walter Kaufmann, "Doubts About Justice," in *Social Responsibility in an Age of Revolution,* ed. L. Finkelstein (New York, Jewish Theological Seminary, Ethics of Today, 1971), 99.

4. Michael Walzer, *Interpretation and Social Criticism* (Cambridge, Harvard U., 1987), 48, 82, n.15.

5. Charles R. Van Patten, "Ethics and War," (unpublished MATS thesis, Gordon-Conwell Theological Seminary, 1984), 98. He also notes the lack of grounds for one state to respect the rights that another state understands itself to possess.

6. Cf. Calvin, *Institutes,* 2.8.1.

7. John Rawls, *A Theory of Justice* (Cambridge, MA, Harvard U., 1971). This would be true of his work up through the publication of that work. Since then, according to David Hollenbach's analysis, he has moved to the position that what one can assert about the good of human life is dependent upon the tradition in which the thinker finds oneself (Hollenbach, "A Communitarian Reconstruction of Human Rights: Contributions from Catholic Tradition," a paper presented to Boston Theological Ethicists' Colloquium, October 17, 1990. (Cambridge U. will publish it in a forthcoming book edited by Hollenbach and R. Bruce Douglass.) This "tradition-dependent" (Hollenbach) position would belong to the social good position described earlier: justice is found in the traditions of one's own group, a position held also by Richard Rorty and, with modification, Alasdair MacIntyre.

8. William Frankena, "The Concept of Social Justice," in *Social Justice,* ed. R. Brandt (Englewood Cliffs, NJ, Prentice-Hall, 1962), 1–29.

9. Cf. ibid., 23, 27–29.

10. Those who contribute the most to the good life have a larger portion of the state (Aristotle, *Pol.* 1281a4–8); correspondingly, the managers of the household will pay more attention to its free members than to its slaves (1259b20–21). Injustice is an excess or deficit of advantage or harm contrary to one's proportional worth (Aristotle, *Nic. Eth.* 1134a7–8). If Aristotle's views of justice were carried out in a society in which equal worth were described to each, the contribution of distributive justice would be significant. Cf. Plato, *Rep.* 558c, 563.

11. *Aristos* serving as the superlative of *agathos* ("good").

12. Paul Tillich, "Man and Society in Religious Socialism," *Christianity and Society* 8,4

(Fall, 1943), 17; cf. Ronald H. Stone, *Paul Tillich's Radical Social Thought* (Atlanta, Knox, 1980), 120.

13. Suggested by John Womack, a former student.

14. Quoted in Maguire, *New American Justice,* 129.

15. Cf. Niebuhr, *Moral Man and Immoral Society,* 257–58;

16. Cf. Wesley, Sermon 4, "Scriptural Christianity" 2.3, in Wesley, *Works 1: Sermons 1,* 166; cf. 3.4, p. 171. John W. Olley suggests "what is right" and "bringing about what is right (and beneficial for all)" as the best translation for ṣeᵈāqāh ("'Righteousness'—Some Issues in Old Testament Translation into English," *Bible Translator* 38 [1987], 311; cf. Ps. 119.121 in *NRSV*). These are effective renderings for justice. Olley states, "Semitic emphasis is upon actions which bring about prosperity, benefit, equal rights for all subjects, including freedom from external oppression and deliverance from enemies" (309). Olley finds in his examination of Isaiah in the Septuagint that when the translators used *dikaiosunē* to translate ṣeᵈāqāh, its Greek meaning of *justice* was very much in mind ("The Translator of the Septuagint of Isaiah and 'Righteousness,'" *Bulletin of the International Organization for Septuagint and Cognate Studies* 13 [1980], 58–74).

17. Cf. John Goldingay, "The Man of War and the Suffering Servant," *Tyndale Bulletin* 27 (1976), 84–85, commenting on Exod. 6.6; 7.4: "The act of God in the exodus was an act of justice, whereby the oppressed were relieved and the oppressors punished."

18. Aristotle, *Eth. Nic.* 1129a31–1130a23; 1130b6–29.

19. Nash, *Freedom, Justice, and State,* 37, 75. Nash is to be commended for addressing the problem, whereas many have ignored it or dismissed the pertinence of the materials of the Hebrew Bible.

20. Refer also to Olley's observations of *dikaiosynē* in the LXX in notes 16 and 28.

21. Aristotle, *Pol.* 1257b43; cf. 1255a23. In addition, against a laissez-faire use of Aristotle, his *general* justice is supported by the law (Eth. Nic. 1130a22–24; 1130b10–16). Similarly, in Thomas Aquinas' use of Aristotle's general justice, the ruler is responsible for implementing it. General justice sets forth actions of the individual virtues, including distributive justice, as they relate to the common good (cf. Normand J. Paulhus, "Uses and Misues of the Term 'Social Justice' in the Roman Catholic Tradition," *Journal of Religious Ethics* 15 [1987], 265–67). A private (voluntary)/public (legal) distinction that Nash sets forth does not belong to the tradition of Aristotle's general and particular justice.

22. I offer a different treatment of the biblical understanding of love and justice in *Biblical Ethics and Social Change* (Chaps. 3–4). There I develop love as an expression of grace and its contribution to universal dignity as a basis of human rights. The impact of love upon justice when justice is an expression of love is discussed in terms of egalitarian theories of justice on the level of distribution according to basic needs for inclusion in community. The treatments in these two books should be regarded as supplementary to each other.

23. Cf. also Prov. 21.3; Isa. 1.1–11; Jer. 7.4–7; Mic. 6.6–8; Matt. 5.23–24; 19.16–22 par.; Jas. 1.27.

24. Cf. Norman H. Snaith, *The Distinctive Ideas of the Old Testament* London, Epworth, 1944), 68, 71–72; James H. Cone, *God of the Oppressed* (New York, Seabury, 1975), 70–71; if theology is to speak for Yahweh, it must side with the poor since Yahweh has already taken that side.

25. Ps. 72.1–4; Prov. 31.8–9; Jer. 22.3, 14–15; 23.1–5; Dan. 4.27; Matt. 23.23; cf. Olley, "'Righteousness,'" 309, 314.

26. Job 29.14–17; Ezek. 18.5, 7; Deut. 24.11–13; Ps. 112.9; Amos 5.7, 11–15.

27. Num. 11.29 with Exod. 18.13–27, especially v. 16; Ps. 11.7; 94.15 (cf. vv. 5–6); Prov. 29.26; Isa. 26.9; 32.15–17; 59.14–16; 2 Cor. 9.9–10.

28. Olley finds that the Septuagint in Isaiah uses *dikaiosynē* where the context does not

refer to Israel's sins but to her being unjustly oppressed; but where the context emphasizes Israel's sins, *eleēmosunē* (mercy) is used ("Translator of the Septuagint," 71).

29. Also Ps. 40.10; 43.1–2; 71.1–2, 24; 72.1–4; 116.5–6; Isa. 46.12–13; 59.11, 17; 45.8; 61.10; 62.1–2; 63.7–8 (LXX); 65.6; 119.123; and frequent. With *pillēt* for "deliver": Ps. 31.1; 37.28, 40.

30. Cf. Job 29.12, 14; Prov. 24.11.

31. Cf. Ps. 107; 113.7–9.

32. Cf. Jer. 23.5–6; 33.15–16.

33. William Temple describes the sense of the unemployed "that they have fallen out of the common life." Worse than their physical needs is the corrupting sense that "they are not wanted" (*Christianity and Social Order* [New York, Seabury, 1976 (1942)], 34. Marx used a similar image when he spoke of the worker having "only a *precarious* right to inherit [civilization], for it [civilization] has become an alien dwelling that may suddenly not be available, or from which he may be evicted if he does not pay the rent" (Marx, "Economic and Philosophical Manuscripts" 3.14–15, p. 169.

34. David Hollenbach, "The Common Good Revisited," *Theological Studies* 50 (1989), 92. Hollenbach finds Alan Gewirth helpful in the latter's view that human rights are the necessary conditions of human agency (*Human Rights,* 1982, 3, 5, 63); but Hollenbach goes beyond Gewirth's "Kantian notion of agency as autonomy" in recognizing agency to be sustained only in community relations.

35. For such mutuality in power, justice needs to be accompanied by other social virtues. Trust and loyalty are required. The existence, needs, and contributions of all groups and their members are recognized (John C. Raines "Toward a Relational Theory of Justice," *Cross Currents* 39[1989], 137–41, 160). Raines describes them as components of justice itself, supplementing its other aspects. Justice would therefore seem, however, to be returning to its classical form as the general justice that sums up the other social virtues.

36. Cf. Hollenbach, "Communitarian Reconstruction of Human Rights," 12.

37. Max L. Stackhouse, *Creeds, Society, and Human Rights. A Study in Three Cultures* (Grand Rapids, MI, Eerdmans, 1984), 5, 44, 104–5.

38. Also Gal 6.15; Col. 3.9–11; Eph. 2.14–16.

39. Niebuhr, *Moral Man and Immoral Society,* 234.

40. Ismael Garcia, *Justice in Latin American Theology of Liberation* [Atlanta, Knox, 1987], 161.

41. Prov. 30.8; Luke 12.15–34; 1 Tim. 6.8.

42. John Calvin, *The Harmony of the Last Four Books of Moses,* 8th Commandment, on Deut. 15.1, following the translation of Höpfl (*Christian Polity of John Calvin,* 158). *Mediocris* would seem to mean here "avoiding the extremes."

43. Cf. Wolff, *Anthropology of the Old Testament,* 187.

44. Cf. Josh. 17.14–15. The same principle of proportionality was used for the taking of cities from the tribes to be cities of refuge (Num. 35.8).

45. 1 Chron. 24.31; 25.8; 26.13 in describing the use of lots in assigning temple duties, indicates that lots are a way of giving all—"small and great alike"—an equal chance, the younger brother as well as the older, the pupil as well as the teacher. Weisman suggests regarding the use of the lot in appointment of the "selected warriers" that the lot may well suit the idea of equality among all the soldiers in the army from whom the selection was made for it left the selection to God's choices. It indicated "equal right and equal duty" among the tribes (Ze'eb Weisman, "The Nature and Background of *bāḥūr* in the Old Testament," *Vetus Testamentum* 31 [1981], 446–47).

46. Cf. Plato's arrangements for the guardians of the Republic. They were given just enough stipend so that there would no superfluity nor any lack (*Rep.* 416e).

47. Cf. Ronald L. Sider, "Toward a Biblical Perspective on Equality. Steps on the Way Toward Christian Political Engagement," *Interpretation* 43 (1989), 167.

48. C. Spicq, *Les Épîtres Pastorales* (Paris, Gabalda, Études Bibliques, 1969⁴), 190 (on 1 Tim. 6.8).

49. Cf. Job 22 where injustice includes the sins of omission of withholding drink from the weary and bread from the hungry (vv. 7, 23; cf. 31.17), as well as the exploiting use of economic power (v. 6a). In 31.19 the omission is failure to provide clothing.

50. The Law gives concrete expression to justice although merely enforcing the law is not the focus of the justice passages. Eryl W. Davies (*Prophesy and Ethics. Isaiah and the Ethical Traditions of Israel* [Sheffield, Journal for the Study of the Old Testament, Supplement Series 16, 1981], 26–27, 68–69, 105, 116) argues that much of what Isaiah protests was not in strict violation of the Mosaic law. A more paradigmatic view of the Law, however, should qualify his still significant argument.

51. Land is the provision of justice in Num. 27.5–6. Moses brings before the Lord their appeal for justice (*mišpaṭ* ["case," *NRSV*], v. 5) in inheritance in the land.

52. One argument against these provisons denoting benefits rights is that they did not function as civil law since there are no sanctions provided. Rather they are moral duties to be carried out voluntarily (a Theonomist position). This interpretation is based on the seemingly arbitrary principle that the laws that do not have enforcement procedures attached to them were not intended as civil laws. While there is a lack of agreement about the civil nature of the Torah, this principle is not one held in general agreement in scholarship on the Hebrew Scriptures. A better interpretation is that whether the Torah was ideal law, as some argue, or actual law, the sphere of application in mind was the civil law where it touches civil matters.

The Torah, like other Ancient Near Eastern laws, is paradigmatic, rather than comprehensive. For this cf. G. R. Driver and John C. Miles, *The Babylonian Laws* (London: Oxford, Ancient Codes and Laws of the Near East, 1952–1955), 1, 45, and Douglas Stuart, "The Law(s)-Covenant Stipulations for Israel," in Gordon D. Fee and Stuart, *How to Read the Bible for All Its Worth* (Grand Rapids, MI: Zondervan, 1981), 140–43. The Torah is not complete, including consistent provisions of mechanisms for enforcement. Arguments from silence are methodologically inappropriate. Thus Nehemiah as governor enforces the prohibition on interest although penalties are not provided in the law (Neh. 5.7), and he sets up a state machinery for transfer payments to the Levites (Neh. 11.23; 12.44–47; 13.10–14) although the Law does not provide enforcement procedures for such. Moreover, there is an indication that redistribution of land, a form of which is the Jubilee, was to be carried out by a political unit, the assembly of the people (Mic. 2.5).

53. The following injunction against the practice of withholding the wages of the hired laborer until the next day prohibits the use of power to the disadvantage of one of the weakest groups in the community. The next verse goes on to deal with abuse of the blind.

54. E.g., Amos 2.6–7 and Job 22.6a.

55. Mic. 2.1–2; Cf. p. 19.

56. C. Francis Belcher, *Logging Railroads of the White Mountains* (Boston, Appalachian Mountain Club, 1980), 205–6.

57. O. Nigel Bolland, "Labour Control and Resistance in Belize in the Century after 1838," *Slavery and Abolition* 7 (1986), 175–87.

58. Davies, *Prophesy and Ethics,* 69, 116.

59. E.g., Carl F. H. Henry, *Aspects of Christian Social Ethics* (Grand Rapids, MI, Eerdmans, 1964), 146–71.

60. On justice as a continuation of the meaning of love, see Mott, *Biblical Ethics and Social Change,* pp. 61–64. Examples of the association of justice with love or grace in addi-

tion to those provided there, cf. Ps. 36.5–6; 40.10; 89.14–17; 111.3–4; 112.4–6; 116.5–7; 119.149, 156; 143.11–12; 145.7–9, 17; Isa. 63.7–8 (LXX).

61. Cf. a similar statement of purpose in Isa. 32.1: J. W. Olley argues that the preposition 1 with *ṣedeq* and *mišpaṭ* should be translated as "for" on the analogy of its use with *ṣᵉdāqāh* in Hos. 10.12 and its seven other uses with *mišpaṭ* in Isaiah. The purpose or function of the promised coming rulers will be justice ("Notes on Isaiah xxxii 1, xiv 19, 23 and lxiii 1," *Vetus Testamentum* 33 [1983], 447–48).

62. Cf. Deut. 1.17; 2 Sam. 23.3; 2 Chron. 19.6, 8; Prov. 16.12; 25.5; 29.14; Isa. 1.11–26; 28.5–6, 14, 17.

63. Cf. Prov. 31.5; Isa. 42.4; 51.4. The plural of *mišpāṭ* is frequent for the particular ordinances of the Torah. The ordinances are concrete expressions of justice.

64. Madison, *Federalist,* No. 51, p. 267.

65. Zeev W. Falk, "Two Symbols of Justice," *Vetus Testamentum* 10 (1960), 72–73. The sceptre and the throne thus become symbols of justice.

66. Cf. the list of maxims of distributive justice by Gregory Vlastos, "Justice and Equality," in *Social Justice,* ed. Brandt, 35. One might say that the maxim governing one's theory of distributive justice provides the *material* content for the *formal* definition of to each, each one's due (cf. Garcia, *Justice in Latin American Theology,* 27).

67. Might or ability would include property, or the ability in the market. Aristotle, whose criterion is merit in terms of contribution to society, refutes property as the criterion since the purpose of community is the good life not wealth (*Pol.* 1280a26–36).

68. Daniel Maquire keeps recognition of what one has earned (ability) and what one needs in closer balance than what I have suggested (*New American Justice,* 60). Cf. the maxim upon which 2 Tim. 2.6 draws in making an analogy: "the farmer who toils should receive the first of the harvest"; note, however, that it is still only "first."

Chapter 6

1. The chapter title is inspired by a 1967 song by the Beatles, "All You Need is Love."

2. Augustine, *Confessions of St. Augustine* 13 (New York, Collier, 1961), 233.

3. Guy de Maupassant, cited by Eustace Chesser, *Love Without Fear* (New York, Signet, 1947), 48.

4. Wesley, Sermon 7, "The Way to the Kingdom" 1.8, in Wesley, *Works 1: Sermons 1,* 222.

5. Reinhold Niebuhr, "The Ethic of Jesus and the Social Problem," in Niebuhr, *Love and Justice,* ed. D. B. Robertson (Gloucester, MA, Peter Smith, 1957), 32 (also in *Religion in Life* 1 [1932])

6. Erich Fromm, *The Sane Society* (New York, Rinehart, 1955), 31.

7. Aristotle, *Eth. Nic.* 1171a10–12.

8. Nicholas Berdyaev, *The Destiny of Man* (New York, Harper, 1960), 106.

9. Gene Outka, *Agape. An Ethical Analysis* (New Haven, CT, Yale U., 1972), 274–79.

10. Garth L. Hallett, *Christian Neighbor-Love. An Assessment of Six Rival Versions* (Washington, D. C., Georgetown U., 1989), 7, 93.

11. Jonathan Edwards, *Works of Jonathan Edwards, Vol. 2: Religious Affections,* ed. J. Smith (New Haven, CT, Yale U., 1959), 240–48. Cf. Stephen Post, "Disinterested Benevolence: An American Debate over the Nature of Christian Love," *Journal of Religious Ethics* 14 (1986), 356–60, 364–65. The contrast to Edwards was his follower, Samuel Hopkins, who argued for a love devoid of self-regard, including in love a willingness to be damned.

12. John Howard Yoder, *The Christian Witness to the State* (Newton, KS, Faith and Life, Institute of Mennonite Studies 3, 1964), 14.

13. Hallet, *Christian Neighbor Love,* particularly 5, 53–61, 109. The texts which speak of not seeking one's own good or not pleasing oneself (Rom. 15.1; 1 Cor.10.24; 33; 13.5) should be interpreted in this context that one should "give precedence to others' good, and only seek [one's] own when it does not conflict with others'" (Hallet, 61). These texts go beyond parity with others and even prefering others unless the gain to ourselves would be significantly greater.

14. In love we wash one another's feet (John 13.14; cf. Gal. 5.13). We are to consider others better than oneself in having the attitude that we possess in our relationship to Jesus, who did not cling to equality with God but took the form of a slave and became obedient unto death (Phil. 2.3–7).

15. Temple, *Christianity and Social Order,* 14.

16. Yvonne Goulet, "The Church Shouldn't Let Caesar Off the Hook," *Salt* 3, 7 (July/August, 1983), 2.

17. Niebuhr, *Human Destiny,* 69.

18. Niebuhr, "Why the Church is not Pacifist," in Niebuhr, *Christianity and Power Politics,* 14.

19. A. Cressy Morrison, *Man Does Not Stand Alone* (New York, Fleming, 1944), 79.

20. Niebuhr, "Justice and Love," in Niebuhr, *Love and Justice,* 28 (also in *Christianity and Society* 15 [Fall, 1950]).

21. George H. Tavard, *A Way of Love* (Maryknoll, NY, Orbis, 1977), 75.

22. Míguez Bonino, *Christians and Marxists,* 112.

23. H. Richard Niebuhr, *Christ and Culture* (New York, Harper, 1951), 16.

24. Reinhold Niebuhr, "Is There Another Way?" in Niebuhr, *Love and Justice,* 300 (also in *Progressive* 19 [Oct., 1955]).

25. For a fuller account of the continuity between love and justice, cf. Mott, *Biblical Ethics and Social Change,* 48–54, 59–64.

26. Arthur J. Dyck, "Loving Impartiality in Moral Cognition," in *Annual of the Society of Christian Ethics,* 1989, ed. D. M. Yeager (Knoxville, TN, Society of Christian Ethics, 1989), 55–72. For the experiences from combat in Southeast Asia, Dyck cites Robert Jay Lifton, *Home from War* (1973), 103–4, 346–50.

27. Niebuhr, "Why the Church is not Pacifist," 14.

28. Nash, *Freedom, Justice, and State,* 75–76.

29. Karl Mannheim, *Ideology and Utopia. An Introduction to the Sociology of Knowledge* (New York, Harcourt, 1936), 194–95.

30. Tavard, *Way of Love,* 147.

31. Boesak, *Farewell to Innocence,* 11.

32. J. Ramsey Michaels, *Servant and Son. Jesus in Parable and Gospel* (Atlanta, Knox, 1981), 224–25.

33. Martin Luther King, Jr., *Where Do We Go from Here: Chaos or Community?* (Boston, Beacon, 1967), 37.

34. E.g. Ezek. 34.16, 23–24; Ps. 146.7. See pp. 83–85, 87.

35. Goldingay, "Man of War and Suffering Servant," 84.

36. Exod. 15.6, 12 in light of v. 9 (cp. deliverance [*špṭ*] from power as an act of justice, 2 Sam. 18.31).

37. Goldingay, 96.

38. King, *Where Do We Go,* 37.

39. Niebuhr, "Christian Faith and the World Crisis," in Niebuhr, *Love and Justice,* 280 (also in *Christianity and Crisis* 1 [February 10, 1941]).

40. Niebuhr, *Human Nature,* 298.

Chapter 7

1. Reinhold Niebuhr, *The Nature and Destiny of Man, A Christian Interpretation, Vol. 2: Human Destiny* (New York, Scribner's, 1964 [1943]), 3, 290.

2. Ibid., 28.

3. Eduard Heimann, *Communism, Fascism or Democracy?* (New York, Norton, 1938), 232.

4. Niebuhr, *Human Destiny,* 5, 29,

5. Ibid., 320.

6. Ibid., 211, 321.

7. Ibid., 80, 245, 295; Niebuhr, *Faith and History. A Comparison of Christian and Modern Views of History* (New York, Scribner's, 1949), 233.

8. Niebuhr, *Human Destiny,* 305 (individual death relates also to conditions of finiteness). Augustine's statement is found in his comments on 1 Cor. 15.56a in *On the Merits and Forgiveness of Sins, and the Baptism of Infants,* in *Works, Vol. 4: Anti-Pelagian Works 1,* ed. P. Holmes (Edinburgh, Clark, 1872), 150.

9. Niebuhr, 49. Niebuhr holds that evil does not have an independent history. Rather, to the end it parasitically corrupts or defies the good (318).

10. Cf. ibid, 318.

11. Paul S. Minear, "Ontology and Ecclesiology in the Apocalypse," *New Testament Studies* 12 (1966), 89–105.

12. Cf. Paul Tillich, "The Kingdom of God and History," in H. G. Wood et al., *Church, Community, and State, Vol. 3: The Kingdom of God and History* (London, Allen, 1938), 115.

13. Niebuhr, *Human Destiny,* 36, 38, 46, 212, 295; cf. 4, 22.

14. Ibid., 45–46, 96.

15. Ibid., 295–96.

16. Ibid., 1, 80.

17. Ibid., 1

18. Ibid., 2, 80, 207, 245.

19. James Luther Adams, "The Lure of Persuasion: Some Themes from Whitehead" (1975/76), in Adams, *The Prophethood of All Believers,* ed. G. Beach (Boston, Beacon, 1986), 194.

20. Shawn Carruth, "Ears to Hear," *Bible Today* 21 (1983), 89–95. "Q" presents Jesus as the Son of Man, coming to judge and establish the Reign. For the Gospel of Thomas, the Reign is already present and has nothing to do with time. God has no relationship to the world except to the individual. Cf. also Helmut Koester, *Introduction to the New Testament, Vol. 2: History and Literature of Early Christianity* (New York, Walter de Gruyter, 1982), 152–54.

21. Niebuhr, *Human Destiny,* 2, 15.

22. Jürgen Moltmann, *Theology of Hope. On the Ground and the Implications of a Christian Eschatology* (New York, Harper, 1967), 116.

23. Niebuhr, 46.

24. Ibid., 92.

25. Ibid., 290.

26. Ibid., 295–96, 311.

27. Ibid., 211.

28. J.G.A. Pocock, *The Machiavellian Moment: Florentine Political Thought and the Atlantic Republican Tradition* (Princeton, NJ, Princeton U., 1975). Pp. 211–18 provide a significant summation; cf. 156, 265–71.

29. Heimann, *Reason and Faith in Modern Society,* 157.

30. In addition, Pocock notes that the Aristotelian and humanist tradition lacks a positive

(in contrast to a preservative) approach to power because it evaluates change negatively, as a movement away from the norms which define the change (329, 402).

31. Lugwig Edelstein, *The Idea of Progress in Classical Antiquity* (Baltimore, Johns Hopkins, 1967). Other authors have also warned against overemphazing the negative implications of a cyclical theory for the sense of history (cf. Pocock, 6, with further references). Christian writers were aware of the pessimistic extremes of the cyclical outlook, such as the Stoic position presented by Cicero that "the evolution of time . . . creates nothing new and only unfolds each event in its order" (*Div.* 1.127 [trans. W. A. Falconer (Cambridge, Harvard U., Loeb Classical Library, 1923), 20.363]). The contrast encouraged their fleshing out the historical applications of Christian faith in response. Augustine remarks, "What wonder is it if, entangled in these circles, they find neither entrance nor egress" (*City of God,* 12.14, p. 395); cf. Wolin, *Politics and Vision,* 124.

32. Cf. Pocock, 6, 217, 477

33. Wolin, 124

34. Simon John De Vries, *Yesterday, Today and Tomorrow: Time and History in the Old Testament* (Grand Rapids, MI, Eerdmans, 1975), 281. Robert E. Cooley noted the frequency of conditional clauses that are used in the biblical approach to the future, indicating the variable of the human response to God's will ("The Second Coming: A Taxonomy for a Perfect Society," convocation address, Gordon-Conwell Theological Seminary, September 14, 1984).

35. Cf. Wolin, 32.

36. De Vries, 126, 252, 331. *Yôm* is by the far the most frequent Hebrew expression for a unit of time; it also a unit of experience.

37. Wolff, *Anthropology of the Old Testament,* 88. In Ps. 143.5 "of old" (*NRSV*) is "in front [*miqqedem*] of me." In Jer. 29.11 "future" *(NRSV)* is "that which is behind and which follows one," "at one's back" (*'aḥ³rît*). In contrast note our reference to the past in the expression, "Put those things behind you."

38. De Vries, 34–35.

39. Jim Wayne Miller, "The Brier Sermon," in Miller, *The Mountains Have Come Closer* (Boone, NC, Appalachian Consortion, 1980), 56.

40. Søren Kierkegaard, *Kierkegaard's Writings, Vol. 4: Either/Or 2,* ed. H. Hong and E. Hong (1987), 137–48; Alasdair MacIntyre, *After Virtue. A Study in Moral Theory* (Notre Dame, IN, U. of Notre Dame, 1984²), 40. Kierkegaard: "The healthy individual lives simultaneously in hope and in recollection, and only thereby does his life gain true and substantive continuity" (142).

41. As presented by Garry Wills, *Confessions of a Conservative* (Garden City, NY, Doubleday, 1979), 229: Augustine expressed the idea of recollection in a pun on the Latin words for gather *(cogo)* and reflect *(cogito).*

42. Bruce James Smith, *Politics and Remembrance: Republican Themes in Machiavelli, Burke, and Tocqueville* (Princeton, NJ, Princeton U., 1985), 262, cf. 21.

43. Machiavelli, *The Prince* 5, in Niccolo Machiavelli, *Chief Works,* trans. Gilbert, 1.24; Smith, *Politics and Remembrance,* 12, 55, 57, 82. Karen Lebacqz describes the importance of keeping alive in story, worship, and ritual the memories of past justice received from God and humans and of past injustices for community solidarity in commitment to justice (*Justice in an Unjust World. Foundations for a Christian Approach to Justice* [Minneapolis, MN, Augsburg, 1987], 100–101, 111, 116, 128).

44. De Vries, 153, 275.

45. Lev. 26.39 also states literally that (because of the iniquities of their forebears) "they shall pine away *with* them."

46. Cf. MacIntyre, *After Virtue,* 146, 223.

47. So Augustine contrasts the "straight path [*recti itineris*] of sound doctrine" to the philosophers' false cycles of time (*City of God* 12.14 [*Opera* 14,2, Corpus Christianorum, series Latina 48, 1955], 368 [in Dods' translation it is 12.13, p. 394]).

48. J. L. Russell, "Time in Christian Thought," in *The Voice of Time*, ed. J. T. Fraser (Amherst, University of Massachusetts, 1981²), 63.

49. Friedrich Kümmel, "Time as Succession and the Problem of Duration," in *Voices of Time*, ed. Fraser, 31–55. Kümmel perceives that understanding time merely as a point in movement along a line requires time to be represented by means of a spatial image so that time is transposed into "mere spatial contiguity." Its specific temporal character is thus eliminated (41–42).

50. Moltmann, *Theology of Hope*, 20–21.

51. Cone, *God of the Oppressed*, 130. Cone notes the long history of hope theology among black people. It included hope for justice and judgment on the society which enslaved them (127, 131).

52. Coles, *South Goes North*, 462.

53. Paul Tillich, "Kairos," *A Handbook of Christian Theology* (1958), 193–97. Versus false application of the concept, events must be examined in relationship to the original revelation. An event can be "in kairos" only if it corresponds to the original kairos, which is the cross of Christ and the gospel of the coming Reign of God (Stone, *Paul Tillich's Radical Social Thought*, 89–90).

54. Michael Harrington, *The New American Poverty* (New York, Holt, 1984), 106.

55. Martin Luther King, Jr. "Letter from Birmingham Jail" (April 16, 1963), in King, *Why We Can't Wait* (New York, Signet Books, 1964), 86.

56. I am unsure of the source of this statement.

57. De Vries, *Yesterday, Today and Tomorrow*, 281. Cf. p. 315 for Isa. 2.17.

58. Moltmann, *Theology of Hope*, 100, 118.

59. Plato, *Rep.*, 592.

60. Moltmann, 23, 41. The understanding of time in the Middle Ages was highly influenced by Greek thought. Eschatology was replaced by individual immortality. J. L. Russell describes the sense of "terrestrial cycles of generation and decay, both in the inorganic and biological realms . . . controlled by the eternally repeating cycles of the heavenly bodies" ("Time in Christian Thought," 70).

61. Shriver et al., *Spindles and Spires*, 312. Cf. Robert Penn Warren, also writing of the American South, in the words of Jack Burden, the narrator: "I tried to tell her how if you could not accept the past and its burden there was no future, for without one there cannot be the other, and how if you could accept the past you might hope for the future, for only out of the past can you make the future" (*All the King's Men* [New York, Grosset, 1946], 461). Friedrich Kümmel, in establishing the independent function of each dimension of time, similarly states that what has been repressed without having been freely assimilated never is truly past but breaks in at the slightest pretext. In contrast is the affirming act of memory that brings new significance or influence for the present from the past ("Time as Succession and the Problem of Duration," 51–53).

62. Christopher Lasch, "Orwell," *In These Times*, December 19, 1984–January 8, 1985, 13.

63. William S. Ellis, "Rondônia's Settlers Invade Brazil's Imperiled Rain Forest," *National Geographic* 174 (1988), 779, 787.

64. Alan R. Drengson, "Toward a Redefinition of Progress in Agricultural Technology and Practices: From Industrial Paradigms to Natural Patterns," *Quarterly Journal of Ideology* 11, 2 (1987), 59. For a discussion of similar proposals for a measure of growth and economic welfare alternative to that of the gross national product, including that by Herman

Daly and John Cobb in *For the Common Good* (Beacon, 1989), cf. John Miller, "A Green GNP," *Dollars and Sense* 161 (November 1990), 6–8, 22.

65. Cf. John Horton, "Time and Cool People, *Transaction* 4, 5 (April 1967), 5–12, on fantasies of the future among street people with low income in a black ghetto.

66. David Moberg, "Disappearing Dreams," *In These Times,* February 13–19, 1985.

67. Cf. C. H. Dodd, "The Kingdom of God and History," in H. G. Wood et al., *Church, Community, and State, Vol. 3: The Kingdom of God and History* (London, Allen, 1938), 16, 21.

68. Tillich, "Political Meaning of Utopia," 179.

69. Arthur Koestler as cited by William V. Shannon, "The Long March to a Better Future," *Boston Globe,* January 1, 1985, op-ed.

70. For a fuller treatment of the Reign of God, clarifying its social aspects and implications, cf. Mott, *Biblical Ethics and Social Change,* Chap. 5.

71. Tolkien, *Return of the King,* 196.

72. Cf. Letty M. Russell, *Human Liberation in a Feminist Perspective—A Theology* (Philadelphia, Westminster, 1974), 41–42; Rubem A. Alves, *A Theology of Human Hope* (Washington, D. C., Corpus, 1969), 96.

73. H. Richard Niebuhr, *The Kingdom of God in America* (New York, Harper, 1937), 29.

74. Arthur G. Gish, *The New Left and Christian Radicalism* (Grand Rapids, MI, Eerdmans, 1970), 85.

75. Thomas W. Ogletree, *The Use of the Bible in Christian Ethics. A Constructive Essay* (Philadelphia, Fortress, 1983), 177.

76. H. R. Niebuhr, *Kingdom of God in America,* 27.

77. Cf. Paul in Rom. 13.11–14: We are to know the *kairos* and in light of the approaching day of salvation put off the works of darkness and put on the weapons of light.

78. E.g., George Williamson, Jr., "A Niebuhrian Critique of Niebuhrian Thought," *Andover Newton Quarterly* 15 (1975), 182–95.

79. Langdon Gilkey, "Reinhold Niebuhr's Theology of History," *Journal of Religion* 54 (1974), 363–64, 368, 374, 376. Ronald H. Stone states that all the transforming elements are present in Niebuhr's thought; it is a matter of emphasis (*Realism and Hope* [Washington, D.C., University Press of America, 1977], 127).

80. Bruce J. Malina in an article that is deserving of close attention seeks to prevent a distortion from reading twentieth-century views of time into our understanding of the biblical views of time ("Christ and Time: Swiss or Mediterranean?" *Catholic Biblical Quarterly* 51 [1989], 1–31). He is helpful in showing how the past and future are tied to the present for New Testament believers because the past and future belong to the same context of actual experience that dominates the sense of time (12). In contrast there is also imagined time, past and future, beyond experience and completely in the control of God. He argues that there was not a now and not yet tension because of the orientation to the present. I suggest, however, that several factors, including Paul's struggle with those who could not maintain this tension, would indicate more of a future orientation than Malina suggests, if I have understood him correctly: the promise–fulfilment motifs, the definite closure of history, and the way "imagined time" is used to motivate action in the present. The biblical events of "imagined time" are more closely integrated into history than in the general Mediterranean outlook. While it is helpful to understand how a Mediterranean person would view the Christian message, Christian conversion involved more of a shift in time orientation than he indicates.

81. Cf. Russell, *Human Liberation,* 58: "To view the world as history is to think of it not just as a record of past events but also as a process of change from past, to present, to future."

82. Niebuhr, *Human Destiny,* 321.

83. José Míguez Bonino, *Doing Theology in a Revolutionary Situation* (Philadelphia, For-

tress, Confrontation Books, 1975), 136–42; cf. Tillich, "Kingdom of God and History," 130–31; Hans Schwarz, "Reflection on the Work of the Spirit outside the Church," *Neue Zeitschrift für Systematische Theologie und Religionsphilosophie* 23 (1981), 211.

84. Cf. Bernard Zylstra, "The Bible, Justice and the State," *International Reformed Bulletin* 16, 55 (fall 1973), 3.

85. Martin Luther, *In XV Psalmos graduum* (on Ps. 127.1), in Luther, *Werke. Kritische Gesamtausgabe* (Weimar, Böhlaus 1930), 40.3, p. 210; translation of Schwarz, "Reflection on the Work of the Spirit," 206.

86. Schwarz, 206. As Athanasius wrote Ad Serapion, the continuance of God's works is only secured by God's presence within them (205). The Spirit is without revelatory significance, however, in the world outside of Christ (211).

87. Paul Tillich, "Protestantism as a Critical and Creative Principle" (1929), in *Political Expectation,* 10–39. John H. Yoder provides several perceptive guides for avoiding presumption in claims of where "God is at work." Under the authority of the Torah and incarnation as "moral guides," they include the following: "where oppression gives way not to counter-oppression but to servanthood, where suffering is accepted, not imposed, where human dignity commands respect not alone through anger but through the recreation of community" (although anger and confrontation may be involved in its attainment) ("Discerning the Kingdom of God in the Struggles of the World," *International Review of Mission* 68 [1979], 366–72).

Chapter 8

1. Cf. Reinhold Niebuhr, "Liberalism: Illusions and Realities," *New Republic* 133 (July 4, 1955), 11.

2. Russell Kirk, *The Conservative Mind From Burke to Eliot* (Chicago, Gateway, 1960³), 253, cf. 384, 519.

3. Ibid., 4.

4. Samuel P. Huntington, "Conservatism as Ideology," *American Political Science Review* 51 (1957), 465.

5. Edmund Burke, *Reflections on the Revolution in France* (1790), ed. T. Mahoney (Indianapolis, Library of Liberal Arts, 1955), 10. He stated that the French Revolution was most the astonishing to date (11).

6. Kirk, *Conservative Mind,* 41 (describing the position of Edmund Burke).

7. Huntington, "Conservatism as Ideology," 454–73. Huntington argues that it lacks a substantive ideal of how society should be organized and does not present a universal and permanent appeal. Huntington criticizes the approach of building a paradigm on Burke's thought and establishing a common ideology by discovering its elements in other thinkers. We are nevertheless taking Burke as an exemplary figure, but with the warning that significant differences should be expected in other figures and that one could use a different figure as a basis for comparison.

8. Clinton Rossiter, *Conservatism in America* (New York, Vintage, 1962²), 17, 219; Kirk, *Conservative Mind,* 5: "In any practical sense, Burke is the founder of our conservatism." "Burke represents, by general consent, the seminal moment in the genesis of modern conservative thought" (Michael D. Clark, *Coherent Variety: The Idea of Diversity in British and American Conservative Thought* [Westport, CT, Greenwood, Contributions in Political Science 86, 1983], 48). Burke served as the model for most German conservatives (Karl Mannheim, *Ideology and Utopia. An Introduction to the Sociology of Knowledge* (New York, Harvest Book, 1936 [1929]), 120).

9. Clark, *Coherent Variety;* Kirk, 7.

10. Rossiter, *Conservatism in America,* 61–62, 65; Kirk, 7, 66–71. "Burke maintains that a proper majority can be drawn only from a body qualified by tradition, station, education, property, and moral nature to exercise the political function" (Kirk, 67).

11. Rossiter, 8, 27.

12. Garry Wills, *Confessions of a Conservative,* 64 describing Cardinal Newman. For Burke a state without the means of some change is without the means of its own preservation (*Reflections on the Revolution,* 24). Also note Kirk's comment, "Conservatism never is more admirable than when it accepts changes that it disapproves, with good grace, for the sake of a general conciliation" (*Conservative Mind,* 52).

13. Vigen Guroian, "The Possibilities and Limits of Politics: A Comparative Study of the Thought of Reinhold Niebuhr and Edmund Burke," *Union Seminary Quarterly Review* 36 (1981), 191–92; Reinhold Niebuhr, "The Foreign Policy of American Conservatism and Liberalism," in *Christian Realism and Political Problems* (New York, Scribner's, 1953), 72.

14. Karl Mannheim, "Conservative Thought" [1927], in Mannheim, *Essays in Sociology and Social Psychology* (London, Routledge, 1953), 110.

15. Burke, *Speech on a Motion for a Committee to Inquire into the State of the Representation of the Commons in Parliament* (May 7, 1782), in *Works* (Bohn), 6.146: Prescription gives right to prior use and reflects the antiquity of tradition. Presumption favors a settled scheme of society over an untried idea. Cf. Pocock, *Machiavellian Moment,* 15, 23.

16. Burke, *Reflections on the Revolution,* 102; cf. 89, 103–8.

17. Burke, *Reflections on the Revolution,* 38, 40, 107, 212, 214, 217; Francis P. Canavan, *The Political Reason of Edmund Burke* (Durham, NC, Duke U., Lilly Endowment Research Program in Christianity and Politics, 1960), 102.

18. Mannheim, "Conservative Thought," 90.

19. Louis de Bonald, *Économie sociale* 1.4, in *Oeuvres complètes* (Paris, Migne, 1859), 1.355; cf. Wolin, *Politics and Vision,* 403.

20. Burke, *Thoughts and Details on Scarcity* (1795), in *Works* (Boston, Little, Brown, 1886), 5.151, 157. H. R. Feather interprets the lack of antibourgeois sentiment among English Romantic Conservatism to be due in part to the penetration from 1600 of mercantile capital into the traditional quasi-feudal power and the relatively integrated state of traditional (aristocratic) capital and manufacturing capital after 1800 ("Conservative Thought and the English Bourgeoisie," *Sociological Review* 32 [1984], 274–75).

21. David P. Calleo, *Coleridge and the Idea of the Modern State* (New Haven, Yale U., Yale Studies in Political Science 18, 1966), 13–26; cf. Michael Levin, "Marxism and Romanticism: Marx's Debt to German Conservatism," *Political Studies* 22 (1974), 404, 412. The English Romanticists, however, had only a partial affinity to conservative principles. Some also espoused a contrasting optimism, utopianism, and support of idiosyncrasy for its own sake (Clark, *Coherent Variety,* 78–79; cf. Richard Weaver, *Ideas Have Consequences* [Chicago, U. of Chicago, 1948], 80–83). Richard Weaver, a twentieth century American Southern conservative, was strongly critical of the values, exploitation, and abstract forms of ownership of capitalism (cf. ibid, 15, 32, 51, 74–75, 112, 132–33).

22. Edmund Burke, *A Notebook of Edmund Burke. Poems, Characters, Essays and Other Sketches in the Hands of Edmund and William Burke,* ed. H.V.F. Somerset (Cambridge, Cambridge U., 1957), 96; cf. Canavan, *Political Reason of Edmund Burke,* 57.

23. Guroian, "Possibilities and Limits of Politics," 191.

24. Reinhold Niebuhr, "Liberalism and Conservatism," *Christianity and Society* 20 (Winter 1954–55), 3. Liberty is *social* freedom and is not antithetical to coercion and authority (Canavan, *Political Reason of Edmund Burke,* 90).

25. Rossiter, *Conservatism in America,* 35, 41–42; Clark, *Coherent Variety,* 15. Burke

states that rendering government feeble provides no security for freedom (*Reflections on the Revolution*, 33–34).

26. Canavan, *Political Reason of Edmund Burke*. Richard Weaver *(Ideas Have Consequences)* presents a less immanent epistemology than does Burke and decries the attack upon "abstract ideas and speculative inquiry" by those attuned only to present experience (13). Their similarities are veiled by the wording, however. Weaver is speaking of transcendent first principles of the eternal world, which is close to Burke's universal order; Weaver also finds these principles manifested in the wisdom from the past. Nevertheless, Weaver is more Platonic.

27. Burke, "Speech on the Impeachment of Warren Hastings," Second Day of Reply (May 30, 1794), *Works* (Bohn), 8.8–9; cf. Canavan, *The Political Reason of Edmund Burke*, 58.

28. Burke, *Thoughts on French Affairs* (1791), in *Works* (London, Bohn, 1862–94), 3.372; cf. Canavan, *Political Reason of Edmund Burke*, 13.

29. J.G.A. Pocock shows how historical skepticism can become a conservative weapon against the radical use of history as a critique of the present. The continuity of behavior with the past is said to be a matter of style realized in action rather than of conceptualization (evaluating the position of Michael Oakeshott) ("Time, Institutions and Action; An Essay on Traditions and Their Understanding," in Pocock, *Politics, Language, and Time* [Chicago, U. of Chicago, 1989], 269–71 [also in *Politics and Experience*, M. Oakeshott Fest., 1968]). The difference between a historical and a traditional outlook is that history ascribes "a relation to the present more complex than mere transmission" to the past (253).

Some of the hesitation to describe history and social life in terms of universal principles derives from a pragmatic viewpoint. Burke writes as the experienced statesman impatient with the academician. He prefers to talks about the actual policy that can be negotiated rather than abstract principles (e.g., Burke, *Reflections on the Revolution*, 71; cf. his comparison of the professor and the statesman, in *Speech on a Bill to Repeal and Alter Certain Acts Representing Religious Opinions* [May 11, 1792], *Works* [Bohn], 6.114.)

30. Burke, *Reflections on the Revolution*, 97–98.

31. Cf. Leo Strauss, *Natural Right and History* (Chicago, U. of Chicago, 1953), 13. Canavan (*Political Reason of Edmund Burke*, e.g., 133–35) argues that Strauss has underplayed Burke's sense of a universal rational moral order in his warning that Burke's defining rights as historical opened the door for an historicism that denied eternal principles (although this was prevented in Burke's case by his devotion to classical and Christian virtues) (Strauss, 316–23, cf. 6, 12–14, 18; cf. Clark, *Coherent Variety*, 80–81).

32. Guroian, "Possibilities and Limits of Politics," 200; Richard John Neuhaus, *The Naked Public Square. Religion and Democracy in America* (Grand Rapids, MI, Eerdmans, 1984), 136.

33. Wills, *Confessions of a Conservative*, 214–15.

34. Levin, "Marxism and Romanticism," 407–8.

35. Canavan, *Political Reason of Edmund Burke*, 61.

36. Guroian, 201.

37. Clark, *Coherent Variety*, 10, 86–87, 197. Clark cites as liberal examples John Stuart Mill (*On Liberty* [Appleton, 1947], 72–73) and David Riesman (*The Lonely Crowd* [Yale U., 1969] xl, lix–lx).

38. G. K. Chesterton, *The Uses of Diversity* (London, Methuen, Fountain Library, 1937⁶), 128–29; cf. Clark, 39.

39. Clark, *Coherent Variety*, 6–7, 21.

40. Weaver, *Ideas Have Consequences*, Chap. 2 (quotation from p. 45).

41. E. Digby Baltzell, *Puritan Boston and Quaker Philadelphia* (New York, Free, 1979),

26–29. The differences began in religious bases, later lost, in which the Puritan covenant theology nurtured a sense of responsibility. This was lacking in an individualism rooted in the Quaker apprehension of the Inner light. Cf. Weaver on the "gentleman" (*Ideas Have Consequences,* 54–55).

42. Burke, *Reflections on the Revolution,* 56.

43. Wolin, *Politics and Vision,* 230, cf. 202.

44. Burke, *Speech on State of the Representation of the Commons in Parliament,* 6.147.

45. Cf. Paul Tillich, *The Socialist Decision* (New York, Harper, 1977 [1933]), 4–5, 20–21, 141. Lord Acton's complaint of Burke was that "he looked for what ought to be in what is" (quoted in Smith, *Politics and Remembrance,* 111). This is true in terms of the reliance upon continuity. Burke, however, was not without criticism of evil in the present and from the past.

46. James Russell Lowell, "Democracy," in *Writings,* Vol. 6: *Literary and Political Addresses* (Boston, Houghton, 1890), 36; cf. Kirk, *Conservative Mind,* 390. Properly developing institutions are in tune with the mysterious decreed order of the world (Burke, *Reflections on the Revolution,* 38).

47. John Adams, Letter to Abigail Smith Adams (wife), February 4, 1794, in *Works, Vol. 1: A Life of the Author,* by Charles Francis Adams (Boston, Little, Brown, 1856), 462; cf. Rossiter, *Conservatism in America,* 112.

48. Levin, "Marxism and Romanticism," 407–8.

49. Canavan, *Political Reason of Edmund Burke,* 86.

50. Burke, *Reflections on the Revolution,* 36–37, 67, 70–71

51. Burke, *Reflections on the Revolution,* 42, 69–70.

52. Burke, *Speech on Certain Acts Representing Religious Opinions,* 114, 116; cf. Clark, *Coherent Variety,* 40, 45.

53. Mannheim, "Conservative Thought," 106.

54. Plato, *Rep.* 421c, 433a. For Aristotle slavery was valid when not based on unjust force but based on natural differences; there can then be mutual advantage and *philia* between master and slave (*Pol.* 1255b7–8, 13–15).

55. Thomas Aquinas, *Summa Theologiae,* 2a2ae. 61, 2, ed. T. Gilby (New York, McGraw-Hill, 1975), 37.93; cf. Christine E. Gudorf, *Catholic Social Teaching on Liberation Themes* (Lanham, MD, University Press of America, 1980), 37–41. Cf. Aristotle: Those who have a larger portion of the state are those who contribute the most to the good life (*Pol.* 1281a39). Justice is according to worth (*Pol.* 1301b36–39).

56. Cf. Guroian, "Possibilities and Limits of Politics," 196.

57. Robert Coles, *Children of Crisis, Vol. 5: Privileged Ones. The Well-Off and the Rich in America* (Boston, Little, Brown, 1977), 495. He also restates that viewpoint more severely, "If there is to be a redistribution of wealth, let the haves choose when, where, how much, and to whom" (512).

58. Burke, *Reflections on the Revolution,* 42, 86.

59. Cf. Mannheim, "Conservative Thought," 107–8.

60. T. S. Eliot, *The Idea of a Christian Society* (London, Faber, 1939), 47.

61. Burke, *Letter to Sir H. Langrishe* (1792), in *Works* (Bohn), 3.301; cf. Cavanan, *Political Reason of Edmund Burke,* 98.

62. Cf. Pocock, *Machiavellian Moment,* 515. Burke stated that if aristocracy meant "adherence to the rich and powerful against the poor and weak" (rather than the Peers), his face was set against any act of pride and power that impinges on "the smallest rights of the poorest people in the kingdom." If it came to "the last extremity, and to a contest of blood," he would take his "fate with the poor, and low, and feeble" (Burke, *Speech on a Bill for Repeal of the Marriage Act* [1781], in *Works* [Bohn], 6.170–71; cf. Kirk, *Conservative Mind,* 70).

63. Canavan, *Political Reason of Edmund Burke,* 97. Burke wrote that power, authority and distinction are not confined to blood, names, and titles; "virtue and wisdom, actual or presumptive are the qualifications." A proper legislative body should be respectably composed, "in point of condition in life or permanent property," as well as education and such habits as liberalize the understanding (Burke, *Reflections on the Revolution,* 47, 57). Those with substantial amounts of property needed to be well represented so as to prevent assaults on it. In discussing inherited wealth, he states that some preeminence and preference given to birth is not unnatural or unjust (59).

64. Burke, *Reflections on the Revolution,* 67; cf. Guroian, "Possibilities and Limits of Politics, 195. "Government is a contrivance of human wisdom to provide for human *wants.* Men have a right that these wants should be provided for by this wisdom" (Burke, 68 [his emphasis], cf. 69).

65. Burke, *Thoughts and Details on Scarcity,* 166.

66. Guroian, 195–96.

67. Burke, *Thoughts and Details on Scarcity.* Niebuhr, however, noted in Burke a lack of the prejudice against the welfare state often found in American conservatives ("Liberalism: Illusions and Realities," 11). Burke is thinking of the central state and gives indication of more confidence in local governments in such matters, which he regards as local, even private matters (167).

68. Carl Cone, *Burke and the Nature of Politics* (n.p., U. of Kentucky, 1957–1964), 2.490–91; cf. Guroian, 196. Coleridge despite his severe critique of capitalism is similarly hesitant about government interference. The response rather must be the restoration of a conscious concern for the general good through the slow influence of cultural and religious values (Calleo, *Coleridge and the Idea of the Modern State,* 21, 26).

69. Such elements of the bourgeois liberalism of his century were lacking in the Continental conservatives, Louis de Bonald and Joseph de Maistre (Guroian, 199). Likewise in Germany Burke was interpreted reactionarily without the concept of liberty that he retained (Mannheim, "Conservative Thought," 82; cf. Levin, "Marxism and Romanticism, 403).

70. Burke, *Reflections on the Revolution,* 67. For both Burke and Aristotle, the differing awards received from the community according to one's contribution is primarily discussed in terms of the privileges of sharing in political decisions.

71. Wills, *Confessions of a Conservative,* 199.

72. Canavan, *Political Reason of Edmund Burke,* 126.

73. Kirk, *Conservative Mind,* 72.

74. Weaver, *Ideas Have Consequences,* 137; Kirk, 7–8.

75. Wiles, *Economic Institutions Compared,* 35.

76. Ibid., 41.

77. In the provisions of the Jubilee the emphasis is upon the land, as fruitful soil (i.e., as productive property), not as territory per se (cf. Lev. 25.3–5, 19). In Lev. 27.22 a purchased field is distinguished from one's possession (understanding *ᵃḥuzzāh* as *possession,* not *inheritance* ["landed inheritance," *NRSV*]), perhaps because such a field would need to be given up in the Jubilee and was not really one's possession even though purchased legally. (Gillis Gerlemann argues, however, that even in *ᵃḥuzzāh* the emphasis is upon usage, the territory made available for cultivation, rather than upon property per se ["Nutzrecht und Wohnrecht. Zur Bedeutung von נחלה," *Zeitschrift für Alttestamentliche Wissenschaft* 89 (1977), 315–18].)

78. Burke, *Reflections on the Revolution,* 58 (his emphasis).

79. R. H. Tawney, *Equality. Halley Stewart Lectures, 1929* (New York, Harcourt, 1931), 176.

80. Heimann, *Reason and Faith in Modern Society,* 8

81. Niebuhr, *Children of Light,* 109. Some forms of power lend themselves more to power over others, such as that of landlords and large scale agricultural production. Other forms protect against aggrandizement of others and the caprice of nature and life. Still others are primarily the power to perform one's social function (116).

82. Seifert, *Ethical Resources,* 39.

83. Weaver, *Ideas Have Consequences,* 132–33. Aristotle commends the Spartan law for making it wrong to sell the family's land but notes that by permitting it to be given away, it allowed it to become concentrated (*Pol.* 1270a19–23). He argues that agricultural people make the best supporters of democracy and observes that to make a people democratic, laws have been enacted to keep the land in the hands of the people through limits on the maximum amount that could be owned, prohibiting sale of the original allotments, prohibiting mortgages on certain portions of the estate, or through tax reductions (*Pol.* 1319a7–19).

84. Gudorf, *Catholic Social Teaching,* 118–27.

85. Augustine, *Sermons* 178.8–9, and *In Johan. Evang. Tract* 6.25–26, in Augustine, *Political Writings,* ed. Paolucci, 160–61. Goods that are "possessed badly," although legally acquired, lose their claim of being justly possessed. They are another's property. Restitution ought to be made, and we do not intercede to prevent it; in this life the situation instead is endured although civil laws make this misuse of property less injurious (Letter 153, "To Madedonius," in Augustine, *Letters, Vol. 3,* trans. W. Parsons [New York, Fathers of the Church, 1953, 302–3; cf. José Míguez Bonino, *Toward a Christian Political Ethic* [Philadelphia, Fortress, 1983], 82–83).

86. Arthur M. Okun, *Equality and Efficiency: The Big Tradeoff* (Washington, DC, Brookings Institution, 1975), 37. However, short of the commendable goal of all families possessing their own decent dwelling, it is socially more significant that all families have a home than that there is opportunity for some to own a home at the price of others having something less for shelter.

87. James Luther Adams, "Art, Psyche, and Society," in Adams, *On Being Human Religiously,* 143–44 (also in *Perkins Journal* 26, 1 [fall 1972], 20). Cf. Robin M. Williams: Every legitimized right of access to scarce values is at least potentially a form of property (*American Society* [New York, Knopf, 1959], 174).

88. Richard Hooker, *Works, Vol. 1: Of the Laws of Ecclesiastical Polity* (1593), ed. G. Edelen (Cambridge, Harvard U, Folger Library Edition, 1977), 1.10.8, p. 105; cf. Wolin, *Politics and Vision,* 276. Hooker here is speaking of bonding through laws, customs, and corporations. Huntington states that Hooker's defence of the civil and religious establishment two hundred years before Burke delineated every significant strand of Burkean thought ("Conservatism as Ideology," 464).

89. Walter Lippmann, *The Public Philosophy* (New York, Mentor, 1955), 105; cf. Smith, *Politics and Remembrance,* 23.

90. Burke, *Reflections on the Revolution,* 110. Society is a contract and partnership in all science, art, virtue, and perfection.

91. Smith, *Politics and Remembrance,* 245. Burke writes of the awful gravity as well as self-respect that comes from a respectful consciousness of one's forebears (Burke, *Reflections on the Revolution,* 39, 41).

92. Neuhaus, *Naked Public Square,* 196.

93. Wills, *Confessions of a Conservative,* 76–77. Although Burke stated that "corporate bodies are immortal for the good of the members, but not for their punishment" (*Reflections on the Revolution,* 161), taking positive responsibility for wrongs of the past ensures that corporate bonding across time does provide good to those suffering from past deeds from which we benefit.

94. Alexis de Tocqueville, *Democracy in America*, ed. J. P. Mayer (Garden City, NY, Doubleday, 1969), 2.2.2, p. 507.

95. Burke, *Reflections on the Revolution*, 108.

96. Mannheim, *Ideology and Utopia*, 233, 250.

97. Mannheim, "Conservative Thought," 103.

98. Moltmann, *Theology of Hope*, 23, citing R. Musil.

99. Burke, *Reflections on the Revolution*, 104. The British Constitution stood on such a "nice equipoise" that removing a dangerous leaning on one side might upset it on the other (*Thoughts on the Cause of the Present Discontents* (1770), in *Works* (Bohn), 1.368; cf. Canavan, *Political Reason of Edmund Burke*, 163).

100. Tillich, "Political Meaning of Utopia," 131.

101. Burke, *Thoughts and Details on Scarcity*, 136, 165–66. He suggested that in good times even more would have died from causes such as accidents.

102. David Thompson, *Europe Since Napolean* (New York, Knopf, 1962²), 135.

103. Coles, *Privileged Ones*, 526.

104. Gudorf, *Catholic Social Teaching on Liberation Themes*, 6–16.

105. Wesley interpreted the passage as rebuking ingratitude for God's gracious provisions in the present (Sermon 102, "Of Former Times" 23, in Wesley, *Works 3: Sermons 3*, 453).

106. Edward Farley, *The Fragility of Knowledge. Theological Education in the Church and the University* (Philadelphia, Fortress, 1988), 27.

107. Pocock, "Time, Institutions and Action," 233–72.

108. Smith, *Politics and Remembrance*, 15.

109. Ibid., 116–17.

110. Cf. Niebuhr, "Foreign Policy of American Conservatism," 66.

Chapter 9

1. David G. Smith, "Liberalism," *International Encyclopedia of the Social Sciences* (1968), 9:276–77.

2. Engels could describe Adam Smith as the Luther of political economy. As Luther brought the individual into the sphere of religion as a matter belonging to one's very person, so Smith brought the individual into the sphere of property (as cited in Marx, "Economic and Philosophical Manuscripts" 3.1 in *Early Writings*, ed. Bottomore, 147–48).

3. Engels noted that Dissenters in the Puritan tradition were the main strength of the progressive middle class even to his day (Frederick Engels, *Socialism, Utopian and Scientific* [London, Allen, 1892], Introduction to the English edition, xxvi). Troeltsch made a similar observation (Troeltsch, *Social Teaching of the Christian Churches*, 681).

4. Consent as the essential mode for government in the U.S. Constitution, for example, has the premise that each individual should acquiesce in the association since each possesses the inviolable element of reason (Roland H. Bainton, "The Appeal to Reason and the American Constitution" [1938], in Bainton, *Collected Papers in Church History, Vol. 3: Christian Unity and Religion in New England* [Boston, Beacon, 1964], 202).

5. John Dunn, *The Political Thought of John Locke. An Historical Account of the Argument of the "Two Treatises of Government"* (Cambridge, Cambridge U., 1969), 245, 264–65. Dunn's very influential work shows the continuing importance of a Calvinist derived sense of objective moral order in Locke's thought, reflecting his Puritan upbringing. The conception of the purposes of God has an "axiomatic centrality" in his entire intellectual construction (12).

6. Cf. Smith, "Liberalism," 278.

7. Wiles, *Politics and Vision,* 373–74. This concept is found in particularly extreme fashion in Rousseau: The state of nature involves dependency on impersonal entities rather than persons. "There are two kinds of dependence: dependence on things, which is the work of nature; and dependence upon men, which is the work of society. Dependence on things, being nonmoral, does no injury to liberty and begets no vices; dependence on men, being out of order, gives rise to every kind of vice, and through this master and slave become mutually deprived" (Jean Jacques Rousseau, *Émile,* trans. B. Foxley [London, Dent, Everyman's Library 518, 1911], 49; cf. Wolin, 374). The cure, he goes on to state, is to substitute the impersonal system of law for the individual.

8. Smith, "Liberalism," 276.

9. Wolin, *Politics and Vision,* 236, 280, 301, 304–5.

10. Heimann, *Reason and Faith in Modern Society,* 212.

11. Leo Tolstoi describes Stepan Arkadyevitch of whom "liberalism" was in his blood: "He treated all men perfectly equally and exactly the same, whatever their fortune or calling might be" (*Anna Karenina* [Philadelphia, Macrae, 1919], 23).

12. Dunn, *Political Thought of John Locke,* Chap. 10. People have a natural "executive power" for the "legislative power" of God in the law of nature (126–27).

13. Cf. John H. Hallowell, *The Decline of Liberalism as an Ideology. With Particular Reference to German Politico-Legal Thought* [London, Keagan Paul, International Library of Sociology and Social Reconstruction, 1946], 4–7.

14. Dunn, *Political Thought of John Locke,* 121.

15. Bainton also notes a recoil from reason already in the eighteenth century due to earlier extravagant claims and uses of reason; thus, alongside government by consent was the need for restraint upon the contracting parties (Bainton, "Appeal to Reason and the American Constitution," 204–5).

16. Jeremy Bentham, *Handbook of Political Fallacies,* ed. H. Larrabee (Baltimore, Johns Hopkins, 1952), 213; cf. Wolin, *Vision and Politics,* 298, 332, 341. The emotions to which Bentham refers here are "hopes and fears." Wolin distinguishes the restraint about reason in the liberals from the optimism of democratic radicalism molded by eighteenth century rationalism and the French Revolution, 293–98. His distinction is valuable, but the matter is in part one of definition of who is to be included within liberalism.

17. Reinhold Niebuhr, "A Faith for History's Greatest Crisis," *Fortune* 26 (July, 1942), 125.

18. Anthony Arblaster, *The Rise and Decline of Western Liberalism* (Oxford, Blackwell, 1985), 35–36.

19. Reinhold Niebuhr, "The Reunion of the Church Through the Renewal of the Churches," *Christianity and Crisis* 7 (Nov. 24, 1947), 6; Reinhold Niebuhr, "The Blindness of Liberalism," *Radical Religion* 1,4 (Autumn, 1936), 4.

20. Reinhold Niebuhr, "Ten Years That Shook My World," *Christian Century* 56 (April 26, 1939), 543.

21. Reinhold Niebuhr, "Two Forms of Utopianism," *Christianity and Society* 12 (Autumn, 1947), 6.

22. Niebuhr, "Ten Years That Shook My World," 543.

23. One contrast were the current economic liberals, such as Dudly North and Nicholas Barbon, who argued that the goad for trade and industry lay in the human being as consuming animal with boundless appetites, particularly the wants of the mind, such as envy, rather than natural needs (Joyce Appleby, "Ideology and Theory: The Tension between Political and Economic Liberalism in Seventeenth-Century England," *American Historical Review* 81 [1976], 505–7).

24. K. R. Minogue, *The Liberal Mind* (London, Methuen, 1963), 44–49.

25. Harold J. Berman, *The Interdependence of Law and Religion* (Nashville, Abingdon, 1974), 67.

26. A.S.P. Woodhouse, "Introduction," to *Puritanism and Liberty,* ed. Woodhouse (Chicago, U. of Chicago, [69]–[80]).

27. John Milton, *The Doctrine and Discipline of Divorce,* in *Prose Works* (London, Bohn, 1848), 3.171; cf. *The Reason of Church Government Urged against Prelaty,* in *Prose Works,* 2.503. Cf. John Stuart Mill's reference to "the despotism of custom" (*On Liberty,* ed. D. Spitz [New York, Norton, Norton Critical Editions in the History of Ideas, 1975], 66).

28. Woodhouse, "Introduction," [50].

29. Ibid., [95], referring particularly to the development among the Levellers. Richard Overton stated, "Reason hath no precedent; for reason is the fountain of all just precedents" (An Appeal from the Commons to the Free People" (1647), in *Puritanism and Liberty,* ed. Woodhouse, 323). Precedence was also countered by Scripture. As Milton stated, "Let them chant while they will of prerogatives. We shall tell them of scripture; of custom, we of scripture; of acts and statutes, still of scripture" (Milton, *Reason of Church Government,* 485; cf. Woodhouse, [51]). E. Clinton Gardner notes that the Puritan grounding in covenantal theology added a profound basis for expecting new developments of justice: The Puritan's conception of the mystery and transcendence of God countered a static rationalism as one expected "new disclosures of the divine will in the ordering processes of history" ("Justice in the Puritan Covenant Tradition," 104).

30. Cf. Reinhold Niebuhr, "The Sickness of American Culture," *Nation* 166 (1948), 267.

31. Patricia Hollis, *The Pauper Press. A Study in Working-Class Radicalism of the 1830's* (London, Oxford U., 1970), Chaps. 6–7. Writers in 1819 placed manufacturers among the productive classes, which they favored. It was not until 1826 that manufacturers were included instead among the "parasitic" (205, 209).

32. Robert Browning, "Why I am a Liberal" (from "Ferishtah's Fancies"), in *Poems and Plays of Robert Browning* (New York, Modern Library, 1934), 1138.

33. Smith, "Liberalism," 276.

34. Christine Gudorf, *Catholic Social Teaching,* 29.

35. Ramsay Muir as cited in Rossiter, *Conservatism in America,* 58 (emphasis added). Cf. Ramsay Muir, *Liberalism and Industry, Towards A Better Social Order* (Boston, Houghton Mifflin, 1921), 197, 201.

36. For Locke and others the initiation of any dangerous disruption of the social order had been confined to the behavior of rulers (Dunn, *Political Thought of John Locke,* 238).

37. Smith, "Liberalism," 281.

38. Karl Marx, *Capital, A Critical Analysis of Capitalist Production,* ed. F. Engels (New York, International, 1967 [1889–1894]), Afterward to the Second German Edition (1873), I.15. Mill thought that significant inequalities in distribution could only be justified if all had equal starting points in life, but that this was prevented by the inequalities of capitalist society (John Stuart Mill, *Principles of Political Economy,* ed. W. Ashley [New York, Kelley, Reprints of Economic Classics, 1969 (1909, using the 7th ed.)], 208–9; cf. Richard Lichtman, "The Façade of Equality in Liberal Democratic Theory," *Inquiry* 12 [1969], 194).

39. Mill, *On Liberty,* 70–86 (Chap. 4), 88. Adam Smith expressed the preventive aspect in more utilitarian terms; natural liberty must be restrained when it endangers the security of the whole society (*Works and Correspondence, Vol. 2: An Inquiry into the Nature and Causes of the Wealth of Nations,* ed. R. H. Campbell and A. S. Skinner [Oxford, Oxford U., 1976], 2.2.94, p. 324).

40. Earlier markings of such a principle can be see in Calvin's distinction of manifest or public sins, which are dealt with publically, from private sins (Höpfl, *Christian Polity of John*

Calvin, 117). Aquinas stated that a person is not bound by human obedience in those matters which "depend upon the interior movements of the will," but one is bound in matters which relate to the ordering of human affairs and actions (Thomas Aquinas, *Summa Theologiae,* 2a2ae. 104, 5, in Aquinas, *Selected Political Writings,* 177).

41. Minogue, *Liberal Mind,* 49.

42. Seifert, *Ethical Resources,* 21.

43. Cf. Augustus, *Res Gestae Divi Augusti* 1.5.33–34, in Frederick W. Danker, *Benefactor* (St. Louis, Clayton, 1982), 260: "I liberated our people from fear and threatening peril" through careful administration of the grain supply during a severe food shortage.

44. Pope John XXIII, *Pacem in Terris* 11, in *Papal Encyclicals, Vol. 5: 1958–1981,* ed. C. Carlen (n.p., Consortium, 1981), 108.

45. Smith, "Liberalism," 281.

46. Rossiter, *Conservatism in America,* Chap. 5; cf. Heimann, *Reason and Faith in Modern Society,* 8. Regarding appeals to Locke's treatment of property, Dunn notes that what Locke was responding to was the threat of nonparliamentarian taxation and the confiscation of freeholds in 1680 or 1685–1688, not a determined policy of redistributive social justice (*Political Thought of John Locke,* 216).

47. Cf. Daniel Levine's comparison of the limited affirmation of human goodness in the rational self-interest of Lockean liberalism with Jane Addams' conviction that the human being was naturally good and generous, hindered only by their environment (*Jane Addams and the Liberal Tradition* [Madison, WI, State Historical Society of Wisconsin, 1971], 170–74). This Romantic strand, which goes beyond the caution of Lockean self-interest, is also part of the liberal tradition.

48. Niebuhr, *Children of Light,* 27.

49. Tillich, *Socialist Decision,* 50. Note Joseph S. Clark's references to the government as "the organized intelligence of the community," "the agent of our collective national wisdom" which anticipates and prevents crises that demean the human spirit ("The Case for Democratic Liberalism," *Saturday Review* (July 11, 1964), 14–15.

50. Tillich, 72.

51. Wills, *Nixon Agonistes,* 318–19. Each idea has an equal chance to establish itself. Wills quotes Kingman Brewster, then president of Yale, in 1970: "Practical progress relies most of all on the evolution of the better by the survival of the fittest among ideas tossed in the blanket of debate, dispute, and disagreement." Wills also sees an experience oriented version: Unguided authentic experiences would produce truth and goodness by an invisible hand (346).

52. Ibid., 541.

53. Istvan Deak, *Weimar Germany's Left-Wing Intellectuals: A Political History of the Weltbühne and Its Circle* (Berkeley, U. of California, 1968), 181–82. *Die Weltbühne* was a weekly political journal, established in 1905, by intellectuals dedicated to socialism (in that regard not really in the vision we are treating here), democracy, and human goodness (1, 6).

54. Niebuhr, "Sickness of American Culture," 267.

55. Saul D. Alinsky, *Reveille for Radicals* (New York, Vintage, 1969 [1946]), 22.

56. Harrington, *New American Poverty,* 103–4, 107.

57. Marvin E. Olsen, "Social Pluralism as a Basis for Democracy," in *Power in Societies,* ed. Olsen (New York, Macmillan, 1970), 185–86.

58. This was Theodore J. Lowi's critique of "interest group" liberalism (*The End of Liberalism, Ideology, Policy, and the Crisis of Public Authority* [New York, Norton, 1969], 288, 290, 294–95). He also notes the harm to racial minorities who are not included in the contending groups that set public policy. He neglects, however, the vital role of the pressure

groups that have risen from the otherwise neglected groups. Viewing democracy also as automatically effective can encourage irresponsibility and an apathy of which special interests can take advantage (Muelder, *Foundations of a Responsible Society,* 113).

59. Heimann, *Reason and Faith in Modern Society,* 38–39.

60. Bob Goudzwaard, *Capitalism and Progress. A Diagnosis of Western Society* (Grand Rapids, MI, Eerdmans, 1979²), 191, 200.

61. Charles S. Maier, "The Politics of Time: Changing Paradigms of Collective and Private Time in the Modern Era," in *Changing Boundaries of the Political,* ed. Maier (Cambridge, Cambridge U, Cambridge Studies in Modern Political Economics, 1987), 165.

62. Mannheim, *Ideology and Utopia,* 219, 224; cf. Tillich, "Political Meaning of Utopia," 139. Time is seen as only linear and constant, and the future can be calculated in contrast to God's control of time.

63. Tocqueville, *Democracy in America,* 2.2.2, p. 508; cf. Dennis P. Hollinger, *Individualism and Social Ethics, An Evangelical Syncretism* (Lanham, MD, University Press of America, 1983), 14.

64. David W. Wills, "Racial Justice and the Limits of American Liberalism," *Journal of Religious Ethics* 6 (1978), 188.

65. Tillich, *Socialist Decision,* 71, 74. The rationalistic view of human nature neglects the center of the person that is more primordial than abstract reason or the objective drive mechanism. Reinhold Niebuhr stated that the exhortations of the liberal church have "no understanding . . . of the agony of rebirth required if the individual would turn from self-love to love" ("Reunion of the Church," 6).

66. Robert F. Drinan, *ADA For Your Information* [newsletter] (August, 1981), 1.

67. John Rawls, *A Theory of Justice* (Cambridge, Harvard U., 1971), 302. Rawls himself does not see the principles themselves to assume a liberal rather than a socialist economy (258), but the argument on the whole appears to address the mixed economy associated with modern liberalism. Cf. the extensive summary, review of literature, and critique in Karen Lebacqz, *Six Theories of Justice. Perspectives from Philosophical and Theological Ethics* (Minneapolis, Augsburg, 1986), Chap. 2.

68. Cf. David B. Fletcher, "Christian Social Justice and Rawl's Liberalism," *Christian Scholar's Review* 19 (1990), 231–42.

69. Cf. Wolin, *Politics and Vision,* 301.

70. From the standpoint of perceiving reality in the context of God's grace, that ability may be treated as a special obligation rather than as a claim upon others. Jeremy Taylor wrote, "Whatsoever other difference there is between thee and thy neighbor . . . if it be good, thou hast received it from God; and then thou art more obliged to pay duty and tribute, use and principal to him: and it were a strange folly for a man to be proud of being more in debt than another" (Jeremy Taylor, *The Rules and Exercises of Holy Living,* 2.4.8 [London, Bell, 1857 (1650)], 107–8; cf. Herbert Spiegelberg, "A Defence of Human Equality," *Philosophical Review* 53 [1944], 122, n.25. Spiegelberg notes that greater gifts often mean not greater rights but decreased privileges as the consequence of increased duties [109].)

71. Wolff, *Anthropology of the Old Testament,* 194–205.

72. Cf. Julian B. Kaye, *Bernard Shaw and the Nineteenth Century Tradition* (Norman, OK, U. of Oklahoma, 1958), 42.

73. Paul Marshall, "Liberalism, Pluralism and Christianity: A Reconceptualization," *Fídes et Hístoría* 21, 3 (October 1989), 7.

74. Cf. Thomas Luckman, *The Invisible Religion. The Problem of Religion in Modern Society* (New York, Macmillan, 1967); Neuhaus, *Naked Public Square.*

75. Cf. Walter G. Muelder, "Contradictions in Capitalistic Triumphalism," *Theology and*

Public Policy 2, 2 (Fall, 1990), 4–16. "It is not the GNP and the average per capita income measured in gross terms that display whether the economic order is working, but it is the life of the poor, hungry, the homeless, and the oppressed who are its true measure" (15).

76. Karl Marx, "Bruno Bauer, *Die Judenfrage,*" in *Karl Marx: Early Writings,* 13–15.

77. Cf. John H. Yoder, who notes that while we are still governed by an elite, "of all the forms of oligarchy, democracy is the least oppressive because it provides the strongest language of justification and therefore of critique which the subjects may use to mitigate its oppressiveness" ("The Christian Case for Democracy," *Journal of Religious Ethics* 5 [1977], 221).

78. Gunnar Myrdal, *An American Dilemma* (New York, Harper, 1962²), 3–25.

79. Robert Paul Wolff, *The Poverty of Liberalism* (Boston, Beacon, 1968), Chap. 5.

80. Wills, "Racial Justice and the Limits of American Liberalism," 188–95.

81. Heimann, *Reason and Faith in Modern Society,* 220. Cf. Wilson Carey McWilliams, who sees that one of the great failures of liberalism was that, unlike classical political thought and the Judeo-Christian tradition, fraternity, rather than being an essential means to liberty and equality, is postulated only as their end, allowing the present pursuit of self-interest (*The Idea of Fraternity in America* [Berkeley, CA, U. of California, 1973], 5, 99–100, 109–10, 620).

82. Dunn, *Political Thought of John Locke,* 249–50, cf. 213, 257. Locke was preceded in this by Thomas Hobbes who influenced later thought on rights by presenting "a view of society as based on and reducible to relationships between private individuals as part of the order of things" (Ian Shapiro, *The Evolution of Rights in Liberal Theory* [Cambridge, Cambridge U., 1986], 60). On Locke and the Puritan tradition, cf. n. 5, earlier.

83. Heimann, 39.

84. Marshall, "Liberalism, Pluralism," 8–9.

85. Cf. Joseph P. Fitzpatrick, "Values, Ethics, and Family Life," in *Helping the Family in Urban Society,* ed. F. Delliquadri (New York, Columbia U., 1963), 73–74. The contract of divorce also reflects society viewed as a fabric of contracts, which expire automatically or at given notice (Heimann, 37–38). One should note, however, that earlier there was a positive impact of liberalism that is now assumed. Relationships between generations became more natural and intimate as the social links of rule and authority were loosened (Tocqueville, *Democracy in America,* 2.3.8, p. 587).

86. Rosalind Pollack Petchesky, *Abortion and Woman's Choice: The State, Sexuality, and Reproductive Freedom* (Boston, Northeastern U., Northeastern Series in Feminist Theory, 1990²), xxii–xxvi, 3–13, 358, 389–401 (quotation from p. 7). Recognizing the necessary social framework for the abortion debate does not settle it in one way or the other. Petchesky herself sees abortion as a positive benefit, like education and health, that society should provide for women. She views it as indispensable as one of the many social conditions that encompass their lives. The sense of being a person with personal and bodily integrity is essential to a woman's social participation and responsibility. Others would want the claims of the fetus or the moral claims and ends involved in sexual intercourse to be visible within this social network.

87. Bernard Zylstra, "The Bible, Justice, and the State," *International Reformed Bulletin* 16, 55 (fall 1973), 16. The state must recognize these rights and prevent one sphere from destroying another.

88. Marx, "Bruno Bauer," 26.

89. Margaret Farley, Review of *The Theory of Morality,* by Alan Donagan, *Religious Studies Review* 7 (1981), 233–37.

90. An aspect involved in the support for human rights in early liberalism was that the

reason in each individual must be inviolate as corresponding to and a part of the reason of the universe (Bainton, "Appeal to Reason and the American Constitution," 205).

91. Farley, 237.

92. David Hollenbach, "The Common Good Revisited," *Theological Studies* 50 (1989), 92–93.

93. Elisha Williams, *The Essential Rights and Liberties of Protestants* (1744), in *Puritan Political Ideas,* ed. Morgan, 271–70.

94. Jefferson is chosen for effect. Jefferson, however, is not the best selection to represent the contrast of individualism and community. He represents, in fact, one within the liberal tradition who had a perception of and commitment to fraternity, despite serious flaws in his total conception and response (such as slavery; cf. McWilliams, *Idea of Fraternity,* 209–23). Jefferson wrote that "the earth belongs in usufruct to the living." For both the individual and each generation of humanity, at death the portion used reverts to the society. So each generation can manage the earth and what proceeds from it as they please during their usufruct. They are not bound by any perpetual laws of property coming from previous generations (Letter to James Madison, September 6, 1789, in Jefferson, *Life and Selected Works,* ed. A. Koch and W. Peden [Modern, 1944], 488, 491).

95. A. P. D'Entrèves, "Introduction," to Aquinas, *Selected Political Writings,* xxxi.

96. R. H. Tawney, *The Acquisitive Society* (London, Bell, 1922), 14. Private rights now are the pillars of society and other aspects of society are subordinate to them.

97. Thomas Aquinas, *Summa Theologiae,* 2a2ae. 66, 2; in Aquinas, *Selected Political Writings,* ed. D'Entrèves, 169, 171; cf. 1a2ae. 94, 5, p. 127. Property is a matter of administration and distribution, not of exclusive use. Cf. Gudorf, *Catholic Social Teachings,* 114–15; Temple, *Christianity and Social Order,* 28–29.

98. D'Entrèves, "Introduction," xxxii.

99. McWilliams, *Idea of Fraternity in America.* On the Puritan covenant as making abstract values concrete, cf. 125–26. Covenant is also an aspect of the identity, unity, and vocation of a people (James Luther Adams, "God and Economics" [1978], in Adams, *Voluntary Associations,* 391). As the agreement is made before God, covenant binds the agreement and the values in God.

100. Heimann, *Reason and Faith in Modern Society,* 214, 219–20, 224; V. A. Demant, *Religion and the Decline of Capitalism* (New York, Scribner's, 1952), 30–31, 179–82; Max Weber, *The Protestant Ethic and the Spirit of Capitalism* (New York, Scribner's, 1958), 180–83. Note also J. H. Hallowell: Liberalism requires a belief in objective truth and value, transcending all individuals and binding upon each in order to reconcile its freedom from arbitrary authority with the idea of a ordered commonwealth (*The Decline of Liberalism as an Ideology,* 23). John Dunn makes a similar observation of the consequences of accepting Locke's politics without his framework of duties based in divine calling (*Political Thought of John Locke,* 266–67).

101. Heimann, 224–32, 236–44.

Chapter 10

1. Hannah Arendt, *On Revolution* (New York, Viking, 1965), 41, cf. Paul Lehmann, *The Transfiguration of Politics* (New York, Harper, 1975), 9.

2. Cf. Thorkild Jacobsen, "Primitive Democracy in Ancient Mesopotamia," in Jacobsen, *Toward the Image of Tammuz and Other Essays on Mesopotamian History and Culture* (Cambridge, MA, Harvard U., Harvard Semitic Series 21, 1970), 157–72 (also in *Journal of*

Near Eastern Studies 2 [1943], 159–72). Particularly important was the consent role of the popular assembly, which also had judicial functions. Jacobsen sees abundant parallels elsewhere, especially in early European materials (169).

3. R. K. Sinclair estimates the portion of political citizens in Athens to be 14–17 percent of the population in the period 450–322 B.C. (*Democracy and Participation in Athens* [Cambridge, Cambridge U., 1988], 200).

4. Harry F. Ward, *Democracy and Social Change* (New York, Modern Age, 1940), 52.

5. Reinhold Niebuhr, "Democracy, Secularism, and Christianity," in Niebuhr, *Christian Realism and Political Problems* (New York, Scribner's, 1953), 101.

6. Jürgen Moltmann, *The Crucified God. The Cross of Christ as the Foundation and Criticism of Christian Theology* (New York, Harper, 1974²), 328.

7. Reinhold Niebuhr, *The Children of Light and the Children of Darkness. A Vindication of Democracy and a Critique of Its Traditional Defense* (New York, Scribner's, 1944), 151; cf. Jacques Ellul, *The Political Illusion* (New York, Vintage, 1967), 235.

8. Cf. Ludwig Koehler, *Hebrew Man* (London, SCM, 1956), Appendix, "Justice in the Gate."

9. Many of the materials to be cited in this section are disputed as to where they should be placed within the history of Israel. Their value for us in this discussion is that such ideals and practices were present within that history, not their particular dating.

10. Georg Fohrer, "Der Vertrag zwischen König und Volk in Israel," in Fohrer, *Studien zur alttestamentlichen Theologie und Geschichte* (Berlin, Gruyter, Beihefte zur Zeitschrift für die alttestamentliche Wissenschaft 115, 1969), 330–51 (also in *Zeitschrift für die alttestamentliche Wissenschaft* 71 [1959], 1–22).

11. 1 Sam. 10.21–27; 2 Kgs. 9.12–13; 11.17; 23.1–3.

12. Robert Gordis, "Primitive Democracy in Ancient Israel," in Gordis, *Poets, Prophets, and Sages* (Bloomington, IN, Indiana U., 1971), 45–60. Gottwald describes in premonarchic Israel a network of assemblies of all males (certain charismatic leadership roles were open to women) and heads of extended families, protective associations, and tribes in various combinations and jurisdictions assuring decentralization and diffusion of power (*Tribes of Yahweh*, 322, 613–14).

13. Fohrer, 331–33.

14. Albrecht Alt, "Micha 2, 1–5 *Gēs Anadasmos* in Juda," in Alt, *Kleine Schriften zur Geschichte des Volkes Israel,* Vol. 3 (Munich, Beck, 1959), 377, 380.

15. Gordis, 56: Through the Bible it entered the fabric of Western civilization.

16. Fohrer, 350.

17. (a) the election by lot of Matthias to complete the Twelve: Acts 1.14 [including the women], 15, 26; (b) the choice of the seven deacons: 6.2–6; (c) the decision of the Jerusalem Council regarding the Gentile Christians: 15.12, 22. Cp. Didache 15.1. Rudolf Schnackenburg, "Community Co-operation in the New Testament," *Concilium* 77 (1972), 9–13, 17 (quotation).

18. George W. MacRae, "Shared Responsibilities—Some New Testament Perspectives," *Chicago Studies* 9 (1970), 115–27. 1 Corinthians (5.4) and Matthew (18.20) are similar in that the community decisions are made in the presence of the power and authority of Christ. *Shared* means consent not only among the other members of the community but also that the decision is supported by the leaders. This is seen clearly in Acts and 1 Corinthians.

19. 1 Cor. 5.4. Similar is the choice of someone to act as judge between the members (1 Cor. 6.5) and the final decision on veils (11.13).

20. Schnackenburg, 15, 17, citing also 1 Peter, Hebrews, Revelation, and 1 John.

21. Cf. pp. 46–47; Adams, "Indispensable Discipline of Social Responsibility," 257–59.

22. J. D. Dengerink, "The Christian and Modern Democracy," *International Reformed Bulletin* 7 (July, 1964), 21; cf. Wolin, *Politics and Vision* (on Luther, particularly Luther's earlier writings), 255.

23. Rhys Isaac, *The Transformation of Virginia: 1740–1790* (Chapel Hill, NC, U. of North Carolina, 1982), 164–72.

24. Charles Chauncy, *Seasonable Thoughts on the State of Religion in New England* (Hicksville, NY, Regina, Rise of Modern Religious Ideas in America, 1975 [1743]), 226; cf. Mark A. Noll, "God and the Colonies," in *Eerdmans' Handbook to Christianity in America* (1983), 121.

25. Harry S. Stout, "The Transforming Effects of the Great Revival," in *Eerdmans' Handbook to Christianity in America* (1983), 130.

26. The best example is the *Defensor Pacis* by Marsilius of Padua (1324); cf. Troeltsch, *Social Teaching of the Christian Churches*, 373.

27. H. R. Niebuhr, *Kingdom of God in America*, 79.

28. Calvin, *Institutes*, 4.20.8. *Plures* is fairly strong, often with a stronger sense than Calvin appears to have meant. It can mean *the mass, the multitude, the majority* (Lewis and Short, *multus*, IIB2b). This is not a metaphysical argument about the people, but a theologically and ethically pragmatic argument. For the early Calvinists the people who have sovereignty is singular not plural. It is not an assemblage of individuals bearing rights (Carney, "Associational Thought in Early Calvinism, 46).

29. Ezra Stiles, Letter to Benjamin Gale, October 1, 1766, quoted in Edmund S. Morgan, *The Gentle Puritan. A Life of Ezra Stiles, 1727–1795* (New Haven, Yale U., 1962), 250. (Stiles was later president of Yale.) For John Owen, religious adviser to Cromwell, it was better for 500 errors to be scattered among individuals than for one error to have power and jurisdiction over all the others (John Adair, *Founding Fathers, The Puritans in England and America* [Grand Rapids, MI, Baker, 1982], 218). This was an Aristotelian concept. The multitude is more incorruptible than the single individual, who is more quickly swayed by emotion (Aristotle, *Pol.* 1286a32, 36).

30. "The Whitehall Debates" (1648), in *Puritanism and Liberty*, ed. Woodhouse, 161.

31. Calvin, *Sermons sur le Deuteronome*, in *Opera*, ed. Baum et al., 25.635 (Sermon 3, on Deut. 1.9–15, 1555); Höpfl, *Christian Polity of John Calvin*, 157–60. Calvin states that "to be in a free state [*estat*] is much better than to be under a prince" (Sermon 105, on Deut. 17.14–18, 1555, in *Opera*, 27.458). Liberty is a singular and inestimable gift when God permits a people "to elect judges and magistrates." Thus the condition of the people of God was "much better than their neighbors, who had kings and princes and no liberty" (Sermon 101, on Deut. 16.18–19, 1555, in *Opera*, 27.410–11). Höpfl notes Calvin's hostile references to the conduct of princes and courts in his sermons—stronger in the unpublished ones. The people in Geneva elected from nominees selected by the experienced predecessors in office. Thus it was, as Calvin described it, a compound of aristocracy and democracy (McNeill, "John Calvin on Civil Government," 84).

32. Troeltsch, *Social Teachings of the Christian Churches*, 628.

33. Engels, *Socialism, Utopian and Scientific* (1892), Introduction to the English Edition, xxii.

34. John Wise, *A Vindication of the Government of New England Churches* (1717), in *Puritan Political Ideas*, ed. Morgan, 252–53.

35. "The Putney Debates" (1647), in *Puritanism and Liberty*, 53.

36. John Lilburne, *The Free-man's Freedom Vindicated* (1646), in *Puritanism and Liberty*, 317.

37. John Saltmarsh, *Smoke in the Temple* (1646), in *Puritanism and Liberty*, 184.

38. Also in New England as the distinction of the saints from the unregenerate was under-

mined, the democracy of the saints flowed out to include all the people (Sidney E. Mead, "The Nation with a Soul of a Church," in *American Civil Religion,* ed. R. Russell and D. Jones [New York, Harper, 1974], 52 [also in *Church History* 36 (1967)]). Friedrich Engels: "Calvin's church constitution was thoroughly democratic and republican; and where the kingdom of God was republicanised could the kingdoms of this world remain subject to monarchs, bishops, and lords?" ("On Historical Materialism," 56).

39. John Cotton, "Letter to Lord Say and Seal in the Year 1636," in *Puritan Political Ideas,* 169.

40. Niebuhr, *Kingdom of God in America,* 79–80.

41. James Luther Adams, "The Enduring Validity of Congregational Polity" (1978), in Adams, *Prophethood of All Believers,* 131–32.

42. H. R. Niebuhr, *Kingdom of God in America,* 124.

43. Reinhold Niebuhr, *Children of Light,* xi.

44. Bennett, *Christians and State,* 155.

45. Cf. Niebuhr, "Democracy, Secularism, and Christianity," 101.

46. A. D. Lindsay, *The Essentials of Democracy* (London, Oxford U., William J. Cooper Foundation Lectures, 1935^2), 13. As Rainborough said, even the poorest person "hath a life to live" (see note 35).

47. Spiegelberg, "Defense of Human Equality," 110.

48. Tillich, *Socialist Decision,* 50, 142; Tillich, "State as Expectation and Demand," 109.

49. Ward, *Democracy and Social Change,* 51.

50. Cf. Devlin, *Enforcement of Morals,* 100.

51. Niebuhr, *Children of Light,* xi.

52. Ellul, *Political Illusion,* 236.

53. Lindsay, *Essentials of Democracy,* 1, 35.

54. Ibid, 37, 40, 67, 78.

55. De Tocqueville, *Democracy in America,* 2.2.5, p. 513.

56. Bennett, *Christians and State,* 158; Adams, "Indispensable Discipline of Social Responsibility," 258.

57. Lindsay, 1.

58. De Tocqueville, 2.2.7, pp. 521–22.

59. Mill, *Considerations on Representative Government* (Indianapolis, IN, Bobbs-Merrill, Library of Liberal Arts, 1958 [1865^3]), 36, 38, 47–48, 54, 130 (first quotation is from p. 128). Lichtman notes the similarity here of Mill to Rousseau ("Façade of Equality in Liberal Democracy," 187). Mill felt that the lack of participation under a despot also negatively affected religion by removing its social consideration and compassion and transforming it into merely a personal affair between the individual and God focused upon personal salvation (39).

60. Abraham Lincoln, Speech at Peoria, IL, October 16, 1854, in *Collected Works,* ed. R. Basler (New Brunswick, NJ, Rutgers U., 1953), 2.266 [his emphasis]. He is discussing slavery, "a total violation of this principle." All the governed have an equal voice in government— that, and that only, is self-government.

61. John C. Bennett, *Christian Ethics and Social Policy* (New York, Scribner's, 1956), 71.

62. Madison, *Federalist,* No. 51, p. 265. Madison in this context is describing dividing the distributions of power that are subordinate to the state so "that each may check on the other."

63. Alinsky, *Reveille for Radicals,* 55.

64. Lindsay, *Essentials of Democracy,* 49.

65. Reinhold Niebuhr, "The Anomaly of European Socialism" (1952), in *Christian Realism and Political Problems,* 51.

66. Kornhauser, *Politics of Mass Society,* 230.

67. Adams, "Indispensable Discipline of Social Responsibility," 260; Robert Michels, *Political Parties. A Sociological Study of the Oligarchical Tendencies of Modern Democracy* (Glencoe, IL, Free, 1958 [1915]). The law is stated concisely on p. 418.

68. Tillich, *Socialist Decision,* 51.

69. Karl R. Popper, *The Open Society and Its Enemies,* (Princeton, NJ, Princeton U., 1950), 119–24; cf. Bryan Magee, *Popper* (London, Fontana, Modern Masters, 1975), 78. It requires constitutional protection of speech, organization, press, and regular free general elections.

70. Robert H. Trudeau, "The Guatemalan Elections of 1985. Prospects for Democracy," in *Elections and Democracy in Central America,* ed. J. Booth and M. Seligson (Chapel Hill, NC, U. of North Carolina, 1989), 100, 106.

71. John A. Booth, "Elections and Democracy in Central America. A Framework for Analysis," in idem, 13, 18.

72. Trudeau, 105, 118. Since 1954 no Guatemalan regime has successfully adopted any scheme of income redistribution to turn Guatemalan workers into consumers (113).

73. "During the presidential campaign [of 1985], no candidate touched on issues such as corruption within the military or its human rights violations; none suggested that such violators be punished for past crimes or proposed dialogue with the insurgents. All contenders pledged not to pursue major socioeconomic reforms, and all acknowledged the special status of the military" (Trudeau, 106).

74. Booth, "Elections and Democracy in Central America," 13.

75. Trudeau, 98, 101, 104, 112; Booth, 28.

76. John A. Peeler, "Democracy and Elections in Central America: Autumn of the Oligarchs?" in *Elections and Democracy in Central America,* 190, 194.

77. Ward, *Democracy and Social Change,* 48.

78. Henry Sumner Maine, *Popular Government* (London, Murray, 1885), 59, 61.

79. García, *Justice in Latin American Theology,* 177.

80. Bong-Ho Son, "Response to 'Democracy—A Christian Imperative,'" *Transformation* 7, 4 (October/December, 1990), 5.

81. Alinsky, "Introduction to Vintage Edition," *Reveille for Radicals,* xiv.

82. Miroslav Volf, "Democracy and the Crisis of the Socialist Project. Toward a Post-Revolutionary Theology of Liberation," *Transformation* 7, 4 (October/December, 1990), 13.

83. Cf. idem.

84. Heimann, *Reason and Faith in Modern Society,* 284.

85. Niebuhr, *Children of Light,* 45–46 (cf. p. 73).

86. James Fenimore Cooper, *The American Democrat* (New York, Knopf, 1931 [1838]), 79. Versus the tyrant, the majority involves one's own neighbor (139). Majority rule replaces statutes with "the prejudice, provincialism, ignorance, and passion of a neighborhood" (141). Tocqueville expressed the thought in this way: Giving "the majority the sovereign right to rule society ... considerably increases the dominion it has anyhow over men's minds." "I am no better inclined to pass my head under the yoke because a million men hold it for me" (Tocqueville, *Democracy in America,* 2.1.2, p. 436).

87. Tocqueville, *Democracy in America,* 1.1.6, pp. 100–101; 1.1.8, pp. 149–50. Tocqueville saw provincial governments providing the guarantee against the excesses of despotism that aristocratic forces had provided previously (1.1.5, p. 96).

88. Franklin Sherman, "Christian Theology and American Democracy," in *Belonging and Alienation,* ed. P. Hefner and W. W. Schroeder (Chicago, Center for the Scientific Study of Religion, Studies in Religion and Society, 1976), 151. Sherman notes in particular Lutheran contributions to democracy.

89. Cf. James Skillen, *Justice for Representation. A Proposal for Revitalizing our System*

of Political Representation (Washington, D.C., Association for Public Justice, 1979), 10, 12, 14; Herbert J. Gans, "We Won't End the Urban Crisis Until We End 'Majority Rule,'" *New York Times Magazine* (August 3, 1969), 28. Gans also suggests that lower level administrative bodies include those affected on their policy setting boards, and he recommends the voucher system of financing education to allow minorities the opportunity of controlling their own schools. Proportional representation systems have been the norm, however, in Latin America, and it has meant that candidates are typically selected by national party elites (Booth, "Elections and Democracy in Central America," 18). This, perhaps, is further evidence that political democracy requires a democratic society, with internal democracy within a genuine pluralism. Lijphart, however, makes a similar evaluation of candidate selection in the proportional system of the Netherlands (Arend Lijphart, *The Politics of Accommodation. Pluralism and Democracy in the Netherlands* [Berkeley, CA, U. of California, 1975²], 141–44). A change to districts from the Netherlands' countrywide system would help (218). The required percentage of the vote for a party to get a seat in the Second Chamber in the Netherlands after 1956 was only .67 percent (162).

90. Heimann, *Reason and Faith in Modern Society,* 285.

91. Plato, *Rep.* 557b, 561a.

92. Gans, "We Won't End the Urban Crisis Until We End 'Majority Rule,'" 14–15; cf. Roger Shinn, "The Locus of Authority: Participatory Democracy in the Age of the Expert," in *Erosion of Authority,* ed. C. Manschreck (Nashville, Abingdon, 1971), 113.

93. De Tocqueville, *Democracy in America,* 1.2.7, p. 253.

94. Lindsay, *Essentials of Democracy,* 52, 74. Most effective are nonpolitical associations in the society that exist for their own purpose yet are concerned for the public welfare. Churches and universities have done much to create a disinterested public opinion (81).

95. Thomas Jefferson, *Notes on the State of Virginia,* Query 18, in *The Complete Jefferson,* ed. S. Padover (New York, Duell, 1943), 677. He is discussing slavery.

96. Tocqueville, *Democracy in America,* 1.2.9, p. 292. "How could society escape destruction, if, when political ties are broken, moral ties are not tightened? And what can be done with a people master of itself if it is not subject to God?" (294). Cf. Burke, *Reflections on the Revolution,* 107, on the need of religion for the people to empty themselves of self-interest.

97. Heimann, 286. "Pure ethicists and humanists" in a Christian climate often are the most sensitive members of the community. "They err only in inferring that the existence of an unreligious ethic in a religious environment proves the possibility of such an unreligious ethic without the religious environment."

98. Lasch, "Orwell," 13, 22.

99. Dengerink, "The Christian and Modern Democracy," 20.

Chapter 11

1. Adam Smith, *Works and Correspondence. Vol. 2: An Inquiry into the Nature and Causes of the Wealth of Nations,* ed. R. H. Campbell and A. S. Skinner (Oxford, Oxford U., 1976), 4.5b.43, p. 540; cf. Irving Kristol, "A Capitalist Conception of Justice," in *Ethics, Free Enterprise, and Public Policy,* ed. R. De George and J. Pichler (New York, Oxford U., 1978), 58: "Capitalism says that equal opportunity will result in everyone's bettering his or her condition."

2. "Capitalism has almost no ideology and tolerates virtually all political movements not actively bent on its destruction." Economic freedom, however, is a precondition for, and a

stimulant to political freedom (Wiles, *Economic Institutions Compared,* 460–61, cf. 5). Chile would be an example from the 1970s and 1980s of capitalism combined with a nondemocratic government.

3. Cf. Demant, *Religion and the Decline of Capitalism,* 179–80. *Market* in this discussion means the economic exchanges of the society.

4. English abstract in *Sociological Abstracts* 37 (1989), 957, of Borko Yuriy Antonovich, "O mekhanizmakh samorazvitiya sovaremennogo kapitalizma" ["Apropos of Modern Capitalism's Mechanisms for Self-Development"] *Kommunist* 15 (October, 1988), 105–116, which I have not seen.

5. The discussion of the propriety of capitalism is characterized by people talking past each other to an unusual degree. Most of the leading advocates of democratic capitalism affirm the type of liberalism represented by the New Deal. What they are opposing is a naïve attraction to the collectivistic command economy although it is true that they inconsistently use this framework to critique aspects of the mixed economy and too often assume that the command economy is the alternative for critics of capitalism. Their critics often are advocates of a democratic socialism, often without extensive state planning. The critics, however, suppose that their idea of socialism is under attack, yet their neoconservative targets have failed to consider it, perhaps dismissing its relevance. The critics wrongly assume that the neoconservatives are espousing a strictly laissez-faire outlook, partly because the freedom motifs are pushed so hard in refutation of the collectivistic spector.

6. This background is delightfully presented by Robert L. Heilbroner, *The Worldly Philosophers. The Lives, Times, and Ideas of Great Economic Thinkers* (New York, Simon and Schuster, 1953), 13–15, 22; also see Smith, *Wealth of Nations* 1.10c.6, p. 136.

7. Smith, 4.1.2, 9–10; 4.3c.10; 4.5a.23, pp. 429, 433–34, 494, 515; cf. Heilbroner, 45.

8. W. Cargill Thompson, *Politics of Martin Luther,* 163–65. Luther did not make the concessions of late medieval thought. He included in usury commercial transactions that resulted in undue profit and excommunicated a Wittenburg citizen for such a sale of a horse. Because of the temptation by greed to charge extortionate prices, commerce was almost a necessary evil. The Christian nobility in luxury trades such as spices and silk were involved in the indulgence of vanity and greed.

9. Interest is allowed only in productive loans. Interest could not be taken from the needy, yet the needy were not to be refused loans for lack of securities. The debtor should gain as much as the creditor. The law of cheapness should prevail everywhere (Troeltsch, *Social Teachings,* 648).

10. H. R. Niebuhr, *Kingdom of God in America,* 85.

11. William Perkins, "Treatise of the Vocations," in *Puritan Political Ideas,* ed. Morgan, 39, 56–57. Pursuit of profit is directly contrary to the end of every calling to contribute to the common good (39). Cf. John Winthrop, "A Model of Christian Charity" (1630), in ibid., 92–93, in his presentation of "a city upon a hill."

12. Weber, *Protestant Ethic and Spirit of Capitalism,* 181–82.

13. Robert N. Bellah, Richard Madsen, William M. Sullivan, Ann Swidler, and Steven M. Tipton, *Habits of the Heart, Individualism and Commitment in American Life* (New York, Perennial Library, 1985), esp. chaps. 2 and 11; cf. Bellah, "Religion and Polity in America," *Andover Newton Quarterly* 15 (1974), 107–23.

14. Demant, *Religion and the Decline of Capitalism,* 180.

15. Smith, *Wealth of Nations* 2.3.25; 2.5.31; 4.8.49, pp. 340, 372, 660; cf. Heilbroner, *Worldly Philosophers,* 45; Joyce Appleby, "Ideology and Theory: The Tension between Political and Economic Liberalism in Seventeenth-Century England," 499–515. In the new model workers were driven by envy and emulation; in the old model, they were idle and willing to work only for survival (513).

16. Calvin B. Hoover, "Capitalism," *International Encyclopedia of the Social Sciences* [1968], 2:295.

17. Smith, 2.1.2; 2.2.86; 4.2.3, pp. 278, 320, 453; Peter L. Berger, *The Capitalist Revolution: Fifty Propositions about Prosperity, Equality, and Liberty* (New York, Basic, 1986), 18–19.

18. C. B. MacPherson, *The Political Theory of Possessive Individualism: Hobbes to Locke* (London, Oxford U., 1962), 55. Capitalism is intrinsically linked with a new stratification system based solely on relationship to the production system (Berger, 27, 52).

19. Cf. Heilbroner, *Worldly Philosophers,* 46.

20. Goudzwaard, *Capitalism and Progress,* 27.

21. Herbert Spencer described the recognition of "some unseen, but universally diffused influence determining . . . buyings and sellings . . . in a way most advantageous to all parties" as part of the "conquest of faith in impersonal agencies over the faith in personal agencies" (*Social Statics* [New York, Appleton, 1865 (1850)])], 23.3, p. 333).

22. Smith, *Wealth of Nations* 4.2.9, p. 456.

23. Ibid., 1.2.2, p. 27; Heilbroner, *Worldly Philosophers,* 46–47.

24. Adam Smith, *Works and Correspondence, Vol. 1: The Theory of Moral Sentiments,* ed. D. D. Raphael and A. L. Macfie (Oxford, Oxford U., 1976), 4.1.10, pp. 184–85.

25. Charles K. Wilbur and Roland Hoksbergen, "Ethical Values and Economic Theory: A Survey," *Religious Studies Review* 12 (1986), 211.

26. Cf. Robert Benne, *The Ethic of Democratic Capitalism. A Moral Reassessment* (Philadelphia, Fortress, 1981), 143. Benne states that the value system of some is not imposed on others. In the market, however, the consumers who outbid others are able to impose their values, (e.g., as expressed in luxury housing, even to the detriment of those who need low cost housing).

27. Heilbroner, *Worldly Philosophers,* 53–59.

28. Smith, *Wealth of Nations* 4.2.10, p. 456.

29. Ibid., 4.7b.44, p. 582.

30. Heilbroner, *Worldly Philosophers,* 60–62.

31. Félix-Paul Codaccioni, *De l'inégalité sociale dans une grande ville industrielle: Le drame de Lille de 1850 à 1914* (Université de Lille III, éditions universitaires, 1976), 210, 430. The figures are for 1891–1893. They are a mean. Even at the beginning of the twentieth century, if the fifty most privileged workers were taken out, the ratio to the industrialists for the remaining 3,227 workers covered would be 59,513 to 1 (431).

32. S. J. Bastomsky estimates that the gulf between the free laborers and the wealthy was considerably greater in the time of Cicero than in Victorian England. He estimates from income data that in Ancient Rome the extraordinarily rich were 10,476 times better off than the poor while in the 1880s they were 6,000 times better off ("Rich and Poor: The Great Divide in Ancient Rome and Victorian England," *Greece & Rome* 37 [1990], 40–41). Bastomsky measures income, while the Lille figures measure wealth. The distribution of wealth, which is harder to measure for large groups, is more unequal than the distribution of income (Russell W. Rumberger, "The Influence of Family Background on Education, Earnings, and Wealth," *Social Forces* 6 [1983], 759).

33. Cf. R. H. Campbell and A. S. Skinner, "General Introduction," to Smith, *Wealth of Nations,* 50. Smith did see that the laborers might gain less in prosperity than the proprietors, and that no order suffered so cruely from economic decline (*Wealth of Nations* 1.11p.9, p. 266).

34. Carl N. Degler, *Place Over Time: The Continuity of Southern Distinctiveness* (Baton Rouge, Louisiana State U., Walter Lynwood Fleming Lectures in Southern History, 1977), 89–90.

35. Richard Hofstadter, *Social Darwinism in American Thought* (New York, Braziller,

1955²), 34: Over 300,000 copies of Spencer's works were sold in the last four decades of the nineteenth century. No foreign philosopher ever had a more visible effect on American thought.

36. Thomas C. Cochran and William Miller, *The Age of Enterprise. A Social History of Industrial America* (New York, Harper, 1961²), 122.

37. Hofstadter, 45, 57; Rockfeller quoted in W. J. Ghent, *Our Benevolent Feudalism* [New York, Macmillan, 1902], 29.

38. "Communism Denounced: Henry Ward Beecher's Opinions on the Labor Question," *The New York Times,* July 30, 1877, 8.

39. William Graham Sumner, quoted in Rossiter, *Conservatism in America,* 144.

40. Herbert Spencer, *The Study of Sociology* (New York, Appleton, 1891), 401; cf. Roland Warren, *Types of Purposive Social Change at the Community Level* (Waltham, MA, Brandeis U., Florence Heller Graduate School for Advanced Studies in Social Welfare, Brandeis U. Papers in Social Welfare 11, 1965), 3–4. Spencer again made the analagy to a natural organism.

41. Spencer, *Social Statics* 25.6, p. 354. Cf. William Graham Sumner, "The Influence of Commercial Crises on Opinions about Economic Doctrines" (1879), in Sumner, *Essays,* ed. A. G. Keller and M. Davie (n.p., Archon, 1969 [1934]), 2.56: To the alternatives of the survival of the fittest or the survival of the unfittest, no one will ever find the third alternative that the socialists desire—nourishing the unfittest while advancing civilization. Sumner wrote of the poor who cannot be helped as long as they "insist on remaining in the slums of great cities" or on exhausted land ("The Challenge of Facts," in Sumner, *The Challenge of Facts and the Other Essays,* ed. A. G. Keller [New York, AMS 1971 (1914)]), 52. Russell Conwell in his famous *Acres of Diamonds* address stated that "number of poor who are to be symphathized with is very small" and warned that it is wrong to help those whom God has punished for their sins ([New York, Harper, 1915)], 21). To the National Association of Manufacturers, welfare redistribution subsidized "the idle, spendthrift, incompetent, and inefficient." By despoiling the thrifty, it dried up the source of capital, producing more poverty (National Association of Manufacturers, Economic Principles Commission, *The American Enterprise System. Its Nature, Evolution, and Future* [New York, McGraw-Hill, 1946], 1019).

42. Herbert Spencer, *Principles of Biology* (New York, Appleton, 1899²), 2.527–33 (quotation about "forcible burdening" on 533); *Social Statics* 25.5–6, pp. 352, 357; cf. Cochran and Miller, *Age of Enterprise,* 125. Since it is limited and voluntary, charity does not suspend the "natural relation between merit and benefit which constitutes justice" (533). Welfare, a mechanical replacement of sympathy, is what is unnatural (352).

43. Nicholas Murray Butler, "Hebert Spencer's 'The Great Political Superstition'," *Forum* 55 (1916), 83; cf. Cochran and Miller, *Age of Enterprise,* 126. For this reason, Butler states, the government should not do anything that is not by substantial common consent its task.

44. Spencer, *Social Statics* 28.2–5, 9 and pp. 412–14, 431 (quotation: 28.4, p. 413).

45. Ibid., 28.4, p. 414.

46. Wills' description in *Nixon Agonistes,* 228.

47. Loren E. Lomasky, *Persons, Rights, and the Moral Community* (New York, Oxford U., 1987), 180–81, 250–52; Robert Nozick, *Anarchy, State, and Utopia* (New York, Basic, 1974), 235–36.

48. Spencer, *Social Statics,* chs. 26, 29. Public education interfered with parental choice between different schools and between wisdom and ignorance.

49. Milton Friedman, *Capitalism and Freedom* (Chicago, U. of Chicago, 1982), 2; cf. Hollinger, *Individualism and Social Ethics,* 43.

50. Hofstadter, *Social Darwinism in American Thought,* 50, 203.

51. For example, a representative of the American Industrial Health Council, Dr. Francis Roe, testified before the Occupational Health and Safety Administration in 1979 that "cancer is probably one of nature's ways of eliminating sexually effete individuals who would otherwise, in nature's view, compete for available food resources without advantage to the species as a whole" (*In These Times,* April 8–14, 1981, 2).

52. Wills, *Nixon Agonistes,* 160, 166, 291, 531.

53. Berger, *Capitalist Revolution,* 33.

54. Cf. Marx, "Economic and Philosophical Manuscripts," 2.62, p. 143. Capitalism by its application of science increases surplus labor time to allow for the development of individual development (Karl Marx, *Grundrisse. Foundations of the Critique of Political Economy* (1857–1858), trans. M. Nicolaus (New York, Vintage, 1973), 7, p. 708). For both Marx and Engels a high level of technology and high labor productivity is an absolute prerequiste for the communist society (Richard N. Hunt, *The Political Ideas of Marx and Engels, Vol. 2: Classical Marxism, 1850–1895* [Pittsburgh, U. of Pittsburgh, 1984], 257).

55. "For is not the first task of an economic order to economize, to be as efficiently productive as possible? Its job is to produce the wealth which provides the possibility for civilization in its material and a good deal of its nonmaterial aspect" (Benne, *Ethic of Democratic Capitalism,* 127; cf. 135–36).

56. M. Douglas Meeks, *God the Economist. The Doctrine of God and Political Economy* (Minneapolis, Fortress, 1989), 60, 172, 174.

57. Heimann, *Reason and Faith in Modern Society,* 26; Hoover, "Capitalism," 295–96, 298; Berger, *Capitalist Revolution,* esp. Chaps. 2 and 6, and p. 288; Karl Marx and Frederick Engels, *Manifesto of the Communist Party* (1848) 1, in Marx and Engels, *Collected Works* 6.489.

58. Tocqueville, *Democracy in America,* 1.2.10, p. 403.

59. Fromm, *Fear of Freedom,* 93.

60. Robert J. Samuelson, "Enter Gorbanomics," *Boston Globe,* December 27, 1988, 36.

61. The high turnover is particularly true of new companies that are initially innovative. In addition they frequently lack funds to finance product development. The short-term focus is also encouraged by profit-related bonus and stock options to business executives geared to yearly or even semiannual performance of company earnings. This is coupled with a new management style that focuses on turning a company around through short-term financial restructuring to bolster profits. The managers' skills are accordingly financial and legal, but they lack sufficient knowledge about the products, markets, and production processeses of the particular industry to lead in technological innovation for the long term (MIT Commission on Industrial Productivity, *Made in America. Regaining the Productive Edge* [Cambridge, MA, MIT, 1989], 62–65).

62. MIT Commission on Industrial Productivity, 53–66.

63. Advertisement by W. P. Grace and Co., *Harvard Magazine* 86, 1 (September/October, 1983), 5.

64. Reinhold Niebuhr, "The Christian Faith and the Economic Life of Liberal Society," in *Goals of Economic Life,* ed. A. D. Ward (New York, Harper, Ethics and Economic Life, 1953), 446.

65. Friedrich A. Hayek, "Individualism: *True and False,*" in Hayek, *Individualism and Economic Order* (Chicago, U. of Chicago, 1948), 12.

66. Andrew Young, "Implications of the 1984 United States Elections for Christian Ethics and the Churches," address to the Society of Christian Ethics, Atlanta, GA, January 18, 1985. In an interesting exchange, Joseph E. Lowery responded that the question is not between the government pig and the private pig but between a few people owning all the pigs and too many people having no pigs [to stay up with].

67. Niebuhr, *Children of Light,* 76.

68. Goudzwaard, *Capitalism and Progress,* 126.

69. Michael Novak, *The Spirit of Democratic Capitalism* (New York, Simon & Schuster, 1982), 351; George Gilder, *Wealth and Poverty* (New York, Basic, 1981), x, 27. Cf. Adam Smith's position, particularly in his *Theory of Moral Sentiments,* that self-interest leads to the common good when it can be assumed that most people in society accept a general moral law as the guide of their actions (Charles K. Wilber and Laura K. Grimes, "The Moral Defense of Market Capitalism: A Critique of the Literature," a paper presented to the Biblical Perspectives on a Mixed Market Economy consultation, Wheaton, IL, September 8–10, 1987, 52).

70. Reinhold Niebuhr, "Coercion, Self-Interest, and Love," commentary in Kenneth E. Boulding, *The Organizational Revolution* (New York, Harper, 1953), 238.

71. Cf. Reinhold Niebuhr's critique that this historic ability of traditional conservatism was "conspicuously absent" in the leading manifestations of American conservatism ("American Conservatism and the World Crisis, I: A Study in Vacillation," *Yale Review* 40 [1951], 390).

72. Reinhold Niebuhr, "Has the Church Any Authority?" *Christianity and Crisis* 10 (1950), 36.

73. Cf. Niebuhr, *Children of Light,* 76; Prentiss L. Pemberton and Daniel Rush Finn, *Toward a Christian Economic Ethic. Stewardship and Social Power* (Minneapolis, Winston, 1985), 135, 188 (quotation).

74. Walter George Muelder, *Religion and Economic Responsibility* (New York, Scribner's, 1953), 169.

75. Hayek, "Individualism: *True and False,*" 13–15. This rendering is preferable to another attempt to clarify self-interest by linking it to any goals in which the individual has an interest. Thus it might be one of great philanthropic motivation (cf. Michael Novak, *The Spirit of Democratic Capitalism,* 94–95). Daniel Rush Finn, however, points out that the idea of self-interest then becomes vacuous in that "no action could be anything but self-interested" since it rises out of the interest of a self who is an actor ("Self-Interest, Markets, and the Four Problems of Economic Life," in *Annual of the Society of Christian Ethics,* 1989, ed. D. M. Yeager [Knoxville, TN, Society of Christian Ethics, 1989], 36).

76. Paul Tillich, *The Religious Situation* (New York, Living Age, 1932), 109; cf. Stone, *Paul Tillich's Radical Social Thought,* 78.

77. Hayek, "Individualism: *True and False,*" 14.

78. Cf. Adams, "Freedom and Association," 84. For a classic case study of the power of local industry particularly upon the churches, cf. Liston Pope, *Millhands and Preachers. A Study of Gastonia* (New Haven, Yale U., 1942), 143–61. Cf. Wiles, *Economic Institutions Compared,* 447.

79. Complete laissez-faire and pure and perfect competition have never occurred. The old feudal, guild, and mercantile customs had not fully been eliminated when new processes that were inconsistent with laissez-faire were developed (Hoover, "Capitalism," 296). In the United States a state-supported infrastructure spread across the land. Government units of all sizes provided finance and free land. In nearly all countries, the industrial revolution was a state capitalist affair. The exceptional period of "pure capitalism" was ca. 1815–1870 and was dominated by one country, Britain (Wiles, *Economic Institutions Compared,* 339, 519; cf. Wills, *Confessions of a Conservative,* 125).

80. Banton, *Racial and Ethnic Competition,* 117.

81. Goudzwaard, *Capitalism and Progress,* 11; cf. Robert Heilbroner's statement that the largely uncritical worship of the idea of economic growth is central to the nature of capitalism ("Reflections: The Triumph of Capitalism," *New Yorker* 64 [1989], 102).

82. Eric J. Hobsbawm, *Labouring Men: Studies in the History of Labour* (London, Weidenfeld, 1964), 65. Berger states that "the early period of industrial capitalism in England, and probably other Western countries exacted considerable human costs, if not in an actual decline in material living standards then in social and cultural dislocation" (*Capitalist Revolution,* 41).

83. Charles Spahr (*An Essay on the Present Distribution of Wealth in the United States, 1890* [based on the 1890 census taken close to the peak of pre-Depression worker prosperity]) estimated 1 percent of all families held half of the aggregate wealth of the country; seven-eighths held only one-eighth of the wealth (Cochran and Miller, *Age of Enterprise,* 261; Walter Rauschenbusch, *Christianity and the Social Crisis* [Boston, Pilgrim, 1907], 263). Three out of every five American males did not hold any real estate.

84. Alexander Keyssar, *Out of Work. The First Century of Unemployment in Massachusetts* (Cambridge, Cambridge U., Interdisciplinary Perspectives on Modern History, 1986), 59: From 1870 to 1920 about 20 percent of the labor force experienced idleness at one point or another during the year in Massachusetts.

85. For example, the Pullman Car Company in the 1894 depression (Alfred H. Kelly and Winfred A. Harbison, *The American Constitution, Its Origins and Development* [New York, Norton, 1955^2], 561.

86. Cochran and Miller, 18–19, 231–32. In 1913 death from industrial accidents amounted to 25,000 people. The total for injuries was close to 1 million.

87. Frank Friedel, "America Enters the Modern Era," *National Geographic* 128 (1965), 538. In England the importance of child labor did not diminish until late in the nineteenth century (Hobsbaum, *Labouring Men,* 294).

88. Cochran and Miller, 264. New York City's Sanitary District "A" in 1894 averaged 986.4 people to the acre.

89. Ibid., 262, 265. Infant mortality in New York City in 1870 was 65 percent higher than it had been in 1810.

90. Cochran and Miller, 138–50; cf. Goudzwaard, *Capitalism and Progress,* 89–117.

91. Gudorf, *Catholic Social Teaching,* 10, 38.

92. Cf. Goudzwaard, 100–101.

93. Adams, "Enduring Validity of Congregational Polity," 133. The relationship, Adams suggests, needs further research, but it makes sense "to assume that the people who were promoting free enterprise in business were also members of the small conventicles."

94. Stackhouse, *Public Theology and Political Economy,* 113–37 (Chap. 7, "Spirituality and the Corporation"); Max L. Stackhouse and Dennis P. McCann, "Public Theology After the Collapse of Socialism," *Christian Century* 108 (1991), 44, 46.

95. André Brink, *Rumors of Rain* (Harmondsworth, Middlesex, Penguin, 1978), 339.

96. Cf. Stackhouse, 133–35.

97. Marx, *Capital* 1.32, p. 764; cf. Marx and Engels, *Manifesto of the Communist Party* 1, p. 496; 2, p. 499; Marx, *The Eighteenth Brumaire of Louis Bonaparte* (1852) 7, in *Collected Works* 11.187.

98. Nozick, *Anarchy, State, Utopia,* 149, 159. The conclusion that therefore no pattern of distributive justice is needed does not follow. Explicit attention to distributive justice is needed for basic needs not met in the massive process of voluntary exchange, which needs supplementation but not replacement.

99. Paul Johnson, "The Capitalism & Morality Debate," *First Things* (March 1990), 20.

100. Daniel Bell, *Cultural Contradictions of Capitalism,* (New York, Basic, 1976), 276.

101. This application was made by Pemberton and Finn, *Toward a Christian Economic Ethic,* 190.

102. Niebuhr, "Has the Church Any Authority?" 34.

103. A. D. Lindsay, *Essentials of Democracy,* 43.

104. Heimann, *Reason and Faith in Modern Society,* 102.

105. Seifert, *Ethical Resources,* 41–42. Other reasonable choices that Seifert describes as being denied the consumer as a voter include items they would like to have produced with a subsidy, with losses covered by profits from other items.

106. No one can buy a share of clean air in the market. Indeed, economic growth results when smoking goes up or lung cancer increases (Bell, 276–77; Robert Lekachman, "Is America Fair? Ethics and Current Economic Prospects," address to the American Society of Christian Ethics, New York, January 18, 1980; Schumacher, *Small is Beautiful,* 47).

107. J. Philip Wogaman, *The Great Economic Debate. An Ethical Analysis* (Philadelphia, Westmnister, 1977), 92–93, 96–97.

108. Cf. Bell, 222–23. In contrast the ancient economy was oriented toward needs.

109. Marx, "Economic and Philosophical Manuscripts" 3.42–43, in Marx, *Early Writings,* 192.

110. Thea Lee, "Choose Your Poison: Competition or Concentration," *Dollars & Sense* (July/August, 1989), 7.

111. George Gilder's defense of entrepreneurship undercuts the democratic argument for the market. Instead, he states, "supply creates its own demand." Contemporary business persons may have less need of planning ahead since investment decisions, including market and advertising, determine the essential pattern of consumer purchases. Democratic masses can merely react, ratify, or reject (*Wealth and Poverty,* 36, 38). Cf. Goudzwaard, *Capitalism and Progress,* 98–99, 193, 214.

112. Goudzwaard, 97–99.

113. Edmund A. Opitz, *Religion and Capitalism: Allies, Not Enemies* (New Rochelle, NY, Arlington House, 1970), 103. ". . . In the last resort competition has to be circumscribed and mitigated by moral forces within the market parties" (Wilhelm Röpke, *A Humane Economy. The Social Framework of the Free Market* [Indianapolis, IN, Liberty Fund, 1960], 129).

114. Okun, *Equality and Efficiency,* 13–14.

115. "That which is carried on for the benefit of the poor and the indigent, is too often, either neglected, or oppressed" (Smith, *Wealth of Nations* 4.8.4, p. 644). Further, he notes that one-half of the children die before adulthood (1.8.15, p. 85). Higher wages produce more active, diligent, and expeditious workers (1.8.44, p. 99). When society declines, workers' wages fall even below the subsistence level (1.11p.10, p. 266).

116. Ibid., 4.8.30, p. 654.

117. Johnson, "Capitalism & Morality Debate," 19. Johnson notes that this competitive aspect of capitalism is an adjunct to the basic liberal commitment to equality before the law. While Adam Smith would be one with later followers of his vision in seeing the task of government of supporting only what is "for the general benefit of the whole society" (*Wealth of Nations* 5.1i.1, p. 814), he supported higher taxes on those more able to pay (5.1d.5; 5.2k.31, pp. 725, 883). The public provision of elementary education was needed by the common people, not by those of rank and wealth. Some parts of society need the attention of government "to prevent the almost total corruption and degeneracy of the great body of people" (5.1f.49, 53, pp. 781, 784). While such instruction of the lower classes provides considerable benefit to the state, even without that advantage "it would still deserve its attention that they should not be altogether uninstructed." (5.1f.61, p. 788). Smith here moves beyond utilitarianism to a conviction of human entitlement.

118. Erich Fromm, *The Sane Society* (New York, Holt, 1955), 173.

119. Opitz, *Religion and Capitalism,* 235–41.

120. Hayek, "Individualism: *True and False,*" 14.

121. Smith, 1.10c.12, 44–45, 59, pp. 138, 152, 157.

122. Jon P. Gunnemann, "Capitalism and Commutative Justice," in *Annual of the Society of Christian Ethics,* 1985, ed. A. Anderson (Vancouver, B.C., Society of Christian Ethics, 1986), 101–22 (quotation, 119).

123. José Miranda, *Marx and the Bible* (Maryknoll, NY, Orbis, 1976), 26; Okun, *Equality and Efficiency* (1975), 80.

124. Robert Nozick's description of this principle of ability in the market as "from each as they choose, to each as they are chosen" (*Anarchy, State, Utopia,* 160) underplays the involuntarily aspects of economic and social life.

125. Herbert Spencer, "The Sins of the Legislators," in Spencer, *The Man versus the State* (London, Williams, 1884), 65; cf. Yehoshua Arieli, *Individualism and Nationalism in American Ideology* (Cambridge, Harvard U., 1964), 334; Maguire, *New American Justice,* 20. For Spencer, merit and desert are the ability to fulfill all the requirements of securing physical life. "Capitalism thrives on meritocracy" as the market identifies and rewards objective merit. What the market "cannot be made to do, at least without wrecking it, is to discriminate in favor of failure" (Johnson, "Capitalism & Morality Debate," 20, 21).

126. "Communism Denounced," 8. A descent into poverty should be born with dignity. They are still humans even if they die of hunger. "I don't say that one dollar per day is enough to support a working man, but it is enough to support a man." This ridicule and other gibes in this sermon take away from Beecher's declaration of being on the side of the working person. His biographer, Paxton Hibben, notes that with Beecher making $20,000 a year and at least that amount again in lectures (i.e., $128 per working day [assuming a six day working week]), this sermon after four years of depression following the panic of 1873 did go over well in circles less refined than Plymouth Church where he gave it (*Henry Ward Beecher: An American Portrait* [New York, Doran, 1927], 326).

127. Spencer, *Social Statics* 25.2, pp. 344–45.

128. Niebuhr, "Coercion, Self-Interest, and Love," 228, describing the position of Boulding, who found the market approach therefore to be closer to Christian ideals of justice, love, and freedom.

129. Description of Milton Friedman's position by Warren R. Copeland, *Economic Justice: The Social Ethics of U.S. Economic Policy* (Nashville, Abingdon, 1988), 27.

130. Gunnemann, "Capitalism and Commutative Justice," 106; Okun, *Equality and Efficiency,* 6–7, 9–10, 19–22.

131. It is true that unlike other rights, such as benefit rights, "liberty is unique . . . in that it *must be provided by others* if it is to be enjoyed by all" (Lomasky, *Persons, Rights, and the Moral Community,* 97, 100 [emphasis his]). This need makes the protection of liberty a profoundly important task of the government, but it does not follow that liberty therefore has primacy. For those lacking other conditions of community such as food or shelter, those needs are equally urgent and raise a claim upon society with just as powerful a moral force. Lomasky argues for primacy on the grounds that in this everyone needs the help of the government. It would reflect his statement that nothing is a basic right unless the vast majority of community members are better off if it is respected (83). Rights, however, are also for situations of potential deprivation of the conditions of communal life for the smallest minority of the community, whether torture or hunger. Such provisions may not always appear to the advantage of the vast majority.

132. Cf. Daniel Bell, "On Meritocracy and Equality," *Public Interest* 29 (Fall, 1972), 63–68. These are two fears by those who would not depart from market distribution. According to our approach, there are some results that justice does secure in terms of the basic conditions for life in the community, but not across the board equality in results.

133. Cf. Okun, *Equality and Efficiency,* 41.

134. As Marx stated, those who possess no other property than their labor power will be

dominated by those who own the material conditions of labor ("Critique of the Gotha Program, Marginal Notes on the Programme of the German Workers' Party" (1875) 1, in Marx and Engels, *Collected Works,* 24.81).

135. Hugo, *Les Misérables,* 1.51.

136. Okun, 43.

137. Wiles, *Economic Institutions Compared,* 420; Irving Fisher, *Elementary Principles of Economics* (New York, Macmillan, 1912), 482. (Fisher was an influential Yale economist in the early twentieth century.) Sumner recognized the existence of fortune, but saw it as an irrational force about which nothing could be done apart from insurance. It modifies merit, the significant factor (William Graham Sumner, "What Makes the Rich Richer and the Poor Poorer?" [1887] in Sumner, *Challenge of Facts,* 68; "The Power and Beneficence of Capital" [1889], in Sumner, *Essays,* ed. Keller and Davie, 2.22–23; cf. Kristol, "Capitalist Conception of Justice," 60).

138. Russell W. Rumberger, "The Influence of Family Background on Education, Earnings, and Wealth," *Social Forces* 61 (1983), 755–73. In a longitudinal study of 482 fathers and sons, this finding was true of white males, for whom parental wealth was the most significant component of family background influences. It was not true of black males, indicating perhaps that wealth has to be up to a certain level to be significant (765).

139. Okun, *Equality and Efficiency,* 46; cf. E. F. Schumacher, *Small is Beautiful: Economics as If People Mattered* (New York, Harper, 1973), 248. The choice that Opitz presents is thus inaccurate: Wealth is acquired either by producing it or "helping yourself to someone else's production" (*Religion and Capitalism,* 110). All production is in part someone else's.

140. Niebuhr, *Children of Light,* 65–66.

141. Reward is solely on the basis of the value of the results of one's actions to others (Hayek, "Individualism: *True and False,*" 22). Hayek perceives that this does not adequately express "our views of distributive justice," but a full satisfaction of distributive justice is incompatible with the preservation of individual freedom. Justice, however, is therefore no longer the supreme social virtue, but is subordinated to freedom; therefore, this understanding of either justice or of freedom or of both needs to be reconsidered.

142. Kristol, "Capitalist Conception of Justice," 67.

143. E.g., Popes Pius XI and Leo XII, cf. Gudorf, *Catholic Social Teaching,* 38.

144. Niebuhr, *Moral Man and Immoral Society,* 125.

145. To William Graham Sumner, however, capital should be in few hands since the millionaires had been prepared by natural selection to handle a great accumulation of capital, a wisdom that very few have. Their high wages and luxury are a bargain for society ("Power of Capital," 28–29; Rossiter, *Conservatism in America,* 134–35).

146. Norman J. Faramelli, "Neo-Conservatives in the Church," *Ecumenist* 21 (1982), 4–5. Strikingly, Spencer held to the radical concept that people do have equal rights to the use of the earth. This could be preserved for them by making society the joint stock owner of the earth to provide land by lease (*Social Statics,* 9.8, p. 141). Correcting the wrong of the loss of this birthright is the only long-term solution, but that will take many generations (25.3, p. 346).

147. Cf. Wiles, *Economic Institutions Compared,* 39. The result is class conflict and a rupture in the human community (Tillich, *Religious Situation,* 110).

148. Cf. the recommendation of a Catholic study of industrial problems in the early twentieth century: The majority must somehow become owners, at least in part, of the instruments of production (National Catholic War Council, Committee on Special War Activities, *Social Reconstruction. A General Review of the Problems and Survey of Remedies* [Washington, D.C., National Catholic War Council, Reconstruction Pamphlets, 1919], 22). As Wil-

liam Booth put it, capital is good; "it is the congestion of capital that is evil, and the labour question will never be finally solved until every labourer is his [or her] own capitalist" (*In Darkest England and the Way Out* [London, International Headquarters of the Salvation Army, 1890], 229).

149. Susanne Gowan et al., *Moving Toward a New Society* (Philadelphia, New Society, 1976), 128. Public stock accounted for only 2 percent of the total wealth of the lower ninetieth percentile (according to total net worth) of American households, according to the 1983 Survey of Consumer Finances (U.S. House of Representatives, Committee on Ways and Means, *1991 Green Book: Overview of Entitlement Programs* [U. S. Government, 1991], 1330–1331). (I am in debt to Professor John Mason for this reference.) According to a survey of the New York Stock Exchange, only 21.1 percent of the American population had any stock at all in 1990 (*Boston Globe,* May 22, 1991, 69).

150. F. A. Hayek, *The Road to Serfdom* (London, Routledge, 1944), 55: A society can agree on the means—the use of the market—when it has difficulty coming to a consensus on basic values and ends, short of which somebody's views are imposed on others in planning.

151. Lomasky, *Persons, Rights, and the Moral Community,* 26–27, 32, 49, 83 (quotation), 102, 105.

152. Heimann, *Reason and Faith in Modern Society,* 28.

153. Rauschenbusch, *Christianity and the Social Crisis,* 310–11. In China the loss of community values was quickly felt as economic freedom expanded (Rich Levy, "Why China Exploded: Five Views," *Dollars & Sense* [September, 1989], 14).

154. J. R. McCulloch, *The Principles of Political Economy* (Edinburgh, Tait, 1825), 402; cf. Wolin, *Politics and Vision,* 325. McCulloch was assured that the greed would be controlled by its negative consequences in producing poverty and degradation. Cf. the American spirit as praised by the National Association of Manufacturers: "Individuals, conscious of unbounded opportunities, inflamed by the love of achievement, inspired by hope of profit, ambitious of the comfort, power, and influence that wealth brings, turned with vim and vigor to producing and offering goods and services in competitive markets" (National Association of Manufacturers, *American Enterprise System,* 1018; cf. Arieli, *Individualism and Nationalism,* 336; Maguire, *New American Justice,* 20).

155. Prov. 23.4; cf. 28.8, 20, 22; Ps. 10.3

156. Wesley, Sermon 28, "Sermon on the Mount, VIII" 1, in Wesley, *Works 1: Sermons 1,* 612, quoting William Law, *A Serious Call to a Devout and Holy Life* (1729), 4.33. For Aquinas, profit is only acceptable when it is to be used for the upkeep of one's household, for assisting the poor, or for providing the necessities of life for the public welfare. It is condemned when it is pursued for its own sake in the desire for gain (Aquinas, *Summa Theologiae,* 2a2ae. 77.4, in Aquinas, *Selected Political Writings,* 173). For the similar attitude among the Puritans, see p. 164.

157. Brian Griffiths, *The Creation of Wealth. A Christian's Case for Capitalism* (Downers Grove, IL, InterVarsity, 1984), 20. The accumulation of capital and successful economic development require the entreprenuer to think over the long term (35). He cites Alfred Marshall for whom saving is associated with human "prospectiveness, that is, [the] facility of realizing the future" (*Principles of Economics* [1961], 193).

158. Smith, *Wealth of Nations* 2.3.15, 17, p. 337.

159. Bell, *Cultural Contradictions of Capitalism,* 69–76.

160. David Mehegan, "Boomers' Shopping Matures," *Boston Globe,* August 30, 1988, 27.

161. Smith, 2.3.25, p. 340.

162. Cf. Miranda, *Marx and the Bible,* 25.

163. Aristotle, *Pol.* 1334b1, 1338a3.

164. Paul Tillich, *Theology of Culture* (New York, Oxford U., 1959), 43–44; cf. Richard

Quinney, *Providence. The Reconstruction of Social Moral Order* (New York, Longman, 1980), 4. God is excluded from determining property, access to livelihood, and the definition of needs (Meeks, *God the Economist,* 47–48, 109, 158; cf. 20, 52). The medieval regulations regarding just prices and prohibition of usury as conclusions from a vertical perspective constituted such interference (Goudzwaard, *Capitalism and Progress,* 11). For many, but not all, the preference for the impersonality of the market reflects a view that values are relativistic, merely reflecting personal preferences (Pemberton and Finn, *Toward a Christian Economic Ethic,* 128). In addition, some thinkers express their liberal individualism in an agnoticism about a group's ability to come to a conclusion that expresses genuine social morality. A necessary and wholesome aspect of group life is undercut.

165. Cf. Griffiths, *Creation of Wealth,* 107; Wogaman, *Great Economic Debate,* 2; Stackhouse and McCann, "Public Theology After the Collapse of Socialism," 45.

Chapter 12

1. Marx, "Critique of the Gotha Program" 1.3, in Marx and Engels, *Collected Works,* 24.87.

2. Branko Horvat notes that the formula had been used previously in the socialist tradition (*The Political Economy of Socialism: A Marxist Social Theory* [Armonk, NY, Sharpe, 1982], 115).

3. Heilbroner, *Worldly Philosophers,* Chap. 4, and pp. 119–26, 153.

4. Heilbroner, 147–53.

5. Marx, "Theses on Feuerbach" (1845) 11, in Marx and Engels, *Collected Works,* 5.5; cf. "Economic and Philosophical Manuscripts" 3.39.19, in Marx, *Early Writings,* ed. Bottomore, 176.

6. Cf. Heimann, *Communism, Fascism, or Democracy?* 231.

7. Marx, "Critique of the Gotha Program" 1.3, pp. 86–87.

8. Ibid. 1.3, p. 87; Sanford A. Lakoff, *Equality in Political Philosophy* (Boston, Beacon, 1964), 223. Not only are there needs of the worker and of the worker's family, there are also social needs for further production and for education, health, and those unable to work ("Gotha Program" pp. 84–85).

9. This priority of needs over work is reinforced in an earlier text in which Marx and Frederick Engels critique the position that superior faculties and capacities should be rewarded. "The differences of brain and of intellectual ability do not imply any differences whatsoever in the nature of the stomach and of physical needs; therefore the false tenet, based on existing circumstances, 'to each according to his abilities', must be changed . . . into the tenet, 'to each accoring to his need.'" A different form of labor does not confer any privileges in property and enjoyment (Marx and Engels, *The German Ideology* [1845–1846] 2.5, in Marx and Engels, *Collected Works* 5.535, 537; cf. Hunt, *Political Ideas of Marx and Engels, Vol. 2: Classical Marxism,* 263–64).

10. Cf. Karl Marx, *Grundrisse,* trans. Nicolaus, Introduction, p. 118, where Marx divides distribution between "the instruments of production" and "the products" themselves and shows that one cannot separate the two forms in analyzing distribution; cf. Zizad I. Husami, "Marx on Distributive Justice," in *Marx, Justice, and History,* ed. M. Cohen et al. (Princeton, Princeton U., 1980), 46 (also in *Philosophy and Public Affairs* 8 [1978]).

11. Karl Marx, "Bruno Bauer, *Die Judenfrage*" (1843), in Marx, *Early Writings,* ed. Bottomore, 13–14.

12. Idem, 15. Cf. the positive reference to the freedoms of ballot, press, association, jury

trial by peers in Marx, *The Class Struggles in France, 1848–1850* (1850), in Marx and Engels, *Collected Works* 10.1, p. 67; 2, p. 73; cf. note 14. Freedom of religion existed in the Paris Commune (Marx, *The Civil War in France* [1871] 3, in Marx and Engels, *Collected Works,* 22.337.

13. Hal Draper, *Karl Marx's Theory of Revolution, Vol. 1: State and Bureaucracy* (New York, Monthly Review, 1977), 31, 59 (quotation, emphasis his). The pre-Marxian socialists were proponents of a "socialism from above," the installation of the new order by a benevolent elite (59).

14. Marx, *Class Struggles in France* 3, p. 125.

15. Draper, 282–310. The affirmation of freedoms in later writings, such as those on the Paris communes, were characteristic of Marx's earlier advocacy. Draper documents them from Marx's articles in 1848–1849, particularly in the *Neue Rheinische Zeitung.*

16. Karl Marx, "The Chartists" (1852), in Marx and Engels, *Collected Works* 11.335–36; Marx, *Class Struggles in France* 2, p. 79; Shlomo Avineri, *Political and Social Thought of Marx* (London, Cambridge U., 1969), 213–14.

17. Marx and Engels, *Manifesto of the Communist Party* 2, in Marx and Engels, *Collected Works* 6:504; Karl Marx, "On the Hague Congress" (1872), in Marx and Engels, *Collected Works* 23.255; cf. Avineri, 211, 213–14.

18. Marx, *Class Struggles in France* 3, p. 127. In this context *dictatorship* means the time when the proletatariat are in charge in contrast to having to seek concessions from the ruling bourgeoisie (126). Its counterpart is the "bourgeois dictatorship" (125).

19. Marx and Engels, *Manifesto of the Communist Party,* 2, p. 504; 1, p. 495; cf. Marx, *Capital* 1. 32, p. 764.

20. For the emancipation of society at large, not merely the proletariat, cf. Marx and Engels, *Manifesto of the Communist Party* 1, p. 495; 2, pp. 505–6; Engels, preface to the English edition of 1888 of *Manifesto of the Communist Party,* in Karl Marx and Engels, *Basic Writings on Politics and Philosophy,* ed. L. Feuer (Garden City, NY, Anchor, 1959), 4.

21. Richard N. Hunt, *The Political Ideas of Marx and Engels, Vol. 1: Marxism and Totalitarian Democracy, 1818–1850* (Pittsburgh, U. of Pittsburgh, 1974), 295. These appear in Marx's and Engels' articles in the *Neue Rheinische Zeitung.* For example, in "The Crisis and the Counter-Revolution" (No. 100, September 12, 1848) (in Marx and Engels, *Collected Works* 7.431; cf. Hunt, 293), Marx states that in the provisional condition of the state, "dictatorship" "smashed up and removed the remains of the old state." "In any unconstitutional state of affairs it is solely . . . the public welfare, and not this or that principle that is the decisive factor."

22. Hunt, 302. Cf. Marx, *Class Struggles in France* 3, p. 127. Frederick Engels makes explicit the comparison to Louis Auguste Blanqui (perhaps the most famous of the nineteenth-century French revolutionists) in "Programme of the Blanquist Commune Refugees" (1874), in Marx and Engels, *Collected Works* 24.13; cf. Hunt, 310–12.

23. Friedrich Engels, Introduction to *The Civil War in France* (1891), in Marx and Engels, *Basic Writings on Politics and Philosophy,* 361–62; cf. Marx, *Civil War in France* 3, p. 331.

24. Marx, *Civil War in France* 3, pp. 332, 334–35, 339.

25. Cf. Heimann, *Reason and Faith in Modern Society,* 165; Paul Tillich, *The Socialist Decision* (New York, Harper, 1977 [1933]), 60.

26. Marx, *Civil War in France* 3, pp. 332–33; Avineri, *Political and Social Thought of Marx,* 209.

27. Cf. Heimann, 107. This was all the more true in communism's development in an undeveloped, preindustrial country (132–33). In addition, Marx indicates that at the time of his writing the proletariat in France was outnumbered by the peasants, who were the majority class *Class Struggles in France* 1, pp. 57, 61; *Eighteenth Brumaire of Louis Bonaparte* 7, p.

187). In England, however, he perceived the proletariat to form the large majority (Marx, "The Chartists," 335).

28. Carol C. Gould, *Marx's Social Ontology: Individuality and Community in Marx's Theory of Social Reality* (Cambridge, MA, MIT, 1978), 171 ("the conditions of positive freedom"). (Self-realization is "real freedom" [Marx, *Grundrisse* 6, p. 611].)

29. Marx, *Grundrisse* 2, p. 244. Marx was particularly interacting with Aristotle's prescription that "reciprocal" justice required *koinonia* and *philia,* "community" and "friendship", so that the parties in the exchange could be equal (*Nicomachean Ethics* 1133b17–19; 1133a10–19). Marx saw, as Aristotle failed to see, that this required equalizing the participants' status, not merely their products. He also saw as the socialists failed to see that justice required more than a demand of rights, but a community fulfilling Aristotle's qualities for justice (Michael DeGolyer, "Marx's Theory of Justice," *Fides et Historia* 16,2 [1984], 18–37).

30. Marx, *Grundrisse* 2, p. 247; cf. p. 275; cf. Gould, 150–52.

31. *Grundrisse* 3, p. 307; Gould, 46–47, 50.

32. *Grundrisse* 4, p. 453; 7, p. 705; Gould, 152, 154, 158–60. Alien labor is appropriated "without an equivalent" (*Grundrisse* 4, p. 458). This critique merges with that of violation of distribution according to labor contribution (Husami, "Marx on Distributive Justice," 62)

33. Gould, 123. DeGolyer shows that Marx's insistence that the exchange in capitalism was not free and equal reflected the stipulation for this prerequisite by thinkers from Aristotle to Adam Smith ("Marx's Theory of Justice," 23).

34. "We shall have an association, in which the free development of each is the condition of the free development of all" (Marx and Engels, *Manifesto of the Communist Party* 6.2, 506).

35. Gould, 162–66; Marx stated that "a communal production, communality, is presupposed as the basis of production" and speaks of the "social conditions of production within which the individual is active" (*Grundrisse* 1, p. 172).

36. Gould, 171.

37. Heilbroner, *Worldly Philosophers,* 155, 159–60.

38. Cf. José Míguez Bonino, *Christians and Marxists: The Mutual Challenge to Revolution* (Grand Rapids, MI, Eerdmans, 1976), 57, 148 (n.6).

39. Ibid.

40. Marx, "Economic and Philosophical Manuscripts" 1.25, p. 132; 3.39.3, p. 153; cf. Lakoff, *Equality in Political Philosophy,* 231. Marx wrote of the replacement of life and humanity by money and wealth ("Economic and Philosophical Manuscripts" 3.39.15–16, p. 171).

41. Marx, "Economic and Philosophical Manuscripts" 3.39, p. 153

42. Fromm, *Sane Society,* 216–36; cf. Fromm, *Marx's Concept of Man* (New York, Ungar, Milestones of Thought, 1961), 45.

43. Cf. Paul Tillich, "Basic Principles of Religious Socialism," in Tillich, *Political Expectation,* 76.

44. Marx, "Economic and Philosophical Manuscripts" 3.20, pp. 177–78.

45. Ibid. 3.39.7, p. 160; 3.43, pp. 193–94; "Bruno Bauer, *Die Judenfrage,*" p. 30.

46. Marx, "Critique of the Gotha Program" 1.3, p. 87; cf. Marx, Letter to *Otechestvenniye Zapiski,* November, 1877, in Marx and Engels, *Collected Works* 24.201.

47. Marx, "Economic and Philosophical Manuscripts" 1.22, p. 123; 1.24, pp. 126–27 (cf. 129); 3.39.5, p. 157; cf. "Critique of the Gotha Program" 1.1, p. 81.

48. Marx, *Grundrisse* 6, p. 694; cf. Gould, *Marx's Social Ontology,* 24. Adam Smith had also spoken of torpor of mind, and the loss of social and martial values, that affect those whose life in the factories was spent in doing a few simple operations. In contrast, in tribal society

one's capacity was pushed by the breadth of tasks. That has been lost in civilized society for most individuals although the variety of tasks in the total society has been greatly multiplied (*Wealth of Nations* 5.1f.51, p. 783). The Southern traditional conservative, Richard Weaver, describes how modern organization has driven a wedge between the worker and her or his product. The worker does not express one's self in "producing quantity for the market" (*Ideas Have Consequences,* 74). A worker related to me how he felt like a thing and like cattle when after signing for a mortgage, the bank attorney put his hand on the worker's shoulder and said, "There is a lot of years of production left in this shoulder."

49. Marx, "Economic and Philosophical Manuscripts" 1.3, p. 72; 1.23–24, pp. 125, 128; cf. 1.25, p. 132.

50. Ibid. 1.22–23, pp. 122–24; 1.3, p. 72; cf. 1.25, p. 130.

51. Gould, 42, 52, 55, 75, 114. Labor properly creates self-realization, which is "real freedom" (Marx, *Grundrisse* 6, p. 611).

52. Marx, "Economic and Philosophical Manuscripts" 1.24, p. 129; "Bruno Bauer, *Die Judenfrage,*" p. 26.

53. MacPherson, *Political Theory of Possessive Individualism,* 55.

54. Marx, "Economic and Philosophical Manuscripts" 2.40, pp. 137–38; 3.39, p. 155.

55. Ibid. 3.14, p. 168; cf. 1.24, p. 129; *Grundrisse* 2, p. 243; cf. Gould, 54.

56. Marx, "Economic and Philosophical Manuscripts" 3.39.7, pp. 159–60.

57. Goudzwaard, *Capitalism and Progress,* 31, 201, 207.

58. A conscious "species-being" treats the species as one's own being (Marx, "Economic and Philosophical Manuscripts" 1.14, p. 128).

59. Marx, "Economic and Philosophical Manuscripts" 3.39.4, 8, 19, pp. 154, 165, 176.

60. Marx, "Bruno Bauer, *Die Judenfrage,*" 24, 26, 31.

61. Gould, 56.

62. Marx, "Economic and Philosophical Manuscripts" 3.39.4, p. 155.

63. Ibid. 3.39.6, p. 158. The human being ("man") is a unique individual and also "the subjective existence of society": The human being is where society comes to expression and where society becomes conscious and activated.

64. Ibid.

65. Gould, 35.

66. Marx, "Economic and Philosophical Manuscripts" 3.39.4, p. 154. A society is only free insofar as the individuals within it are free (Gould, 108).

67. Marx, "Critique of the Gotha Program" 1.1, p. 82.

68. Marx, *Capital* 1.1.4, pp. 78–79; cf. MacIntyre, *After Virtue,* 261.

69. Marx, *Eighteenth Brumaire of Louis Bonaparte* 1, p. 103.

70. Marx, "Theses on Feuerbach" 3, p. 4.

71. Cf. Maximilien Rubel, "Marx, Karl," *International Encyclopedia of the Social Sciences* (1968), 10:36.

72. Marx, *Capital,* preface to first German edition, p. 10; 1.10.5, p. 270; "Economic and Philosophical Manuscripts" 3.39.20, p. 178; *Grundrisse,* 1, p. 164.

73. Karl Marx, *A Contribution to the Critique of Political Economy* (1859), preface, in Marx and Engels, *Collected Works* 29.263–64.

74. Avineri correctly notes that it is Engels, not Marx, who used the term *withering away* [*Absterben*]. Marx's term, *abolition* [*Aufhebung*] includes the idea of transcending; the contents are preserved on the higher level (*Political and Social Thought of Marx,* 37, 202). In the context of Engels' one use of *Absterben* (*Anti-Duhring* 3.2, in Marx and Engels, *Collected Works,* 25.268), it is the milder term, indicating gradualness in contrast to the abruptness there of *Aufhebung*. Richard N. Hunt notes that the question is the impact of all the terms

used by Marx and Engels in conjunction with the disappearance of the state, which Hunt documents: "breaks to pieces, falls away of itself, ceases to exist, is *aufgehoben,* comes to an end; also: disappears, dissolves, falls asleep, and is surmounted" (*Classical Marxism,* 242).

75. Cf. the previous note.

76. Karl Marx, "First Draft of *The Civil War in France*" (1871), in Marx and Engels, *Collected Works* 22.486–87; cf. Hunt, 235. For both of these paragraphs: Hunt, 213–35.

77. Karl Marx, "Notes on Bakunin's Book *Statehood and Anarchy*" (1874–1875), in Marx and Engels, *Collected Works* 24.517 (Marx's emphasis), 519; cf. Hunt, 237.

78. Frederick Engels, "On Authority" (1874), in Marx and Engels, *Collected Works* 23.423–24; cf. Hunt, 247. Elsewhere he writes of "the future conversion of political rule over [persons] into an administration of things and a direction of processes of production" (*Socialism: Utopian and Scientific* 1 [1880], in Marx and Engels, *Collected Works* 24.292).

79. Marx, "Inaugural Address of the Working Men's International Association" (1864), in Marx and Engels, *Collected Works* 20.11–12; "Instructions for the Delegates of Provisional General Council: 5. Co-operative Labour" (1866), in *Collected Works* 20.190 (first quotation); *Capital* 3.27, p. 440; 3.23, p. 387; "Notes on Bakunin," in *Collected Works* 24.519 (second quotation); cf. 520; cf. Hunt, 248–52.

80. Marx, *Communist Manifesto,* 505; cf. Hunt 247.

81. Marx, *Civil War in France* 3, 332–33; cf. Avineri, 202. Correspondingly, in the *Critique of the Gotha Programme* (4a, p. 95) he implies continuing "social functions . . . similar to present state functions" (Hunt, 246–47).

82. Cf. Shlomo Avineri in "Are We Entering a Post-Marxist Age?" *Commonweal* 111 (1984), 527. Adam Smith stated that there is no need of civil government where there is no property or none that "exceeds two or three days labor" (*Wealth of Nations* 5.1b.2, p. 710). Jon P. Gunnemann suggests that Marx may be reflecting a position by Smith that market relations would gradually replace all traditional forms of morality and all traditional institutions, including family and political authority (review of *Politics and Markets,* by Charles E. Lindblom, *Religious Studies Review* 9 [1983], 212).

83. MacIntyre, *After Virtue,* x.

84. Cf. Levin, "Marxism and Romanticism," 400–13.

85. Paul Tillich, "Religious Socialism," in Tillich, *Political Expectation,* 43.

86. Marx and Engels, *Manifesto of the Communist Party* 3.3, p. 515; Marx, *Class Struggles in France* 3, p. 127.

87. Marx, "Critique of the Gotha Program" 1.3, p. 88.

88. *Manifesto of the Communist Party* 4, p. 519.

89. Niebuhr, *Moral Man and Immoral Society,* 163.

90. Marvin E. Olsen states that in these thoughts of Marx lie the beginnings of a general power theory of social organization ("Marx as a Power Theorist," in *Power in Societies,* ed. Olsen, 71, 74).

91. Marx, "Economic and Philosophical Manuscripts" 3.14, p. 168; 3.39, p. 154 (capitalism); 1.18, p. 115 (feudalism).

92. Heimann, *Reason and Faith in Modern Society,* 112.

93. Karl R. Popper, "Prediction and Prophecy in the Social Sciences," in *Theories of History,* ed. P. Gardiner (Glencoe, IL, Free, 1959), 284; cf. Gilkey, "Reinhold Niebuhr's Theology of History," 375–76. The leaders' interests are independent from those of the proletariat. To believe that power will be voluntarily given up after being used and that it will overcome itself by reason is a belief in miracles (Tillich, *Socialist Decision,* 76).

94. An example regarding democracy would be his confidence that the two "infallible means" of election and recall would achieve a healthy turnover in office (Hunt, *Classical*

Marxism, 262). In support of maximal legislative power he advocated a single representative assembly and the control of the executive by the legislature (Draper, *State and Bureaucracy,* 296, 300–303).

95. Gould, *Marx's Social Ontology,* 3, 34.

96. Gould, 34, 40.

97. Gould's interpretation is similar. Human self-realization is freedom. "Freedom has no ground as a value outside of itself and all other values are grounded on it" (119). The capacity of freedom by its very nature demands its realization through activity. Whatever serves this end as a condition of freedom has value (171). Husami cites as an example of the ideal of humanity as the basic measuring principle, Marx's critique of distribution according to one's labor as regarding individuals as workers and nothing more ("Critique of the Gotha Program" 1.3, p. 87; Husami, "Marx on Distributive Justice," 60).

98. Eric Voegelin, *From Enlightenment to Revolution,* ed. J. Hallowell (Durham, NC, Duke U., 1975), 301–2. The life of the spirit is devalued so that science and pragmatic acts are believed appropriate in dealing with the realm of substance in contrast to their reasonable limitation to the realm of phenomena. Cf. Ernest Becker, *The Structure of Evil* (New York, Free, 1968), 136.

99. Carmen Sirianni, *Workers' Control and Socialist Democracy* (London, Verso, 1982), 281, 296, 300–304. Sirianni argues that the confidence in science was such that the content of bourgeois culture was not contested. Rather it was to be appropriated and democratized.

100. Hunt, *Classical Marxism,* 261.

101. Niebuhr, *Children of Light,* 60.

102. Niebuhr, *Faith and History,* 212.

103. Míguez Bonino, *Christians and Marxists,* 109–10.

104. Marxism also shares with liberalism, specifically with laissez-faire thought, the view that economic and social life is and should be controlled by autonomous economic forces (Heimann, *Reason and Faith in Modern Society,* 278).

105. François Bloch-Lainé, "The Utility of Utopias for Reformers," in *Utopia and Utopian Thought,* ed. F. Manuel (Boston, Beacon, 1971), 211; cf. Popper, "Prediction and Prophecy in the Social Sciences," 284; Mannheim, *Ideology and Utopia,* 240, 247.

106. Paul Tillich, "Christianity and Marxism" (1960), in Tillich, *Political Expectation,* 94.

107. Tillich, 92; cf. Heimann, 157.

108. Alasdair MacIntyre, *Marxism and Christianity* (Notre Dame, IN, U. of Notre Dame, 1968²), 115.

109. Marx, "Bruno Bauer, *Die Judenfrage,*" 16–17 (his emphasis).

110. Cf. Paul Tillich, "Religious Socialism," in Tillich, *Political Expectation,* 48–49.

Chapter 13

1. John Cort, "Can Socialism be Distinguished from Marxism?" *Cross Currents* 29 (1980), 423–24.

2. Tillich, "Kingdom of God and History," 133; Reinhold Niebuhr, "Why A New Quarterly?" *Radical Religion* 1, 1 (Autumn, 1935), 3, 5.

3. Cf. Niebuhr, *Moral Man and Immoral Society,* 200–209.

4. Cf. Cort, 433–34.

5. Gregory Baum, review of *The Spirit of Democratic Capitalism,* by Michael Novak, *Religious Studies Review* 10 (1984), 109.

6. Michael Harrington, *Socialism* (New York, Saturday Review, 1972), 198–216. "One immediate result was to rescue some of the most inefficient capitalists . . . by socializing their losses" (202). Niebuhr noted that when enterprises are taken over piecemeal, there is a danger of a chaos, which compounds the vices of both systems, rather than developing a systematic and coherent scheme of social ownership (*Moral Man and Immoral Society,* 210).

7. Fromm, *Sane Society,* 247–48. In both the worker owns nothing (Wiles, *Economic Institutions Compared,* 39).

8. Wiles, 52.

9. Branko Horvat, *The Political Economy of Socialism: A Marxist Social Theory,* 21.

10. Heimann, *Reason and Faith in Modern Society,* 248–49. Peter L. Berger's influential critique of socialism in developing countries in *Pyramids of Sacrifice* (New York, Basic, 1975) is of a revolutionary form of statism of which the former Soviet Union was the leading example and dominating influence (cf. 80–81, 89–91). His alternatives of either public or private ownership (73) misses the socialists' third way of social ownership. An example of a reduction of socialism to state ownership, although within a thoroughly democratic context, is in Garcia, *Justice in Latin American Theology of Liberation,* 146–47. He perceptively critiques "syndicate control, cooperatives, and municipal ownerships" as not making the good of society as a whole their primary concern. The alternative, however, is not state ownership but cooperative forms culturally or legally normative and combined with social planning. An expression of this third way is Marx's distinction of social property from state and private property.

11. Goudzwaard, *Capitalism and Progress,* 217.

12. Walzer, *Radical Principles, Reflections of an Unreconstructed Democrat* (New York, Basic, 1980), 17, 274–75.

13. Horvat, 155, 232. The exceptions according to Horvat are the Chinese and Cuban revolutions. In addition he states that workers' management was not produced in some African and Asian military coups and movements of national liberation that claimed association with socialism.

14. Cornel West, *Prophesy Deliverance!* (Philadelphia, Westminster, 1982), 112, 122.

15. Walzer, "Town Meetings and Workers' Councils: A Story for Socialists" (1978), in Walzer, *Radical Principles,* 277, 279–84, 287.

16. Henry Ireton in "Putney Debates," in *Puritanism and Liberty,* ed. Woodhouse, 58, 60, 69.

17. Cf. Woodhouse, "Introduction," to *Puritanism and Liberty,* [69], [99].

18. Interview of Gerrard Winstanley and William Everard before Lord Fairfax, April 20, 1649, in Bulstrode Whitelocke, *Memorial of English Affairs,* 397, quoted in Lewis Henry Berens, *The Digger Movement in the Days of the Commonwealth as Revealed in the Writings of Gerrard Winstanley, the Digger, Mystic and Rationalist, Communist and Social Reformer* (London, Holland, 1961), 38.

19. In the Spanish Mondragon cooperatives, 85 percent of the profits are retained for reinvestment (Joyce Rothschild and J. Allen Whitt, *The Cooperative Workplace, Potentials and Dilemmas of Organizational Democracy and Participation* [Cambridge, Cambridge U., Arnold and Caroline Rose Monograph, 1986], 161).

20. Alec Nove, *The Economics of Feasible Socialism Revisited* (London, Harper Collins Academic, 1991²), xiv–xv, 211–20, 245–46.

21. Cf. Horvat, *Political Economy of Socialism,* 238–39.

22. Marx and Engels, *Manifesto of the Communist Party* 2, in *Collected Works* 6:497–98; Marx, *Civil War in France* 3, in *Collected Works,* 22.335. For cooperative property in "the conditions of production" distinguished from property as the "means of consumption," cf. Marx, "Critique of the Gotha Program" 1.3, in *Collected Works,* 24.87–88.

23. George D. Herron, *Between Caesar and Jesus* (New York, Crowell, 1899), 100. Herron, an American Congregational minister and college professor, was an early member of the Social Gospel movement.

24. Rauschenbusch, *Christianity and the Social Crisis,* 396.

25. Marx, *Civil War in France,* 337. On the objection, cf. Aristotle, *Pol.* 1263b11–14: Common property denies the virtue of liberality.

26. Albert T. Mollegan, "The Religious Basis of Western Socialism," in *Socialism and American Life,* ed. D. Egbert and S. Persons (Princeton, NJ, Princeton U., 1952), 1.107.

27. Norman Cohn, *The Pursuit of the Millennium* (New York, Oxford U., 1970²).

28. Bell, "Socialism," *International Encyclopedia of the Social Sciences* (1968), 14:507.

29. Baum, review of *The Spirit of Democratic Capitalism,* 109.

30. Cf. Arthur DiQuattro, "Alienation and Justice in the Market," *American Political Science Review* 72 (1978), 881.

31. Fromm, *Sane Society,* 247–48.

32. Ibid., 249–53; Heilbroner, *Worldly Philosophers,* 102, 108. In addition to those discussed by Fromm mention must be made of Henri Saint-Simon, in whom, Engels states, "almost all the ideas of later Socialists, that are not strictly economic, are found . . . in embryo" (*Socialism: Utopian and Scientific* 1, in Marx and Engels, *Collected Works* 24.292).

33. Horvat, 270–71

34. Rothschild and Whitt, *Cooperative Workplace,* 59.

35. Horvat, 266–69. Favorable factors not due to work include the rent from land or mines, interest, advantages for working in a favorable locale or in an industry with a more efficient technology.

36. Tillich, *Socialist Decision,* 135–36.

37. E.g., Horvat, *Political Economy of Socialism,* xiv; Gordon Fellman, "Socialism and Religion in Israel," *Religious Socialism* 10, 4 (Fall, 1986), 4.

38. Wiles, *Economic Institutions Compared,* 155.

39. Mollegan, "Religious Basis of Western Socialism," 118. Human nature is viewed in terms of a primitive and uncorrupted lack of artificiality or as the perfected actualization of capacities.

40. Cf. James Dombrowski, *The Early Days of Christian Socialism in America* (New York, Columbia U., 1936), 26, 104–5.

41. Mollegan, 120.

42. Dombroski, 26.

43. E.g., Ward, *Democracy and Social Change,* 113: Unless there democratic control of both economic and state power, "the invisible government of economic power will continue to encroach upon the democratic state."

44. E.g., A. T. Mollegan, "The Common Convictions of the Fellowship of Socialist Christians," *Christianity and Society* 8, 2 (1943), 22; Niebuhr, "Why A New Quarterly?" 5. The most well known of this particular circle of Christian socialist realists were Reinhold Niebuhr, Eduard Heimann, and Paul Tillich. They brought together both European and American traditions of religious socialism.

45. Horvat, *Political Economy of Socialism,* 207, 239.

46. Heimann, *Reason and Faith in Modern Society,* 245.

47. Bell, "Socialism," 524.

48. Cf. Heimann, 266–67.

49. See pp. 171–72. Cf. also Ivan Szelenyi, "Recent Contributions to the Political Economy of State Socialism," *Contemporary Sociology* 14 (1985), 284, who notes agreement among several current authors on state socialism that centralized planning has an irreducible problem of shortages due to underproduction and overinvestment.

50. DiQuattro, "Alienation and Justice in the Market," 886. Central planning also means that individuals must subsidize benefits desired by others that they themselves do not want (880). DiQuattro argues that the alienation and great inequalities of capitalist society are due to the class structure and not the market (871–87).

51. Horvat, *Political Economy of Socialism,* 208–9.

52. Cf. Wogaman, *Great Economic Debate,* 18.

53. Severyn T. Bruyn, *The Social Economy, People Transforming Modern Business* (New York, Wiley-Interscience, 1977), 371–79.

54. Cf. Horvat, *Political Economy of Socialism,* 239–50.

55. Ibid., 163.

56. Uri Leviatan, "Organizational Effects of Managerial Production Branches," in *Work and Organization in Kibbutz Industry,* ed. Leviatan and M. Rosner (Norwood, Pa, Norwood, Kibbutz, Communal Society, and Alternative Social Policy 3, 1980), 140; Dov Eden, "Assessment," in *Quality of Worker Life and the Kibbutz Experience,* ed. A. Cherns (Norwood, Pa, Norwood, Kibbutz, Communal Society, and Alternative Social Policy 2, 1978), 272; Melford E. Spiro, *Kibbutz: Venture in Utopia. Studies in the Libertarian and Utopian Tradition* (New York, Schocken, 1970³), 77.

57. Herbert Marcuse, *One Dimensional Man. Studies in the Ideology of Advanced Industrial Society* (Boston, Beacon, 1964), 44; cf. R. H. Tawney, *The Acquisitive Society* (London, Bell, 1922), 206.

58. Horvat, 189–90, 241.

59. "Is Good Politics Bad Business? An Update on Worker Ownership," *Dollars & Sense* (September, 1986), 14.

60. Horvat, 244, 247.

61. Ibid., 241, 251.

62. Ibid., 244.

63. Rothschild and Whitt, *Cooperative Workplace,* 99.

64. Louis Putterman, "Some Behavioral Perspectives on the Dominance of Hierarchical over Democratic Forms of Enterprise," *Journal of Economic Behavior and Organization* 3 (1982), 145–46, 151, 157–58; cf. Oliver E. Williamson, *The Economic Institutions of Capitalism, Firms, Markets, Relational Contracting* (New York, Free, 1985), 268. Putterman is studying worker-controlled, not worker-owned, enterprises. Moreover, a worker-run system needs more managerial talent than the capitalistic alternative. The necessary solution may be making democratic worker control normative through legislation to the degree that it is not established as a social norm (Putterman, 140, 151, 158). Rothschild and Whitt state, "It is among those who perceive that they are making the greatest sacrifice by remaining in the co-op that attrition is highest" (99).

65. N. Scott Arnold, "Marx and Disequilibrium in Market Socialist Relations of Production," *Economics and Philosophy* 3 (1987), 23–48; cf. his responses, 320–30, 335–38.

66. David Schweickart, "Market Socialist Capitalist Roaders. A Comment on Arnold," *Economics and Philosophy* 3 (1987), 308–19; cf. his response, 331–34; DiQuattro, "Alienation and Justice in the Market," 879.

67. DiQuattro, 879.

68. Horvat, *Political Economy of Socialism,* 256–59.

69. Rothschild and Whitt, *Cooperative Workplace,* 156–57.

70. Horvat, 261.

71. Heimann, *Reason and Faith in Modern Society,* 270–71.

72. Horvat, 230, 355, 360.

73. Ibid., 293

74. Gowan et al., *Moving Toward a New Society,* 176; Horvat, 242.

75. Hoover, "Capitalism," 300.

76. Horvat, 173.

77. "What is the Purpose of Farm Cooperatives?" *Center for Rural Affairs Newsletter* (April, 1987), 3–4. The guiding Rochdale principles provide for one person, one vote to give the small farmer the same influence as the larger farmer. This article suggests expanded services of market planning and risk control, as well as including nonmanagement employees in membership.

78. Henry Hansmann, "A General Theory of Corporate Ownership" (Cambridge, MA, Harvard University Law School, Program in Law and Economics, Discussion Paper 33, 1987), 31–33, 54. For example, 50 percent of hardware wholesalers are retailer owned (e.g., True Value and Ace).

79. Cf. *Social Report* 1, 2, p. 7. Cf. Paul Johnson' support of worker co-ownership through purchase of stock as making ordinary people secure actors in the system and diminishing class divisions. It is an alternative to public ownership. For him, it does not mean worker control, however ("Capitalism & Morality Debate," *First Things* [March, 1990], 20).

80. Griffiths, *Creation of Wealth,* 32.

81. Walzer, *Radical Principles,* 16.

82. Wiles, *Economic Institutions Compared,* 482.

83. Cf. p. 175. In Latin America, where most businesses are family-owned, employee share-holding is rare.

84. Hansmann, "General Theory of Corporate Ownership," 6. He feels that *lender* expresses more accurately than *investor* the true nature of the relationship of the owners. The advantage of this standard form of corporation is that each shareholder's stake is only a fraction of his or her wealth. Another common associational phenomenon within capitalism and mixed economies is insurance, which is a collective good, the production of which is made possible by the pooling of risk among a group of policyholders (Michael Hechter, review of *Reactive Risk and Rational Action,* by Carol A. Heimer, *Contemporary Sociology* 15 [1986], 586).

85. Robert Jackall and Joyce Crain, "The Shape of the Small Worker Cooperative Movement," in *Worker Cooperatives in America,* ed. Jackall and H. Levin (Berkeley, CA, U. of California, 1984), 88; cf. Rothschild and Whitt, *Cooperative Workplace,* 11. The number of producer cooperatives were estimated to be 750–1,000 in 1980. This was considered to be a great increase from 1970 when few existed (Jackall and Crain, ibid.).

86. John Simmons, "ESOP on the Move," *Workplace Democracy* [Summer, 1989], 6. In 1989 there were over 10,000 ESOPs. ESOPs, however, leave workers without a direct say in basic decisions that normally go with ownership, those which deal with hiring, firing, wages, long-term planning, and workplace rules. Their only right of ownership is to vote in the election of the company's board of directions, but that often leaves the worker representation in a minority position, even when workers own a majority of stock, an example of worker ownership without worker control ("The ESOP Fable: Employee Stock Ownership Falls Short," *Dollars & Sense* [July/August, 1983], 13; "Is Good Politics Bad Business?" 12). Rath Packing Company is cited as such a company in which as a result workers' pensions were eliminated after they had already accepted wage cuts and deferrals to finance the reorganization of the company. In only about 10–15 percent of the ESOPs do workers have or will have control of a majority of the voting stock (Corey M. Rosen et al., *Employee Ownership In America. The Equity Solution* [Lexington, MA, Lexington, 1986], 1; cf. cf. Rothschild and Whitt, *Cooperative Workplace,* 175). Higher-paid and managerial workers usually own most of the ESOPs stock since the amount of stock is based on salary level and seniority. An area in which worker ownership without control is extreme is union pensions, in which most unions lack *any* control or input into the investment of their pension fund capital (Vince Valvano,

"Investing Labor's Capital: An Update on Union Penson Fund Strategies," *Dollars & Sense* [September, 1987], 10). Fromm describes the principle as "'sharing of profits,' not 'sharing of work'" (*Sane Society,* 246).

87. About 15 percent of American companies have profit sharing. About 10 percent have subsidized employee sharing. Stephen C. Smith, "On the Incidence of Profit and Equity Sharing. Theory and an Application to the High Tech Sector," *Journal of Economic Behavior and Organization* 8 (1987), 2.

88. Gary J. Dorrien, *The Democratic Socialist Vision* (Totowa, NJ, Rowman, 1986), 147–49.

89. Horvat, *Political Economy of Socialism,* 450.

90. Ibid., 167. By 1977 nine nations had such laws: West Germany, Sweden, Norway, Denmark, Austria, the Netherlands, France, Luxemburg, Spain.

91. Coal, iron, and steel companies employing over 1,000 persons must provide workers with equal representation with shareholders on the supervisory board. In all joint stock companies with more than 2,000 employees, workers elect one-third of the members of the supervisory board. Companies with 100 or more employees also must have economic committees, to which each side appoints half of the members, to promote cooperation between the work councils and the employers (Horvat, 160).

92. David Moberg, "Beyond the Images of Nuts and Dilettantes," *In These Times* (December 17–23, 1980), 2.

93. More than one of every five Americans receive their electricity from one of 2,194 public power systems. Nine hundred of these are consumer owned cooperatives, serving 9 percent of the populace (Richard Morgan et al., *Taking Charge: A New Look at Public Power* [Washington, D. C., Environmental Action Foundation, 1976], 9–10, 15; Richard Rudolph and Ridley Scott, *Power Struggle: The Hundred-Year War over Electricity* [New York, Harper, 1986], 13). Municipal systems on average provide electricity at rates 30 percent less than those charged by private utilities. The rates charged by consumer-owned utilities are 10 percent lower. The savings for residential users were even higher (37 percent and 21 percent, respectively). Forty-two percent of the savings offered by municipals were due to their lack of profit margins (Morgan et al., 15, 17–18; Rudolph and Scott, 248). At the same time, cooperatively owned, and especially municipally owned, electric utilities have been shown to be less profitable than privately owned ones, at least among those using coal, gas, and internal combustion fuels (Daniel R. Hollas and Stanley R. Stansell, "An Examination of the Effect of Ownership Form on Price Efficiency: Proprietary, Cooperative and Municipal Utilities," *Southern Economic Journal* 55 [1988], 336–50). (Morgan et al. had argued that in 1973 municipal utilities spent 7 percent less than private on operation, maintenance, and production expenses [17]). Hollas and Stansell's exclusion of nuclear and hydro generation from their study is significant (343).

94. Cf. Paul M. Minus, *Walter Rauschenbusch. American Reformer* (New York, Macmillan, 1988), 66–68, 72.

95. Aristotle, *Pol.* 1261b33–37.

96. Alinsky, *Reveille for Radicals,* 40.

97. Paul Blumberg, *Industrial Democracy. The Sociology of Participation* (New York, Schocken, 1969), 123, 130–31.

98. Samuel Bowles, *Workplace Democracy* 10, 3 (Summer, 1983), 12. Horvat cites studies showing less supervision in worker managed firms than in traditional firms (*Political Economy of Socialism,* 207, 581, n.73).

99. In a firm of 4,000 workers, there may be eleven layers of authority (Horvat, *Political Economy of Socialism,* 193, citing a study of the Lockheed Missiles and Space Company in the 1960s).

100. Smith, "Incidence of Profit and Equity Sharing," 4–5.

101. For example, Horvat (173, 571, n.90) cites a study by J. Cable and J. Fitzroy of forty-two German enterprises classified into high-participatory and low-participatory firms. The former outperformed the latter by 5 percent in terms of output per person, 177 percent in output per unit of capital, and 33 percent in rate of return on capital ("Cooperation and Productivity: Some Evidence from West German Experience," mimeographed).

102. Rothschild and Whitt, *Cooperative Workplace*, 26.

103. Williamson cites several studies from 1958 to 1976 that show little or no association between job satisfaction and productivity (Williamson, *Economic Institutions of Capitalism,* 270).

104. "A systematic study that controls for firm size, industry, and internal structure is needed before we can draw firm conclusions about the economic performance of co-ops" (Rothschild and Whitt, 167).

105. Corey Rosen, "Conference Set On Unions and Employee Ownership," *Social Report* 2, 2 (December, 1981), 8.

106. Rothschild and Whitt, 166.

107. Ibid., 161.

108. The correlation between democratic decision-making procedures and economic vitality is also demonstrated in Derek C. Jones, "Producer Co-Operatives in Industrialised Western Economies," *British Journal of Industrial Relations* 18 (1980), 143–47, 151; Rothschild and Whitt, 167, also cite personal communications from Ann Olivarius of Oxford University on her survey of 400 producer cooperatives. A 1986 study by the General Accounting Office showed that ESOPs that have employees involved in decision-making have 52 percent higher productivity than do companies without participative management (Simmons, "ESOP on the Move," 6).

109. Rothschild and Whitt, *Cooperative Workplace,* 178.

110. Dorrien, *Democratic Socialist Vision,* 165. Since its beginning, sixty-one additional cooperatives have been added. No enterprise has been closed or jobs lost. Increasingly sophisticed technology has been added (Jones, "Producer Co-Operatives in Industrialised Western Economies," 143).

111. Menachem Rosner and A. S. Tannenbaum, "Organizational Efficiency and Egalitarian Democracy in an Intentional Community Society: The Kibbutz," *British Journal of Sociology* 38 (1987), 523; Amos Epshtein, *lgud hatassiyah hakibbutzit 1987* (Tel Aviv, igud hatassiyah hakibbutzit), 9, 18; cf. S. C. Mott, "The Kibbutz's Adjustment to Industrialization and Ideological Decline: Alternatives for Economic Organization," *Journal of Religious Ethics* 19 (1991), 158–60.

112. Diane Barthel, "The American Commune and the American Mythology," *Qualitative Sociology* 12 (1989), 241–60.

113. Mott, "Kibbutz's Adjustment to Industrialization and Ideological Decline," 153–58.

114. Rothschild and Whitt, *Cooperative Workplace,* 121.

115. Horvat, *Political Economy of Socialism,* 164–65, 203, 205. In 1965 there was a revival of the laissez-faire approach with the dismantling of government investment funds and specialized federal banks. The rate of growth fell below zero and unemployment increased rapidly. In 1971 the laissez-faire market was replaced with parastate arrangements for social compacts. The rate of growth remained substantially below the former achievement, even when making allowance for world inflation and recession after 1972. Despite these trials and errors, there still was relatively high economic prosperity (206–7).

116. Harrington, *Socialism,* 241, 308, 351.

117. Cited by Michael Walzer, "A Day in the Life of a Socialist Citizen" (1968), in Walzer, *Radical Principles,* 129.

118. Horvat, 252.
119. Charles R. Walker and Robert H. Guest, *The Man on the Assembly Line* (Cambridge, Harvard U., 1952), 32–37, 81–91. This study is limited by its date and by the fact those studied were only those who had left the previous jobs, not those who chose to stay. In addition, 50 of 180 workers had left their previous job because it was terminated or about to be. The study is cited, however, by Amitai Etzioni, *A Comparative Analysis of Complex Organizations* (New York, Free, 1975²), 34–35, and Williamson, *Economic Institutions of Capitalism* (1985), 269.
120. Blumberg, *Industrial Democracy,* 133.
121. Horvat, 261.
122. Walzer, *Radical Principles,* 10, 12.
123. Booth, "Election and Democracy in Central America," 21.
124. Walzer, 10, 12.
125. Dale Vree, "Religious Socialism," *Religious Socialism* 9, 2 (Spring, 1985), 8.
126. Rothschild and Whitt, *Cooperative Workplace,* 121.
127. Bell, "Socialism," 531.

Epilogue

1. Karl Otto Hondrich, "Politische Herrschaft und wirtschaftliche Entwicklung. Macht und Herrschaft als Kategorien der Entwicklungssoziolgie," *Kölner Zeitschrift für Soziologie und Sozialpsychologie* Suppl. 13 (1969), 371–84. He cites fascist Germany and Japan as examples.
2. Ralph H. Bowen, review of *The Scientific Origins of National Socialism,* by Daniel Gasman, *American Historical Review* 78 (1973), 712.
3. Karl Dietrich Bracher, *The German Dictatorship: The Origins, Structure, and Effects of National Socialism* (New York, Praeger, 1970), 490–91.
4. Helmut Krausnick and Hans-Heinrich Wilhelm, *Die Truppe des Weltanschauungskrieges: Die Einsatzgruppen der Sicherheitspolizei und des SD 1938–1942* (Stuttgart, Deutsche, Quellen und Darstellungen zur Zeitgeschichte 22, 1981), 281–84, 644.
5. Cf. Robert Jay Lifton, *The Nazi Doctors, Medical Killing and the Psychology of Genocide* (New York, Basic, 1986). A National Socialist doctor was asked how he could reconcile his actions with his Hippocratic oath. He stated that to preserve and to respect human life, "I would remove a gangrenous appendix from a diseased body. The Jew is the gangrenous appendix in the body of mankind" (16).
6. William Ebenstein, "National Socialism," *International Encyclopedia of the Social Sciences* (1968), 11:48. Identifying the rise of National Socialism in Germany with the severity of the economic depression is insufficient to explain why it arose in this nation and not elsewhere.
7. Ibid. The liberal and humanistic tradition that we tend to associate with German thought—that of Lessing, Kant, Humboldt—and Goethe, was never dominant. It was more influential in the academy than in the court of the decision makers. New political orientations influenced by this tradition in 1848 and 1918 were squelched (49).
8. Ibid., 49.
9. Bracher, *The German Dictatorship,* 10. Jean Steinberg, Bracher's translator, notes that *völkisch* does not have an equivalent in English. It includes ethnocentric, racial, and national elements (10, note).
10. Ibid., 29–31.

11. Ebenstein, "National Socialism," 48.

12. Ernst Wolf, "Political and Moral Motives behind the Resistance," in *The German Resistance to Hitler,* ed. H. Graml et al. (Berkeley, CA, U. of California, 1970), 204. The Christian theologian Paul Althaus, who later endorsed the National Socialist regime, stated in 1919 in criticism of individualism, "Man's greatest possession is his nation."

13. Ebenstein, 48.

14. Roderick Stackelberg, *Idealism Debased: From völkisch Ideology to National Socialism* (Kent, OH, Kent State U., 1981), 4. The novelist, Friedrich Lienhard, traced class antagonism, not to economic exploitation, but to the loss of love and sympathy between people. His prescription was a hierarchical society in which an elite would be freed to pursue self-fulfillment through the deference accorded to them by the masses (80, 92).

15. Bracher, *German Dictatorship,* 11.

16. Stackelberg, *Idealism Debased,* 5.

17. Bracher, 10, 23, 35–36.

18. Ebenstein, "National Socialism," 49.

19. Geoffrey G. Field, *Evangelist of Race: The Germanic Vision of Houston Stewart Chamberlain* (NY, Columbia U., 1981), 5, 226; Stackelberg, *Idealism Debased,* 106. "No single publication was more instrumental in legitimating racial anti-Semitism among educated people" (Stackelberg, 11). Selling a quarter of a million copies by 1938, it became a classic of the literature of National Socialism, of which he became an adherent before his death in 1927 (114). Chamberlain reported that every morning before he immersed himself in writing this book, he knelt and prayed for God's guidance (Field, 173).

20. Heimann, *Communism, Fascism, or Democracy?* 238.

21. Ebenstein, 49.

22. Bracher, *German Dictatorship,* 47.

23. Hans Barth, *Truth and Ideology* (Berkeley, CA, U. of California, 1976^2 [1961; 1st ed., 1945]), 194.

24. Bracher, 10.

25. Heimann, 237–38.

26. Hilmar Linnenkamp, "Die sozialen Voraussetzungen des italienischen Faschismus," *Schmollers Jahrbuch* 88 (1968), 574, 589–91.

27. Bracher, 13–16, 47 (quotation from p. 15).

28. Heimann, 181–82; Barrington Moore, Jr., *Social Origins of Dictatorship and Democracy. Lord and Peasant in the Making of the Modern World* (Boston, Beacon, 1966), 450.

29. Richard F. Hamilton, *Who Voted for Hitler?* (Princeton, Princeton U., 1982), 422–23, 432.

30. Mario Einaudi, "Fascism," *International Encyclopedia of the Social Sciences* (1968), 5:335.

31. Bracher, *German Dictatorship,* 145.

32. Einaudi, 334, 336.

33. Bracher, 10, 145.

34. Bell, "Socialism," 523.

35. Heimann, *Communism, Fascism, or Democracy?* 190, 242.

36. Einaudi, "Fascism," 335.

37. Cf. Heimann, *Communism, Fascism, or Democracy?* 243.

38. Einaudi, "Fascism," 337.

39. Bracher, *German Dictatorship,* 10.

40. Description by José Comblin, cited in Frank Maurovich, "The Hot War for Minds in South America," *Boston Globe,* January 30, 1977, A3.

41. Bracher, 18 (quotation); Stackelberg, *Idealism Debased,* 6.

42. Bracher, 47.

43. Einaudi, 336–37.

44. Bracher, 138, 341, 351

45. Einaudi, 337.

46. Bracher, 231.

47. Richard C. Lukas, *The Forgotten Holocaust: The Poles under German Occupation 1939–1944* (Lexington, KY, University of Kentucky, 1986), 232, n. 174. This was 22 percent of Poland's population. Of the deaths, 89.9 percent were victims of prisons, death camps, raids, executions, annihilation of ghettoes, epidemics, starvation, excessive work, and ill treatment (39).

48. B. A. Sijes et al., *Vervolging van Zigeuners in Nederland, 1940–1945,* cited in a review by Werner E. Braatz, *American Historical Review* 85 (1980), 650.

49. Steven E. Aschheim, review of *The Holocaust and the German Elite,* by Rainer C. Baum, *American Historical Review* 87 (1982), 1124.

50. Three corporate actions should be mentioned. A memorandum submitted to the government by the Second Provisional Administration of the Confessing Church in 1936 criticized racist anti-Semitism. Later in 1936, a proclamation of the Reich Council of Brethren restated against "every authority in the German nation" the charges of the memorandum. Finally, a statement of the Twelfth Prussian Confessional Synod in 1943 condemned "the annihilation of people merely . . . because they belong to another race" (Wolf, "Political and Moral Motives behind the Resistance," 215–17).

51. Hamilton, *Who Voted for Hitler?* 422, 420.

52. Bracher, *German Dictatorship,* 387.

53. Michael R. Marrus and Robert O. Paxton, *Vichy France and the Jews* (New York, Basic, 1981), 201.

54. Ethel Mary Tinnemann, "Attitudes of the German Catholic Hierarchy toward the Nazi Regime: A Study in German Psychopolitical Culture," *Western Political Quarterly* 22 (1969), 334–35, 337, 346–48. The protests were confined to individual measures. When they spoke against the claims of race or blood superiority, they never specifically mentioned the Jews or condemned anti-Semitism. They knew of the deportations by 1942.

55. November 22, 1942 entry, cited by Donald M. McKale, *Curt Prüfer: German Diplomat from the Kaiser to Hitler* (Kent, OH, Kent State U., 1987), 175. Prüfer's only concern appears to be the hatred against the German people that would result.

56. Marrus and Paxton, *Vichy France and the Jews,* 199.

57. Richard V. Pierard, "The Lutheran Two-Kingdom Doctrine and Subservience to the State in Modern Germany," *Journal of the Evangelical Theological Society* 29 (1986), 195–203; cf. Wolf, "Political and Moral Motives behind the Resistance," 208–9, 212–13.

58. Albert Speer, *Inside the Third Reich* (New York, Macmillan, 1970), 134–35; cf. 38–39.

59. William Harlan Hale, "Der Fuehrer Dead Center," *Saturday Review* (August 29, 1970), 21.

60. Tocqueville, *Democracy in America,* 2.2.14, p. 541.

61. Pierard, 201.

62. Bracher, *German Dictatorship,* 381.

63. Ibid., 381; Wolf, "Political and Moral Motives behind the Resistance," 212–13, 219.

64. Wolf, 202.

65. Bracher, 389. Nearly all the military conspirators were religious people (Wolf, 227).

66. Bracher, 494.

BIBLIOGRAPHY

Acton, Lord John E. Letter to Mandell Creighton, April 5, 1887. Acton, *Essays on Freedom and Power*, ed. Gertrude Himmelfarb. Gloucester, MA, Peter Smith, 1948.

Adair, John. *Founding Fathers. The Puritans in England and America*. Grand Rapids, MI, Baker, 1982.

Adams, Charles Francis. John Adams, *Works, Vol. 1: A Life of the Author*. Boston, Little, Brown, 1856.

Adams, James Luther. "Art, Psyche, and Society." Adams, *On Being Human Religiously*, ed. Max L. Stackhouse. Boston, Beacon, 1976, 139–50.

Adams, James Luther. "Blessed are the Powerful." *Christian Century* 86 (June 18, 1969), 838–41.

Adams, James Luther. "The Enduring Validity of Congregational Polity" (1978). Adams, *The Prophethood of All Believers*, ed. G. Beach. Boston, Beacon, 1986, 127–35.

Adams, James Luther. "Freedom and Association." Adams, *On Being Human Religiously*, 57–88.

Adams, James Luther. "God and Economics" [1978]. Adams, *Voluntary Associations. Socio-cultural Analyses and Theological Interpretation*, ed. J. R. Engel (Chicago, Exploration, 1986, 389–404.

Adams, James Luther. "Indispensable Discipline of Social Responsibility: Voluntary Associations" (1966). Adams, *Prophethood of All Believers*, 255–63.

Adams, James Luther. "The Lure of Persuasion: Some Themes from Whitehead" (1975/76). Adams, *Prophethood of All Believers*, 186–205.

Adams, James Luther. "Mediating Structures and the Separation of Powers." *Democracy and Mediating Structures*, ed. Michael Novak. Washington, American Enterprise Institute, AEI Symposia 80A, 1980, 1–28.

Adams, James Luther. "Religion and the Ideologies." *Confluence* 4 (1955), 72–84.

Adams, James Luther. "Theological Bases of Social Action." Adams, *Taking Time Seriously*. Glencoe, IL, Free, 1957, 42–58.

Alinsky, Saul D. *Reveille for Radicals*. New York, Vintage, 1969 (1946).

Allen, Irving Lewis. "A Retrospective Note on Urban 'Neighborhood School' Ideology." *Urban Education* 12 (1977), 205–12.

Alt, Albrecht. "Micha 2,1–5 Gēs Anadasmos in Juda." Alt, *Kleine Schriften zur Geschichte des Volkes Israel*, Vol. 3. Munich, Beck, 1959, 373–81.

Althusius, Johannes. *The Politics of Johannes Althusius*, 3rd ed. (1614), ed. Frederick S. Carney. Boston, Beacon, Beacon Series in the Sociology of Politics and Religion, ed. J. L. Adams, 1964.

Alves, Rubem A. *A Theology of Human Hope*. Washington, D.C., Corpus, 1969.

Antonovsky, Aaron. *Health, Stress, and Coping*. San Francisco, Jossey-Bass, 1979.

Appleby, Joyce. "Ideology and Theory: The Tension between Political and Economic Liberalism in Seventeenth-Century England." *American Historical Review* 81 (1976), 499–515.

Aquinas, Thomas. "On Princely Government." Aquinas, *Selected Political Writings*, ed. A. D'Entrèves. Oxford, Blackwell, Blackwell's Political Texts, 1959.

Aquinas, Thomas. *Selected Political Writings,* ed. A. D'Entrèves. Oxford, Blackwell, Blackwell's Political Texts, 1959.

Aquinas, Thomas. *Summa Theologiae,* ed. T. Gilby. New York, McGraw-Hill, 1975.

Arblaster, Anthony. *The Rise and Decline of Western Liberalism.* Oxford, Blackwell, 1985.

Arendt, Hannah. *On Revolution.* New York, Viking, 1965.

Arieli, Yehoshua. *Individualism and Nationalism in American Ideology.* Cambridge, Harvard U., 1964.

Arnold, N. Scott. "Marx and Disequilibrium in Market Socialist Relations of Production," *Economics and Philosophy* 3 (1987), 23–48.

Aschheim, Steven E. Review of *The Holocaust and the German Elite,* by Rainer C. Baum. *American Historical Review* 87 (1982), 1124.

Augustine. *The City of God,* trans. M. Dods. New York, Modern Library, 1950.

Augustine. *De civitate Dei. Opera* 14, 2, Corpus Christianorum, Series Latina 48, 1955.

Augustine. *Confessions of St. Augustine.* New York, Collier, 1961.

Augustine. *De Musica.* Augustine, *Opera Omnia,* ed. Migne. Paris, Montrouge, 1841, 1.1081–1191.

Augustine. Letter 153, "To Macedonius" (414). Augustine, *Letters,* Vol. 3, trans. W. Parsons. New York, Fathers of the Church, 1953, 281–303.

Augustine. Letter 155, "To Macedonius." *The Political Writings of St. Augustine,* ed. H. Paolucci. Chicago, Gateway, 1962, 266–76.

Augustine. *On the Merits and Forgiveness of Sins, and the Baptism of Infants.* Augustine, *Works, Vol. 4: Anti-Pelagian Works 1,* ed. P. Holmes. Edinburgh, Clark, 1872, 3–154.

Augustine. *The Political Writings of St. Augustine,* ed. H. Paolucci. Chicago, Gateway, 1962.

Avineri, Shlomo. "Are We Entering a Post-Marxist Age?" *Commonweal* 111 (1984), 526–27.

Avineri, Shlomo. *Political and Social Thought of Marx.* London, Cambridge U., 1969.

Bainton, Roland H. "The Appeal to Reason and the American Constitution" (1938). Bainton, *Collected Papers in Church History, Vol. 3: Christian Unity and Religion in New England.* Boston, Beacon, 1964.

Baltzell, E. Digby. *Puritan Boston and Quaker Philadelphia.* New York, Free, 1979.

Banton, Michael. *Racial and Ethnic Competition.* Cambridge, Cambridge U., Comparative Ethnic and Race Relations Series, 1983.

Barth, Hans. *Truth and Ideology.* Berkeley, CA, U. of California, 1976² (1961; 1st ed.: 1945).

Barthel, Diane. "The American Commune and the American Mythology." *Qualitative Sociology* 12 (1989), 241–60.

Bartley, Numan V. Review of *In Search of the Silent South,* by Morton Sosna. *American Historical Review* 83 (1978), 840.

Bastomsky, S. J. "Rich and Poor: The Great Divide in Ancient Rome and Victorian England." *Greece & Rome* 37 (1990), 37–43.

Baum, Gregory. Review of *The Spirit of Democratic Capitalism,* by Michael Novak. *Religious Studies Review* 10 (1984), 107–12.

Becker, Ernest. *The Structure of Evil.* New York, Free, 1968.

Beiner, Ronald. "The Classical Method of Political Science, and its Relation to the Study of Contemporary Politics." *Government and Opposition* 19 (1984), 471–85.

Belcher, C. Francis. *Logging Railroads of the White Mountains.* Boston, Appalachian Mountain Club, 1980.

Bell, Daniel. *The Cultural Contradictions of Capitalism.* New York, Basic, 1976.

Bell, Daniel. "On Meritocracy and Equality." *Public Interest* 29 (Fall, 1972), 63–68.

Bell, Daniel. "Socialism." *International Encyclopedia of the Social Sciences* (1968), 14:506–34.

Bellah, Robert N. "Religion and Polity in America." *Andover Newton Quarterly* 15 (1974), 107–23.

Bellah, Robert N., Richard Madsen, William M. Sullivan, Ann Swidler, and Steven M. Tipton. *Habits of the Heart, Individualism and Commitment in American Life.* New York, Perennial Library, 1985.

Benne, Robert. *The Ethic of Democratic Capitalism. A Moral Reassessment.* Philadelphia, Fortress, 1981.

Bennett, John C. *Christian Ethics and Social Policy.* New York, Scribner's, 1956.

Bennett, John C. *Christians and the State.* New York, Scribner's, 1958.

Bentham, Jeremy. *Handbook of Political Fallacies,* ed. H. Larrabee. Baltimore, Johns Hopkins, 1952).

Berdyaev, Nicholas. *The Destiny of Man.* New York, Harper, 1960.

Berens, Lewis Henry. *The Digger Movement in the Days of the Commonwealth as Revealed in the Writings of Gerrard Winstanley, the Digger, Mystic and Rationalist, Communist and Social Reformer.* London, Holland, 1961.

Berger, Peter L. *Capitalist Revolution: Fifty Propositions about Prosperity, Equality, and Liberty.* New York, Basic, 1986.

Berger, Peter L. *Pyramids of Sacrifice.* New York, Basic, 1975.

Bergstrom, Charles V. "When the Self-Righteous Rule, Watch Out!" *FOCUS on Governmental Affairs* 13, 12 (December, 1979), 3.

Berman, Harold J. *The Interdependence of Law and Religion.* Nashville, Abingdon, 1974.

Bernstein, Richard J. *The Restructuring of Social and Political Theory.* Philadelphia, U. of Pennsylvania, 1978.

Béteille, André. "Ideologies: Commitment and Partisanship." *L'Homme* 18, 3/4 (July/December, 1978), 47–67.

Beyerhaus, Gisbert. *Studien zur Staatsanschauung Calvins.* Berlin, Trowitzsch, Neue Studien zur Geschichte der Theologie und der Kirche 7, 1910.

Bierstedt, Robert. "An Analysis of Social Power." *American Sociological Review* 15 (1950), 730–78.

Bird, Otto. *The Idea of Justice.* New York, Praeger, 1967.

Bloch-Lainé, François. "The Utility of Utopias for Reformers." *Utopia and Utopian Thought,* ed. F. Manuel. Boston, Beacon, 1971, 201–18.

Blumberg, Paul. *Industrial Democracy. The Sociology of Participation.* New York, Schocken, 1969.

Blumrosen, Alfred W. "Quotas, Common Sense, and Law in Labor Relations: Three Dimensions of Equal Opportunity." *Rutgers University Law Review* 27 (1974), 675–703.

Boesak, Allan Aubrey. *Farewell to Innocence. A Socio-Ethical Study on Black Theology and Black Power.* Maryknoll, NY, Orbis, 1977.

Bolland, O. Nigel. "Labour Control and Resistance in Belize in the Century after 1838." *Slavery and Abolition* 7 (1986), 175–87.

Bolt, Christine. *Victorian Attitudes to Race.* Toronto, U. of Toronto, Studies in Social History, 1971.

Bonald, Louis de. *Économie sociale. Oeuvres complètes.* Paris, Migne, 1859. Vol. 1.

Boobyer, G. H. "New Testament Perfectionism and Christian Citizenship." *Hibbert Journal* 51 (1952/53), 143–48.

Booth, John A. "Elections and Democracy in Central America. A Framework for Analysis." *Elections and Democracy in Central America,* ed. Booth and M. Seligson. Chapel Hill, NC, U. of North Carolina, 1989, 7–39.

Booth, William. *In Darkest England and the Way Out.* London, International Headquarters of the Salvation Army, 1890.

Bourdieu, Pierre. *Distinction: A Social Critique of the Judgement of Taste.* Cambridge, MA, Harvard U., 1984.

Bowen, Ralph H. Review of *The Scientific Origins of National Socialism,* by Daniel Gasman. *American Historical Review* 78 (1973), 712.

Braatz, Werner E. Review of *Vervolging van Zigeuners in Nederland, 1940–1945,* by B. A. Sijes et al. *American Historical Review* 85 (1980), 650.

Bracher, Karl Dietrich. *The German Dictatorship: The Origins, Structure, and Effects of National Socialism.* New York, Praeger, 1970.

Brink, André. *Rumors of Rain.* Harmondsworth, Middlesex, Penguin, 1978.

Browning, Robert. "Why I am a Liberal" (from "Ferishtah's Fancies"). *Poems and Plays of Robert Browning.* New York, Modern Library, 1934, 1138.

Bruyn, Severyn T. *The Social Economy, People Transforming Modern Business.* New York, Wiley-Interscience, 1977.

Burke, Edmund. *A Notebook of Edmund Burke, Poems, Characters, Essays and Other Sketches in the Hands of Edmund and William Burke,* ed. H.V.F. Somerset. Cambridge, Cambridge U., 1957.

Burke, Edmund. *Letter to Sir H. Langrishe* (1792). *Works.* London, Bohn, 1855–1894, 3.298–344.

Burke, Edmund. *Reflections on the Revolution in France* (1790), ed. T. Mahoney. Indianapolis, Library of Liberal Arts, 1955.

Burke, Edmund. *Speech on a Bill for Repeal of the Marriage Act* (1781). *Works* (Bohn), 6.168–72.

Burke, Edmund. *Speech on a Bill to Repeal and Alter Certain Acts Representing Religious Opinions* (May 11, 1792). *Works* (Bohn), 6.113–26.

Burke, Edmund. *Speech on a Motion for a Committee to Inquire into the State of the Representation of the Commons in Parliament* (May 7, 1782). *Works* (Bohn), 6.144–54.

Burke, Edmund. "Speech on the Impeachment of Warren Hastings," Second Day of Reply (May 30, 1794). *Works* (Bohn), 8.1–53.

Burke, Edmund. *Thoughts and Details on Scarcity* (1795). *Works* (Boston, Little, Brown, 1886), 5.133–69.

Burke, Edmund. *Thoughts on French Affairs* (1791). *Works* (Bohn), 3.347–93.

Burke, Edmund. *Thoughts on the Cause of the Present Discontents* (1770). *Works* (Bohn), 1.306–81.

Butler, Nicholas Murray. "Hebert Spencer's 'The Great Political Superstition.'" *Forum* 55 (1916), 81–108.

Calleo, David P. *Coleridge and the Idea of the Modern State.* New Haven, Yale U., Yale Studies in Political Science 18, 1966.

Calvin, John. *Commentary on the Book of Prophet Isaiah.* Edinburgh, Calvin Translation Society, 1851.

Calvin, John. *Institutes of the Christian Religion,* ed. J. McNeill. Philadelphia, Westminster, Library of Christian Classics 20–21, 1960.

Calvin, John. *Joannis Calvini opera selecta,* ed. P. Barth and W. Niesel. Munich, Kaiser, 1928–1936.

Calvin, John. *Sermons sur le Deuteronome,* in *Joannis Calvini opera quae supersunt omnia,* ed. G. Baum et al. Brunswick, Schwetschke, 1863–1900. Vol. 27.

Campbell, R. H. and A. S. Skinner. "General Introduction." Adam Smith, *Works and Corresponence, Vol. 2: An Inquiry into the Nature and Causes of the Wealth of Nations,* ed. R. H. Campbell and A. S. Skinner. Oxford, Oxford U., 1976, 1–60.

Canavan, Francis P. *The Political Reason of Edmund Burke.* Durham, NC, Duke U., Lilly Endowment Research Program in Christianity and Politics, 1960.

Cargill Thompson, W.D.J. *The Political Thought of Martin Luther,* ed. P. Broadhead. Sussex, Harvester, 1984.

Carney, Frederick S. "Associational Thought in Early Calvinism." *Voluntary Associations,* James Luther Adams Fest., ed. D. B. Robertson. Richmond, VA, John Knox, 1966, 39–53.

Carruth, Shawn. "Ears to Hear." *Bible Today* 21 (1983), 89–95.

Chase, Allan. *The Legacy of Malthus. The Social Costs of the New Scientific Racism.* Urbana, IL, U. of Illinois, 1980.

Chauncy, Charles. *Seasonable Thoughts on the State of Religion in New England.* Hicksville, NY, Regina, Rise of Modern Religious Ideas in America, 1975 (1743).

Chesser, Eustace. *Love Without Fear.* New York, Signet, 1947.

Chesterton, G. K. *The Uses of Diversity.* London, Methuen, Fountain Library, 1937[6].

Cicero. *De Senectute, De Amicitia, De Divinatione,* trans. W. A. Falconer. Cambridge, Harvard U., Loeb Classical Library, 1923.

Clark, Joseph S. "The Case for Democratic Liberalism." *Saturday Review* (July 11, 1964), 14–17, 26.

Clark, Michael D. *Coherent Variety: The Idea of Diversity in British and American Conservative Thought.* Westport, CT, Greenwood, Contributions in Political Science 86, 1983.

Cochran, Thomas C. and William Miller. *The Age of Enterprise. A Social History of Industrial America.* New York, Harper, 1961[2].

Codaccioni, Félix-Paul. *De l'inégalité sociale dans une grande ville industrielle: Le drame de Lille de 1850 à 1914.* Université de Lille III, éditions universitaires, 1976.

Cohn, Norman. *The Pursuit of the Millennium.* New York, Oxford U., 1970[2].

Coles, Robert. *Children of Crisis, Vol. 3: The South Goes North.* Boston, Little, Brown, 1971; *Vol. 5: Privileged Ones. The Well-Off and the Rich in America.* Boston, Little, Brown, 1977.

"Communism Denounced: Henry Ward Beecher's Opinions on the Labor Question." *The New York Times,* July 30, 1877, 8.

Cone, Carl. *Burke and the Nature of Politics.* N.p., U. of Kentucky, 1957–1964.

Cone, James H. *God of the Oppressed.* New York, Seabury, 1975.

Conrad, Joseph. *Nostromo.* New York, Signet, 1904.

Conwell, Russell. *Acres of Diamonds.* New York, Harper, 1915.

Cooper, James Fenimore. *The American Democrat.* New York, Knopf, 1931 (1838).

Copeland, Warren R. *Economic Justice: The Social Ethics of U.S. Economic Policy.* Nashville, Abingdon, 1988.

Cort, John. "Can Socialism be Distinguished from Marxism?" *Cross Currents* 29 (1980), 423–34.

Coser, Lewis A. *The Functions of Social Conflict.* New York, Free, 1956.

Cotton, John. "An Exposition upon the Thirteenth Chapter of Revelation" (1658). *Puritan Political Ideas,* ed. E. Morgan. Indianapolis, IN, Bobbs-Merrill, American Heritage Series, 1965, 174–77.

Cotton, John. "Letter to Lord Say and Seal in the Year 1636." *Puritan Political Ideas,* ed. E. Morgan, 167–73.

D'Entrèves, A. P. "Introduction." *Aquinas. Selected Political Writings.* Oxford, Blackwell, 1948, vii–xxxiii.

Danker, Frederick W. *Benefactor.* St. Louis, Clayton, 1982.

Davies, Eryl W. *Prophesy and Ethics. Isaiah and the Ethical Traditions of Israel.* Sheffield, Journal for the Study of the Old Testament, Supplement Series 16, 1981.

De Vries, Simon John. *Yesterday, Today and Tomorrow: Time and History in the Old Testament*. Grand Rapids, MI, Eerdmans, 1975.

Deak, Istvan. *Weimar Germany's Left-Wing Intellectuals: A Political History of the Welt-bühne and Its Circle*. Berkeley, U. of California, 1968.

Degler, Carl N. *Place Over Time: The Continuity of Southern Distinctiveness*. Baton Rouge, Louisiana State U., Walter Lynwood Fleming Lectures in Southern History, 1977.

DeGolyer, Michael. "Marx's Theory of Justice." *Fides et Historia* 16, 2 (1984), 18–37.

DeJong, Peter, and Donald Wilson. *Husband & Wife. The Sexes in Scripture and Society*. Grand Rapids, MI, Zondervan, 1979.

Demant, V. A. *Religion and the Decline of Capitalism*. New York, Scribner's, 1952.

Dengerink, Jan D. "The Christian and Modern Democracy." *International Reformed Bulletin* 7 (July, 1964), 13–23.

Dengerink, Jan D. *The Idea of Justice in Christian Perspective*. Toronto, Wedge, 1978.

Devlin, Patrick. *The Enforcement of Morals*. London, Oxford U., 1965.

DiQuattro, Arthur. "Alienation and Justice in the Market." *American Political Science Review* 72 (1978), 871–87.

Dodd, C. H. "The Kingdom of God and History." H. G. Wood et al., *Church, Community, and State. Vol. 3: The Kingdom of God and History*. London, Allen, 1938, 13–36.

Dombrowski, James. *The Early Days of Christian Socialism in America*. New York, Columbia U., 1936.

Dooyeweerd, Herman. *Roots of Western Culture: Pagan, Secular and Christian Options*. Toronto, Wedge, 1979.

Dorrien, Gary J. *The Democratic Socialist Vision*. Totowa, NJ, Rowman, 1986.

Douglass, Frederick. *Life and Times of Frederick Douglass*. New York, Collier, 1962^2.

Draper, Hal. *Karl Marx's Theory of Revolution, Vol. 1: State and Bureaucracy*. New York, Monthly Review, 1977.

Drengson, Alan R. "Toward a Redefinition of Progress in Agricultural Technology and Practices: From Industrial Paradigms to Natural Patterns." *Quarterly Journal of Ideology* 11, 2 (1987), 59–66.

Driver, G. R. and John C. Miles. *The Babylonian Laws*. London: Oxford, Ancient Codes and Laws of the Near East, 1952–1955.

Druster, Troy. "Conditions for Guilt-Free Massacre." Nevitt Sanford, Craig Comstock, et al., *Sanctions for Evil: Sources of Social Destructiveness*. San Francisco, Jossey-Bass, Behavioral Science Series, 1971, 25–36.

Dubey, S. N. "Powerlessness and Orientations towards Family and Children: A Study in Deviance." *Indian Journal of Social Work* 32 (1971), 35–43.

Dumbrell, William J. "Genesis 1–3, Ecology, and the Dominion of Man." *Crux* 21,4 (December, 1985), 16–26.

Dunn, John. *The Political Thought of John Locke, An Historical Account of the Argument of the "Two Treatises of Government"*. Cambridge, Cambridge U., 1969.

Dyck, Arthur J. "Loving Impartiality in Moral Cognition." *Annual of the Society of Christian Ethics,* 1989, ed. D. M. Yeager. Knoxville, TN, Society of Christian Ethics, 1989, 55–72.

Eagleton, Terry. "What is Politics About? Terry Eagleton Replies to Bernard Bergonzi." *New Blackfriars* 47 (1966), 372–73.

Ebenstein, William. "National Socialism." *International Encyclopedia of the Social Sciences* (1968), 11:45–50.

Edelstein, Lugwig. *The Idea of Progress in Classical Antiquity*. Baltimore, Johns Hopkins, 1967.

Eden, Dov. "Assessment." *Quality of Worker Life and the Kibbutz Experience,* ed. A. Cherns.

Norwod, Pa, Norwood, Kibbutz, Communal Society, and Alternative Social Policy 2, 1978, 270–75.

Edwards, Jonathan. "Some Thoughts Concerning the Revival." Edwards, *Works of Jonathan Edwards, Vol. 4: The Great Awakening,* ed. C. Goen. New Haven, CT, Yale U., 1972, 289–530.

Edwards, Jonathan. *Works of Jonathan Edwards. Vol. 2: Religious Affections,* ed. J. Smith. New Haven, CT, Yale U., 1959.

Einaudi, Mario. "Fascism," *International Encyclopedia of the Social Sciences* (1968), 5:334–41.

Eliot, T. S. "Choruses from 'The Rock.'" Eliot, *Collected Poems 1909–1962.* San Diego, CA, Harcourt, 1970, 145–71.

Eliot, T. S. *The Idea of a Christian Society.* London, Faber, 1939.

Ellis, William S. "Rondônia's Settlers Invade Brazil's Imperiled Rain Forest." *National Geographic* 174 (1988/89), 772–99.

Ellul, Jacques. *The Meaning of the City.* Grand Rapids, MI, Eerdmans, 1970.

Ellul, Jacques. *The Political Illusion.* New York, Vintage, 1967.

Emerson, Ralph Waldo. "The Conservative" (1841). Emerson, *Works,* Concord ed., Vol. 1: *Nature: Addresses and Lectures.* Boston, Houghton, 1903, 295–326.

Emerson, Richard M. "Power-Dependence Relations." *American Sociological Review* 27 (1962), 31–41.

Engels, Frederick. *Anti-Duhring* (1878). Marx and Engels, *Collected Works.* New York, International, 1978, 25.5–309.

Engels, Frederick. Introduction to *The Civil War in France* (1891). Karl Marx and Engels, *Basic Writings on Politics and Philosophy,* ed. L. Feuer. Garden City, NY, Anchor, 1959, 349–62.

Engels, Frederick. Introduction to the English edition of *Socialism. Utopian and Scientific.* London, Allen, 1892, v–xxxix.

Engels, Frederick. "On Authority" (1874). Marx and Engels, *Collected Works,* 23.422–25.

Engels, Frederick. Preface to the English edition of 1888 of *Manifesto of the Communist Party.* Marx and Engels, *Basic Writings on Politics and Philosophy,* 1959, 1–6.

Engels, Frederick. "Programme of the Blanquist Commune Refugees" (1874). Marx and Engels, *Collected Works,* 24.12–18.

Engels, Frederick. *Socialism: Utopian and Scientific* (1880). Marx and Engels, *Collected Works,* 24.281–325.

Epshtein, Amos. *Igud hatassiyah hakibbutzit 1987.* Tel Aviv, igud hatassiyah hakibbutzit.

"The ESOP Fable: Employee Stock Ownership Falls Short." *Dollars & Sense* (July/August, 1983), 12–14.

Etzioni, Amitai. *The Active Society. A Theory of Societal and Political Processes.* New York, Free, 1968.

Etzioni, Amitai. *Comparative Analysis of Complex Organizations.* New York, Free, 1975².

Falk, Zeev W. "Two Symbols of Justice." *Vetus Testamentum* 10 (1960), 72–74.

Faramelli, Norman J. "Neo-Conservatives in the Church." *Ecumenist* 21 (1982), 1–5.

Farley, Edward. *The Fragility of Knowledge. Theological Education in the Church and the University.* Philadelphia, Fortress, 1988.

Farley, Margaret. Review of *The Theory of Morality,* by Alan Donagan. *Religious Studies Review* 7 (1981), 233–37.

Fasenfast, David and Stephen Rose. "A Growing Gap: Income Distribution in The 80's." *Blueprint for Social Justice* 42, 10 (June, 1989), 1–7.

Feather, H. R. "Conservative Thought and the English Bourgeoisie." *Sociological Review* 32 (1984), 266–84.

Feeley, Malcolm. "Coercion and Compliance. A New Look at an Old Problem." *Law and Society Review* 4 (1970), 505–19.

Fellman, Gordon. "Socialism and Religion in Israel." *Religious Socialism* 10, 4 (Fall, 1986), 4.

Fensham, F. Charles. "Widow, Orphan, and the Poor in Ancient Near Eastern Legal and Wisdom Literature." *Journal of Near Eastern Studies* 21 (1962), 129–39.

Field, Geoffrey G. *Evangelist of Race: The Germanic Vision of Houston Stewart Chamberlain.* NY, Columbia U., 1981.

Fife, Eric S. and Arthur F. Glasser. *Missions in Crisis.* Chicago, Inter-Varsity, 1962.

Finn, Daniel Rush. "Self-Interest, Markets, and the Four Problems of Economic Life." *Annual of the Society of Christian Ethics,* 1989, ed. D. M. Yeager. Knoxville, TN, Society of Christian Ethics, 1989, 23–53.

Finney, Charles. *Lectures on Systematic Theology,* ed. J. H. Fairchild. Oberlin, OH, Goodrich, 1878.

Fisher, Irving. *Elementary Principles of Economics.* New York, Macmillan, 1912.

Fitzpatrick, Joseph P. "Values, Ethics, and Family Life." *Helping the Family in Urban Society,* ed. F. Delliquadri. New York, Columbia U., 1963, 66–78.

Fletcher, David B. "Christian Social Justice and Rawl's Liberalism." *Christian Scholar's Review* 19 (1990), 231–42.

Fohrer, Georg. "Der Vertrag zwischen König und Volk in Israel." Fohrer, *Studien zur alttestamentlichen Theologie und Geschichte.* Berlin, Gruyter, Beihefte zur Zeitschrift für die alttestamentliche Wissenschaft 115, 1969, 330–51.

Frankena, William. "The Concept of Social Justice." *Social Justice,* ed. R. Brandt. Englewood Cliffs, NJ, Prentice-Hall, 1962, 1–29.

Friedel, Frank. "America Enters the Modern Era." *National Geographic* 128 (1965), 537–77.

Friedenberg, Edgar Z. *Coming of Age in America. Growth and Acquiescense.* New York, Vintage, 1965.

Friedman, Milton. *Capitalism and Freedom.* Chicago, U. of Chicago, 1982.

Fromm, Erich. *Fear of Freedom.* London, Kegan Paul, International Library of Sociology and Social Reconstruction, 1942.

Fromm, Erich. *Marx's Concept of Man.* New York, Ungar, Milestones of Thought, 1961.

Fromm, Erich. *The Sane Society.* New York, Holt, 1955.

Furtado, Celso. *Economic Development of Latin America. Historical Background and Contemporary Problems.* Cambridge U., Cambridge Latin American Studies 8, 1976².

Gans, Herbert J. "We Won't End the Urban Crisis Until We End 'Majority Rule.'" *New York Times Magazine* (August 3, 1969), 12–28.

García, Ismael. *Justice in Latin American Theology of Liberation.* Atlanta, Knox, 1987.

Gardner, E. Clinton. "Justice in the Puritan Covenant Tradition." *Annual of the Society of Christian Ethics,* 1988, ed. D. M. Yeager. Knoxville, TN, Society of Christian Ethics, 1988, 91–111.

Gerlemann, Gillis. "Nutzrecht und Wohnrecht. Zur Bedeutung von נחלה." *Zeitschrift für Alttestamentliche Wissenschaft* 89 (1977), 313–25.

Ghent, W. J. *Our Benevolent Feudalism.* New York, Macmillan, 1902.

Gilder, George. *Wealth and Poverty.* New York, Basic, 1981.

Gilkey, Langdon. "Reinhold Niebuhr's Theology of History." *Journal of Religion* 54 (1974), 360–86.

Gilkey, Langdon. *Shantung Compound. The Story of Men and Women under Pressure.* New York, Harper, 1966.

Gilligan, Carol. *In a Different Voice. Psychological Theory and Women's Development.* Cambridge, MA, Harvard U., 1982.

Gish, Arthur G. *The New Left and Christian Radicalism.* Grand Rapids, MI, Eerdmans, 1970.

Goldingay, John. "The Man of War and the Suffering Servant." *Tyndale Bulletin* 27 (1976), 79–113.

Goodenough, E. R. *Introduction to Philo Judaeus.* Oxford, Blackwell, 1962².

Gordis, Robert. "Primitive Democracy in Ancient Israel." Gordis, *Poets, Prophets, and Sages.* Bloomington, IN, Indiana U., 1971, 45–60.

Gottwald, Norman K. *The Tribes of Yahweh. A Sociology of the Religion of Liberated Israel 1250–1050 B.C.E.* Maryknoll, NY, Orbis, 1979.

Goudzwaard, Bob. *Capitalism and Progress. A Diagnosis of Western Society.* Grand Rapids, MI, Eerdmans, 1979².

Gould, Carol C. *Marx's Social Ontology: Individuality and Community in Marx's Theory of Social Reality.* Cambridge, MA, MIT, 1978.

Goulet, Yvonne. "The Church Shouldn't Let Caesar Off the Hook." *Salt* 3,7 (July/August, 1983), 2.

Gowan, Susanne et al. *Moving Toward a New Society.* Philadelphia, New Society, 1976.

Griffiths, Brian. *The Creation of Wealth. A Christian's Case for Capitalism.* Downers Grove, IL, InterVarsity, 1984.

Gudorf, Christine E. *Catholic Social Teaching on Liberation Themes.* Lanham, MD, University Press of America, 1980.

Gunnemann, Jon P. "Capitalism and Commutative Justice." *Annual of the Society of Christian Ethics,* 1985, ed. A. Anderson. Vancouver, B. C., Society of Christian Ethics, 1986, 101–22.

Gunnemann, Jon P. Review of *Politics and Markets,* by Charles E. Lindblom. *Religious Studies Review* 9 (1983), 212–19.

Guroian, Vigen. "The Possibilities and Limits of Politics: A Comparative Study of the Thought of Reinhold Niebuhr and Edmund Burke." *Union Seminary Quarterly Review* 36 (1981), 189–203.

Gutman, Herbert G. *The Black Family in Slavery and Freedom, 1750–1925.* New York, Pantheon, 1976.

Habermas, Jürgen. *Theory and Practice.* Boston, Beacon, 1973⁴.

Hale, William Harlan. "Der Fuehrer Dead Center." *Saturday Review* (August 29, 1970), 19–21, 47.

Hallett, Garth L. *Christian Neighbor-Love. An Assessment of Six Rival Versions.* Washington, D.C., Georgetown U., 1989.

Hallowell, John H. *The Decline of Liberalism as an Ideology. With Particular Reference to German Politico-Legal Thought.* London, Keagan Paul, International Library of Sociology and Social Reconstruction, 1946.

Hamilton, Alexander, James Madison, and John Jay. *The Federalist.* New York, Everyman's Library, 1970.

Hamilton, Richard F. *Who Voted for Hitler?* Princeton, Princeton U., 1982.

Hansmann, Henry. "A General Theory of Corporate Ownership." Cambridge, MA, Harvard University Law School, Program in Law and Economics, Discussion Paper 33, 1987.

Harrington, Michael. *The Long-Distance Runner. An Autobiography.* New York, Holt, 1988.

Harrington, Michael. *The New American Poverty.* New York, Holt, 1984.

Harrington, Michael. *Socialism.* New York, Saturday Review, 1972.

Hatfield, Mark. *Between a Rock and a Hard Place.* Waco, TX, Word, 1976.

Hawley, Amos H. "Community Power and Urban Renewal Success." *American Journal of Sociology* 68 (1963), 422–23.

Hayek, Friedrich A. "Individualism: *True and False.*" Hayek, *Individualism and Economic Order.* Chicago, U. of Chicago, 1948, 1–32.

Hayek, Friedrich A. *The Road to Serfdom.* London, Routledge, 1944.

Hechter, Michael. Review of *Reactive Risk and Rational Action,* by Carol A. Heimer. *Contemporary Sociology* 15 (1986), 584–86.

Heilbroner, Robert L. "Reflections: The Triumph of Capitalism." *New Yorker* 64 (1989), 98–109.

Heilbroner, Robert L. *Worldly Philosophers. The Lives, Times, and Ideas of Great Economic Thinkers.* New York, Simon and Schuster, 1953.

Heimann, Eduard. *Communism. Fascism or Democracy?* New York, Norton, 1938.

Heimann, Eduard. *Reason and Faith in Modern Society. Liberalism, Marxism, and Democracy.* Middletown, CT, Wesleyan U., 1961.

Henry, Carl F. H. *Aspects of Christian Social Ethics.* Grand Rapids, MI, Eerdmans, 1964.

Herron, George D. *Between Caesar and Jesus.* New York, Crowell, 1899.

Hertz, Karl. "The Nature of Voluntary Associations." *Voluntary Associations,* James Luther Adams Fest., ed. D. B. Robertson. Richmond, VA, Knox, 1966, 17–35.

Heymann, Philip B. "How Government Expresses Public Ideas." *The Power of Public Ideas,* ed. R. Reich. Cambridge, MA, Ballinger, 1988, 85–107.

Hibben, Paxton. *Henry Ward Beecher: An American Portrait.* New York, Doran, 1927.

Hobsbawm, Eric J. *Labouring Men: Studies in the History of Labour.* London, Weidenfeld, 1964.

Hocking, William Ernest. *Man and the State.* Hamden, CT, Archon, 1968.

Hofstadter, Richard. *Social Darwinism in American Thought.* New York, Braziller, 1955^2.

Hollas, Daniel R. and Stanley R. Stansell. "An Examination of the Effect of Ownership Form on Price Efficiency: Proprietary, Cooperative and Municipal Utilities." *Southern Economic Journal* 55 (1988), 336–50.

Hollenbach, David. "A Communitarian Reconstruction of Human Rights: Contributions from Catholic Tradition." Paper presented to the Boston Theological Ethicists' Colloquium, October 17, 1990.

Hollenbach, David. "The Common Good Revisited." *Theological Studies* 50 (1989), 70–94.

Hollinger, Dennis P. *Individualism and Social Ethics. An Evangelical Syncretism.* Lanham, MD, University Press of America, 1983.

Hollis, Patricia. *The Pauper Press. A Study in Working-Class Radicalism of the 1830's.* London, Oxford U., 1970.

Hondrich, Karl Otto. "Politische Herrschaft und wirtschaftliche Entwicklung. Macht und Herrschaft als Kategorien der Entwicklungssoziolgie." *Kölner Zeitschrift für Soziologie und Sozialpsychologie* Suppl. 13 (1969), 367–87.

Hooker, Richard. *Works. Vol. 1: Of the Laws of Ecclesiastical Polity* (1593), ed. G. Edelen. Cambridge, Harvard U, Folger Library Edition, 1977.

Hoover, Calvin B. "Capitalism." *International Encyclopedia of the Social Sciences* (1968), 2:294–301.

Horn, Robert A. *Groups and the Constitution.* Stanford, Stanford U., 1956.

Horton, John. "Time and Cool People." *Transaction* 4, 5 (April 1967), 5–12.

Horvat, Branko. *The Political Economy of Socialism: A Marxist Social Theory.* Armonk, NY, Sharpe, 1982.

Höpfl, Harro. *The Christian Polity of John Calvin.* Cambridge, Cambridge U., Studies in the History and Theory of Politics, 1982.

Hugo, Victor. *Les Misérables.* London, Dent, 1909.

Hunt, Richard N. *The Political Ideas of Marx and Engels. Vol. 1: Marxism and Totalitarian Democracy, 1818–1850.* Pittsburgh, U. of Pittsburgh, 1974; *Vol. 2: Classical Marxism, 1850–1895.* Pittsburgh, U. of Pittsburgh, 1984.

Hunter, Floyd. *Community Power Structure. A Study of Decision Makers.* Garden City, NY, Doubleday, 1963.

Huntington, Samuel P. "Conservatism as Ideology." *American Political Science Review* 51 (1957), 454–73.

Husami, Zizad I. "Marx on Distributive Justice." *Marx, Justice, and History,* ed. M. Cohen et al. Princeton, Princeton U., 1980, 42–79.

Hügel, Friedrich von. "On the Place and Function, within Religion, of the Body, of History, and of Institutions" (1913). Hügel, *Essays and Addresses on the Philosophy of Religion.* London, Dent, 1926), 2.57–88.

Interfaith Action for Economic Justice. *Networker.* July/August, 1990, 1–2.

"Is Good Politics Bad Business? An Update on Worker Ownership." *Dollars & Sense* (September, 1986), 12–14, 21.

Isaac, Rhys. *The Transformation of Virginia: 1740–1790.* Chapel Hill, NC, U. of North Carolina, 1982.

Jackall, Robert, and Joyce Crain. "The Shape of the Small Worker Cooperative Movement." *Worker Cooperatives in America,* ed. Jackall and H. Levin. Berkeley, CA, U. of California, 1984, 88–108.

Jacobsen, Thorkild. "Primitive Democracy in Ancient Mesopotamia." Jacobsen, *Toward the Image of Tammuz and Other Essays on Mesopotamian History and Culture.* Cambridge, MA, Harvard U., Harvard Semitic Series 21, 1970, 157–72.

Janeway, Elizabeth. *Powers of the Weak.* New York, Knopf, 1980.

Janis, Irving L. "Groupthink Among Policy Makers." Nevitt Sanford, Craig Comstock, et al., Sanctions for Evil: Sources of Social Destructiveness. San Francisco, Jossey-Bass, Behavioral Science Series, 1971, 71–89.

Jefferson, Thomas. Letter to James Madison, September 6, 1789. Jefferson, *Life and Selected Works,* ed. A. Koch and W. Peden. New York, Modern, 1944, 488–91.

Jefferson, Thomas. *Notes on the State of Virginia* (1781–1785). *The Complete Jefferson,* ed. S. Padover. New York, Duell, 1943, 567–697.

Johnson, Paul. "The Capitalism & Morality Debate." *First Things* (March 1990), 18–22.

Jones, Derek C. "Producer Co-Operatives in Industrialised Western Economies." *British Journal of Industrial Relations* 18 (1980), 141–54.

Junker, Théo. "Paul Tillich: Une théorie du pouvoir pour le socialisme." *Studies in Religion* 12 (1983), 325–36.

Kaufmann, Walter. "Doubts About Justice." *Social Responsibility in an Age of Revolution,* ed. L. Finkelstein. New York, Jewish Theological Seminary, Ethics of Today, 1971, 95–127.

Kaye, Julian B. *Bernard Shaw and the Nineteenth Century Tradition.* Norman, OK, U. of Oklahoma, 1958.

Kelly, Alfred H. and Winfred A. Harbison. *The American Constitution. Its Origins and Development.* New York, Norton, 1955².

Kelman, Steven. "Why Public Ideas Matter." *The Power of Public Ideas,* ed. R. Reich. Cambridge, MA, Ballinger, 1988, 31–53.

Keyssar, Alexander. *Out of Work. The First Century of Unemployment in Massachusetts.* Cambridge, Cambridge U., Interdisciplinary Perspectives on Modern History, 1986.

Kierkegaard, Søren. *Kierkegaard's Writings. Vol. 4: Either/Or 2,* ed. H. Hong and E. Hong (1987).

Kierkegaard, Søren. *Kierkegaard's Writings. Vol. 19: The Sickness unto Death. A Christian Psychological Exposition for Upbuilding and Awakening,* ed. H. Hong and E. Hong. Princeton, Princeton U., 1980.

King, Martin Luther, Jr. "Letter from Birmingham Jail" (April 16, 1963). King, *Why We Can't Wait.* New York, Signet Books, 1964, 76–95.

King, Martin Luther, Jr. *Stride Toward Freedom.* New York, Harper, 1958.

King, Martin Luther, Jr. *Where Do We Go from Here: Chaos or Community?* Boston, Beacon, 1967.

Kirk, Russell. *The Conservative Mind From Burke to Eliot.* Chicago, Gateway, 1960³.

Kline, Meredith G. *Kingdom Prologue.* Hamilton, MA, Meredith G. Kline, 1983.

Kline, Meredith G. "Oracular Origin of the State." *Biblical and Near Eastern Studies,* ed. G. Tuttle. Grand Rapids, Eerdmans, 1976, 132–41.

Koehler, Ludwig. *Hebrew Man.* London, SCM, 1956.

Koester, Helmut. *Introduction to the New Testament. Vol. 2: History and Literature of Early Christianity.* New York, Walter de Gruyter, 1982.

Koester, Helmut. "Outside the Camp: Hebrews 13:9–14." *Harvard Theological Review* 55 (1962), 299–315.

Kolakowski, Leszek. "The Priest and the Jester." Kolakowski, *Toward a Marxist Humanism. Essays on the Left Today.* New York, Grove, 1968, 9–37.

Kornhauser, William. *The Politics of Mass Society.* New York, Free, 1959.

Krausnick, Helmut and Hans-Heinrich Wilhelm. *Die Truppe des Weltanschauungskrieges: Die Einsatzgruppen der Sicherheitspolizei und des SD 1938–1942.* Stuttgart, Deutsche, Quellen und Darstellungen zur Zeitgeschichte 22, 1981.

Kristol, Irving. "A Capitalist Conception of Justice." *Ethics, Free Enterprise, and Public Policy,* ed. R. De George and J. Pichler. New York, Oxford U., 1978, 57–69.

Kuyper, Abraham. *Lectures on Calvinism.* Grand Rapids, MI, Eerdmans, Stone Foundation Lectures, 1931 (1898).

Kümmel, Friedrich. "Time as Succession and the Problem of Duration." *The Voice of Time,* ed. J. T. Fraser. Amherst, University of Massachusetts, 1981², 31–55.

Lakoff, Sanford A. *Equality in Political Philosophy.* Boston, Beacon, 1964.

Lambrecht, Jan. "Dienende Macht." *Erbe und Auftrag* 60 (1984), 434–41.

Lasch, Christopher. "Orwell." *In These Times,* December 19, 1984–January 8, 1985, 12–13, 22.

Le Goff, Jacques. "Is Politics Still the Backbone of History?" *Daedalus* 100 (Winter, 1971), 1–19.

Lebacqz, Karen. *Justice in an Unjust World. Foundations for a Christian Approach to Justice.* Minneapolis, MN, Augsburg, 1987.

Lebacqz, Karen. *Six Theories of Justice. Perspectives from Philosophical and Theological Ethics.* Minneapolis, Augsburg, 1986.

Lee, Thea. "Choose Your Poison: Competition or Concentration." *Dollars & Sense* (July/August, 1989), 6–8.

Lehmann, Paul. *Transformation of Politics.* New York, Harper, 1975.

Leviatan, Uri. "Organizational Effects of Managerial Production Branches." *Work and Organization in Kibbutz Industry,* ed. Leviatan and M. Rosner. Norwood, PA, Norwood, Kibbutz, Communal Society, and Alternative Social Policy 3, 1980, 139–52.

Levin, Michael. "Marxism and Romanticism: Marx's Debt to German Conservatism." *Political Studies* 22 (1974), 400–13.

Levine, Daniel. *Jane Addams and the Liberal Tradition.* Madison, WI, State Historical Society of Wisconsin, 1971.

Levy, Rich. "Why China Exploded: Five Views," *Dollars & Sense* (September, 1989), 14.

Lewin, Kurt. "Background of Conflict in Marriage" (1940). Lewin, *Resolving Social Con-flicts. Selected Papers on Group Dynamics,* ed. Gertrud Weiss Lewin. New York, Harper, 1948, 84–102.

Lewin, Kurt. "Self-Hatred among Jews" (1941). Lewin, *Resolving Social Conflicts,* 186–200.

Lewis, Lionel S. *Cold War on Campus: A Study of the Policies of Organizational Control.* New Brunswick, NJ, Transaction, 1988.

Lichtman, Richard. "The Façade of Equality in Liberal Democratic Theory." *Inquiry* 12 (1969), 170–208.

Lifton, Robert Jay. "Existential Evil." Nevitt Sanford, Craig Comstock, et al., *Sanctions for Evil: Sources of Social Destructiveness.* San Francisco, Jossey-Bass, Behavioral Sci-ence Series, 1971, 37–48.

Lifton, Robert Jay. *The Nazi Doctors. Medical Killing and the Psychology of Genocide.* New York, Basic, 1986.

Lijphart, Arend. *The Politics of Accommodation. Pluralism and Democracy in the Nether-lands.* Berkeley, CA, U. of California, 1975².

Lilburne, John. *The Free-man's Freedom Vindicated* (1646), in *Puritanism and Liberty,* ed. Woodhouse, 317–18.

Lincoln, Abraham. Speech at Peoria, IL, October 16, 1854. *Collected Works,* ed. R. Basler. New Brunswick, NJ, Rutgers U., 1953, 2.247–83.

Lindsay, A. D. *The Essentials of Democracy.* London, Oxford U., William J. Cooper Foun-dation Lectures, 1935².

Linnenkamp, Hilmar. "Die sozialen Voraussetzungen des italienischen Faschismus." *Schmollers Jahrbuch* 88 (1968), 561–97.

Lippmann, Walter. *The Public Philosophy.* New York, Mentor, 1955.

Lipset, Seymour Martin, Martin A. Trow, and James S. Coleman. "Union Democracy and Secondary Organization." *American Social Patterns,* ed. W. Petersen. Garden City, NY, Doubleday Anchor, 1956, 171–218.

Lloyd, Peter C. *Classes, Crises and Coups: Themes in the Sociology of Developing Countries.* London, MacGibbon, 1971.

Lomasky, Loren E. *Persons, Rights, and the Moral Community.* New York, Oxford U., 1987.

Loomer, Bernard. "Two Kinds of Power." *Criterion* 15,1 (Winter, 1976), 11–29.

Lovelace, Richard F. *Dynamics of Spiritual Life. An Evangelical Theology of Renewal.* Downers Grove, IL, Inter-Varsity, 1979.

Lowell, James Russell. "Democracy." Lowell, *Writings,* Vol. 6: *Literary and Political Addresses.* Boston, Houghton, 1890, 7–37.

Lowi, Theodore J. *The End of Liberalism, Ideology, Policy, and the Crisis of Public Author-ity.* New York, Norton, 1969.

Luckman, Thomas. *The Invisible Religion. The Problem of Religion in Modern Society.* New York, Macmillan, 1967.

Lukas, Richard C. *The Forgotten Holocaust: The Poles under German Occupation 1939–1944.* Lexington, KY, University of Kentucky, 1986.

Lundsgaarde, Henry P. *Murder in Space City: A Cultural Analysis of Houston Homicide Pat-terns.* New York, Oxford U., 1977.

Luther, Martin. *In XV Psalmos graduum* (1532–1533). Luther, *Werke. Kritische Gesam-tausgabe.* Weimar, Böhlaus, 1930, 40, 3.9–475.

Machiavelli, Niccolo. *Discourses.* Machiavelli, *The Chief Works and Others,* trans. A. Gil-bert. Durham, NC, Duke U., 1989, 1.175–529.

Machiavelli, Niccolo. *The Prince.* Machiavelli, *Chief Works.* 1.5–96.

MacIntyre, Alasdair. *After Virtue. A Study in Moral Theory.* Notre Dame, IN, U. of Notre Dame, 1984².

MacIntyre, Alasdair. *Marxism and Christianity.* Notre Dame, IN, U. of Notre Dame, 1968².

MacIver, R. M. *Society. A Textbook of Sociology.* New York, Farrar, 1937.

MacIver, R. M. *The Web of Government.* New York, Macmillan, 1947.

MacPherson, C. B. *The Political Theory of Possessive Individualism: Hobbes to Locke.* London, Oxford U., 1962.

MacRae, George W. "Shared Responsibilities—Some New Testament Perspectives." *Chicago Studies* 9 (1970), 115–27.

Magee, Bryan. *Popper.* London, Fontana, Modern Masters, 1975.

Maguire, Daniel C. *A New American Justice. Ending the White Male Monopolies.* Garden City, NY, Doubleday, 1980.

Maier, Charles S. "The Politics of Time: Changing Paradigms of Collective and Private Time in the Modern Era." *Changing Boundaries of the Political,* ed. Maier. Cambridge, Cambridge U, Cambridge Studies in Modern Political Economies, 1987, 151–75.

Maine, Henry Sumner. *Popular Government.* London, Murray, 1885.

Malina, Bruce J. "Christ and Time: Swiss or Mediterranean?" *Catholic Biblical Quarterly* 51 (1989), 1–31.

Malinowski, Bronislaw. "Culture." *Encyclopaedia of the Social Sciences* (1931), 4:621–46.

Mannheim, Karl. "Conservative Thought" (1927). Mannheim, *Essays in Sociology and Social Psychology.* London, Routledge, 1953, 74–164.

Mannheim, Karl. *Ideology and Utopia. An Introduction to the Sociology of Knowledge.* New York, Harcourt, 1936.

Marcuse, Herbert. *One Dimensional Man. Studies in the Ideology of Advanced Industrial Society.* Boston, Beacon, 1964.

Maritain, Jacques. *Man and the State.* Chicago, U. of Chicago, 1962.

Marrus, Michael R. and Robert O. Paxton. *Vichy France and the Jews.* New York, Basic, 1981.

Marshall, Paul. "Liberalism, Pluralism and Christianity: A Reconceptualization." *Fides et História* 21, 3 (October 1989), 4–17.

Martin, Roderick. *The Sociology of Power.* London, Routledge, International Library of Sociology, 1977.

Marx, Karl. "Bruno Bauer, *Die Judenfrage*" (1843). *Karl Marx: Early Writings,* ed. T. B. Bottomore. New York, McGraw-Hill, 1963, 3–31.

Marx, Karl. *Capital. A Critical Analysis of Capitalist Production,* ed. F. Engels. New York, International, 1967 (1889–94).

Marx, Karl. "The Chartists" (1852). Marx and Frederick Engels, *Collected Works.* New York, International, 1978, 11.333–41.

Marx, Karl. *The Civil War in France* (1871). Marx and Engels, *Collected Works,* 22.307–58.

Marx, Karl. "The Class Struggles in France, 1848 to 1850." Marx and Engels, *Collected Works,* 10.45–145.

Marx, Karl. *A Contribution to the Critique of Political Economy* (1859). Marx and Engels, *Collected Works,* 29.257–417.

Marx, Karl. "The Crisis and the Counter-Revolution" (1848). Marx and Engels, *Collected Works,* 7.427–33.

Marx, Karl. "Critique of the Gotha Program, Marginal Notes on the Programme of the German Workers' Party" (1875). Marx and Engels, *Collected Works* 24.75–99.

Marx, Karl. "Economic and Philosophical Manuscripts." Marx, *Early Writings,* ed. T. B. Bottomore. New York, McGraw-Hill, 1963, 61–219.

Marx, Karl. *The Eighteenth Brumaire of Louis Bonaparte* (1852). Marx and Engels, *Collected Works,* 11.99–326.

Marx, Karl. "First Draft of *The Civil War in France*" (1871). Marx and Engels, *Collected Works,* 22.437–514.

Marx, Karl. *Grundrisse. Foundations of the Critique of Political Economy* (1857–1858), trans. M. Nicolaus. New York, Vintage, 1973.

Marx, Karl. "Inaugural Address of the Working Men's International Association" (1864). Marx and Engels, *Collected Works,* 20.5–13.

Marx, Karl. "Instructions for the Delegates of the Provisional General Council" (1866). Marx and Engels, *Collected Works,* 20.185–94.

Marx, Karl. Letter to *Otechestvenniye Zapiski,* November, 1877. Marx and Engels, *Collected Works,* 24.196–201.

Marx, Karl. "Notes on Bakunin's Book *Statehood and Anarchy*" (1874–1875). Marx and Engels, *Collected Works,* 24.485–526.

Marx, Karl. "On the Hague Congress" (1872). Marx and Engels, *Collected Works,* 23.254–56.

Marx, Karl. "Theses on Feuerbach" (1845). Marx and Engels, *Collected Works,* 5.3–5.

Marx, Karl and Frederick Engels. *The German Ideology* (1845–1846). Marx and Engels, *Collected Works,* 5.15–539.

Marx, Karl and Frederick Engels. *Manifesto of the Communist Party* (1848). Marx and Engels, *Collected Works,* 6.477–519.

May, Larry. *The Morality of Groups: Collective Responsibility. Group-Based Harm, and Corporate Rights.* Notre Dame, IN, U. of Notre Dame, 1987

May, Rollo. *The Art of Counseling.* New York, Abingdon, 1939.

May, Rollo. *Power and Innocence. A Search for the Sources of Violence.* New York, Norton, 1972.

McCulloch, J. R. *The Principles of Political Economy.* Edinburgh, Tait, 1825.

McKale, Donald M. *Curt Prüfer: German Diplomat from the Kaiser to Hitler.* Kent, OH, Kent State U., 1987.

McNeill, John T. "John Calvin on Civil Government." *Journal of Presbyterian History* 42 (1964), 71–91.

McWilliams, Wilson Carey. *The Idea of Fraternity in America.* Berkeley, CA, U. of California, 1973.

Mead, Sidney E. "The 'Nation with a Soul of a Church.'" *American Civil Religion,* ed. R. Russell and D. Jones. New York, Harper, 1974, 45–75.

Meeks, M. Douglas. *God the Economist. The Doctrine of God and Political Economy.* Minneapolis, Fortress, 1989.

Mendelsohn, I. "Samuel's Denunciation of Kingship in the Light of the Akkadian Documents from Ugarit." *Bulletin of the American Schools of Oriental Research* 143 (1956), 17–22.

Michaels, J. Ramsey. *Servant and Son. Jesus in Parable and Gospel.* Atlanta, Knox, 1981.

Michels, Robert. *Political Parties. A Sociological Study of the Oligarchical Tendencies of Modern Democracy.* Glencoe, IL, Free, 1958 (1915).

Mill, John Stuart. *Considerations on Representative Government.* Indianapolis, IN, Bobbs-Merrill, Library of Liberal Arts, 1958 (1865³).

Mill, John Stuart. *On Liberty,* ed. D. Spitz. New York, Norton, Norton Critical Editions in the History of Ideas, 1975.

Mill, John Stuart. *Principles of Political Economy,* ed. W. Ashley. New York, Kelley, Reprints of Economic Classics, 1969 (1909, using the 7th ed.).

Miller, Eugene F. "Political Philosophy and Human Nature." *Personalist* 53 (1972), 209–21.

Miller, Jim Wayne. "The Brier Sermon." Miller, *The Mountains Have Come Closer.* Boone, NC, Appalachian Consortion, 1980, 52–64.

Miller, John. "A Green GNP." *Dollars and Sense* 161 (November 1990), 6–8, 22.

Milton, John. *The Doctrine and Discipline of Divorce.* Milton, *Prose Works.* London, Bohn, 1848, 3.169–273.

Milton, John. *The Reason of Church Government Urged against Prelaty.* Milton, *Prose Works,* 2.438–548.

Minear, Paul S. "Church, Idea of." *Interpreter's Dictionary of the Bible* (1962), 1.607–17.

Minear, Paul S. "Ontology and Ecclesiology in the Apocalypse." *New Testament Studies* 12 (1966), 89–105.

Minogue, K. R. *The Liberal Mind.* London, Methuen, 1963.

Minus, Paul M. *Walter Rauschenbusch. American Reformer.* New York, Macmillan, 1988.

Miranda, José Porfirio. *Marx and the Bible. A Critique of the Philosophy of Oppression.* Maryknoll, NY, Orbis, 1974.

MIT Commission on Industrial Productivity. *Made in America. Regaining the Productive Edge.* Cambridge, MA, MIT, 1989.

Míguez Bonino, José. *Christians and Marxists. The Mutual Challenge to Revolution.* Grand Rapids, Eerdmans, 1976.

Míguez Bonino, José. *Doing Theology in a Revolutionary Situation.* Philadelphia, Fortress, Confrontation Books, 1975.

Míguez Bonino, José. *Toward a Christian Political Ethic.* Philadelphia, Fortress, 1983.

Mollegan, A. T. "The Common Convictions of the Fellowship of Socialist Christians." *Christianity and Society* 8, 2 (1943), 22–28.

Mollegan, Albert T. "The Religious Basis of Western Socialism." *Socialism and American Life,* ed. D. Egbert and S. Persons. Princeton, NJ, Princeton U., 1952, 1.99–123.

Moltmann, Jürgen. *The Crucified God. The Cross of Christ as the Foundation and Criticism of Christian Theology.* New York, Harper, 1974[2].

Moltmann, Jürgen. *Theology of Hope. On the Ground and the Implications of a Christian Eschatology.* New York, Harper, 1967.

Moore, Barrington, Jr. *Social Origins of Dictatorship and Democracy. Lord and Peasant in the Making of the Modern World.* Boston, Beacon, 1966.

Moore, George Foot. *Judaism in the First Centuries of the Christian Era. The Age of the Tannaim.* Cambridge, Harvard U., 1927.

Morgan, Richard, et al. *Taking Charge: A New Look at Public Power.* Washington, D. C., Environmental Action Foundation, 1976.

Morgan, Edmund S. *The Gentle Puritan. A Life of Ezra Stiles, 1727–1795.* New Haven, Yale U., 1962.

Morrison, A. Cressy. *Man Does Not Stand Alone.* New York, Fleming, 1944.

Mott, S. C. *Biblical Ethics and Social Change.* New York, Oxford U., 1982.

Mott, S. C. "How Should Christian Economists Use the Bible? A Study in Hermeneutics." *Bulletin of the Association of Christian Economists* 13 (Spring, 1989), 7–19.

Mott, S. C. "The Kibbutz's Adjustment to Industrialization and Ideological Decline: Alternatives for Economic Organization." *Journal of Religious Ethics* 19 (1991), 151–73.

Mott, S. C. "The Use of the New Testament for Social Ethics." *Journal of Religious Ethics* 15 (1987), 225–60.

Mott, S. C. "Where Is the Cross? A Political Reflection on Hebrews 13." *The Other Side* 10, 2 (March/April, 1974), 39–42.

Mouw, Richard J. *Political Evangelism.* Grand Rapids, MI, Eerdmans, 1973.

Mouw, Richard J. *Politics and the Biblical Drama.* Grand Rapids, MI, Eerdmans, 1976.

Muelder, Walter George. "Contradictions in Capitalistic Triumphalism." *Theology and Public Policy* 2, 2 (Fall, 1990), 4–16.

Muelder, Walter George. *Foundations of the Responsible Society.* New York, Abingdon, 1959.

Muelder, Walter George. *Religion and Economic Responsibility.* New York, Scribner's, 1953.

Muir, Ramsay. *Liberalism and Industry. Towards A Better Social Order.* Boston, Houghton Mifflin, 1921.

Murray, John Courtney. "Leo XII: Two Concepts of Government." *Theological Studies* 14 (1953), 552–56.

Myrdal, Gunnar. *An American Dilemma.* New York, Harper, 1962².

Nash, Ronald H. *Freedom, Justice and the State.* Lanham, MD, University Press of America, 1980.

National Association of Manufacturers, Economic Principles Commission. *The American Enterprise System. Its Nature, Evolution, and Future.* New York, McGraw-Hill, 1946.

National Catholic War Council, Committee on Special War Activities. *Social Reconstruction. A General Review of the Problems and Survey of Remedies.* Washington, D. C., National Catholic War Council, Reconstruction Pamphlets, 1919.

National Commission on Testing and Public Policy. *From Gatekeeper to Gateway: Transforming Testing in America.* Chestnut Hill, MA, National Commission on Testing and Public Policy, 1990.

Nelson, John O. "The Function of Government." *Personalist* 52 (1971), 161–85.

Neuhaus, Richard John. *The Naked Public Square. Religion and Democracy in America.* Grand Rapids, MI, Eerdmans, 1984.

Niebuhr, H. Richard. *Christ and Culture.* New York, Harper, 1951.

Niebuhr, H. Richard. *The Kingdom of God in America.* New York, Harper, 1937.

Niebuhr, Reinhold. "The Age between the Ages." Niebuhr, *Discerning the Signs of the Times.* London, SCM, 1946, 40–54.

Niebuhr, Reinhold. "American Conservatism and the World Crisis, I: A Study in Vacillation." *Yale Review* 40 (1951), 385–99.

Niebuhr, Reinhold. "The Anomaly of European Socialism" (1952). Niebuhr, *Christian Realism and Political Problems.* New York, Scribner's, 1953, 43–51.

Niebuhr, Reinhold. "The Blindness of Liberalism." *Radical Religion* 1, 4 (Autumn, 1936), 4–5.

Niebuhr, Reinhold. *The Children of Light and the Children of Darkness. A Vindication of Democracy and a Critique of Its Traditional Defence.* New York, Scribner's, 1972.

Niebuhr, Reinhold. "Christian Faith and the Economic Life of Liberal Society." *Goals of Economic Life,* ed. A. D. Ward. New York, Harper, Ethics and Economic Life, 1953, 433–59.

Niebuhr, Reinhold. "Christian Faith and the World Crisis." Niebuhr, *Love and Justice,* ed. D. B. Robertson. Gloucester, MA, Peter Smith, 1957, 279–85.

Niebuhr, Reinhold. "The Christian Perspective on the World Crisis." *Christianity and Crisis* 4, 7 (May 1, 1944), 2–5.

Niebuhr, Reinhold. *Christian Realism and Political Problems.* New York, Scribner's, 1953.

Niebuhr, Reinhold. "Coercion, Self-Interest, and Love." Commentary in Kenneth E. Boulding, *The Organizational Revolution.* New York, Harper, 1953, 228–44.

Niebuhr, Reinhold. "A Dark Light on Human Nature," *Messenger* 13 (April 27, 1948), 7.

Niebuhr, Reinhold. "Democracy, Secularism, and Christianity." Niebuhr, *Christian Realism and Political Problems,* 95–103.

Niebuhr, Reinhold. "The Ethic of Jesus and the Social Problem." Niebuhr, *Love and Justice,* 29–40.

Niebuhr, Reinhold. *Faith and History. A Comparison of Christian and Modern Views of History.* New York, Scribner's, 1949.

Niebuhr, Reinhold, "A Faith for History's Greatest Crisis." *Fortune* 26 (July, 1942), 99–100, 122–31.

Niebuhr, Reinhold. "The Foreign Policy of American Conservatism and Liberalism." *Christian Realism and Political Problems,* 53–73.

Niebuhr, Reinhold. *The Irony of American History.* New York, Scribner's 1952.

Niebuhr, Reinhold. "Is There Another Way?" Niebuhr, *Love and Justice,* 299–301.

Niebuhr, Reinhold. "Justice and Love." Niebuhr, *Love and Justice,* 27–29.

Niebuhr, Reinhold. "Liberalism and Conservatism." *Christianity and Society* 20 (Winter, 1954–1955), 3–4.

Niebuhr, Reinhold. "Liberalism: Illusions and Realities." *New Republic* 133 (July 4, 1955), 11–13.

Niebuhr, Reinhold. *Moral Man and Immoral Society.* New York, Scribner's, 1960.

Niebuhr, Reinhold. *The Nature and Destiny of Man. A Christian Interpretation. Vol. 1: Human Nature; Vol. 2: Human Destiny.* New York, Scribner's, 1964.

Niebuhr, Reinhold. "Our Moral and Spiritual Resources for International Cooperation." *Social Action* 22 (February, 1956), 5–24.

Niebuhr, Reinhold. "Pacifism and Sanctions: A Symposium" (with John Nevin Sayre). *Radical Religion* 1, 2 (Winter, 1936), 27–30.

Niebuhr, Reinhold. "The Reunion of the Church Through the Renewal of the Churches." *Christianity and Crisis* 7 (Nov. 24, 1947), 5–7.

Niebuhr, Reinhold. *The Self and the Dramas of History.* New York, Scribner's, 1955.

Niebuhr, Reinhold. "The Sickness of American Culture." *Nation* 166 (1948), 267–270.

Niebuhr, Reinhold. *The Structure of Nations and Empires. A Study of the Recurring Patterns and Problems of the Political Order in Relation to the Unique Problems of the Nuclear Age.* New York, Scribner's, 1959.

Niebuhr, Reinhold. "Synthetic Barbarism." Niebuhr, *Christianity and Power Politics.* New York, Scribner's, 1940, 117–30.

Niebuhr, Reinhold. "Ten Fateful Years." *Christianity and Crisis* 11, 1 (February 5, 1951), 1–4.

Niebuhr, Reinhold. "Ten Years That Shook My World." *Christian Century* 56 (April 26, 1939), 542–46.

Niebuhr, Reinhold. "Two Forms of Utopianism." *Christianity and Society* 12 (Autumn, 1947), 6–7.

Niebuhr, Reinhold. "Why A New Quarterly?" *Radical Religion* 1, 1 (Autumn, 1935), 3–5.

Niebuhr, Reinhold. "Why the Church is not Pacifist." Niebuhr, *Christianity and Power Politics,* 1–32.

Noll, Mark A. "God and the Colonies." *Eerdmans' Handbook to Christianity in America* (1983), 1–156.

Novak, Michael. *The Spirit of Democratic Capitalism.* New York, Simon & Schuster, 1982.

Nove, Alec. *The Economics of Feasible Socialism Revisited.* London, Harper Collins Academic, 1991^2.

Nozick, Robert. *Anarchy, State, and Utopia.* New York, Basic, 1974.

Nyerere, Julius K. "The Economic Challenge: Dialogue or Confrontation?" *International Development Review* 18, 1 (January, 1976), 2–9.

Ogletree, Thomas W. *The Use of the Bible in Christian Ethics. A Constructive Essay.* Philadelphia, Fortress, 1983.

Okun, Arthur M. *Equality and Efficiency: The Big Tradeoff.* Washington, D.C., Brookings Institution, 1975.

Olivier, J.P.J. "The Sceptre of Justice and Ps. 45:7b." *Journal of Northwest Semitic Languages* 7 (1979), 45–54.

Olley, John W. "Notes on Isaiah xxxii 1, xlv 19, 23 and lxiii 1." *Vetus Testamentum* 33 (1983), 446–53.

Olley, John W. "'Righteousness'—Some Issues in Old Testament Translation into English." *Bible Translator* 38 (1987), 307–15.

Olley, John W. "The Translator of the Septuagint of Isaiah and 'Righteousness.'" *Bulletin of the International Organization for Septuagint and Cognate Studies* 13 (1980), 58–74.

Olsen, Marvin E. "Marx as a Power Theorist." *Power in Societies,* ed. Olsen. New York, Macmillan, 1970, 70–77.

Olsen, Marvin E. "Social Pluralism as a Basis for Democracy." *Power in Societies,* ed. Olsen, 182–88.

Opitz, Edmund A. *Religion and Capitalism: Allies, Not Enemies.* New Rochelle, NY, Arlington House, 1970.

Orren, Gary R. "Beyond Self Interest." *The Power of Public Ideas,* ed. R. Reich. Cambridge, MA, Ballinger, 1988, 13–29.

Outka, Gene. *Agape. An Ethical Analysis.* New Haven, CT, Yale U., 1972.

Overton, Richard. "An Appeal from the Commons to the Free People" (1647). *Puritanism and Liberty,* ed. Woodhouse, 323–34.

Papal Encyclicals. Vol. 5: 1958–1981, ed. C. Carlen. N.p., Consortium, 1981.

Paris, Peter J. *The Social Teachings of the Black Churches.* Philadelphia, Fortress, 1985.

Pascal, Blaise. *Pensées.* Paris, Garnier, Classiques Garnier, 1958.

Paulhus, Normand J. "Uses and Misues of the Term 'Social Justice' in the Roman Catholic Tradition." *Journal of Religious Ethics* 15 (1987), 261–82.

Peeler, John A. "Democracy and Elections in Central America: Autumn of the Oligarchs?" *Elections and Democracy in Central America,* ed. J. Booth and M. Seligson. Chapel Hill, NC, U. of North Carolina, 1989, 185–200.

Pemberton, Prentiss L. and Daniel Rush Finn. *Toward a Christian Economic Ethic. Stewardship and Social Power.* Minneapolis, Winston, 1985.

Perkins, William. "A Treatise of the Vocations or Callings of Men." *Puritan Political Ideas 1558–1794,* ed. E. Morgan. Indianapolis, IN, Bobbs-Merrill, American Heritage Series, 1965, 35–59.

Petchesky, Rosalind Pollack. *Abortion and Woman's Choice: The State, Sexuality, and Reproductive Freedom.* Boston, Northeastern U., Northeastern Series in Feminist Theory, 1990[2].

Pierard, Richard V. "The Lutheran Two-Kingdom Doctrine and Subservience to the State in Modern Germany." *Journal of the Evangelical Theological Society* 29 (1986), 195–203.

Plaskow, Judith. *Sex, Sin and Grace: Women's Experience and the Theologies of Reinhold Niebuhr and Paul Tillich.* Washington, D. C., University Press of America, 1980.

Plato. *The Republic,* trans. P. Shorey. Cambridge, Harvard U., Loeb Classical Library, 1935.

Pocock, J.G.A. "Time, Institutions and Action; An Essay on Traditions and Their Understanding." Pocock, *Politics, Language, and Time.* Chicago, U. of Chicago, 1989, 233–72.

Pocock, J.G.A. *The Machiavellian Moment: Florentine Political Thought and the Atlantic Republican Tradition.* Princeton, NJ, Princeton U., 1975.

Pope, Liston. *Millhands and Preachers. A Study of Gastonia.* New Haven, Yale U., 1942.

Popper, Karl R. *The Open Society and Its Enemies.* Princeton, NJ, Princeton U., 1950.

Popper, Karl R. "Prediction and Prophecy in the Social Sciences." *Theories of History.* ed. P. Gardiner. Glencoe, IL, Free, 1959, 276–85.

Post, Stephen. "Disinterested Benevolence: An American Debate over the Nature of Christian Love." *Journal of Religious Ethics* 14 (1986), 356–68.

Powell, Cyril H. *The Biblical Concept of Power.* London, Epworth, Fernley-Hartley Lectures, 1963.

Putterman, Louis. "Some Behavioral Perspectives on the Dominance of Hierarchical over Democratic Forms of Enterprise." *Journal of Economic Behavior and Organization* 3 (1982), 139–60.

Quinney, Richard. *Providence. The Reconstruction of Social Moral Order.* New York, Longman, 1980.

Rahner, Karl. "The Theology of Power." Rahner, *Theological Investigations.* Baltimore, Helicon, 1966), 4.391–409.

Raines, John C. "Sin as Pride and Sin as Sloth." *Christianity and Crisis* 29, 1 (February 3, 1969), 4–8.

Raines, John C. "Toward a Relational Theory of Justice." *Cross Currents* 39 (1989), 137–41, 160.

Ramsey, Paul. *Who Speaks for the Church? A Critique of the 1966 Geneva Conference on Church and Society.* Nashville, Abingdon, 1967.

Rauschenbusch, Walter. *Christianity and the Social Crisis.* Boston, Pilgrim, 1907.

Rauschenbusch, Walter. *The Righteousness of the Kingdom,* ed. Max L. Stackhouse. Nashville, Abingdon, 1968.

Rawls, John. *A Theory of Justice.* Cambridge, MA, Harvard U., 1971.

Rocher, Guy. "Le Droit et l'imaginaire social." *Recherches sociographiques* 23 (1982), 65–74.

Rogers, Mary F. "Instrumental and Infra-Resources." *American Journal of Sociology* 79 (1974), 1418–33.

Rosen, Corey M. "Conference Set On Unions and Employee Ownership." *Social Report* 2, 2 (December, 1981), 8.

Rosen, Corey M. et al. *Employee Ownership In America. The Equity Solution.* Lexington, MA, Lexington, 1986.

Rosner, Menachem and A. S. Tannenbaum. "Organizational Efficiency and Egalitarian Democracy in an Intentional Community Society: The Kibbutz." *British Journal of Sociology* 38 (1987), 521–45.

Rossiter, Clinton. *Conservatism in America. The Thankless Persuasion.* New York, Vintage, 1962².

Rothschild, Joyce and J. Allen Whitt. *The Cooperative Workplace. Potentials and Dilemmas of Organizational Democracy and Participation.* Cambridge, Cambridge U., Arnold and Caroline Rose Monograph, 1986.

Röpke, Wilhelm. *A Humane Economy. The Social Framework of the Free Market.* Indianapolis, IN, Liberty Fund, 1960.

Rubel, Maximilien. "Marx, Karl." *International Encyclopedia of the Social Sciences* (1968), 10:34–37.

Rudolph, Richard, and Ridley Scott. *Power Struggle: The Hundred-Year War over Electricity.* New York, Harper, 1986.

Rumberger, Russell W. "The Influence of Family Background on Education, Earnings, and Wealth." *Social Forces* 61 (1983), 755–73.

Russell, J. L. "Time in Christian Thought." *The Voice of Time,* ed. J. T. Fraser. Amherst, University of Massachusetts, 1981², 59–76.

Russell, Letty M. *Human Liberation in a Feminist Perspective—A Theology.* Philadelphia, Westminster, 1974.

Saltmarsh, John. *Smoke in the Temple* (1646), in *Puritanism and Liberty,* ed. Woodhouse, 179–85.

Sample, Tex S. "Toward a Christian Understanding of Power." *Toward a Discipline of Social Ethics,* Walter Muelder Fest., ed. P. Deats. Boston, Boston U., 1972, 117–41.

Sanford, Nevitt, Craig Comstock, et al. *Sanctions for Evil: Sources of Social Destructiveness.* San Francisco, Jossey-Bass, Behavioral Science Series, 1971.

Schaller, Lyle E. *The Change Agent.* Nashville, TN, Abingdon, 1972.

Schnackenburg, Rudolf. "Community Co-operation in the New Testament." *Concilium* 77 (1972), 9–19.

Schnackenburg, Rudolf. "Macht, Gewalt und Friede nach dem Neuen Testament." Schnackenburg, *Massstab des Glaubens.* Freiberg, Herder, 1978, 231–55.

Schoeck, Helmut. *Envy: A Theory of Social Behaviour.* New York, Harcourt, 1969.

Schumacher, E. F. *Small is Beautiful: Economics as If People Mattered.* New York, Harper, 1973.

Schwarz, Hans. "Reflection on the Work of the Spirit outside the Church." *Neue Zeitschrift für Systematische Theologie und Religionsphilosophie* 23 (1981), 197–211.

Schweickart, David. "Market Socialist Capitalist Roaders. A Comment on Arnold." *Economics and Philosophy* 3 (1987), 308–19.

Segundo, Juan Luis. *A Theology for Artisans of a New Humanity,* Vol. 2: *Grace and the Human Condition.* New York, Orbis, 1973.

Seifert, Harvey. *Ethical Resources for Political and Economic Decision.* Philadelphia, Westminster, 1972.

Seneca. *Epistulae Morales.* trans. R. Gummere. Cambridge, Harvard U., Loeb Classical Library, 1962. Vol. 2.

Shapiro, Ian. *The Evolution of Rights in Liberal Theory.* Cambridge, Cambridge U., 1986.

Sherman, Franklin. "Christian Theology and American Democracy." *Belonging and Alienation,* ed. P. Hefner and W. W. Schroeder. Chicago, Center for the Scientific Study of Religion, Studies in Religion and Society, 1976, 145–57.

Shinn, Roger. "The Locus of Authority: Participatory Democracy in the Age of the Expert." *Erosion of Authority.* ed. C. Manschreck. Nashville, Abingdon, 1971, 92–122.

Shriver, Donald W., Jr., et al. *Spindles and Spires: A Re-Study of Religion and Social Change in Gastonia.* Atlanta, Knox, 1976.

Sider, Ronald L. "Toward a Biblical Perspective on Equality. Steps on the Way Toward Christian Political Engagement." *Interpretation* 43 (1989), 156–69.

Simmons, John. "ESOP on the Move." *Workplace Democracy* (Summer, 1989), 6.

Sinclair, R. K. *Democracy and Participation in Athens.* Cambridge, Cambridge U., 1988.

Sirianni, Carmen. *Workers' Control and Socialist Democracy.* London, Verso, 1982.

Skillen, James. *Justice for Representation. A Proposal for Revitalizing our System of Political Representation.* Washington, D.C., Association for Public Justice, 1979.

Smedes, Lewis B. *Love Within Limits. A Realist's View of 1 Corinthians 13.* Grand Rapids, MI, Eerdmans, 1978.

Smith, Adam. *Works and Correspondence. Vol. 1: The Theory of Moral Sentiments,* ed. D. D. Raphael and A. L. Macfie. Oxford, Oxford U., 1976.

Smith, Adam. *Works and Correspondence. Vol. 2: An Inquiry into the Nature and Causes of the Wealth of Nations,* ed. R. H. Campbell and A. S. Skinner. Oxford, Oxford U., 1976.

Smith, Bruce James. *Politics and Remembrance: Republican Themes in Machiavelli, Burke, and Tocqueville.* Princeton, NJ, Princeton U., 1985.

Smith, David G. "Liberalism." *International Encyclopedia of the Social Sciences* (1968), 9:276–82.

Smith, Stephen C. "On the Incidence of Profit and Equity Sharing. Theory and an Application to the High Tech Sector." *Journal of Economic Behavior and Organization* 8 (1987), 1–14.

Snaith, Norman H. *The Distinctive Ideas of the Old Testament.* London, Epworth, 1944.

Son, Bong-Ho. "Response to 'Democracy—A Christian Imperative.'" *Transformation* 7, 4 (October/December, 1990), 5–6.

Sosna, Morton. *In Search of the Silent South: Southern Liberals and the Race Issue.* New York, Columbia U., Contemporary American History Series, 1977.

Speer, Albert. *Inside the Third Reich.* New York, Macmillan, 1970.

Spencer, Bob, as interviewed by Ed Wojcicki. "Good Citizens Can't Be Cynics." *Salt* 11, 4 (April, 1991), 19–24.

Spencer, Herbert. *Principles of Biology.* New York, Appleton, 1899².

Spencer, Herbert. *Social Statics.* New York, Appleton, 1865 (1850]).

Spencer, Herbert. "The Sins of the Legislators." Spencer, *The Man versus the State.* London, Williams, 1884, 44–77.

Spencer, Herbert. *The Study of Sociology.* New York, Appleton, 1891.

Spicq, C. *Les Épîtres Pastorales.* Paris, Gabalda, Études Bibliques, 1969⁴.

Spiegelberg, Herbert. "A Defence of Human Equality." *Philosophical Review* 53 (1944), 101–24.

Spiro, Melford E. *Kibbutz: Venture in Utopia. Studies in the Libertarian and Utopian Tradition.* New York, Schocken, 1970³.

Stackelberg, Roderick. *Idealism Debased: From völkisch Ideology to National Socialism.* Kent, OH, Kent State U., 1981.

Stackhouse, Max L. *Creeds, Society, and Human Rights. A Study in Three Cultures.* Grand Rapids, MI, Eerdmans, 1984.

Stackhouse, Max L. *Public Theology and Political Economy. Christian Stewardship in Modern Society.* Grand Rapids, MI, Eerdmans, Library of Christian Stewardship, 1987.

Stackhouse, Max L., and Dennis P. McCann. "Public Theology After the Collapse of Socialism." *Christian Century* 108 (1991), 33, 44–47.

Stone, Ronald H. *Paul Tillich's Radical Social Thought.* Atlanta, Knox, 1980.

Stone, Ronald H. *Realism and Hope.* Washington, D.C., University Press of America, 1977.

Stout, Harry S. "The Transforming Effects of the Great Revival." *Eerdmans' Handbook to Christianity in America* (1983), 127–30.

Strauss, Leo. *Natural Right and History.* Chicago, U. of Chicago, 1953.

Stuart, Douglas. "The Law(s)-Covenant Stipulations for Israel." Gordon D. Fee and Stuart, *How to Read the Bible for All Its Worth.* Grand Rapids, MI: Zondervan, 1981, 135–47.

Sumner, William Graham. "The Challenge of Facts." Sumner, *The Challenge of Facts and the Other Essays,* ed. A. G. Keller. New York, AMS 1971 (1914), 17–62.

Sumner, William Graham. "The Influence of Commercial Crises on Opinions about Economic Doctrines" (1879). Sumner, *Essays,* ed. A. G. Keller and M. Davie. N.p., Archon, 1969 (1934), 2.44–66.

Sumner, William Graham. "The Power and Beneficence of Capital" (1889). Sumner, *Essays,* ed. Keller and Davie, 2.14–30.

Sumner, William Graham. "What Makes the Rich Richer and the Poor Poorer?" (1887). Sumner, *Challenge of Facts,* 65–77.

Szelenyi, Ivan. "Recent Contributions to the Political Economy of State Socialism." *Contemporary Sociology* 14 (1985), 284–87.

Tavard, George H. *A Way of Love.* Maryknoll, NY, Orbis, 1977.

Tawney, R. H. *Equality. Halley Stewart Lectures, 1929.* New York, Harcourt, 1931.

Tawney, R. H. *The Acquisitive Society.* London, Bell, 1922.

Taylor, Jeremy. *The Rules and Exercises of Holy Living.* London, Bell, 1857 (1650).

Taylor, John V. *Enough Is Enough.* Minneapolis, Augsburg, 1975.

Temple, William. *Christianity and Social Order*. New York, Penguin, 1942.

Temple, William. *Christianity and the State*. London, Macmillan, 1928.

Thompson, David. *Europe Since Napolean*. New York, Knopf, 1962^2.

Tillich, Paul. "Basic Principles of Religious Socialism" (1923). Tillich, *Political Expectation*, ed. James Luther Adams. New York, Harper, 1971, 58–88.

Tillich, Paul. "Christianity and Marxism" (1960). Tillich, *Political Expectation*, 89–96.

Tillich, Paul. "Kairos." *A Handbook of Christian Theology* (1958), 193–97.

Tillich, Paul. "The Kingdom of God and History." H. G. Wood et al., *Church, Community, and State. Vol. 3: The Kingdom of God and History*. London, Allen, 1938, 105–42.

Tillich, Paul. *Love, Power, and Justice. Ontological Analyses and Ethical Applications*. New York, Oxford U., 1954.

Tillich, Paul. "Man and Society in Religious Socialism." *Christianity and Society* 8, 4 (Fall, 1943), 10–21.

Tillich, Paul. "The Political Meaning of Utopia" (1951). Tillich, *Political Expectation*, 125–80.

Tillich, Paul. "The Problem of Power" (1931). Tillich, *The Interpretation of History*. New York, Scribner's, 1936, 179–202.

Tillich, Paul. "Protestantism as a Critical and Creative Principle" (1929). Tillich, *Political Expectation*, 10–39.

Tillich, Paul. *The Religious Situation*. New York, Living Age, 1932.

Tillich, Paul. "Religious Socialism" (1930). Tillich, *Political Expectation*, 40–57.

Tillich, Paul. "Shadow and Substance: A Theory of Power" (1965). Tillich, *Political Expectation,*, 115–24.

Tillich, Paul. *The Socialist Decision*. New York, Harper, 1977 (1933).

Tillich, Paul. "The State as Expectation and Demand" (1930). Tillich, *Political Expectation*, 97–114.

Tillich, Paul. *Theology of Culture*. New York, Oxford U., 1959.

Tinnemann, Ethel Mary. "Attitudes of the German Catholic Hierarchy toward the Nazi Regime: A Study in German Psychopolitical Culture." *Western Political Quarterly* 22 (1969), 333–49.

Tocqueville, Alexis de. *Democracy in America*, ed. J. P. Mayer. Garden City, NY, Doubleday, 1969.

Tolkien, J. R. *The Lord of the Rings*. Boston, Houghton Mifflin, 1965^2. Pt. 1: *The Fellowship of the Ring;* Pt. 3: *The Return of the King*.

Tolstoi, Leo. *Anna Karenina*. Philadelphia, Macrae, 1919.

Troeltsch, Ernst. *The Social Teaching of the Christian Churches*. New York, Harper, 1960 [1911].

Trudeau, Robert H. "The Guatemalan Elections of 1985. Prospects for Democracy." *Elections and Democracy in Central America*, ed. J. Booth and M. Seligson. Chapel Hill, NC, U. of North Carolina, 1989, 93–125.

U.S. House of Representatives, Committee on Ways and Means. *1991 Green Book: Overview of Entitlement Programs*. U. S. Government, 1991.

Valvano, Vince. "Investing Labor's Capital: An Update on Union Penson Fund Strategies." *Dollars & Sense* (September, 1987), 10–12.

Van Patten, Charles R. "Ethics and War." Unpublished MATS thesis, Gordon-Conwell Theological Seminary, 1984.

Vannoy, J. Robert. *Covenant Renewal at Gilgal: A Study of I Samuel 11:14–12:25*. Cherry Hill, NJ, Mack, 1978.

Vlastos, Gregory. "Justice and Equality." *Social Justice*, ed. R. Brandt. Englewood Cliffs, NJ, Prentice-Hall, 1962, 31–72.

Voegelin, Eric. *From Enlightenment to Revolution,* ed. J. Hallowell. Durham, NC, Duke U., 1975.

Volf, Miroslav. "Democracy and the Crisis of the Socialist Project. Toward a Post-Revolutionary Theology of Liberation." *Transformation* 7, 4 (October/December, 1990), 11–16.

Vree, Dale. "Religious Socialism." *Religious Socialism* 9, 2 (Spring, 1985), 8.

Walker, Charles R. and Robert H. Guest. *The Man on the Assembly Line.* Cambridge, Harvard U., 1952.

Walsh, J.P.M. *The Mighty From Their Thrones.* Philadelphia, Fortress, Overtures to Biblical Theology 21, 1987.

Walzer, Michael. "A Day in the Life of a Socialist Citizen" (1968). Walzer, *Radical Principles.* New York, Basic, 1980, 128–38.

Walzer, Michael. *Interpretation and Social Criticism.* Cambridge, Harvard U., 1987.

Walzer, Michael. *Radical Principles, Reflections of an Unreconstructed Democrat.* New York, Basic, 1980.

Walzer, Michael. "Town Meetings and Workers' Councils: A Story for Socialists" (1978). Walzer, *Radical Principles,* 273–90.

Ward, Harry F. *Democracy and Social Change.* New York, Modern Age, 1940.

Warren, Robert Penn. *All the King's Men.* New York, Grosset, 1946.

Warren, Roland. *Types of Purposive Social Change at the Community Level.* Waltham, MA, Brandeis U., Florence Heller Graduate School for Advanced Studies in Social Welfare, Brandeis U. Papers in Social Welfare 11, 1965.

Watts, Craig M. "Dealing Responsibly with Power." *Cross Currents* 36 (1986), 74–84.

Weaver, Richard. *Ideas Have Consequences.* Chicago, U. of Chicago, 1948.

Weber, Max. *Economy and Society. An Outline of Interpretative Sociology,* ed. G. Roth and C. Wittick. New York, Bedminster, 1968[4].

Weber, Max. *The Protestant Ethic and the Spirit of Capitalism.* New York, Scribner's, 1958.

Weber, Max. "Religious Rejections of the World and Their Directions." *From Max Weber: Essays in Sociology,* ed. H. Gerth and C. W. Mills. New York, Oxford U., 1946, 323–59.

Weisman, Ze'eb. "The Nature and Background of *bāḥūr* in the Old Testament." *Vetus Testamentum* 31 (1981), 441–50.

Wesley, John. Letter to Charles Wesley, June 27, 1766. *The Letters of the Rev. John Wesley, A. M.* ed. J. Telford. London, Epworth, 1931, 5.16.

Wesley, John. Sermon 4, "Scriptural Christianity." Wesley, *The Works of John Wesley, Vol. 1: Sermons 1* (Bicentennial Ed.). Nashville, Abingdon, 1984, 159–80.

Wesley, John. Sermon 7, "The Way to the Kingdom." Wesley, *Works 1: Sermons 1,* 218–32.

Wesley, John. Sermon 28, "Sermon on the Mount, VIII." Wesley, *Works 1: Sermons 1,* 612, 31.

Wesley, John. Sermon 102, "Of Former Times." Wesley, *Works 3: Sermons 3,* 1986, 442–53.

Wesley, John. Sermon 108, "On Riches." Wesley, *Works 3: Sermons 3,* 519–28.

Wesley, John. Sermon 128, "The Deceitfulness of the Human Heart." Wesley, *Works 4: Sermons 4,* 1987, 150–60.

Wesley, John. Sermon 129, "Heavenly Treasures in Earthen Vessels." Wesley, *Works 4: Sermons 4,* 162–67.

Wesley, John. Sermon 142, "The Wisdom of Winning Souls." Wesley, *Works 4: Sermons 4,* 306–17.

Wesson, Robert G. *The Imperial Order.* Berkeley, CA, U. of California, 1967.

West, Cornel. *Prophesy Deliverance!* Philadelphia, Westminster, 1982.

"What is the Purpose of Farm Cooperatives?" *Center for Rural Affairs Newsletter* (April, 1987), 3–4.

Wilber, Charles K., and Laura K. Grimes. "The Moral Defense of Market Capitalism: A Critique of the Literature." Paper presented to the Biblical Perspectives on a Mixed Market Economy consultation, Wheaton, IL, September 8–10, 1987.

Wilbur, Charles K., and Roland Hoksbergen. "Ethical Values and Economic Theory: A Survey." *Religious Studies Review* 12 (1986), 208–14.

Wiles, P.J.D. *Economic Institutions Compared.* New York, Halsted, 1977.

Williams, Elisha. *The Essential Rights and Liberties of Protestants* (1744). *Puritan Political Ideas,* ed. E. Morgan. Indianapolis, IN, Bobbs-Merrill, American Heritage Series, 1965, 268–304.

Williams, Robin M. *American Society.* New York, Knopf, 1959.

Williamson, George, Jr. "A Niebuhrian Critique of Niebuhrian Thought." *Andover Newton Quarterly* 15 (1975), 182–95.

Williamson, Oliver E. *The Economic Institutions of Capitalism. Firms, Markets, Relational Contracting.* New York, Free, 1985.

Wills, David W. "Racial Justice and the Limits of American Liberalism." *Journal of Religious Ethics* 6 (1978), 187–220.

Wills, Garry. *Confessions of a Conservative.* Garden City, NY, Doubleday, 1979.

Wills, Garry. *Nixon Agonistes: The Crisis of the Self-Made Man.* New York, American Library, 1970.

Winthrop, John. "A Model of Christian Charity" (1630). *Puritan Political Ideas.* ed. E. Morgan. Indianapolis, IN, Bobbs-Merrill, American Heritage Series, 1965, 76–93.

Wise, John. *A Vindication of the Government of New England Churches* (1717). *Puritan Political Ideas,* ed. E. Morgan. Indianapolis, IN, Bobbs-Merrill, American Heritage Series, 1965, 251–67.

Wogaman, J. Philip. *Christian Perspectives on Politics.* Philadelphia, Fortress, 1988.

Wogaman, J. Philip. *The Great Economic Debate. An Ethical Analysis.* Philadelphia, Westminster, 1977.

Wolf, Ernst. "Political and Moral Motives behind the Resistance." *The German Resistance to Hitler,* ed. H. Graml et al. Berkeley, CA, U. of California, 1970, 193–234.

Wolff, Hans Walter. *Anthropology of the Old Testament.* Philadelphia, Fortress, 1974.

Wolff, Robert Paul. *The Poverty of Liberalism.* Boston, Beacon, 1968.

Wolin, Sheldon. *Politics and Vision. Continuity and Innovation in Western Political Thought.* Boston, Little, Brown, 1960.

Wolverton, Wallace I. "The King's 'Justice' in Pre-Exilic Israel." *Anglican Theological Review* 41 (1959), 276–86.

Wood, James E., Jr. "A Theology of Power." *Journal of Church and State* 14 (1972), 107–24.

Woodhouse, A.S.P. "Introduction." *Puritanism and Liberty,* ed. Woodhouse. Chicago, U. of Chicago, [11]–[100].

Woolman, John. "A Plea for the Poor." *The Journal and Major Essays of John Woolman,* ed. P. Moulton. New York, Oxford U., Library of Christian Thought, 1971, 224–49.

Wright, Christopher J. H. *An Eye for An Eye. The Place of Old Testament Ethics Today.* Downers Grove, IL, InterVarsity, 1983.

Wrong, Dennis. *Power: Its Forms, Bases and Uses.* New York, Harper, Key Concepts in the Social Sciences, 1979.

Yinon, Yoel et al. "Escape from Responsibility and Help in Emergencies among Persons Alone or Within Groups." *European Journal of Social Psychology* 12 (1982), 301–5.

Yoder, John H. "Discerning the Kingdom of God in the Struggles of the World." *International Review of Mission* 68 (1979), 366–72.

Yoder, John H. "The Christian Case for Democracy." *Journal of Religious Ethics* 5 (1977), 209–23.

Yoder, John Howard. *The Christian Witness to the State.* Newton, KS, Faith and Life, Institute of Mennonite Studies 3, 1964.

Zylstra, Bernard. "The Bible, Justice and the State." *International Reformed Bulletin* 16, 55 (Fall, 1973), 2–18.

Name Index

Acton, Lord John E., 20, 233n.50, 260n.45
Adair, John, 271n.29
Adams, James Luther, 13, 15, 16, 23, 48, 63,
    127, 229–44 passim, 253n.19, 262n.87,
    269n.99, 270n.21, 272n.41, 273n.67,
    279n.78, 280n.93
Adams, John, 122, 260n.47
Addams, Jane, 266n.47
Adler, Alfred, 60
Alinsky, Saul, 140, 157, 159, 266n.55,
    272n.63, 273n.81, 295n.95
Allen, Irving Lewis, 241n.60
Alt, Albrecht, 270n.14
Althaus, Paul, 298n.12
Althusius, Johannes, 44, 239n.15
Alves, Rubem A., 256n.72
Antonovich, Borko Yuriy, 275n.4
Antonovsky, Aaron, 232nn.37, 41, 233n.54
Appleby, Joyce, 264n.23, 275n.15
Aquinas, Thomas, 5, 44, 122, 147–48,
    238n.73, 239n.8, 260n.55, 266n.40,
    269n.97, 284n.156
Arendt, Hannah, 150, 269n.1
Arieli, Yehoshua, 282n.125, 284n.154
Aristotle, 34, 52, 58, 65, 76, 78, 90, 123, 182,
    188, 233n.45, 237nn.45, 49, 238n.72,
    240n.18, 243n.4, 247nn.1, 10, 248nn.18,
    21, 251nn.7, 67, 260n.54, 261n.70,
    262n.83, 284n.163, 287nn.29, 33,
    292n.25, 295n.95
Arnold, N. Scott, 293n.65
Ascheim, Steven E., 299n.49
Athanasius, 257n.86
Augustine, 30, 32–33, 41, 55, 58, 62, 89, 104,
    235n.24, 236nn.28, 32, 237nn.42, 44,
    240n.22, 243n.7, 246n.83, 247n.94,
    251n.2, 253n.8, 255n.47, 262n.85
Augustus, 266n.43
Avineri, Shlomo, 286nn.16, 17, 26, 289nn.81,
    82

Ball, John, 4
Baltzell, E. Digby, 120, 259n.41

Bainton, Roland H., 263n.4, 264n.15,
    269n.90
Banton, Michael, 241n.61
Barbon, Nicholas, 264n.23
Barth, Hans, 221, 298n.23
Barthel, Diane, 296n.112
Bartley, Numan V., 242n.83
Bastomsky, S. J., 276n.32
Baum, Gregory, 246n.76, 271n.31, 290n.5,
    292n.29
Becker, Ernest, 290n.98
Beecher, Henry Ward, 167, 179, 277n.38,
    282n.126
Beiner, Ronald, 229n.14
Belcher, C. Francis, 250n.56
Bell, Bernard Iddings, 204, 280n.100,
    281n.108
Bell, Daniel, 282n.132, 284n.159, 292nn.28,
    47, 297n.127, 298n.34
Bellah, Robert N., 275n.13
Benne, Robert, 276n.26, 278n.55
Bennett, John C., 240n.26, 244n.32,
    272nn.44, 56, 61
Bentham, Jeremy, 133, 195, 264n.16
Berdyaev, Nicolas, 90, 251n.8
Berens, Lewis Henry, 129n.18
Berger, Peter, 170, 276nn.17, 18, 278nn.53,
    57, 280n.82, 291n.10
Bergstrom, Charles V., 238n.78
Berman, Harold J., 265n.25
Bernstein, Richard J., 229n.16
Béteille, André, 229n.4, 7, 8, 230n.25
Beyerhaus, Gisbert, 246n.73
Bierstedt, Robert, 230nn.4, 7, 9, 231n.14,
    232n.31
Bird, Otto, 247n.2
Blanqui, Louis, 186, 286n.22
Bloch-Lainé, François, 290n.105
Blumberg, Paul, 213–14, 295n.97, 297n.120
Blumrosen, Alfred W., 242n.82
Boesak, Allan, 24, 94, 232n.33, 234n.68,
    252n.31
Bolland, O. Nigel, 250n.57

Subject Index